*Emergence: Complexity & Organization*
VOLUME 9, Numbers 1-2, 2007
Special issue: *Complexity Thinking & Systems Theory*

Guest edited by: Kurt A. Richardson, Wendy J. Gregory & Gerald Midgley

ISSN: 1521-3250 (print)
ISSN: 1521-7000 (online)

ISBN10: 0-9791688-5-6
ISBN13: 978-09791688-5-7

Library of Congress Control Number: 2007932124
© ISCE Publishing, 2007

D1560411

Published and distributed by:

395 Central Street
Mansfield, MA 02048, USA

*ISCE Publishing* is very grateful for the generous financial support it receives from the
*Recursionst Fund* (http://recursionist.org) and Scott Harris.

*Emergence: Complexity & Organization*

Subscription prices (2006, volume 8, 4 issues) not including postage and handling: US$795.00 Corporate/US$495.00 Institutional/US$98.50 Individual (complementary print on request and electronic access to all previous issues). Members of the Complexity Society and the ISSS can subscribe to this journal at a concessionary rate. They must declare that the subscription is for their own private use, it will not replace any institutional subscription, and it will not be put at the disposal of any library. Subscriptions should be sent directly to the ISCE Publishing, 395 Central Street, Mansfield, MA 02048, USA, or to any subscription agent.

A journal of the *Institute for the Study of Coherence and Emergence,*
the *Complexity Society*, and the *Cognitive Edge*

VOLUME 9, Numbers 1-2, 2007
*Complexity Thinking & Systems Theory*

CONTENTS

Editorial
E:CO Vol. 9 Nos. 1-2 2007 pp. vi-viii

# Editorial introduction to the special double issue on *Complexity Thinking and Systems Theory*

Kurt A. Richardson, Wendy J. Gregory and Gerald Midgley

Welcome to Volume 9! To begin this new look volume of *E:CO* we have, among others, brought together a special collection of papers and articles that are drawn from no less than three recent complexity conferences. All of the academic and practitioner section papers were selected from the recent ANZSYS/ISCE collaboration that resulted in the International 11th ANZSYS / Managing the Complex V conference that was held December 5-7, 2005 in Christchurch, New Zealand. The purpose of this event was to provide a lively forum for discussion and debate for a wide range of academics and practitioners in the fields of systems thinking, complexity science and management. People from other disciplines who had an interest in the application of systems thinking and complexity approaches were also invited to participate. The event brought together thinkers and practitioners in the fields of systems and complexity as it seemed to the organizers that there had been a significant international resurgence in these areas in recent years.

The fields of systems and complexity have many similarities, yet they are being developed by two overlapping research communities that have unique insights to bring to bear on the management of 'wicked' problems. By providing forums in which people working at the frontiers of complexity and systems thinking can learn from one another, significant new insights for action can emerge. At the end of the day, it is important to the vast majority of those working with complexity and systems ideas that they are able to make a positive difference in people's lives. It is therefore vitally important that we share our insights and build a community of practitioners that can take the research agenda forward. A primary goal of the 11th ANZSYS / Managing the Complex V event was to bring together as many people as possible engaged in complex environmental, social and business issues, with the intention of promoting an intense and lively debate with real implications for systems and complexity practice. The hope of the organizers is that this conference was a step in the right direction.

It is no secret that in recent issues of *E:CO* we have attempted to raise awareness amongst complexity thinkers of the extensive systems thinking literature, and its relevance to our community. The Christchurch event was a major step in this endeavor. From the complex systems perspective, papers were submitted by experienced complexity thinkers, as one would expect. A series of papers were also submitted by systems researchers who took the opportunity at ANZSYS 11 to attempt to use the language and ideas of complexity thinking in their systems research. This led to some interesting syntheses in which complexity ideas were applied in ways not necessarily familiar to *E:CO*'s audience. One reason to be particularly interested in these papers is because they emerge at the boundary between 'systems' and 'complexity'. Purists might argue that if people want to use complexity concepts differently, this should be discouraged. Such linear thinking is often associated with calls for the solidification of definitions that can enable measurable progress. Apparently, flexible and fluid applications hinder such efforts. For some reason the need to measure progress often accompanies the need to establish boundaries - actually the need for boundaries is derived from the need to measure. So measuring progress in complexity thinking requires that we first determine exactly what we mean by the term 'complexity', thus allowing us to define exactly what complexity thinking is; its tools, its methods, its areas of applications, etc. If we accept this, then complexity thinking would be squeezed into the form of a nice and neat '-ism', such as reductionism or holism. To those purists who would support such an endeavor, the following quote from Dewey is offered:

*"For in spite of itself any movement that thinks and acts in terms of an 'ism becomes so involved in reaction against other 'isms that it is unwit-*

*tingly controlled by them. For it then forms its principles by reaction against them instead of by a comprehensive, constructive survey of actual needs, problems, and possibilities.*" (Dewey, 1938: 6).

Essentially what this is saying is that reference to external issues gets lost in the drive for boundary solidification. We would hate to think that the apparent ignorance of the systems literature in the complexity community is the result of the solidification, or institutionalization, of our topical boundaries. As soon as that happens, our approach(es) will slowly become irrelevant, and we will begin to think for the sake of thinking and not for the sake of solving problems in an effort to improve the lives of ourselves and others. We may kid ourselves into thinking that 'complexity' is important, but the moment we allow the rigid application of language to dominate over fluid application, we have essentially removed external reference from the equation and replaced it with an increasingly irrelevant idealization. The editors of *E:CO* hope that this argument justifies our loosening of the 'complexity' boundaries for this particular issue.

The first seven papers are all taken from the 11th ANZSYS / Managing the Complex V (although they have been significantly revised since their birth as conference papers), and yet they do not represent even half of the material on offer in this special double issue. Our other familiar sections are bursting at the seams. For example, the Complexity and Philosophy section contains three (rather than the two that would usually be expected in a double issue) thought-provoking articles, the first of which offers an analysis of complexity theory using complexity theory itself. The continued relevance of complexity theory / thinking relies heavily on our willingness to dissect rather than protect it. Fortunately, complexity thinking itself actually encourages such a critical stance.

Complexity and Philosophy also explores how the field of ecology (a close cousin of complexity) is different from the mechanistic sciences in terms of the role of (and even the possibility of establishing) Natural Laws. This is followed by a thorough analysis of the concept at the heart of *E:CO* - emergence: a term which has so far resisted being pinned down and rigidly defined.

This issue's Classic Paper section contains two fascinating papers written by Frederick A. von Hayek. The inclusion of these papers was originally suggested by Neel Chamilall. Neel was in the process of writing an extended introduction for these papers, but was unfortunately involved in a serious car accident that prevented him from finishing. We wish Neel all the best and hope he makes a full and speedy recovery. We would also like to express our gratitude to Rodrigo Zeidan and Mihnea Moldoveanu who volunteered to prepare introductions for the two Hayek papers selected. They both did a very competent job under a very tight time restriction. Many thanks indeed!

The first article of the Forum section concludes the ongoing series on Systems Theory and Complexity by introducing an edited transcription of a lecture given by Gerald Midgley at the 1st International Workshop on Complexity and Policy Analysis which was held June 22-24, 2005 in Cork, Ireland, hosted by the ETHOS Project, Department of Government, University College, Cork. The aim of the Systems Thinking and Complexity series was to explore general systems laws in terms of complexity theory, and to highlight the similarities in the evolution of the complexity and systems literatures. Gerald's presentation provides a fitting finale.

Webb *et al.* explore the role that swarming models play in learning about complexity, suggesting that they are very useful indeed, even if they are regarded by some as flawed natural science models, imported and overused within the social sciences.

It is often assumed in the modern technological world that 'being connected' is a good thing. Our next article explores the limits of this assumption by presenting the early results in a study that investigates the relationship between connectivity and behavior / function. It would seem that 'being connected' is only beneficial to a limited degree, again illustrating the central role of 'balance' in complexity thinking.

Ken Baskin gives us his views on the third conference to be mentioned in this issue - the 3rd International Workshop on Complexity and Philosophy held February 22-23, 2007, in Stellenbosch, South Africa, which was hosted by the Stellenbosch Institute for Advanced Study (STIAS). Ken's review of this event illustrates the growing maturity with which the implications of complexity for philosophy are being explored. Roll on number 4!

Before reviews of some recent contributions to the complexity booklist are offered, Ron Schultz, in his ongoing Adjacent Opportunities, illustrates the importance of 'applied chutzpah' in the first steps of initiating radical change. Change often begins with someone have the foresight as well as the effrontery to suggest something quite different. Emergent processes then take over and determine whether change will follow, or whether the initial input of creative and emotional energy is dissipated.

To finish, there have been some rather obvious changes to the aesthetics of *E:CO* for Volume 9. However, a more significant change is the inclusion of embedded web links in the reference sections of each paper. These of course can only be exploited via the online edition that all subscribers have access to. A cursory glance at the reference section of almost any 'complexity' paper is all that is needed to witness the range of written sources used to inspire explorations in complexity thinking. From this issue onwards, every reference will contain a link that will take the online reader to an Amazon.com link for books (where summaries and reviews can be found - and in many cases selected pages from the books can be seen... and of course, the books can be purchased); to a journal summary page for journal articles (from which one can often get to the journal's homepage); as well as for regular internet web page sources. We hope you find this feature a useful tool in your exploration of 'complexity space'.

### References

Dewey, J. (1938). *Experience and Education*, ISBN 9780684838281.

### Relevant links

**11th ANZSYS Conference / Managing the Complex V: Systems Thinking and Complexity Science - Insights for Action.**
*Co-hosted by ISCE Events, USA and the Institute of Environmental Science and Research Limited, NZ.*
5-7 December, 2005, Christchurch, New Zealand.

http://isce.edu/ISCE_Group_Site/web-content/ISCE_Events/Christchurch_2005/Proceedings/index.html

**1st International Workshop on Complexity and Policy Analysis.**
*Co-hosted by ISCE Events, Department of Government University College Cork ETHOS Project, and School of Public Affairs, Penn State, Harrisburg.*
22-24 June 2005, Cork, Ireland.

http://isce.edu/ISCE_Group_Site/web-content/ISCE_Events/Cork_2005.html

**3rd International Workshop on Complexity and Philosophy.**
*Co-Hosted by Stellenbosch Institute for Advanced Study (STIAS), South Africa, ISCE Events, USA, and Cathedra for the Study of Complexity (Instituto de Filosofia de La Habana), Cuba.*
22-23 February, 2007, Stellenbosch, South Africa.

http://isce.edu/ISCE_Group_Site/web-content/ISCE_Events/Stellenbosch_2007.html

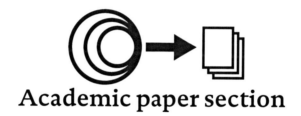

Academic paper section

Academic

# Systemic planning: Dealing with complexity by a wider approach to planning

Steen Leleur
Technical University of Denmark

On the basis of the author's latest book, *Systemic Planning*, this paper addresses systems thinking and complexity in the context of planning. Specifically, renewal of planning thinking on this background is set out as so-called systemic planning (SP). The principal concern of SP is to provide principles and methodology that can be helpful for planning under circumstances characterized by complexity and uncertainty. It is argued that compared to conventional planning – referred to as systematic planning – there is a need for a wider, more systemic approach to planning that is better suited to current real-world planning problems, often characterized by complex issues.

## Introduction

On the basis of the author's latest book, *Systemic Planning* (Leleur, 2005), this paper presents an overview of the ideas behind systemic planning (SP). The principal concern of SP is to set out – by making use of systems science – some principles and methodology that can be helpful for planning under circumstances characterized by complexity and uncertainty. The paper is arranged as follows: After an introductory overview, the second section gives the main ideas behind the SP approach, with an outline of different categories of change processes and of three principal types of complexities that can make a conventional planning approach inappropriate. Then systems science is used to formulate the basic SP principles. In this respect, the paradigms of simplicity and complexity thinking as set out by the French philosopher of science Edgar Morin are called on, and a generic, methodological framework for SP is formulated.

The following section presents SP as an appropriate multimethodological approach characterized, among other things, by combining "soft" and "hard" operations research (OR)

methods to set up an exploration and learning cycle that can guide planners and decision makers in a real case. A comprehensive set of relevant tools is presented, and it is discussed how this SP toolbox can be made use of together with the general principles of SP. In the subsequent section an example is dealt with. This concerns the complex public decision whether or not to build the Øresund Fixed Link at a cost of €3.2 billion for road and rail traffic between Copenhagen and Malmoe. This ex-post study – carried out four years after the opening of the link in 2000 – has been found relevant to demonstrate a planning case where the planning environment can be described as complex and uncertain. The case is treated with the emphasis on presenting the applicability of SP in general; that is, as being of interest also for other societal sectors than transport and infrastructure. The final section gives some findings and a perspective on further work.

## Simplicity, complexity, and systemic decision making

Based on work carried out by the British organizations and complexity researcher Ralph Stacey, change processes in general can be categorized as closed change, contained change, and open-ended change (Stacey, 1993; Leleur, 2005: 16–17). These processes, described below, will influence the kind of planning approach that should be made use of when dealing with planning tasks relating to specific change processes.

- *Closed change*: The key features of closed change are unambiguous problems, opportunities, and issues; clear connections between cause and effect; and the possibility of accurately forecasting the consequences of change. Faced with such change, people tend to behave in easily understandable ways. The decision maker can use rational planning techniques and the processes of control are formal, analytical and quantitative. There is a clear purpose with clear preferences, and alternative ways of achieving the purpose are known.

- *Contained change*: The key features of contained change derive from those change situations where it is possible to make probabilistic forecasts based on actions taken now and their most likely consequences. This is made possible because the consequences appear to some degree as repetitions of what has happened in the past or relate to large numbers of essentially the same event. As a planner looks into the future, accurately predictable closed change declines in relative importance, while less reliably predictable contained change increases in relative importance.

- *Open-ended change*: Planning and control in open-ended situations in practice means something completely different from what it means in closed and contained situations. In such situations, the future consequences are to some extent unknown and forecasting is made difficult due to the sometimes ambiguous purposes and equivocal preferences of the planning agents involved. The whole situation may be ill structured and accompanied by inadequate information that is more or less subjective and conditioned by personal ambitions, beliefs, and values. There can be considerable problems interpreting data and applying statistical techniques in uniquely uncertain conditions, for which reason forecasting and simulation become problematic.

Planning methodology and problem solving can in many cases be reasonably well specified and developed so they can facilitate planning-based decision making relating to closed and contained change, whereas open-ended change remains a challenge for several reasons. One basic consideration in this respect is that the uncertainties involved in complex decision making are principally of a generic type that cannot be satisfactorily dealt with by detailing and refining conventional planning methods that work well in situations with closed and contained change. Specifically for complex

planning problems the planning environment when approached by conventional planning thinking is seen to "complexify" along three dimensions, which is why the following complexity categories are relevant to deal with:

- Detail complexity;
- Dynamic complexity;
- Preference complexity.

Basically we will associate detail complexity with "means" and dynamic complexity with "path," whereas preference complexity relates primarily to "ends."

The application of systems science for improving our problem-solving capabilities holds two promises (Leleur, 2005: 22):

- By seeing our problem or study object as a system, we may make use of the systems concepts to create a better representation of it and here capture (and model) various interrelations among elements and so on in a more qualified way.

- By seeing our problem as a system, we may be able to focus less on step-by-step approaches and capture more holistic impressions that can qualify our study.

The first statement above concerns what is sometimes referred to as systems analysis. In an almost generic process we commence by defining our problem and determining the objectives. After this we turn to envisage or model the consequences of various relevant alternatives. Then we appraise the alternatives to make it possible to select the best one. The final step concerns the implementation of this alternative and it may be decided to continue the process by monitoring it (Leleur, 2000: 18). Our ideal in this undertaking is to be rational in our decision making so that the analytical processing of complete information will lead to an optimal result, be it a decision, design, plan, and so on. We will see this as a systematic approach.

The second statement relating to the use of systems science expresses that wholeness matters and it can therefore be seen as a corrective to the first one. With the systematic

| Simplicity Paradigm | Complexity Paradigm |
|---|---|
| Universality | Multiplicity |
| Determinism | Organization |
| Dependence | Autonomy |
| Necessity | Possibility |
| Lawfulness | Self-organization |
| Prediction | Surprise |
| Separation | Wholeness |
| Identity | Individuality |
| The general | The particular |
| Objects | Subject |
| Elements | Interactions |
| Matter | Life |
| Quantity | Quality |
| Linear causality | Multicausality |
| The automaton | Time |
| Objectivity | Culture |

**Table 1** *The two paradigms of simplicity and complexity*

| SP Method Structure | Systemic | Systematic |
|---|---|---|
| Scanning | Example: Critical systems heuristics | Example: Scenario analysis |
| Assessment | Example: Futures workshop | Example: Multicriteria analysis and simulation |

**Table 2** *The SP structure as four interrelated modes of exploration and learning. Different methods are indicated to illustrate some possible method choice.*

approach we proceed in our planning and problem solving by using a step-by-step approach; with the systemic approach we are concerned with holistic views.

No doubt the systematic approach is tied to the rational-analytical thinking well known to people educated, for example, as engineers and economists, whereas the notion of being systemic is more difficult to understand and come to grips with. In this situation the paradigms about simplicity and complexity by Morin become highly relevant, where a paradigm denotes a basic research orientation and pattern. Fundamentally, Morin sees classic scientific explanation as based on a simplicity paradigm. Although he recognizes the strength of the simplicity paradigm in many respects, he also identifies certain limitations to its explanatory models. As physics and cosmological thinking have always been major suppliers of ideas to other branches of science, it stands out that subnuclear physics is the main example that Morin uses to argue the insufficiency of the simplicity paradigm, as this branch of physics cannot satisfactorily explain new so-

called exotic particles, for example. Against this background, Morin proposes a complexity paradigm to reorient and widen our research activities. Specifically, he suggests principles for the complexity paradigm that are complementary to those contained in the simplicity paradigm. Table 1 indicates Morin's two paradigms by some paired keywords (Morin, 1974, 1986; Leleur, 2005: 24).

As concerns the development of systemic planning, we will see systemic thinking as rooted in the complexity paradigm and systematic thinking as rooted in simplicity thinking. The idea is not to replace systematic thinking with systemic thinking, but to make wider planning possible by applying both. As the conventional planning approach is tied to systematic thinking, we adopt the term systemic for such wider analysis in which we choose to include both systematic and systemic findings and not just the latter. In this way, systemic planning (SP) seeks to generalize the conventional well-known planning approach that in this context can be seen as relating primarily to systematic planning and problem solving.

Another basic complementary relationship behind SP concerns scanning vs. assessment. Dealing with planning and problem solving, exploration and learning will depend on alternating between these two modes; that is, they cannot both be problematized at the same time but will reciprocally influence each other. By cross-referencing the two pairs of complementary relationships we obtain the basic methodological structure behind SP shown in Table 2 (Leleur, 2005: 127):

E:CO Vol. 9 Nos. 1-2 2007 pp. 2-10

| Current Methods Available for SP – Bold Type Indicates the Methods Made Use of in the Øversund Fixed Link Case | |
|---|---|
| Analytical hierarchy process (AHP) | Interactive planning (IP) |
| Computer-aided design (CAD) | Intuitive exploration/brainstorming/meta- |
| Conflict analysis | phor and analogy building |
| Cost–benefit analysis (CBA) and cost-effective- | Linear programming techniques |
| ness analysis (CEA) | **Multicriteria analysis (MCA)** |
| **Critical systems heuristics (CSH)** | Multiple perspectives (MP) |
| Critical path method (CPM) | Network theory |
| Cross-impact analysis | Optimization theory and heuristics |
| Decision analysis (DA) applying SMART and | Program evaluation and review techniques |
| SMARTER | (PERT) |
| Delphi conferencing techniques | **Scenario analysis** |
| Environmental impact assessment (EIA) | Sensitivity analysis |
| Expert systems | **Simulation** |
| Forecasting | Soft systems methodology (SSM) |
| **Futures workshop (FW)** | Statistics, probability and queuing theory |
| Fuzzy set theory | Strengths, weaknesses, opportunities, and |
| Game theory | threats analysis (SWOT) |
| Graph theory | Systems dynamics |
| Input–output analysis | Total systems intervention (TSI) |

**Table 3** *The SP toolbox made up of various hard and soft OR methods*

### The tools of systemic planning

The SP approach is developed by making use of the generic structure shown in Table 2. Generally this is carried out by applying appropriate OR methods (see Table 3) in a self-organizing process that embeds conventional optimization in a wider process of exploration and learning (Leleur, 2005: 35). The ongoing search–learn–debate process moves on by contrasting and interpreting the different findings and insights. The process aims at converging into a satisfactory end result for the decision makers.

Generally, "hard" OR methods can be seen to provide first-order findings based on calculative rationality, whereas second-order findings (or even higher) are associated with "soft" OR methods – based on communicative rationality – that relate to the so-called subworld created around a complex problem by the various stakeholders and participants in the process (Dreyfus & Dreyfus, 1988: 76; Leleur, 2005: 72–73, 107).

The SP exploration and learning cycle makes it possible to deal with a complex problem in a much more explicit way. The example below describes some findings relating to the Øresund Fixed Link, where the set of four methods in Table 2 was applied (Leleur, 2005: 132–136).

### Overview and application example

The Øresund Fixed Link – open since July 2000 – can be regarded as one of the most complex transport investment decisions made in Scandinavia (Leleur, *et al.*, 2004; Leleur, 2005: 119–137). The case work demonstrated how the huge amount of information produced in studies and so on over the years could have formed part of an ex-ante examination of how to apply the SP approach. In this respect the case has functioned as a kind of evaluation research methodology laboratory (Leleur, 2005). The idea of the ex-post study, undertaken three to four years after the opening of the fixed link, is to consider and review the impacts and the ex-ante evaluation methodology to examine whether the latter was appropriate. Therefore, the study aims at informing planning and evaluation methodology and possibly updating it. However, the ex-post study cannot give certain results concerning the ex-ante methodology stemming from the beginning of the 1990s, with the decision to implement being taken back in 1994. Development could have been otherwise if, for example, new issues of high relevance of various types had arisen: Danish and Swedish legislation being counterproductive for integration across the Øresund, an oil supply crisis, and so on. However, saying that a narrow cost–benefit analysis for large infrastructure planning is at best insufficient is a generally relevant finding, which is exemplified by the wider approach presented below that makes use of systemic planning (SP) ideas, which are briefly reiterated.

With an emphasis on a search–learn–debate process that develops around contrasting and interpreting the upcoming intermediate findings and insights of the planning problem, a group of four complementary methodologies was selected after some scrutiny; see Table 2. These SP principles for guiding the search–learn–debate process do not draw on an overarching kind of rationality; in fact, applying German sociologist Niklas Luhmann's view on selection and complex processes, the theme of rationality in the SP process,

*"disintegrates into a typology of distinct rationalities, whose relations to one another can no longer be subsumed under the requirements of rationality – in, for example, some sort of ranking."* (Luhmann, 1996: 171)

Then in SP there is no general rationality blueprint when proceeding and doing this or that in the planning process. This is part of the theoretical underpinnings of systemic planning (SP); further detail behind the formulation of SP relating to, among other things, Luhmann's perception of social systems and his contingency/complexity thinking – perceived as representing third-wave systems science – is given in the book *Systemic Planning* (Leleur, 2005: 40–48, 83–94).

The OR methods that were made use of in the Øresund Fixed Link (see Table 3) were critical systems heuristics (CSH), scenario analysis (SA), futures workshop (FW), multicriteria analysis (MCA), and simulation (SI). Basic methodology references are Jackson (2000); Midgley (2000); Flood (1999); Drewes, *et al.*

(2004); and Goodwin & Wright (1999).

In brief, CSH mapped decision coalitions ("players") and their motives and different responses at certain stages, whereas SA and FW provided a set of interrelating framework and trend scenarios. In that way several future images were constructed and each of these was examined using MCA and SI. These latter methods produced some quantitative expressions that illuminated some aspects of the complex investment project. In addition, the application of MCA and SI also made it relevant to reconsider some of the CSH and FW analyses and results concerning, for example, the integrative role of the new bridge linking not just two major cities across a strait but also two countries and, furthermore, giving all Nordic countries access from Scandinavia to the central part of Europe.

There was general agreement among the participants – representing both researchers and (some of) the identified stakeholders – at a seminar in 2004 where the results were presented that the assessment insights found could not have been achieved by making use of the standard cost–benefit approach that would normally be applied for such a study (Leleur, *et al.*, 2004). In this respect it should be noted that the SP approach has been conducted as a kind of comparative study as, among other things, it has been possible to make comparisons with the actual examination process before the construction work began in 1994. To illustrate the iterative, nonlinear planning process prescribed by SP, Table 4 presents some intermediate findings. As a general characteristic, it can be noted that certain insights gained with one of the applied methods in a particular category trigger new examinations in one or more of the categories. New stakeholder preferences revealed in the systemic assessment category may, for example, lead to new scenarios being relevant in the systematic scanning category and so on. In this way the total process becomes one of exploration and learning.

The outcome of the type of examination outlined above showed that the Øresund Fixed Link was a feasible project from a societal point of view if – as it turned out – different strategic impacts such as European and re-

| Some Intermediate Findings and Specifications that Can Feed Back into the Process | |
|---|---|
| Systemic scanning: Issues of identification and demarcation<br><br>General concerns:<br>• Øresund region one of several spheres<br>• The meaning of national barriers<br>• Drivers: market, clusters, culture, etc.<br>• Infrastructure and development<br><br>Specific concerns:<br>• Limitations of cause-effect model<br>• Interpretation of expressed expectations | Systematic scanning: Issues relating to scenarios<br><br>Regional scenarios:<br>• Economy, regulation, transport, etc.<br>• Local integration vs. nonintegration<br>• Baltic Sea development: trade etc.<br>• Competitive transport development<br><br>EU-wide scenarios:<br>• Economy, regulation, transport<br>• Trends: resources and technology<br>• Trends: modal policies etc. |
| Systemic assessment: Issues relating to stakeholder preferences<br><br>Ex-ante:<br>• Local pro-coalition<br>• Local environmental anti-coalition<br>• National interest<br>• International pro-coalition<br><br>Ex-post:<br>• National interest<br>• Øresund region citizens<br>• Øresund companies<br>• International interest | Systematic assessment: Issues relating to multicriteria analysis<br><br>Narrow feasibility (CBA):<br>• Investment<br>• Time savings<br>• Cost savings<br>• Local emissions and accidents<br><br>Wider feasibility (MCA):<br>• Network and mobility<br>• Global emissions ($CO_2$)<br>• Employment<br>• Logistics and goods effects |

**Table 4** *Intermediate findings and specifications based on SP exploration and learning*

gional mobility, regional employment, climate effects, and so on were considered and included in the assessment. Such wider impacts are not part of a conventional cost–benefit analysis (CBA), which is why the SP approach is found more suitable considering that the actual Øresund case is much more complex than, for example, ordinary medium-sized Danish highway projects that are recurrently examined by CBA (Leleur, 2000). In the case presented here the focus has been on methodology and process aspects; a full account of specific results and a closer description of details and other study information are available in Leleur, *et al.* (2004) and – with emphasis on their principal interpretation as relating to systemic planning – Leleur (2005).

**Findings and perspective**

Below a summary is given of the general findings relating to the formulation of systemic planning principles and methodology (Leleur, 2005: 107–108, 76).

• The systemic planner needs to assess that the actual planning task is really suitable for a systemic approach. This means that simple cause–effect relationships cannot be obtained and that the characterizing features of the problem are complex to some extent along the dimensions of means, path, and ends, expressing varying degrees of detail, dynamic, and preference complexity. Such a problem has earlier been categorized as open ended. The planner ends up perceiving that the planning task is "beyond" a conventional approach and decides to continue with a systemic one.

- Against this background it becomes relevant to start building knowledge about the concrete "subworld" that will unfold in the course of events and to set up a planning team that can be expected to handle this. Some kind of framework to assist in structuring a search–learn–debate process could be relevant and could be developed with different purposes in mind. The generic structure presented in Table 2 makes it possible in a kind of nonlinear "iteration" to contrast subsequent findings and insights based on cross-referencing methodologically the pair scanning and assessment with systemic and systematic, "filled in" with suitable planning methods for the problem. Findings and insights can be highly different in nature: Some may be derived from mathematical modeling as optimization relating to "what-if" considerations; others may concern issues raised by different power coalitions; and still other issues will have to do with implementation and so on. The planning unfolds by making use of findings and insights, be they of first, second, or even higher order. The latter may in some cases be expected if, for example, the "wickedness" of the problem is due to politics and power issues.

- The systemic approach can be built on a major methodological base (see Table 3), and one should expect that in real-life studies highly different methods will sometimes be applied in combination. In the case presented above, among other things, the "soft" critical systems heuristics (CSH) approach is applied together with the "hard" multicriteria methodology. Needless to say, the choice of specific methods is important and ought to be driven by the actual planning problem.

No doubt a systemic planning process should be expected to be demanding in skills, resources, and so on. For this reason alone, undertaking a systemic planning study should be contemplated ahead of its commencement. A general characterization as demanding, compared to conventional planning tasks where suitable planning routines and methods are available, follows from the successive establishment of the necessary subworld around it; from applying and combining different methods it needs to be seen how they perform and provide formation of meaning and understanding in the particular context consisting of the planning problem and its environment, stakeholders, planners, concrete interpretations, narratives, suggestions, paradoxes, and so on.

If a kind of epistemology should be sketched on the background of generalizing planning thinking, we have to move from a hierarchical, well-ordered input–output process toward a wider process that also contains what we may see as networks or heterarchies. What characterizes a heterarchy is that there is no single "monitor" and no single "highest level." The instrumental reason for conventional planning has, furthermore, been embedded in a wider communicative rationality, which can be seen as a move from a foundational hypothetic-deductive orientation toward a nonfoundational perception; that is, the communications-based agreement.

In Table 5 a new outlook for planning as systemic planning is presented in an overview by comparing issues that characterize it – ranging from problem type to the view above on epistemology – with those of conventional planning. In this respect it can be noted that a consequence of applying the thinking of Morin, Luhmann, and Habermas leads to biperspectivism based on both simplicity and complexity orientations as concerns the paradigm of thinking, and to a nonfoundational, so-called sympoietic orientation based on communicative action as concerns epistemology. The concept of sympoiesis – inspired by seeing autopoietic systems forming co-evolutionary networks – has been introduced with the formulation of systemic planning to indicate the phenomenon and outcome of reciprocal relationships between individual entities and ensembles (Leleur, 2005: 97). Whereas Habermas is well established in current systems science theory and practice – see for example Midgley (2000) and Jackson (2000) – the reception and application of Morin and Luhmann are less so. To point to this situation – and to the fact that a

| Issues of Characterization | Conventional Planning | A New Outlook for Planning |
|---|---|---|
| Problem type | Simple, defined as noncomplex | Complex, not just complicated |
| Paradigm of thinking | Simplicity representing monoperspectivism | Both simplicity and complexity representing biperspectivism |
| Rationale of planning | Mainly proactive and optimizing, with emphasis on models | Mainly enabling and mediating, with emphasis also on learning |
| Professions involved | Engineers, economists, geographers, etc. | Also sociologists, political scientists, etc. |
| Planning practice | A linear process of activities ("tasks"), dominated by first-order findings that can be combined to produce a plan | A nonlinear (self-organizing, autocatalytic) process of activities ("events"), both first- and second-order findings |
| Epistemology | Foundational, hypothetico-deductive ("hierarchical input–output"), based on instrumental reason | Nonfoundational, sympoietic ("heterarchical networks"), based on communicative action |

**Table 5** *Comparison of conventional planning with a new outlook for planning*

complexity orientation could provide managers and planners with other insights than those associated with metaphors derived from deterministic, chaotic models ("chaos management"; see Stacey, 1993) – the conceptual underpinnings of systemic planning relating especially to the work of Luhmann are considered further in Leleur (2006).

Whether systemic planning is warranted or not depends on the actual circumstances and our interpretation of these. Clearly, there have been cases where conventional planning has failed as conditions were not right for a systematic approach; and clearly also there can be no guarantees that widening planning into what we have called systemic planning, comprising both "hard" and "soft" methodologies, will be successful. The applications so far, however, are promising. Therefore we argue that SP holds potential as guidance for planning in a context of open-ended, complex problems necessitating proactive decision making. Increasing complexity in society in general and in the professional spheres of administration and business more specifically, combined with the flexibility and adaptability of SP, make it relevant to pursue a further development of the current SP principles and methodology.

**References**

Dreyfus, H. L. and Dreyfus, S. E. (1988). *Mind Over Machine*, ISBN 9780029080610.

Drewes Nielsen, L., Homann Jespersen, P. and Hartmann-Pedersen, K. (2004). "Future workshops on freight transport: A methodology for actor involvement," *World Transport Policy and Practice*, ISSN 1352-7614, 10(3): 36-41.

Flood, R. L. (1999). *Rethinking the Fifth Discipline: Learning within the Unknowable*, ISBN 9780415185301.

Goodwin, P. and Wright, G. (1999). *Decision Analysis for Management Judgment*, 2nd edn, ISBN 9780470861080 (2004).

Jackson, M. C. (2000). *Systems Approaches to Management*, ISBN 9780306465062 (2005).

Leleur, S. (2000). *Road Infrastructure Planning: A Decision-Oriented Approach*, 2nd edn, ISBN 9788750208242.

Leleur, S. (2005). *Systemic Planning: Principles and Methodology for Planning in a Complex World*, ISBN 9788750209652. See www.systemicplanning.dk.

Leleur, S. (2006). "Systems science and complexity: Comparing a complexity-based orientation with other current research orientations," UK Systems Society Annual Conference 2006, September.

Leleur, S., Holvad, T., Jensen, A. V. and Salling, K. B. (2004). *Development of the CLG-DSS Evaluation Model*, ISBN 9788791639012.

Luhmann, N. (1996). *Social Systems*, ISBN 9780804726252.

Midgley, G. (2000). *Systemic Intervention: Philosophy, Methodology, and Practice*, ISBN 9780306464881.

Morin, E. (1974). "Complexity," *International Social Science Journal*, ISSN 0020-8701, 36(4): 555-582.

Morin, E. (1986). "Kompleksitetens bud," *Paradigma*, ISSN 1600-0285, 1(1): 18-20.

Stacey, R. D. (1993). The Chaos Frontier: Creative Strategic Control for Business, ISBN 9780750609500.

**Steen Leleur** is professor of decision support systems and planning at the Centre for Traffic and Transport at the Technical University of Denmark. Currently he is, among other things, involved in research on topics about systems analysis and evaluation methodology in the Centre for Logistics and Goods Transport. His most recent book, *Systemic Planning: Principles and Methodology for Planning in a Complex World*, treats the issues of uncertainty and complexity as relating to strategic planning and evaluation problems. Previously he has published textbooks in Danish and English about traffic planning and highway engineering. He received his MSc in engineering in 1972 at the Technical University of Denmark and his doctoral dissertation about investment planning at the same university in 1984. Over the years Leleur has been involved in many international transport planning and evaluation research projects, several within the European Commission's strategic transport research programs.

Phenomeno-semantic complexity
E:CO Issue Vol. 9 Nos. 1-2 2007 pp. 11-21

Academic

# Phenomeno-semantic complexity:
# A proposal for an alternative notion of complexity as a foundation for the management of complexity in human affairs*

Darek M. Eriksson
Lulea University of Technology, SWE

This paper proposes a novel notion of complexity, derived from the process of semantic and syntactical transformation of message as communicated between sense-making actors. It distinguishes between complexity driven by syntactical transformation and that driven by semantic transformation. This last is also divided into first- and second-order transformation, the former relating to the observing system and the latter to the observed system of an inquiry. The proposed notion of complexity is juxtaposed with the mainstream notion of complex systems, typically understood as the interaction of adaptive agents governed by local rules, yet giving rise to novel unpredictable global behavior. The proposed notion of phenomenological semantic complexity is illustrated with some examples taken from real-life human affairs. The proposed and conventional notions of complexity are regarded as complementary, yet they require different research strategies; some suggestions for further research are therefore put forward here.

## Introduction

This paper presents intermediate findings from ongoing research into the management of complexity in human affairs. A distinction between *ontological syntactic complexity* and *phenomenological semantic complexity* is introduced, where the former refers to conventional approaches to complexity studies, such as the interaction of adaptive agents governed by local rules giving rise to unpredictable global behavior. The latter, on the other hand, refers to complexity that emerges in the process of communication between sense-making actors, resulting in syntactic and/or semantic transformations, and leading to unpredicted complex behavior in human affairs. This distinction gives rise to promising implications for the practical management of complexity in human affairs in general, and so-called knowledge-intensive enterprises in particular. One such central implication of the novel notion of complexity introduced here is the switch of attention from algorithmic simulation resources to linguistic and communicative models and systems supporting human communication processes.

The text continues with a brief characterization of the contemporary mainstream approach to studies of complexity, leading to identification of some of its key characteristics. The proposed model of *phenomeno-semantic complexity* is then introduced. This model serves as a foundation for distinguishing the complexity arising from syntactic and semantic transformations in the communication process between sense-making actors. The latter is further divided into first-order and second-order semantic complexity, referring to the observing system and the observed system respectively. Some illustrations from real-life human affairs are then presented, while suggestions for further research and conclusions end the paper.

## Conventional notion of complexity: Onto-syntactic

An overview of the conventional notions of complexity is presented in this section, ending with an identification of some of its key characteristics. These will be used to contrast the notion of complexity as introduced here, and will thus contribute to the articulation of its novelty and value.

## Outlines of the contemporary theory of complexity

In his classical paper "Science and complexity," Weaver (1948) distinguishes between three classes of phenomena: simple phenomena addressed by science by means of classical mechanics, those of disorganized complexity that are addressed with thermodynamics, and finally those of organized complexity, which could not yet be successfully addressed by science.

Since that time, a large number of proposals have been put forward regarding the notion of complexity, its measurement, and approaches to its management. Early examples include attempts by the founders of cybernetics and systems sciences, such as Ashby's (1962, 1964, 1965) "law of requisite variety," where complexity is understood in terms of variety, and Boulding's (1956) layered model of nine classes of systems, where each successive class is more complex, with emerging properties, yet without providing any explicit definition of complexity. The Nobel Laureate Simon (1969) proposed a general notion of hierarchical structure of complexity. Other notions include computational complexity, addressing the amount of computational resource (time or memory) needed to solve a class of problem (c.f. Hinegardner & Engelberg, 1983) and Kolmogorov complexity, which focuses on the minimum length of a Turing machine program needed to generate a pattern (Kolmogorov, 1965). Kauffman introduced a working definition of complexity for the formal models of self-organization he was investigating, where complexity is the number of conflicting constraints (Kauffman, 1993).

More recently, attempts have been made to formulate general principles that guide the behavior of complex phenomena, such as Bak's "self-organized criticality" (Bak, 1997; Bak et al., 1987; Bak & Sneppen, 1993). In this, many out-of-equilibrium systems naturally organize themselves, without external tuning or prodding, into a state that is at the threshold between complete disorder and complete order. The system can thus be said to organize itself into a critical state. This approach has, however, been challenged by critics (Sneppen & Newman, 1996; Newman, 1996). Today's most promising approach, for the conception of complex systems, seems to be the so-called notion of complex adaptive systems (Holland, 1994).[1]

The behavior of a complex adaptive system (CAS) is regarded as dynamic, out of equilibrium, and thus highly nonlinear. Such systems manifest the emergence of laws and patterns of order through cooperative effects of the subunits, agents of a complex system; that is, local coordination. CAS employ feedback mechanisms, parallel processing, and simple local rules directing adaptive agents, which in turn can give rise to collective or global behavior of great complexity and variety, where deduction of the emergent behavior is very difficult. CAS are typically characterized by internal in-homogeneity of the system (i.e., it consists of a number of different classes of autonomous agents), adaptation of agents in the system, nonlinear interaction between parts of the system, and the net-like causal structure of the system (high connectivity); see Holland, 1995, 1998; Casti, 1997). They are therefore modeled as a set of agents, with local rules for behavior providing local coordination, giving rise to an emerged global behavior and self-organization.

An example of a CAS is an ant colony that organizes itself without a leader; that is, without any central and top-down directed coordination. Each ant appears to go about its own business, following a few simple rules determining its interaction with its environment or its fellow ants. An incredibly complex and organized society emerges from this interaction, displaying adaptation to changing circumstances.

---

1 There have been various reports of successful application of findings from complexity research. Researchers, for example, have discovered that heart fibrillation can be modeled with equations based on chaos theory (Garfinkel et al., 1992). Other interesting applications include Holland's (1994) ECHO, artificial stock markets (Arthur et al., 1997), and Sugarscape, a simulation of social systems (Epstein & Axtell, 1998).

E:CO Vol. 9 Nos. 1-2 2007 pp. 11-21

## Key characteristics of the contemporary theory of complexity

The contemporary notions of complexity as outlined above may be understood in terms of some of their key characteristics. First, *naturalism*, where the empirical observations made as a basis for induction of theoretical propositions are most frequently based in physical, chemical, and biological phenomena. The peculiar characteristics of mental systems, both psychological and socio-psychological, such as sense making or power structures, are not accounted for. Secondly, *syntactic orientation*, where understanding of the complex behavior of studied phenomena emerges from numerical simulation models using a set of rules guiding the interaction of the constituting components. This is shown by syntactic manipulation – that is, representation – rather than focusing on the pragmatic and semantic aspects of the phenomena studied. Thirdly, *objectification*, where studies of complexity focus mainly on the observed system and do not seriously account for the observing system; in this endeavor, such studies typically assume a kind of ontological representation; that is, a direct correspondence between the model and the modeled phenomena. These three characteristics allow us to label the contemporary notions of complexity as "onto-syntactic." We shall soon see that although this notion of complexity is helpful in making various complex phenomena intelligible, it does not do full justice to human affairs and their management, where sense making is a key feature.

## Alternative notion of complexity: Phenomeno-semantic

In this section, we will present the proposed alternative and complementary notion of complexity, labeled the model of "phenomeno-semantic complexity." The argument is built on the conception of complexity and emergence presented by Le Moigne (1990: Chap. 5). However, while Le Moigne's model, of "information that transforms organization," focuses on the syntactic part of emergence and complexity, the approach proposed here takes a further step toward the semantic component of information, giving rise to a novel argu-

ment. Although in a very different manner, a semantic approach to complexity has also been assumed by other investigators, such as Warfield (2004) for example.

In short, the construction of the argument starts by recalling Richards and Ogden's triangle of meaning, and proceeds with Naess's notion of empirical semantics, followed by Shannon's model of communication, and ends with the support from Quastler's model of transmission transformation.

## The inaccessibility of meaning

Ogden and Richards's (1985) *triangle of meaning* (originally published 1923) proposes a conception of meaning as a structure of three components. First, the very meaning, or idea, or mental concept held by a human being in his or her mind. Secondly, a thing, object, or referent, which is supposed to be represented by the mental concept mentioned. Thirdly, the symbol, term, or signal that is supposed to represent the mental concept, and thus also the object; see Figure 1 for an illustration. This notion conforms to contemporary positions within semiotics (e.g., Deeley, 1990; Nöth, 1990) and its recent advances (e.g., Stonier, 1997; Brier, 1998).

Although Ogden's triangle of meaning is well known and accepted as such, it is

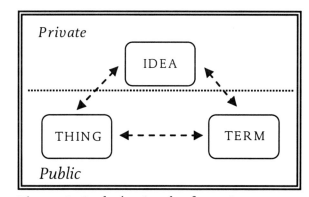

**Figure 1** *Ogden's triangle of meaning, consisting of three related components: (i) the meaning, or mental concept, or Idea; (ii) the object, or referent, or Thing, which the mental concept is about; (iii) the symbol, Term, or signal, representing the mental concept. The Idea is private for the individual as only he or she may access it directly, while the Thing and the Term are public, as they may be accessed by other individuals.*

the very nature of the relationship between its constituting components that creates discussions. We will borrow the proposals of *empirical semantics*, initially pioneered by the Norwegian philosopher Arne Naess (1953), as a kind of reaction against the teachings of the Vienna Circle and their logical positivism, which placed all focus on formalism; that is, formal semantics.

Naess states that there is no one-to-one direct and exclusive relationship between our expressions, clauses, sentences, symbols, and the meaning that we assign to them. For example, the sentence "Putin is ill" and the sentence "Putin is bad" may both mean that [Putin is not healthy]. Yet, the sentence "Putin is bad" may also mean that [Putin is a poor politician]. Further, Naess states that there is no one-to-one direct and exclusive relationship between our mental concepts, ideas, or meanings, on the one hand, and the actual situation, or objects, or facts in the world, on the other. For example, the expression "morning star" typically means [the strongest shining star in the morning, in the east], while in fact it is {the second planet from the sun, in the Milky Way}. A second expression, "evening star," typically means [the strongest shining star in the evening, in the west], while it is in fact {the second planet from the sun, in the Milky Way}. To make the example even more compelling, a third expression, "Venus," typically means [the second planet from the sun, in the Milky Way] and in fact is {the second planet from the sun, in the Milky Way}.

The lack of direct and exclusive relationship between the three components of the meaning triangle gives rise to difficulties in communication and hence understanding between people and in human affairs. An example is the vagueness of terms, such as in the expression "being bald"; a more careful investigation gives rise to the question: How much – or little – hair does a person need to be described as "bald"?

If we accept the propositions presented above, we must conclude that there is a clear risk of misunderstanding the meaning of things in the world, and the terms we use to denote these things, as well as our ideas about these things.

## Communication as unintended transformation of meaning

An instance of Ogden's triangle of meaning, as presented above, is valid for one individual at a time. Thus, if two individuals wish to communicate, we may conceive this in terms of two triangles of meaning attempting to match each other. More specifically: Idea 1 in the mind of Man 1 represents Thing 1 and is represented by Term 1. This term is then communicated to Man 2, who is supposed to interpret it as Idea 1 and refer it to Thing 1. In this, the idea of Man 1 and Man 2 is private – that is, only the conceiving man has direct mental access to the idea – while the Term as well as the Thing are public, as several individuals may perceive them. This situation is valid when the communication is about things existing in the world, for example those that manifest a physical experience. When the communication refers to a design – that is, a thing that is designed and yet not constructed – then the only public referent is the Term – that is, until such time as the construction of the design is realized. Figure 2 illustrates these relationships and directs us to Shannon and Weaver's (1949) classic *model of communication*. We recognize that it was formulated for the conception of machine communication rather than human. When adapting it to the latter, we shall superimpose it onto the above-mentioned two communicating meaning triangles and Naess's notion of empirical semantics.

In Shannon and Weaver's model of communication, the sender, here Man 1, has an Idea 1, which he encodes, resulting in Term 1, a symbol or signal. This is then physically communicated to the receiver, here Man 2, who decodes the symbols received, resulting in Idea 2. Typically, the intention of the sender, here Man 1, is that the receiver, here Man 2, shall have the same idea, hence Idea 1 = Idea 2. Figure 3 illustrates this concept.

The usefulness of Shannon's model of communication is that it facilitates the identification of two types of sources of noise, or transformation of the message, in the process of communication. These are (i) the semantic transformation; and (ii) the syntactic transformation. This is illustrated in Figure 3.

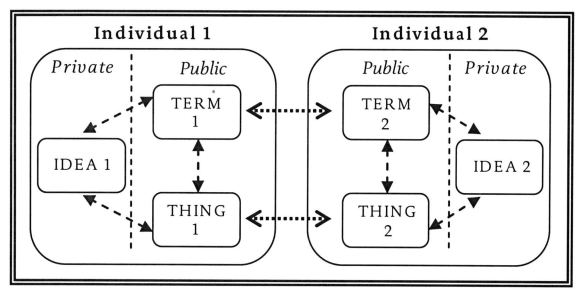

**Figure 2** *The relationship between two triangles of meaning attempting to communicate. The two individuals communicate about the Thing with the help of the Term; where the latter two are public while the individuals' Ideas are private.*

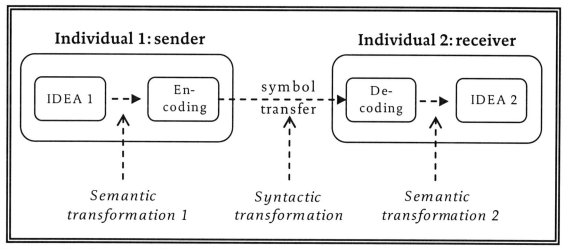

**Figure 3** *The Shannon and Weaver model of communication. In this, a sender, Individual 1, has an Idea 1 that is formalized into a symbol, by means of encoding and then physically transferring it to the receiver, here Individual 2. The latter interprets the received symbol by decoding it, which gives rise to an Idea 2. The purpose of this communication is to secure that the Idea 1 of the sender is the same as the Idea 2 of the receiver. This goal is challenged by two types of transformation: the semantic transformation that occurs during encoding and decoding, and the syntactic transformation that occurs during the physical transfer of the symbol.*

*Syntactic transformation* emerges when the actual syntax, symbol, or signal, here Term 1, is physically transferred from the sender to the receiver. In electronic communication this often occurs as a result of various interferences with other electronic signals. In human mouth-to-mouth communication, this may occur due to interference with other sound waves, for example when a construc-tion machine generates sounds outside an open window to a room where two people are talking. For instance, while the sender, Man 1, says to the receiver, Man 2, "I am not ill," the sound interference may make Man 2 hear "I am ill."

*Semantic transformation* may emerge in two places in the communication model pre-sented. First, when an idea of a sender, here Idea

1 of Man 1, is encoded – that is, formalized into symbols, here Term A – and in the process of encoding or formalization some of the meaning is missed. We can denote that here as formalization noise, or encoding noise. An intuitive example of this is a textbook on how to ski or swim: Anyone who skis or swims knows that even though such a book may be instructive in many aspects, it is not enough merely to read the textbook to acquire sufficient knowledge and skills to be able to ski or swim.

The second instance of semantic transformation is when a receiver decodes a received symbol, hence interpretation noise or decoding noise. Here, Man 2 receives Term 1, which is supposed to give rise to Idea 1. In the process of assigning meaning to a symbol some meaning may be lost, or an alternative meaning may be assigned.

These two processes of formalization and interpretation bring us to phenomenological and constructivist notions of knowledge, as well as to interpretive sociology and to hermeneutics, when we reason about the psychological and social conditions and circumstances of formalization and interpretation. While this is important, it lies outside the scope of this paper; for the purpose of our argument here, it is enough to articulate the intentional, hence psychic quality of the processes mentioned, where syntactic transformation and semantic transformation are understood as unintended transformations of meaning.

Furthermore, to support this unintended transformation of meaning, we would like to recall Quastler's (1964) *model of transition transformation*. This model served to formalize Shannon's model, which states that the receiver does not hear everything expressed by the sender, while the receiver may hear things that the sender does not express; see Figure 4 for an illustration.

While Quastler's model of transition transformation articulates syntactic transformation (i.e., transformation of the code, symbol, signal term), Naess's empirical semantics articulates the semantic transformation (i.e., transformation of the meaning, idea, concept).

To summarize, we have now advanced a model of transformation of both the syntax

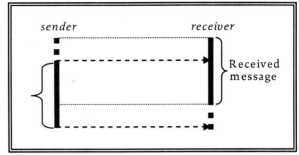

**Figure 4** *A graphical illustration of Quastler's (1964) model of transition transformation. It manifests the sender sending a message which the receiver receives only in part, while the receiver also receives a message that the sender did not send.*

and the semantics of a message. If a message communicated between two sense-making individuals, for example two employees in an organization, is utilized to stimulate the design and execution of actions, hence behavior, the transformation of such a message may be understood as a foundation or driver of the emergence of unpredicted behavior in psychological and social phenomena.

The syntactic transformation provides a foundation for advancing various original notions of emergence, complexity, and self-organization. These include von Foerster's (1959) order from noise model; Atlan's (1972, 1979) complexity from noise model; Varela's (1979) self-in-formation model; and Le Moigne's (1990) model of self-organization. For this reason, we would now like to focus attention on semantic transformation as a source of complexity or emergence of novel and unpredicted behavior.

**First- and second-order semantic complexity**
It follows on from the above that semantic transformation may occur only in the case of communication between two or more sense-making actors with the ability to communicate linguistically. We will thus limit our further inquiry to human activity systems (see Checkland, 1981, for further discussion of the peculiar characteristics of such systems).

Another distinction that we wish to introduce is that between an object system and a subject system. When behavior of a phenomenon such as an enterprise is investigated,

| Key Concept | In Summary |
|---|---|
| Phenomeno-semantic complexity | When communicated meaning is unintentionally transformed – syntactically and/or semantically – in the process of transmission between two sense-making actors, which may lead to an action on the part of the receiver that cannot be predicted by the sender, hence the emergence of complex behavior. |
| Triangle of meaning of sense-making actor | The indirect relationship between an idea conceived by a sense-making actor, and the object that this idea refers to, and then the symbol or signal that aims to represent that idea and hence also the object of reference. |
| Syntactic transformation | Occurs in the process of transferring a message between two sense-making actors, and refers to the experience when the symbols or signals, representing the meaning to be transferred, are transformed or changed unintentionally. |
| Semantic transformation | Occurs in the process of transferring a message between two sense-making actors, and refers to the experience when the meaning that is received by the receiving sense-making actor is unintentionally different from the one that was sent by the sender; is caused by either formalization noise or interpretation noise. |
| Formalization noise | Occurs when a sender assigns a symbol or signal to an idea to be communicated to a receiver, thus formalizing the idea, while the selected formalism cannot represent the intended idea, as perceived by the receiver. |
| Interpretation noise | Occurs when a symbol or signal is received by a sense-making actor, who then assigns some meaning to it, which differs from the one that was intended by the sender of the signal or symbol. |
| First-order semantic complexification | The process of semantic complexification, as described in the first line above, which emerges in the subject system in the inquiry of an object system; i.e., in the process of communication between sense-making actors that investigate a phenomenon, such as a team of business analysts. |
| Second-order semantic complexification | The process of semantic complexification, as mentioned above, which emerges in the object system in the inquiry of an object system; i.e., in the process of communication between sense-making actors constituting the investigated phenomena, such as an enterprise. |

**Table 1** *An overview of the key concepts of the notion of phenomeno-semantic complexity*

the investigated enterprise is the object system, while those investigating it, for example business analysts, are the subject system. This serves as a foundation for defining the first-order and the second-order semantic complexification, or emergence of complexity, respectively.

*First-order semantic complexification* may emerge in any subject system made up of two or more sense-making actors, as they communicate with regard to the investigation of the object system. The unintended semantic transformation induced there may render the conception of the object system complex. In other words, it is the system modelers and analysts – that is, the subject system – that complexify the model of an object system.

*Second-order semantic complexification* may emerge, in contrast, in any object system constituted by two or more sense-making actors, when thy communicate as required by their operations. This implies that only psychological, socio-psychological, and social systems may manifest second-order semantic complexification; it may not be manifested by, for example, a gas, an immune system, or the interaction of planets in a solar system.

Table 1 presents an overview of the key

concepts of the phenomeno-semantic notion of complexity as introduced here.

## Illustrations

Due to limited space we can only briefly describe three empirical illustrations of complexity in human affairs, emerging from the transformation of the semantics of the message.

The first example was observed in the Swedish Road Administration, during a redesign of its organization from functionally organized to process organized. In the midst of the reorganization, it became evident that the key term employed in the offices, "road," was difficult to define. Further investigation revealed that the term was assigned more than ten distinctly different meanings by the organization, plus a set of versions of those ten meanings, depending on the department and the context of usage of the term. For instance, when a unit in the new organization made a request to another unit for approval of reconstruction of a road in the country, this request was not approved as the receiver interpreted it as another type of road than that intended by the sender. This ambiguity of the key term gave rise to misinterpretations when various organizational functions were expected to communicate in a new manner, due to the proposed organizational redesign. These misinterpretations brought about unintended activities, and thus changed behavior. The proposed solution to this situation was to exclude the term "road" from all operations of the Swedish Road Administration, and to introduce new terms that more specifically and in an unambiguous way represent the phenomena intended.

A second example occurred within the Swedish National Defence (SND) organization, which had also emerged from a reorganization. This took place during the 1990s after the collapse of the Soviet bloc. Prior to the reorganization, the SND was organized strictly functionally into three distinct forces: the Navy, the Army, and the Air Force. These forces were instructed and trained to defend Swedish territory from a Soviet bloc invasion, which represented a static enemy. This made it possible for the three forces to develop their operations semi-independently, with only a low degree of coordination. The new organization, on the other hand, was designed for unspecified enemies, and for operations outside the Swedish territory. This in turn called for a closer collaboration between the three forces. In the initial attempts to execute a closer collaboration, it became evident that the term and the concept of an "order" meant slightly different things within the context of the organizations of the respective forces. Within the Air Force the meaning of an order was strictly and explicitly defined, obliging the actors involved to define several variables before an order could be issued. However, an order within the Navy could be reduced to any signal given by a superior officer. This situation showed that when a Navy actor attempted to send an order to an Air Force actor, the latter did not always interpret it as an order, which gave rise to unpredicted behavior in the operations. The solution to this dilemma was to redefine the term "order" within the SND to give a commonly shared meaning within all three forces.

A third example comes from a marketing and sales organization selling a specific pharmaceutical product. This organization had 15 salespeople detailing the product for the targeted physicians. This detailing implied that a salesperson typically conducted a 20–30-minute face-to-face meeting with a particular physician, to inform him or her about the product and its pharmaceutical and therapy-related features. As is common in today's competitive marketing and sales operations, a product is positioned against targeted customers and key competing products. Briefly, this positioning implies that specific key characteristics of a product are explicitly articulated and communicated to the targeted customers. These characteristics are regarded as the product characteristics most relevant for the current market conditions and aim to manifest the attractiveness of the product, thus promoting its sales. In the case of the pharmaceutical product studied here, the marketing officers did define the product's position, which included a side-effect profile that was milder than the competitors'. However, as the projected sales figures were not obtained, the marketers began an investigation to track its cause, including a customer research investigation into their perception of the product. This showed that the customers did not perceive the product as intended; that is, with a focus on its low-side-effect profile. This, in turn, forced the marketers to investigate the message the salespeople gave the customers by means of a test. Each salesperson had to answer a few questions regarding the product's key characteristics. The results showed that 15 different messages were being communicated to the market, one per salesperson, rather than the one intended message of a low-side-effect profile. Hence, the salespeople were unintentionally transforming the intended message, due to a lack of training and discipline. The marketers issued a new strict training program for the salespeople and implemented monitoring procedures for continuous evaluation of the message sent to the market. Some three months later the sales figures had increased and were closer to those projected.

## Summary and further research

Since conventional approaches to sciences – that is, classical mechanics and statistics – cannot help us to understand certain types of behavior of phenomena, such as that of so-called organized complexity, various promising approaches to the theory of complexity have been advanced in order to make such behavior intelligible. The dominant approach is currently the notion of complex adaptive systems. In this, the constituting agents of a system interact in accordance with local rules, with no top-down master plan, leading to the emergence of a typically contra-intuitive complex behavior of the system as a whole. Investigations and studies of such systems focus on the construction of numerical representations for simulation purposes. While this approach has succeeded in making complex systems intelligible, it does have some inherent limitations. One such limitation considered here is the disregard for the peculiar characteristics of systems where human beings constitute its agents; namely, the ability of sense making.

To remedy this limitation, and make complexity emerging in human affairs intelligible, an alternative and complementary notion of complexity is introduced here: the phenomeno-semantic notion. This focuses on the process of communication between sense-making actors, where complexity, or unpredictable behavior, emerges as a result of unintended transformation of the communication between these actors. Complexity may emerge both as a result of transformation of the communicated syntax and semantics. Furthermore, the proposed approach to complexity also makes a distinction between the complexity that emerges in the communication of the investigated object system, and that emerging in the communication of the investigating subject system, in the very interaction between the subject system and the object system.

A key implication of the notion of complexity introduced here is that making complexity intelligible and manageable in human affairs does not necessarily require advanced symbol processors and mathematical formalism, with its strive for explanation, predication, and control of phenomena. Rather, effort should also be put into development of tools for explicit conceptualization and management of conceptual models, which articulate and specify meanings, in order to strive for plausible intelligibility of the phenomena, its inherent communication and sense making, and in addition learning in its evolution. We have only observed some sporadic yet promising contributions in this regard.

In terms of methodologies, we would like to mention Checkland's (1981) soft systems methodology, which offers a set of conceptual tools for the conception of any human activity system in its effort to produce change. A second contribution is systemic enterprise modeling language, developed to support an unambiguous conception of any enterprise and its operations (Eriksson, 2004; Eriksson & Ståhl, 2005). In a somewhat different manner, both contributions focus attention on the semantic and syntactic content of communication between sense-making actors.

In terms of technologies, we would like to mention the so-called spider management information system, based on theories of cognitive modeling (Eden, 1988) and explicitly providing support for groups of people in their articulation and sharing of meanings (Boland *et al.*, 1994, 1995). A second important contribution is "the coordinator," which is also a computerized information system. It is based on the linguistic theories of the so-called speech acts (Searle, 1969; Searle & van der Verken, 1985), with the purpose of explicitly facilitating unambiguous communication and communicative acts between human agents (Flores *et al.*, 1998). In line with the two examples, Simon (1992), in his critical review of contemporary utilization of information and communication technology, calls for a switch of focus from information processing and its syntactic qualities, into decision making and the semantic qualities in the life of human affairs. In this regard, much more research and development are necessary to further develop our understanding and management of complexity in human affairs emerging from unintended transformation of communication; this is in terms of theories, methodologies, and technologies, where this paper aspires to provide a contribution to the first.

One area of theoretical insight that may merit further research into complexity in human affairs is the multifaceted relationship between the syntactic, the semantic, and the pragmatic aspects of communication and the actions it causes. The syntactic and the semantic aspects alone are addressed here.

## References

Arthur, W., LeBaron, B., Palmer, B. and Taylor, R. (1997). "Asset pricing under endogenous expectations in an artificial stock market," in W. Arthur, S. Durlaf, S. and D. Lane (eds.), *The Economy as an Evolving Complex System II*, vol. XXVII of Studies in the Sciences of Complexity, ISBN 9780201959888.

Ashby, W. R. (1962). "Principles of self-organizing systems," in H. von Foester and G. W. Zopf (eds.), *Principle of Self-Organization: Transactions of the University of Illinois Symposium*, London, England: Pergamon Press, 255-278.

Ashby, W. R. (1964). *An Introduction to Cybernetics*, ISBN 9780416683004.

Ashby, W. R. (1965). *Design for a Brain*, ISBN 9780412200908.

Atlan, H. (1972). *L'Organisation Biologique et la Théorie de l'Information*, ISBN 9782705613518.

Atlan, H. (1979). *Entre le Cristal et la Fumée: Essai sur l'Organisation du Vivant*, ISBN 9782020052771.

Bak, P. (1997). *How Nature Works: The Science of Self-Organized Criticality*, ISBN 9780387947914.

Bak, P., Tang, C. and Wiesenfeld, K. (1987). "Self organized criticality," *Physical Review A*, ISSN 1050-2947, 38: 367-374.

Bak, P. and Sneppen, K. (1993). "Punctuated equilibrium and criticality in a simple model of evolution," *Physical Review Letters*, ISSN 0031-9007, 71: 4083-4086.

Boland, R. J., Tenkasi, R. V. and Te'eni, D. (1994). "Designing information technology to support distributed cognition," *Organization Science*, ISSN 1047-7039, 5(3): 456-75.

Boland, R. J. and Tenkasi, R. V. (1995). "Perspective making and perspective taking in communities of knowing," *Organization Science*, ISSN 1047-7039, 4(6): 350-372.

Boulding, K. (1956). "General systems theory: The skeleton of science," *Management Science*, ISSN 0025-1909, 2: 197-208.

Brier, S. (1998). "Cybersemiotics: A transdisciplinary framework for information studies," *BioSystems*, ISSN 0303-2647, 46: 185-191.

Casti, J. (1997). *Would-Be Worlds: How Simulation Is Changing the Frontiers of Science*, ISBN 9780471196938 (1998).

Checkland, P. B. (1981). *Systems Thinking, Systems Practice*, ISBN 9780471279112.

Deeley, J. (1990). *Basics of Semiotics*, ISBN 9780253205681.

Eden, C. (1988). "Cognitive mapping," *European Journal of Operations Research*, ISSN 0377-2217, 13: 1-13.

Epstein, J. and Axtell, R. (1998). *Growing Artificial Societies*, ISBN 9780262050531.

Eriksson, D. M. (2004). *Four Proposals for Enterprise Modeling*, doctoral thesis, Chalmers University of Technology.

Eriksson, D. M. and Ståhl. P. (2005). "Proposal for a systemic enterprise modeling language," *Proceedings of the 38th Hawaii International Conference on Systems Sciences*, ISSN 1530-1605.

Flores, F., Graves, M., Hartfield, B. and Winograd, T. (1988). "Computer system and the design of organizational interaction," *ACM Transactions on Information Systems*, ISSN 1046-8188, 6(2): 153-172.

Foerster, von, H. (1959). "On the self-organizing systems and on their environment," reproduced in H. von Foerster (1984), *Observing Systems*, ISBN 9780914105190.

Garfinkel, A, Spano, M. L., Ditto, W. L. and Weiss,

J. N. (1992). "Controlling cardiac chaos," *Science*, ISSN 0193-4511, 257: 1230-1235.

Hinegardner, R. and Engelberg, J. (1983). "Biological complexity," *Journal of Theoretical Biology*, ISSN 0022-5193, 104: 7-20.

Holland, J. (1994). "Echoing emergence: Objectives, rough definitions, and speculations for ECHO-class models," in G. Crownan, D. Pines and D. Meltzer (eds.), *Complexity: Metaphors, Models, and Reality*, ISBN 9780201626063, pp. 310-334.

Holland, J. (1995). *Hidden Order: How Adaptation Builds Complexity*, ISBN 9780201407938.

Holland, J. (1998). *Emergence: From Chaos to Order*, ISBN 9780201149432.

Kauffman, S. A. (1993). *The Origins of Order: Self-Organization and Selection in Evolution*, ISBN 9780195058116.

Kolmogorov, A. (1965). "Three approaches to the quantitative definition of information," *Problems of Information Transmission*, ISSN 0032-9460, 1(1): 3-11.

Le Moigne, J. L. (1990). La Modélisation des Systèmes Complexes, ISBN 9782100043828.

Naess, A. (1953). *Interpretation and Preciseness: A Contribution to the Theory of Communication*, Oslo: Det norske videnskaps-akademi i Oslo.

Newman, M. (1996). "Self-organized criticality, evolution and the fossil record," *Proceedings of the Royal Society of London B: Biological Sciences*, ISSN 0962-8452, 263: 1605-1610.

Nöth, W. (1990). "Meaning, sense, and reference," in *Handbook of Semiotics*, ISBN 9780253209597 (2006), pp. 92-102.

Ogden, C. K. and Richards, I. A. (1985). *The Meaning of Meaning: A Study of the Influence of Language upon Thought and the Science of Symbolism*, ISBN 9780744800333.

Quastler H. (1964). *The Emergence of Biological Organization*, New Haven, CN: Yale University Press.

Searle, J. R. (1969). *Speech Acts: An Essay in the Philosophy of Language*, ISBN 9780521096263 (1970).

Searle, J. and van der Verken, D. (1985). *Foundations of the Illocutionary Logic*, ISBN 9780521263245.

Shannon, C. E. and Weaver, W. (1949). *A Mathematical Model of Communication*, Urbana, IL: University of Illinois Press.

Simon, H. A. (1969). *The Sciences of the Artificial*, ISBN 9780262193740 (1996).

Simon, H. A. (1992). "On designing information for companies and managements in an electronic age," *Proceedings of the 1992 CEMIT Conference*, Tokyo, September.

Sneppen, K. and Newman, M. (1996). "Avalanches, scaling, and coherent noise," *Physical Review E: Statistical, Nonlinear and Soft Matter Physics*, ISSN 1539-3755, 54(6): 6226-6231.

Stonier, T. (1997). *Information and Meaning: An Evolutionary Perspective*, ISBN 9783540761396.

Varela, F. J. (1979). *Principles of Biological Autonomy*, ISBN 9780444003218.

Warfield, J. N. (2004). "Linguistic adjustments: Precursors to understanding complexity," *Systems Research and Behavioral Science*, ISSN 1092-7026, 21: 123-145.

Weaver, W. (1948). "Science and complexity," *American Scientist*, ISSN 0003-0996, 36: 536-544.

**Darek M. Eriksson** lives in Stockholm, Sweden, where he combines academic work with management consultancy, supplying strategic and operational development advice to organizations and companies. He is an affiliate of several universities and an associate researcher at the Lulea University of Technology in Sweden, where he supervises students and delivers research seminars. Eriksson's current research interests focus on two related areas: enterprise modeling and representation, and enterprise development, including the inherent ethical implications of all design. He has published papers in books and management-related journals, including *Systems Research and Behavioural Science*, *European Journal of Operations Research*, and *Philosophy of Management*. Eriksson has previously served as managing editor of the international journal of *Cybernetics and Human Knowledge*, where he is now consulting editor. He is a member of the board of the journal *Information and Management*, and a member of the Centre for Philosophy, Technology and Social Systems.

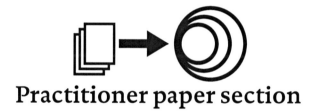

Practitioner paper section

Practitioner

# Complex systems, governance and policy administration consequences*

Jack W. Meek[1], Joe De Ladurantey[1] & William H. Newell[2]
[1]College of Business and Public Management, University of La Verne, US
[2]Western College Program, Miami University, US

This paper combines insights from literature on complex systems theory and the conjunctive state, applies them to new challenges facing public administrators in metropolitan areas, and tests them in a case study of the Peace Officers Association of Los Angeles County (POALAC). The argument is advanced that administrative networks, shared governance, and co-production of public services developed in the conjunctive state are real-world exemplars of the emergent properties of complex adaptive systems (CAS). As the production of social capital and public trust of government decline in response to the increasing inability of hierarchical, top-down, command-and-control institutions to solve complex societal problems, the fundamental nature of associations and relations among citizens, policy makers, civic leaders, and government is changing in metropolitan areas as government slowly shifts toward governance. The case study of POALAC reveals a coordinated networked administrative response to the complexity of regional law enforcement consistent with theoretical predictions.

* An earlier version of this paper, entitled "Complex Systems and the Conjunctive State," appears in K. A. Richardson, W. J. Gregory, & G. Midgley (eds) (2005). *Systems Thinking and Complexity Science: Insights for Action. Proceedings of the 11th ANZSYS/ Managing the Complex V Conference.* Christchurch, New Zealand, 5-7 December, ISBN 9780976681441. A revised version of this paper was presented at the Overman Section on Complexity panel entitled "Advancing complexity thinking for innovation in public administration" at the ASPA Conference held at Denver, Colorado, 1-4 April, 2006.

## Introduction

This paper explores how complex metropolitan systems are evolving through the creation of administrative networks, and how those networks influence public administration and policy formation through the work of public administrators. It draws on previous research (Bogason, 2000; Meek & Newell, 2005; Morcol, 2002; Newell & Meek, 1997) to establish a synthesis of complex systems theories from which we develop central tenets that ground an understanding of complex urban systems. It then sketches out how these conditions have influenced the recent movement toward shared governance in urban environments.

The paper embraces the "conjunctive state" (Frederickson, 1999) as a central feature of public administration. The interplay of administrative conjunction with policy deliberation and administration is then explored through a case study of the collective responses of police officers in Los Angeles county to what is referred to as the "disarticulated state."

One concern of the paper is to examine the characteristic policy deliberation and administration that evolves from complex conditions, and the consequences of such deliberations for public administrators. Collective activities among public administrators – administrative conjunction – greatly influence policy administration. What is yet to be explored in both the policy and administrative network literatures are consequences of administrative conjunction that are a product of complex jurisdictional interdependences as well as a contributor to complex urban system management. The very condition of complexity that draws administrators to work collectively is reflective of their deliberation and collective action. Such influence also has administrative consequences. The goal of this paper is to examine these consequences and highlight their implications for advancing complexity thinking for innovation in public administration.

The paper opens with a review of selected literature on complexity theory and its relevance for public administration, followed by characterization of metropolitan environments as "disarticulated states" full of complexity and self-organization. These forms of collective activities are then discussed within the context of public management network theory. Finally, the paper examines a case study analysis of the POALAC network in order to highlight the central policy administrative consequences that evolve out of conjunctive practices.

Complex systems theory, while developed in the natural sciences, has much to offer the social sciences. While our previous work provided a cautious assessment of the applicability of various complex systems theories to human behavior (Newell & Meek, 2000), this paper provides a summary of findings from recent literature on complex systems that can be applied to the recent movement toward shared governance in urban environments – the so-called conjunctive state. Specifically, we believe that innovations such as "networked" government and co-production of public services are usefully understood as responses to problems posed by the complex inter-jurisdictional nature of urban systems. In another publication, we connect this theory of complexity with our theoretical work on interdisciplinarity to provide pragmatic recommendations for public administrators coping with complex problems and changes in governance (Meek & Newell, 2005).

## Recent developments in complexity theory

Complex systems theory has evolved over the last half dozen years in directions that are, in many ways, useful to public administrators. The good news is that human complex systems are now generally understood to be comprised of many diverse components that are loosely and often nonlinearly linked and that produce emergent patterns of systemic behavior. Complexity is now often distinguished from chaos by theorists interested in human behavior (Anderson, 1999; Lissack, 2002; McDaniel & Driebe, 2005; Mitleton-Kelly, 2003; Newell, 2001, 2003; Newell & Meek, 2000; Smedes, 2004), who now reject as inappropriate to human beings the mindless iteration of simple invariant rules underlying chaos theory. The dominant model has become complex adaptive systems (CAS), which focus on the holistic patterns formed through human interactions. All in all, we have come a long way from models of complexity drawn from the natural sciences and applied to the social sciences without regard for the distinctive characteristics of human beings.

The inferences drawn from CAS models for the management of organizations are considerably more useful than those drawn from earlier natural science-based models (see Newell & Meek, 2000). Of particular interest are the recommendations of Anderson (1999) that managers should influence agents indirectly by changing the "fitness landscape" (e.g., providing longer-term rewards, setting priorities, and choosing the organization's domain) through trial and error; of Weick (2005: 63) that "[t]o prepare for the unexpected means that you have to offset strong cognitive predispositions such as confirmation bias, fallacy of centrality, hubris, normalization, typification, and bottom-up salience of cues"; of Holley (2005: 169) that "[u]nderlying self-organizing systems... are simple design principles," which she enumerates; of Lewin (2000) that organizational practices turn into rules, so keep them few and try small-scale experiments instead of fast, large-scale interventions; of Bonifacio and Bouquet (2002) that knowledge management should be perceived as "the problem of coordinating... multiple sources of knowledge in a distributed (that is, non centralized) way"; and of Espejo (2003) that organizational complexity needs to be embodied in "autonomous systems within autonomous systems within autonomous systems." Authors generally agree on the importance of flattening hierarchies, facilitating informal networks, and diversifying agents.

The implications of complex systems theory for management should be even more useful when the insights of social science disciplines come to be embedded within the complex systems framework. It is a hopeful sign that a few other authors (Bar-Yam & Minai, 2004; Bentley & Maschner, 2003; Jordan in McDaniel & Driebe, 2005; Mitleton-Kelly, 2003) now recognize that complex systems theory has implications for interdisciplinary studies, which hold out the most promise of a comprehensive understanding of individual complex systems.

## Metropolitan administration and complex systems

Luckily for public administrators, complex systems are better behaved, less nonlinear, closer to equilibrium, and less prone to disproportionate effects than are chaotic systems. *Professionals charged with manipulating or, worse, managing complex systems cannot control those systems the way they might a simple or complicated system.* Rigidly hierarchical organizations directed through top-down decision making are likely to be ineffective. But those responsible for working with complex systems need not throw up their hands either, totally abandoning control for self-organization and top-down for bottom-up decision making.

As the behavioral characteristics of complex systems lie between those of complicated and chaotic systems, so too do their managerial characteristics. Managers of complex systems must pay attention to the inherent needs of the system as well as their needs for the system. They must learn to watch and understand systemic patterns as well as set goals and priorities for the system. Lines of communication and decision making must flow up as well as down, so authority and legitimacy become vested in the process as a whole. *Joint prioritizing, decision making, and implementation become essential, and managers (including public administrators) must base them on an appreciation of the system as a whole, not on the perspective from one location within the system.* If this sounds like shared governance and the conjunctive state, then you have reached the same conclusion we have.

## Changes in the association of the citizen and the state

As noted by Putnam (1999), there has been a marked decline in social capital, an institutional cornerstone of functional civic relationships and system cohesion. Putnam, as do complex adaptive systems theorists, focuses on informal networks of individuals, the former on producing social capital and the latter on emergent patterns of behavior. Both promote the functioning and adaptability of "community" to address complex problems. Putnam's new forms of associations are comparable to new networks that emerge spontaneously. Additionally, Nye observed that there has been a steady decline in public trust of government (Nye *et al.*, 1997). This lack of confidence in government means that traditional institutions are less often perceived as problem solvers, or places where some groups of individuals can see their issues being significantly addressed. These groups are turning away from traditional institutions to create unconventional solutions, many of which are new forms of associations.

What is useful to recognize here is the changing fundamental nature of associations and relations among citizens, policy makers, civic leaders, and government in metropolitan arenas. *What seems to be happening is the slow movement away from government toward governance.* Governance is characterized as a facilitative state, one where public administration facilitates the associations of citizens and social organizations in order to produce social goods and services. This is a very different state of affairs from the functionally distinct roles for the state, the citizens, and private institutions, where institutional command and control was familiar. Today government is viewed less as a problem solver and more as a partner and contributor to solution making. It is in this complex environment that new forms of association, especially those formed by institutions whose leadership recognizes the changing nature of problem solutions, and new pathways of governance will emerge.

## The rise of networks and the conjunctive state

Some public administration scholars have observed a new and emerging form of arrangement among citizens, policy makers, and governments (Frederickson, 1997; Goldsmith & Eggers, 2004; Kickert *et al.*, 1997). These new forms of arrangements reflect a recognition of the inability of the state – as government organized through bureaucracies and representing less and less meaningful geographic jurisdictions – to be responsive to citizens' needs and the creation of social good. Simply stated, social problems have outpaced conventional solutions. One form of recognition of this condition is in selected areas of public leadership, where we can witness responsiveness by creative institutional leaders to find solutions that adapt existing institutions to the "disconjunctive state" (Frederickson, 1999), in which social issues overcome bureaucratic solutions or cross public authorities and jurisdictions.

The "conjunctive state" (Frederickson, 1999) is a response to the complex condition. Its characteristics include institutionalism, networks, and governance. It represents an adjustment of the institutional state through the expansion of role definition and actions of and by administrative leaders who recognize the influence and contributions of a broader range of constituencies. As new forms of governance emerge in response to disarticulation, new practices, including the insights from the professional literature on interdisciplinarity (see Newell, 2001), should be of considerable utility to public administrators and other applied social scientists interested in the patterns produced by specific complex systems.

Research on participation in networks indicates that public administrators spend a great deal of time in networks, and view them as valuable to individual success and invaluable to organizational success (Meek, 2002). In addition, network involvement means that many other organizations are involved, power is shared (or central sovereignty is limited), and network and organizational goals are more or less compatible.

Based on grounded theory and a case study research on network management (Agranoff, 2004; Agranoff & McGuire, 2003), emergent lessons for public administration management have been reported to include:

1. Be a representative of your agency and the network.
2. Take a share of the administrative burden.
3. Operate by agenda orchestration.
4. Recognize shared expertise-based authority.
5. Stay within the decision bounds of your network.
6. Accommodate and adjust while maintaining purpose.
7. Be as creative as possible.
8. Be patient and use interpersonal skills.
9. Recruit constantly.
10. Emphasize incentives.

The work of Linden (2002) on cross-boundary collaboration has also been instructive. Based on case study research and individual interviews, Linden identifies a collaborative public management style: maintaining continuity of leadership among all parties, acquiring flexible schedules, and developing open, trusting relationships among all participants (Linden, 2002). Lessons from the experience of public administrators managing and participating in networks correspond to insights in management needs from complexity theorists discussed earlier. Table 1 relates the administrative lessons of conjunctive practice to managerial practices recommended by complexity theorists.

To summarize, the network management literature begins to address the nature of governance in a shared power world. Much of what complexity theorists have posited as important considerations for managing within self-organized environments are also found to have corresponding management "lessons" from fieldwork in public administration networks. These lessons provide the basis for further administrative conjunction that may well serve the practice of public administration in complex environments.

| Author | CAS theorists and management recommendations | PA theorists and managing networks: Findings | Author |
|---|---|---|---|
| Anderson (1999) | Change "fitness landscape" | Stay within the decision bounds of your network | Agranoff (2004) |
| Weick (2005) | "Offset cognitive predispositions" | Accommodate and adjust; open trusting relationships | Agranoff (2004) Linden (2002) |
| Holley (2005) | Rely on "simple design principles" | Leadership follows collaborative principles | Linden (2002) |
| Lewin & Regine (2002) | Rely on few rules | Not found | NA |
| Bonifacio & Bouquet (2002) | Coordinate multiple knowledge sources in a non-centralized way | Maintain continuity of leadership among the parties | Linden (2002) |
| Espejo (2003) | Rely on autonomous systems | Share the administrative burden | Agranoff (2004) |

**Table 1** *CAS management heuristics and PA network literature*

## Policy administration consequences of conjunction

It is important to recognize that networks co-exist with hierarchies. Public administrators must not only manage public hierarchies, but also participate fully in networks. *Administrators now need to be in two places, and the demands of both may lead to conflicting priorities as well as exhaustion.* In addition, networks represent additions to hierarchies or an emergent force in public management where "networks are not about creating order, but rather allowing for ordered chaos" (Mandell, 2004).

The implications of administrative conjunction – and networks created to offer valuable integrative or coordinated services – are that these activities and behaviors also have policy administrative consequences for existing hierarchies and for the system as a whole. We offer empirical evidence of policy administrative consequences in four areas: network and organizational compatibility; the role and nature of shared leadership; network effectiveness; and network influence. To examine these four issue areas, we selected a network case study in the Los Angeles metropolitan area: the Peace Officers Association of Los Angeles County (POALAC). POALAC is a long-standing network of peace officer associations that provides integrative services for a number of associations.

## The cosmopolitan nature of LA County law enforcement

First, it is useful to characterize the public safety issue for which the network was created. The LA County Sheriff's Department (LASD) has jurisdictional responsibility for law enforcement in the over 4,000 square miles of Los Angeles County. Comprised of 88 cities, LA County is further divided by the decision of 46 of the 88 cities to establish their own law enforcement agencies. The remaining 42 have opted to obtain law enforcement services from LASD, as have the 21 community college campuses.

To further compartmentalize law enforcement services in LA County, LASD has 23 geographic stations with strong community identities such as Malibu, Newhall, and San Dimas, in addition to Transit Services and community colleges (Los Angeles County Sheriff's Department, 2005). The City of Los Angeles is comprised of 19 geographic stations for communities such as Hollywood, Wilshire, and Van Nuys (Los Angeles Police Department, 2004). From the perspective of the state of California, there are 336 municipal police agencies in the state and 58 sheriff's

- California Highway Patrol – headquarters plus 10 stations
- Los Angeles School Police
- 12 independent school district PDs
- Cal State Police – CSCLA, CSCLB, CSC Dominguez Hills, CSC Northridge, Cal Poly Pomona
- Los Angeles International Airport PD (also policed by LAPD and Federal TSA)
- USC PD
- UCLA PD
- Los Angeles Port Police
- Los Angeles County Police (separate from LASD)
- Los Angeles County District Attorney Investigators
- Los Angeles County Housing Authority Police

**Table 2** *Law enforcement agencies that operate in Los Angeles County*

departments (California Police Chiefs Association, 2006) that vary greatly in size.

There are a number of other law enforcement agencies that provide their services in LA County and add to the complexity of coordination, as if the above did not suffice. In no order of importance, one may see the uniformed presence of various agencies traversing the streets of the county (see Table 2). In addition, the LA County District Attorney's Office provides prosecutorial services for all felonies and misdemeanors charged in the county. Eleven cities including the City of Los Angeles and Long Beach opt for their own city attorney to prosecute local misdemeanors.

The above description of LA County law enforcement is not intended to be comprehensive but to suggest the complexity of law enforcement in Los Angeles. Morcol (2002) points out that, in general, "the higher the numbers, the higher the degree of complexity." Given the overlapping jurisdictions as well as the sheer number of the organizations listed above, the system of delivering law enforcement services within Los Angeles County represents a complex system. Even if the organizations were to function independently, their activities and interactions would be complex by their very nature.

## Case study: The Peace Officers Association of Los Angeles County

There is one organization in the county that acts as "network manager" to keep the northbound train headed in the intended direction: the Peace Officers Association of Los Angeles County (POALAC).

Through a series of collaborative efforts this entity creates the synergy necessary to ensure that the collective energies of county law enforcement are directed and guided by the principle-centered missions so necessary in today's complex environment.

### Origin

POALAC was formed in 1929 as a forum for the county law enforcement community and to provide training programs for departments throughout the county on common emerging issues. Its officers have been a "who's who" of county law enforcement, from sheriffs to high-profile LA police chiefs, district attorneys, and the California Highway Patrol, and from federal agency heads to corporate security representatives from the utility companies, banking, and the motion picture industry.

### Role and activities

Besides networking and training opportunities for the law enforcement community, POALAC provides a cooperative forum between the private sector and law enforcement, with private-sector members on the board of directors, and jointly sponsored training programs – a concept that was developed well before the community policing (Lundgren, 1995; More *et al.*, 2003; Trojanowicz & Bucqueroux, 1994) and cooperative homeland security initiatives in recent years. Some of the recent training programs have dealt with law enforcement ethics, street racing enforcement, and terrorism investigations. POALAC's traffic committee coordinates DUI enforcement, safety belt usage awareness, and child safety activities with law

| Executive members | President – Los Angeles County Sheriff – Deputy Chief |
| | Vice-President – Reserve Officer Representative |
| | Treasurer – Chief of Police, Irwindale |
| | Past Presidents – Corporate Security Directors (2) |
| Board members | Active law enforcement (6) |
| | Retired law enforcement (3) |
| | Reserve officers (2) |
| | Corporate security (3) |
| | Non-designated (3) |
| | Chaplain (1) |
| | Los Angeles County Chiefs Representative (2) |
| | Chief Special Agents Association (1) |
| | Federal agencies (2) |

**Table 3** *POALAC board membership*

enforcement agencies throughout Los Angeles County. The association will soon embark on a large-scale recruitment project for the entire law enforcement community.

### Board composition

The board is comprised of 23 elected and 3 ex-officio members (the Chief of Police of Los Angeles, the Sheriff of Los Angeles County, and a full-time administrator). The executive board is comprised of the president, vice-president, a treasurer, and two past presidents. The 2005 board is comprised of the agency representatives outlined in Table 3.

### Mission statement

*As the premier professional law enforcement Association in Los Angeles County, it is the Mission of the Peace Officers Association of Los Angeles County (POALAC) to lead, facilitate, inspire, and advocate on behalf of federal, state, county and local law enforcement agencies and those safety professionals in the private sector in our joint responsibility to maximize the safety of those who depend upon us.* (POALAC Strategic Plan, 2005)

### Research questions

Four general research questions addressed how POALAC affects policy administration in the metropolitan arena:

1. How does your involvement in POALAC affect your organization? (network and organizational compatibility);

2. Does POALAC reflect shared leadership? (shared leadership);

3. Is POALAC effective? (network effectiveness);

4. What are the policy administrative consequences of participation in POALAC? (network influence).

Of the board members 22 were interviewed, 5 were unavailable, 2 were not on the board in 2005, and 1 was the researcher.

### Findings
#### Research question 1: Network and organizational compatibility

*Goal compatibility:* All (100 percent) respondents indicated that at no time did their involvement conflict with their organization's goals or responsibilities. On the contrary, some (particularly for the corporate security representatives) commented that network involvement enhanced organizational goals.

- The only concern was **scheduling of time** for 7 (32 percent) who cited competition for calendar space to accommodate busy schedules. Where possible, priority was given to association-related duties.

- Federal and state representatives did cite a potential conflict from political involvement or endorsements; however, the association has never taken a position requiring their abstention.

Overall, membership in POALAC appears highly compatible with individual members' organizational goals.

*Organizational complementarity:* All (100 percent) respondents indicated that their involvement in the association complemented and meshed with their organization's goals. Comments included:

- Provides me with visibility, significantly complements and adds value to everyone in law enforcement-related services;
- Gives me access to information on the other agencies … we are the bridge for all connections and information exchange in LA County.

The phrases used most often were "without a doubt," "absolutely," "most definitely."

*Goal enhancement:* 17 (77 percent) indicated that the association enhances the respondent's organization goals, while 5 (23 percent) were not sure. Comments ranged from "it helps create efficiencies"; "expedites decision-making"; to "provides a voice that is different from the organizational culture worked in."

### Research question 2: Shared leadership
*Shared leadership:* There was support for the shared leadership and self-governance of the network, as 19 (86 percent) reported that decision making varies with the need or issue and is driven by negotiation and consensus of the entire board, while only 3 (14 percent) indicated that decisions emanate from the executive board.

In attempting to identify the most important members of the board, 13 various members were identified as the most important board members. This perception of shared leadership extended to only 9 (41 percent), indicating that the president is the "leader." Others observed, "we do not always need a leader, it is by issue"; "the Executive Board is the leader"; "there are several leaders, not to say we are leaderless but we have many"; "whoever is in the position leads"; "there are a number of leaders, and all presidents are leaders."

When asked to identify the person with the most influence, 12 (55 percent) cited the current president, 5 (23 percent) were undecided, and the remaining responses cited other board members.

*Network functionality:* The board of directors meet monthly, with 90 percent attendance the norm. In addition, meetings are held to recognize one segment of the law enforcement community each month, for example LAPD Day, Chiefs Day, and Corporate Security Day. Interaction is frequent outside these major functions as well. Survey data revealed that, of 22 surveyed, only two had not contacted another board member outside formal meetings, and multiple contacts between meetings are commonplace. Overall, the level of contact and collaboration among participants appears to be strengthened by association membership.

*Personal enhancement:* 21 (95 percent) of the respondents reported that the association increased their value to their own organization. Even the lone exception indicated it has had some value but was difficult to measure.

### Research question 3: Network effectiveness
*Public value:* 19 (86 percent) said the association was contributing to the public value, 2 (10 percent) felt there is little public value in its present state; 7 (32 percent) also commented there is still unmet potential to enhance public value.

The positive contributions of the network were identified in four areas:

- Networking that contributes to training;
- Traffic program coordination as a by-product of the networking;
- Enhancement of career goals (for some);
- Exposure to new concepts.

Additional comments included "we have influence…"; "we are a tent to go under for all agencies and a clearinghouse for ideas"; "we recognize others' efforts." Side comments from federal participants reflected that the network was recommended to them on assignment to the LA area as *the* "go to" organization to immediately get to know those in the business. It appears that organizations that bring leadership from outside the geographic area require an immediate immersion in the region so that they can assimilate as rapidly as possible.

### Research question 4: Network influence

*Agency impact:* Regarding network influence on policies of participating agencies:

- 5 (27 percent) felt that the association is successful in influencing policies to some degree;
- 4 (18 percent) were undecided;
- 9 (41 percent) opined that they have little impact;
- 3 (14 percent) indicated that the association had no impact.

Comments ranged through "we do not directly influence, but it is seen in other ways"; "we do not take on sticky issues"; "we impact the culture more than the policies"; "not sure, I am just not made aware if we are"; "we used to but not now."

*Regional influence:* When asked to determine the regional influence:

- 13 (59 percent) recognized the regional influence as exceptional to modest;
- 7 (32 percent) saw only little regional influence;
- 2 (9 percent) were undecided or saw no regional influence.

Comments: "we can do a better job of developing regional influence"; "the big benefactors are the federal agencies that use the regional influence that exists for them."

*Program impact:* When asked if the programs, work products, and services of the network are having an impact, the consensus was that they do (14 or 64 percent with 2 undecided) and 6 (27 percent) seeing little impact.

*Complementary impact:* An assessment was requested that asked if the network's deci-

sions and programs complicated or enhanced (choose one) current agency operations in LA County in policy considerations. Twenty-one of 22 (95 percent) were of the opinion that it clearly enhanced agency operations and policy considerations, even if the impact is only moderate. Comments: "we are complementary but sometimes it does both"; "it enhances for those who choose to participate and to a lesser extent others"; "not to our potential"; "we are a utility outfielder but could be an all-star shortstop"; "it could be complex but it is not, due to the network"; "that is our value (enhancing)."

*Added value:* When asked if the solutions and programs of the association could have been accomplished by any *one* agency, 20 (91 percent) said a resounding no. One could not respond to the question and the remaining response was that it was difficult to quantify. Comments include: "we are collectively stronger"; "if done by one the final product only benefits one"; "if I would have done it alone, it would not have been as good"; "if done by one agency it would not be accepted"; "we add value due to our diversity, no one could do it themselves."

### Conclusions

County law enforcement services could not function effectively without the coordination, collaboration, and networking provided by POALAC. Through a series of effective programs that establish working relationships among network members, POALAC helps administrative networks function effectively, as evidenced by results from this case study. Its collaborative structure provides the loose couplings required to move among silos, reciprocate and sustain the ability to provide community services, or ensure they are provided through governance. Collaboration is much more than interacting and networking: It is the act of circling around common problems, identifying common issues, and applying resources that individual collaborators bring to the table from their respective areas of expertise and discipline. It is problem identification, an exhaustive effort at alternative solutions from a variety of perspectives, and a working toward solutions that individuals could not

| Policy administrative consequences | Network member responses |
|---|---|
| Network and organizational compatibility | • 100% organizational compatibility<br>• 100% organizational complementarity<br>• 77% enhances organizational goals |
| Shared leadership | • 86% indicates consensus in decision making<br>• 60% of network members listed as leaders<br>• 90% attendance rate<br>• 90% contact rate between meetings |
| Network effectiveness | • 86% network creates public value<br>• 32% more public value can be developed |
| Network influence | • 27% network influenced agency policies<br>• 59% network has regional influence<br>• 64% network programs have impact<br>• 95% network enhances agency operations<br>• 91% network adds value |

**Table 4** *Policy administrative consequences of conjunction*

have imagined on their own.

A summary of our findings with regard to POALAC is represented in Table 4. The focus of our work was on the policy administrative consequences of administrative conjunction as represented by this case study.

Based on survey responses and interview comments, the POALAC administrative network is compatible with and complements agency goals, embraces shared leadership and decision making, creates public value, and enhances agency operations. The challenge faced by complex organizations such as law enforcement services in Los Angeles County cannot be met today without the use of collaborative networks such as POALAC. The sheer volume of services provided by the myriad of agencies, each with its own mission and values, are dependent on a platform of mutual benefit that could be more accurately described as a dynamic reciprocity due to the volatility and the potential for catastrophe that could exist if not for the collaborative network and its structure.

Our study suggests that there is a need to gather those who must be players into networks. Some know it intuitively and volunteer, others need to be requested to join, and still others should be in the network but are not included, either by design or by oversight. There is a constant cycle of membership bringing new players to the network that must be complemented by continuity from past leaders to ensure grounding in the mission of the organization.

The amount of professional time devoted to networking is not seen as burdensome; indeed, it is more valuable for individuals and compatible with their organizations than one might anticipate. The dynamic reciprocity of involvement in the network appears to be shared by both individuals and organizations.

Concerns always arise when networks embark on policy issues within the domain of the silo organizations. However, our study found that there did not appear to be a direct negative impact on the individual agencies. We found that network policies were viewed by network participants as complementary to individual agency policies.

When a network can choose its mission and command loyalty, then shared leadership, with consensus and negotiation as its cornerstone skills, is possible. No single person leads a mission-driven network and conflict is resolved at its lowest levels. Unlike organizational silos, sustainable networks operate effectively through government by consensus.

Working below the organizational lines of formal authority and community responsibility requires collaborative networks to function much as a submarine with a periscope to the landscape. If they surfaced, perhaps they would be the subject of more scrutiny for their style, structure, and makeup. They may be more valuable in contributing their public value from below sea level to others for implementation. Developing too much strength and influence might turn them into the very structures they are attempting to support. Such an effort would require more traditional methods of planning, organization, staffing, directing, coordinating, reporting, and budgeting.

The POALAC organization, and other such networks, cannot be bound by the very structure that nurtures and supports our organizational silos. The ability to set up informal interactions and facilitate problem solving must be considered as well as knowing when and how to contribute without stepping on political toes in the process. Facilitation skills replace command and control while the group strives for shared leadership, consensus, and objectivity.

## Looking ahead

This paper applies insight from recent work of complexity theorists to public administration in the context of metropolitan governance. An emergent trend in governance – conjunction – calls for a reexamination of management and administration. Network researchers based on grounded theory have identified management strategies that overlap with those found in the complexity literature. Our examination of policy administrative consequences found a unique set of positive outcomes related to collective action: organizational compatibility, shared leadership, increased public value, and enhanced agency operations though coordination. The challenge ahead is to understand these emergent features from both analytical and practical perspectives so as to advance our understanding of managing complex environments.

## References

Agranoff, R. (2004). "Leveraging networks: A guide for public managers working across organizations," in J. Kamensky and T. J. Burlin (eds.), *Collaboration: Using Networks and Partnerships*, ISBN 9780742535138, pp. 61-102.

Agranoff, R. and McGuire, R. (2003). *Collaborative Public Management: New Strategies for Local Governments*, ISBN 9780878408962.

Anderson, P. (1999). "Complexity theory and organization science," *Organization Science*, ISSN 1047-7039, 10(3): 216-232.

Bar-yam, Y. and Minai, A. (eds) (2004). *Unifying Themes in Complex Systems: Proceedings of the Second International Conference on Complex Systems*, Vol. II, ISBN 9780813341231.

Bentley, R. A. and Maschner, H. (eds) (2003). *Complex Systems and Archeology: Empirical and Theoretical Applications*, ISBN 9780874807554.

Bogason, P. (2000). *Public Policy and Local Governance: Institutions in Post Modern Society*, ISBN 9781840648911 (2001).

Bonifacio, M. and Bouquet, P. (2002). "Distributed knowledge management: A systemic approach," in G. Minati and E. Pessa (eds.), Emergence in Complex, Cognitive, Social, and Biological Systems, ISBN 9780306473586.

California Police Chiefs Association (2006). http://www.californiapolicechiefs.org.

Espejo, R. (2003). "Social systems and the embodiment of organizational learning," in E. Mitleton-Kelly (ed.), *Complex Systems and Evolutionary Perspectives on Organizations: The Application of Complexity Theory to Organizations*, ISBN 9780080439570, pp. 53-70.

Frederickson, H. G. (1997). *The Spirit of Public Administration*, ISBN 9780787902957 (1996).

Frederickson, H. G. (1999). "The repositioning of American public administration," Political Science and Politics, ISSN 1049-0965, 32(4): 701-711.

Goldsmith, S. and Eggers, W. D. (2004). *Governing by Network: The New Shape of the Public Sector*, ISBN 9780815731290.

Holley, J. (2005). "Transforming your regional economy through uncertainty and surprise: Learning from complexity science, network theory and the field," in R. McDaniel and D. Driebe (eds.), *Uncertainty and Surprise in Complex Systems: Questions of Working with the Unexpected*, ISBN 9783540237730, pp. 165-176.

Kickert, W. J. M., Klijn, E. and Koppenjan, J. F. F. (1997). *Managing Complex Networks: Strategies for the Public Sector*, ISBN 9780761955481.

Lewin, R. (2000). Complexity: Life On the Edge of Chaos, ISBN 9780226476551.

Linden, R. M. (2002). *Working Across Boundaries: Making Collaboration Work in Government and Nonprofit Organizations*, ISBN 9780787964306.

Lissack, M. (ed.) (2002). *The Interaction of Complexity and Management*, ISBN 9781567204278.

Los Angeles County Sheriff's Department (2005). *LASD Strategic Plan*, Los Angeles, CA.

Los Angeles Police Department (2004). *Annual Report of the Los Angeles Police Department*, Los Angeles, CA.

Lundgren, D. E. (1995). *Community Oriented Policing and Problem Solving*, Sacramento, CA: California Department of Justice, Attorney General's Office.

Mandell, M. P. (2004). "The impact of network structures on community-building efforts: The Los Angeles Roundtable for children community studies," in M. Mandell (ed.), *Getting Results Through Collaboration: Network and Network Structures for Public and Policy Management*, ISBN 9781567204551 (2001), pp. 129-153.

McDaniel, R. and Driebe, D. (eds) (2005). *Uncertainty and Surprise in Complex Systems: Questions of Working with the Unexpected*, ISBN 9783540237730.

Meek, J. W. and Newell, W. H. (2005). "Complexity, interdisciplinarity and public administration: Implications for integrating communities," *Public Administration Quarterly*, ISSN 0734-9149, 29(3): 321-349.

Meek, J.W. (1998). "Policy networks: Implications for policy development and implementation," *Presentations: A Journal of Faculty Papers*. Volume Eleven, University of La Verne, La Verne, California.

Minati, G. and Pessa, E. (eds) (2002). *Emergence in Complex, Cognitive, Social, and Biological Systems*, ISBN 9780306473586.

Mitleton-Kelly, E. (2003). *Complex Systems and Evolutionary Perspectives on Organizations: The Application of Complexity Theory to Organizations*, ISBN 9780080439570 (2001).

Morcol, G. (2002). *A New Mind for Policy Analysis: Toward a Post-Newtonian and Postpositivist Epistemology and Methodology*, ISBN 9780275970123.

More, H. W., Wegener, W. F. and Miller, L. (2003). *Effective Police Supervision*, ISBN 9781583605462.

Newell, W. (2001). "Theory of interdisciplinary studies," *Issues in Integrative Studies*, ISSN 1081-4760, 19.

Newell, W. (2003). "Complexity and interdisciplinarity," in "Knowledge management, organizational intelligence and learning, and complexity," *Encyclopedia of Life Support Systems*, Oxford, UK: EOLSS Publishers.

Newell, W. H. and Meek, J. W. (1997). "What can public administration learn from complex systems theory?" *Administrative Theory and Praxis*, ISSN 1084-1806, 19(3): 318-330.

Newell, W. H. and Meek, J.W. (2000). "What can public administration learn from complex systems theory," in G. Morcol and L. F. Dennard (eds.). *New Sciences for Public Administration and Policy: Connections and Reflections*. ISBN 9781574200706.

Nye, J. S., Zelikow, P. D. and King, D. C. (1997). *Why People Don't Trust Government*, ISBN 9780674940574.

Peace Officers Association of Los Angeles County (2005). *Visionquest: A Strategic Plan for POALAC*, Los Angeles, California.

Putnam, R. D. (1999). *Bowling Alone: Civic Disengagement in America*, ISBN 9780743203043 (2001).

Smedes, T. (2004). *Chaos, Complexity, and God: Divine Action and Scientism*, ISBN 9789042915213.

Trojanowicz, R. and Bucqueroux, B. (1994). *Community Policing: How to Get Started*, ISBN 9780870848742.

Weick, K. (2005). "Managing the unexpected: Complexity as distributed sensemaking," in R. McDaniel and D. Driebe (eds.) (2005). *Uncertainty and Surprise in Complex Systems: Questions of Working with the Unexpected*, ISBN 9783540237730, pp. 51-66.

**Jack W. Meek, Ph.D.**, is Professor of Public Administration at the College of Business and Public Management at the University of La Verne, and since 2003, visiting scholar at the School of Policy Planning and Development at the University of Southern California, working on the Civic Engagement Initiative. Professor Meek's research focuses on civic engagement, metropolitan governance including the emergence of cross-jurisdictional administrative connections and relationships, regional collaboration, and policy networks. Professor Meek has published articles in various books and academic journals.

**Joseph C. De Ladurantey** is a third-year doctoral student in Public Administration at the University of La Verne and an Associate Professor of Public Administration in the Graduate School of Public Administration at Cal State College, Northridge. Joe has published two textbooks and several articles. He has been an adjunct faculty member at Cal State Los Angeles, Rio Hondo College, The University of Southern California and Cal Poly Pomona. Joe has over 40 years in law enforcement and served as the Chief of Police of the City of Irwindale and the City of Torrance, and as Law Enforcement Liaison for the LA County District Attorney's Office, as well as spending 27 years with the Los Angeles Police Department achieving the rank of Captain.

**William H. Newell, Ph.D.** is Professor of Interdisciplinary Studies at Miami University (Ohio), Executive Director of the Association for Integrative Studies, and Director of the Institute in Integrative Studies. He has published *Interdisciplinarity: Essays from the Literature* (1998), *Interdisciplinary Undergraduate Programs: A Directory* (1986)*, and Population Change and Agricultural Development in Nineteenth Century France* (1977) and 35 articles and chapters. Over the last two decades, he has served more than a hundred times as consultant or external evaluator to colleges and universities in the United States and Canada. His current research interests include interrelationships among public administration, complex systems theory, and interdisciplinary studies.

Academic

# Complexity challenges of critical situations caused by flooding

Viveca Asproth & Anita Håkansson
Mid Sweden University, Sweden

In cases of flooding many authorities and organizations become involved and it can be a problem to take in the whole situation and have a common picture when many incidents are happening at the same time. There is also a lack of efficient tools that show critical buildings and constructions in combination with actual and forecasted water levels. When handling critical situations people face challenges of complexity, uncertainty, and unpredictably. Such management and decision-making activities are normally supported by various models and support tools. However, complexity is normally not explicitly addressed in such models and tools. In this paper we analyze and discuss different kinds of complexity, which are a challenge in critical situations caused by flooding.

## Introduction

When lakes and watercourses are flooded the water level increases so much that normally dry territories are put under water. Even areas that usually are not bounded by water can be flooded. Globally, flooding is the type of natural catastrophe that every year causes the most victims and the greatest economic effects. In Sweden and other European countries we suffer few big flooding catastrophes and death caused by flooding is relatively unusual. Damage to tangible assets and the cost to society are, however, considerable when flooding does occur.

High water levels and the power of gushing water can cause great damage to settlements and infrastructure. Buildings are often water damaged both by direct flooding and by water rushing in through overloaded systems of water mains and outlets. Ground that is saturated with water combined with erosion can cause landslides, damaging settlements, roads, railways, and bridges. Destroyed and flooded roads cannot be driven down and com-

munications are disturbed. Flooded cables and signalling stations can lead to interruptions in electricity supply and telecommunications. Damaged water supplies and destroyed cables and pipes are a threat to society and if water-purification plants are hit, people's health and the environment might be jeopardized.

As several authorities and organizations become involved in cases of flooding, they may not be able to take in the whole situation and gain a common picture because many incidents are occurring at the same time. Priorities are hard to allocate as there is a lack of efficient tools to show critical buildings and constructions such as roads, railroads, water-purification plants, and so on in combination with actual and forecast water levels. Furthermore, coordination between the authorities and organizations concerned is normally not as effective as it could be.

## The CRISSI project

The aim of the CRISSI project is to present a visualization model for critical situations caused by flooding, and to develop a computerized system for simulations based on the model.

Questions at issue are:

- Which authorities and organizations are affected by such critical situations?

- Which are the critical factors or variables on which the system must be based?

- How can visualization of a critical situation improve the understanding of that situation?

- Can visualization of dynamic processes contribute to understanding?

- In what way can multimedia and GIS (geographic information systems) contribute?

- Which calculation models (for example hydrological) are useful?

| | | |
|---|---|---|
| Secrecy | Laws and regulations | Interfaces |
| Common resources | Sustainability | Production processes |
| Public service provision | Educational systems | R&D systems |
| Innovation systems | Media processes | Soft early warning procedures |
| Historical information | Cultural production | Population processes |
| Physical health | Weather processes | Vegetation processes |
| Water reservoirs | Forest reserves | Soil deposits |
| Energy reserves | Infrastructure | Industries |
| Communication processes | Spreading of the flood | Passable and blocked roads |
| Washed-away roads | Logjams in water courses | Blocked areas |
| Critical or risky industries | Purification plants | Undermining of roads |
| Areas disposed to landslips | Owners of land and buildings | Position of the police |
| Home defense | Military forces | Other actors in the area |
| Water levels | Stream rates | Rising |
| Resources (people, etc.) | Population registers | Precipitation |

**Table 1** *Critical factors in the CRISSI system (Asproth & Håkansson, 2006)*

- How can anticipation contribute to the system?
- Which existing tools are useful for inclusion in the system?

In earlier work we have approached problems concerning decision support for spatial planning (Asproth, *et al.*, 1999, 2002), spatial modeling and simulation (Asproth, *et al.*, 2005b), water regulation (Asproth, *et al.*, 2001), visualization of spatial decision situations (Asproth, *et al.*, 2002), and simulation and anticipation in critical situations caused by flooding (Asproth & Håkansson, 2006). So far in the project, we have identified the critical factors to be included in a model for visualization of situations caused by flooding (see Table 1).

We have used the multi-modal systems method, as developed by J. D. R. de Raadt (2000), to be able to grasp the full width of human life and any human activity system. The main idea of the multi-modal systems method is that for any sociotechnical system to develop in a positive way, all its modalities have to be considered in a balanced fashion. In contrast, if some modalities are constrained while others are overemphasized, the system will express malfunctions and retrogression. The method may be seen in contrast to conventional well-established sciences, which normally focus on just one modality. Figure 1 shows de Raadt's modalities and how they are grouped.

Interviews were carried out with representatives of authorities and organizations with experience of earlier flooding. The interview questions followed the multi-modal systems method in order to cover as many aspects as possible. Documentation of earlier flooding was also examined (Asproth & Håkansson, 2006).

Schwaninger (Espejo & Schwaninger, 1993) has made the interesting observation that control variables at higher logical levels of management have a predictive power over variables at lower levels. However, in multi-modal systems thinking de Raadt (2000) has shown that the influences go in both directions. Higher modalities have an inspirational influence on lower ones and those, in their turn, have a restrictive effect on higher ones. Eriksson (2001) and Veronica de Raadt (2001) have shown practical applications of those insights. When going from operative level to strategic and normative level, the *complexity* increases.

In this paper we discuss the complexity challenges of the critical factors to be included in the model for visualizing situations caused by flooding.

## Complexity

In Asproth, *et al.* (2005a) we identified the core dimensions of complexity for decision making in spatial situations. These are as follows.

E:CO Vol. 9 Nos. 1-2 2007 pp. 37-43

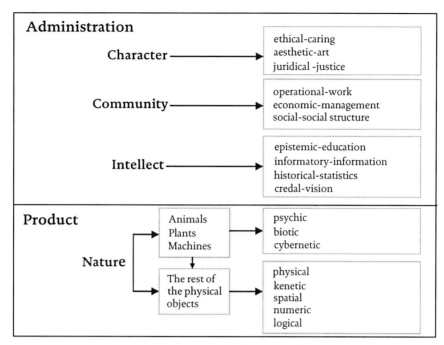

**Figure 1** *De Raadt's modalities*

### Actor and negotiation complexity

One important complexity dimension is due to different actors and their different values and goals. There will often be conflicting interests between organizations and between individuals and groups. Negotiation support systems (Raiffa, 1982; Bacow & Wheeler, 1984) permit different points of view and positions to be joined, differences to be reconciled, and compromise solutions to be suggested.

### Process and structure complexity

One dominating difficulty in managing "geographical space" is the great delays between an action in one point of the system and the effects eventually emerging in quite another one. Furthermore, in any planning system it is necessary to have some sort of model of the geographical space of concern. Such a model is often implemented in the form of a classical geographical information system (GIS), but the model of the space, its activities, and actors may also take the form of a more sophisticated modelling and simulation tool developed by help of the multi-modal systems method.

### Space complexity

Spatial planning is currently facing a multiplicity of challenges. There are problems related to visualization and presentation of geographi-

cal space. In its present classical map form the communicated picture will be far too rigid and "clean," rigid in the sense that only one fixed system state may be expressed.

### Using (model) complexity

A model can be seen as a more or less realistic and objective representation of a part of reality (system in focus). That is probably the most common conception of a model. An alternative conception is to see the model as a representation of a user's current understanding of a situation or system in focus.

### Tools complexity

Turning to artificial planning support tools, the complexity emerges in yet another form. There is an unavoidable tradeoff between relevance, complexity, and uncertainty (Klir, 1996). This means that in order to be relevant, or useful, a tool cannot be too complex at the same time as not exhibiting too great a degree of uncertainty.

Another way to look at the issue of complexity comes from Warfield (1999, 2002). He has identified twenty laws of complexity, which can be categorized in three main categories: behaviorally based, media based, and mathematically based (see Table 2). We have

| Behaviorally Based (70% of the laws) | | | Media Based (10% of the laws) | Mathematically Based (30% of the laws) |
|---|---|---|---|---|
| Physiological | Organizational | Habitual | | |
| Requisite parsimony Structural underconceptualization Limits Requisite saliency | Triadic compatibility Organizational linguistics Vertical incoherence Induced groupthink Forced substitution Precluded resolution | Diverse beliefs Universal priors Inherent conflict Small displays Requisite saliency Induced groupthink Structural underconceptualization | Structural underconceptualization Small displays | Validation Gradation Success and failure Uncorrelated extremes Requisite variety Triadic necessity and sufficiency |

**Table 2** *Categories of the laws of complexity (Warfield, 2002)*

here analyzed the CRISSI system and its critical factors according to the twenty laws.

## Triadic compatibility

Human beings cannot process interrelationships among sets of factors if more than three components are involved. The reason is that the mind is incapable of recalling into the short-term memory more than about seven items.

*Challenge*: To deal with this limitation in the human mind, a computerized system can be of help. In the CRISSI system it is necessary to minimize the number of factors to be handled at the same time. This on the other hand demands that the factors selected must have a high degree of relevance.

## Requisite parsimony

Due to the limitations focused in triadic compatibility, it is essential to have enough time for sequentially presented information to be interpreted.

*Challenge*: Although a critical situation also might be time critical, the decision makers must be able to influence the CRISSI system to get enough interpretation time.

## Structural underconceptualization

The outcomes of ordinary group processes will be underconceptualized.

*Challenge*: To deal with this, some computer support for developing the formal logic structure must be used when developing the CRISSI system.

## Limits

To any activity in the universe there exists a corresponding set of limits on the activity, which determines the feasible extent of the activity.

*Challenge*: It is essential to discover the limits and analyze what effects these limits will have on the CRISSI system and its use.

## Requisite saliency

The situational factors that require consideration are seldom of equal saliency.

*Challenge*: It is necessary to identify which factors should be emphasized more than others. To obtain that a focused dialog and a methodologically well-carried-through design of the system are necessary.

## Organizational linguistics

As an organization grows, linguistic separation grows both laterally and vertically. Higher levels in the organization tend to become progressively disconnected from the relevant components at lower levels. In a strictly hierarchical organization most of the communication occurs within rather than across organizational layers. Intra- and inter-organizational communication is necessary for effective action in emergency situations.

*Challenge*: The planned system must be designed to facilitate communication within and between organizations.

## Vertical incoherence

There are invisible but potentially discoverable patterns of vertical coherence in the organization. A large number of key features can be structured into categories, which in their turn can be structured into areas. The three levels of pattern are strongly correlated to the three organizational levels, operational, tactical, and strategic.

*Challenge*: The planned system must be able to help in the structuring to show the right aggregated level to decision makers at different levels.

### Induced groupthink

Individuals put under pressure by the group to produce results within time limits might end up in induced groupthink. Enough time for interpretation and reasoning must be guaranteed. Every person must act as an independent decision maker.

*Challenge*: Though the time pressure is hard, enough time for interpretation and reasoning must be guaranteed. Every person must be able to act as an independent decision maker.

### Forced substitution

Structural underconceptualization and inherent conflict lead to policy vacuums in an organization. Those in authority then inject forced substitution for absent and inadequate conceptualization.

*Challenge*: There will be significant pressure on the decision makers in an emergency situation, which will be relieved in the short run by taking action. To avoid bad decisions they have to have the most relevant information visualized in order to give the best possible support for the decisions they take.

### Diverse beliefs

The individual members of a group will have diverse beliefs about the issue and the situation will remain uncorrected in the absence of a group learning experience. People must share the same linguistic domain to be able to express the same point of view.

*Challenge*: In a critical situation caused by flooding, people from different organizations have to cooperate. To bridge the differences in views, practice beforehand in using a common tool will help in understanding each other and speaking a common language. The system must hence be developed in a joint structured project.

### Universal priors

The human being, language, reasoning through relationship, and archival representation are universal priors to science.

*Challenge*: When designing the CRISSI system the four parts must have the same priority to be able to succeed.

### Inherent conflict

There will be inherent conflicts within the group stemming from different perceptions of the relative significance of the factors involved in the complex issue. This law reminds us a lot of the law of diverse beliefs.

*Challenge*: Through structured practice and following up the results, it is possible to get a deeper understanding of each other's roles and need for information in the mission.

### Small displays

Complexity cannot be displayed in small display media.

*Challenge*: A system for decision support in complex critical situations cannot be visualized in small media. A headquarters with a large display is necessary.

### Validation

Validity depends on substantial agreement within the community of meaning, but there is no observer-independent "objective knowledge."

*Challenge*: The CRISSI system must be a dynamic system, a system that it is possible to change over time.

### Gradation

Any conceptual body of knowledge can be graded in stages, such that there is one most simple stage, one most comprehensive stage, and intermediate stages whose content lies between the two extremes. The comprehensive stage may be seen as the best alternative, but that takes with it the more comprehensive and the more complex.

*Challenge*: This law affects the entire CRISSI system.

## Success and failure

Inadequacy in any of the seven critical factors that are necessary for success in the design process – leadership, financial support, component availability, design environment, designer participation, documentation support, and design processes that converge to informed agreement – may cause failure.

*Challenge*: All critical factors must be considered to avoid failure.

## Uncorrelated extremes

During the design process, the initial opinion concerning a number of factors and the final opinion about the same factors will be uncorrelated. That shows that significant learning takes place through the application of the design process.

*Challenge*: The answer to that is the same as for validation: The CRISSI system must be a dynamic system, a system that it is possible to change over time.

## Requisite variety

A design specification exhibits requisite variety if the designer has correctly identified and specified the dimensions of the system. That means that the behavior of the design should be that which the situation can absorb and which the designer can control. No more, no less.

*Challenge*: It is necessary to identify and implement requisite variety in the CRISSI system.

## Triadic necessity and sufficiency

Relationships are characterized by the number of distinct relational components, but no matter how many such components a relationship may have, the (complex) relationship can always be expressed by component relationships having no more than three relational components.

*Challenge*: As for triadic compatibility, that demands that the relational components selected must be highly relevant.

## Precluded resolution

An organization must have an effective methodology for learning about the issue, before the design process starts. Either that or the individual's particular uninformed perceptions about the issue will be the basis for the actions. That will definitely exhibit structural underconceptualization, inherent conflict, and diversity of beliefs, dysfunctional organizational linguistics.

*Challenge*: A methodological step for learning about critical situations caused by flooding must be performed.

## Conclusion

In presenting part of the CRISSI project we have analyzed and discussed the complexity challenges in critical situations caused by flooding.

The method used for the inquiry, the multi-modal systems method, was helpful to understand the breadth of the problem, and to catch the most vital input variables to the system, variables that were not obvious in the first place, such as commitment, secrecy, sustainability, and wellbeing.

We chose to use Warfield's (1999, 2002) twenty laws of complexity to understand and cover as many aspects as possible of the complexity in the CRISSI system and its total environment, including organizations and human beings. That is particularly important when developing a system to be used in situations where many organizations, and thereby many individuals, are involved in addition to the advanced system and its complex content (data, models, and calculations). Naturally, we cannot be sure we have covered all aspects of complexity, but when using an approved model we can design a better system, a system that is established among the organizations involved.

## References

Asproth, V., Håkansson, A. (2006). "Simulation and anticipation in critical situations caused by flooding" *International Journal of Computing Anticipatory Systems*, ISSN 1373-5411, 19: 28-36.

Asproth, V., Holmberg, S.C. and Håkansson, A. (1999). "Decision support for spatial planning and management of human settlements," in G. E. Lasker (ed.), *Advances in Support Systems Research*, Volume V, ISBN 9780921836063, The International Institute for Advanced Studies in Systems Research and Cybernetics.

Asproth, V., Holmberg, S. C. and Håkansson, A. (2001). "Applying anticipatory computing in system dynamics," in Dubois D. (ed.), *Computing Anticipatory Systems: CASYS 2000: Fourth International Conference,* ISBN 9780735400122, 573: 578-589.

Asproth, V., Holmberg, S. C. and Håkansson, A. (2002). "Spatial decision support," *Proceedings of the 2002 IEEE International Conference on Fuzzy Systems*, ISBN 9780780372801. 2: 1274-1279

Asproth, V., Holmberg, S. C. and Håkansson, A. (2005a). "Complexity challenges of regional planning and design," in K. A. Richardson, W. J. Gregory and G. Midgley (eds.), *Systems Thinking and Complexity Science: Insight for Action, Proceedings of the 11th ANZSYS/Managing the Complex V conference*, ISBN 9780976681441.

Asproth, V., Håkansson, A. and Révay, P. (2005b). "Visualization and simulation of critical situations caused by flooding," *Proceedings of GeoCAD '05*, Alba Iulia, Romania.

Bacow, L. S. and Wheeler, M. (1984). *Environmental Dispute Resolution*, ISBN 9780306415944 (2003).

Eriksson, D. M. (2001). "Multi-modal investigation of a business process and information system redesign: A post-implementation case study," *Systems Research and Behavioral Science*, ISSN 1092-7026, 18(2): 181-196.

Espejo, R. and Schwaninger, M. (1993). Organizational Fitness: Corporate Effectiveness through Management Cybernetics. ISBN 9783593347837.

Klir, G. J. (1996). *Fuzzy Sets*, ISBN 9782841340125 (1980).

de Raadt, J. D. R. (2000). *Redesign and Management of Communities in Crisis*, ISBN 9781581127218.

de Raadt, V. D. (2001). "Multi-modal systems method: The impact of normative factors on community viability," *Systems Research and Behavioral Science*, ISSN 1092-7026, 18(2): 1171-1180.

Raiffa, H. (1982). *The Art and Science of Negotiation*, ISBN 9780674048133 (2005).

Warfield, J. N. (1999). "Twenty laws of complexity: Science applicable in organizations," *Systems Research and Behavioral Science*, ISSN 1092-7026, 16: 3-40.

Warfield, J. N. (2002). *Understanding Complexity: Thought and Behavior*, ISBN 9789716962093.

**Viveca Asproth** received her doctorate (PhD) and reader (Docent) degree from the University of Stockholm. Currently she is an associate professor in Computer and Systems Science at Mid Sweden University in Östersund, Sweden. She has published papers on visualization, spatial systems, decision support, anticipation, and fuzzy systems. She is member of the Board of Graduate Education and deputy head of the Department of Information Technology and Media at Mid Sweden University. In her current research she is focusing on spatial decision support systems: modeling, simulation, and visualization of critical situations caused by flooding.

**Anita Håkansson** received her doctorate (PhD) and reader (Docent) degree from the University of Stockholm. Currently she is an associate professor in Computer and Systems Science at Mid Sweden University in Östersund, Sweden. She has published papers on spatial systems, decision support, anticipation, and fuzzy systems. She is a member of the Board of Graduate Education and head of the Informatics group at Mid Sweden University. In her current research she is focusing on spatial decision support systems: modeling, simulation, and visualization of critical situations caused by flooding.

Academic

# Mutual empathy, ambiguity, and the implementation of electronic knowledge management within the complex health system*

Martin Orr[1] & Shankar Sankaran[2]
[1]Waitemata District Health Board, Auckland, NZ
[2]University of Technology Sydney, AUS

Healthcare can be characterized as a complex adaptive system. New Zealand is recognized as having one of the highest rates of enmeshed clinical information and communication technology within this complex system. This paper describes the implementation of an integrated series of electronic clinical health knowledge management systems in a large New Zealand District Health Board. In combination with standard project management, the core implementation team utilized an action research reflective learning approach to enhance their capability to cope with emergent issues, and plan for each subsequent project stage. The emergent focus on "process" issues of connectedness, competency, and control were not the "technical" concerns the principal author was initially expecting, but can be understood through an appreciation of individual and group dynamics, system and complexity theories. In particular, mutual empathy for both self and others was identified as a core capability requirement to cope with the inherent ambiguity within complex systems.

## Introduction

Healthcare can be characterized as a complex adaptive system. From the cellular to sociopolitical levels, multiple "agents" and systems interact across shadowy boundaries and contribute to our concepts of health and healthcare. Nonlinear dynamics and sensitivity to initial conditions are inherent; and small changes in one part of the system, or embedded system, can change the context and outcome of another part, leading to significant variability and emergence in health outcomes (Goldberger, 1996; McDaniel et al., 2003; Plesk & Greenhalgh, 2001; Wilson et al., 2001).

If we accept this complexity conceptualization of healthcare (while recognizing doubters and the risk of fadism: e.g., Price, 2004; Reid & Notcutt, 2002), then we need to appreciate the innate unpredictability of health outcomes. We need to appreciate the limitations of healthcare management that is unduly bounded by the search for increasing data analysis and prediction models that will allow this complexity to be controlled. Rather than focusing investment on increasingly complex and costly "rational" control and decision mechanisms, we should be building the capability to cope with and indeed exploit this inherent variability and emergence (Anderson et al., 2000; Fraser & Greenhalgh, 2001; Kurtz & Snowden, 2003; Lemak & Goodrick, 2003; Plesk & Wilson, 2001).

Globally, information and communication technology (ICT) is increasingly being applied to the health system. Objectives and predicted benefits vary by stakeholder and system, but coordination, integration, safety, and efficiency are common themes (Institute of Medicine, 2000). There may be a range of views on the constituent parts or overall makeup of an ideal health knowledge management system. However, recurrent identified core features or principles that may be independent of place, time, or technology can be encapsulated in the mnemonic C.A.R.E. G.A.P.S. F.I.R.S.T.

The system should enhance every stakeholder's "capacity to C.A.R.E."; that is,

*The authors wish to thank and acknowledge the core "Clinical Information System" implementation team and the staff of Waitemata District Health Board, Counties Manukau DHB, Health Alliance, and Orion Systems International, all of whom contributed their knowledge and learning to the success of this project.

perform their integral Clinical, Administrative, Research, and Educational healthcare functions. The system should accommodate the complex and holistic environment in which it is enmeshed, while recognizing, connecting, and enabling all the key stakeholders, primarily General practitioners, Allied health services (including hospitals), Patients and their Supports, as well as being Fast, Intuitive, Robust, Stable, and Trustworthy (Orr, 2004; Standards Australia, 2001; Standards Australia/New Zealand, 2001; Sveiby, 2001; Wyatt, 2001).

Historically, clinician-valued, cost-efficient systems that have sustainably delivered their predicted benefits have proven to be relatively elusive. A failure to recognize complexity, or a focus on trying to control the complexity of healthcare via increasing levels of data collection, analysis, and detailed "decision support" guideline or protocol creation, could explain, at least in part, this relative failure (Ash, 1997; Ash et al., 2004; Berger & Kichak, 2004; Bryant, 1998; Garg, 2005; Heeks et al., 1999; Southon et al., 1997).

The New Zealand health system is recognized as having one of the highest rates of clinical ICT enablement and integration in the world. Clinical information systems are pervasive within primary care (general practice) and the secondary care (hospital-based) systems are rapidly developing both their internal ICT enablement of clinical care and their ability to share information with primary care and other secondary care providers (Orr, 2004; Protti, 2003).

This paper reports on the implementation of an integrated series of electronic clinical health knowledge management systems in a large New Zealand District Health Board. In combination with standard project management, the core implementation team utilized an action research reflective learning approach to enhance their capability to cope with emergent issues and plan for each subsequent project stage. Aspects of this project have been reported in part elsewhere (Orr, 2004, 200b; Orr & Day, 2005; Orr et al., 2005).

However, this paper will detail the team's emergent focus on, and evolving appreciation of, "process" issues of connectedness, competency, and control, particularly with regard to a central metaphor of crossing the "acceptance" or "concept–reality" gap (Heeks et al., 1999; Orr, 2000). The team's journey and their evolving understanding of what was important for their journey can be understood through an appreciation of individual and group dynamics, system and complexity theories. In particular, mutual empathy for both self and others was identified as a core capability requirement to cope with the inherent ambiguity within complex systems.

## Research context

Waitemata District Health Board provides publicly funded primary and secondary care to a population of 450,000. Waitemata, in association with two of its neighboring district health boards, has implemented a series of clinically focused ICT systems. The system developments that were the focus of this project included:

- A single login interface from which all patient demographics, medical alerts, past treatment events, and investigations (blood tests, X-rays, etc.) can be viewed.

- An electronic medical document repository (including the migration of 250,000 historical documents).

- A real-time patient tracking system for the emergency care center.

- A surgical audit system.

- Electronic referral status messaging and discharge summaries for primary care.

- Electronic signoff of laboratory results.

## Action research

Action research is an evolving concept. However, Dick (2001) observes that its name conveys its essence. Its primary goals are action or change and research or understanding, and synergy between the action and research. Action research typically involves cycles of action and critical reflection.

Action research was utilized as a methodology due to its explorative qualitative the-

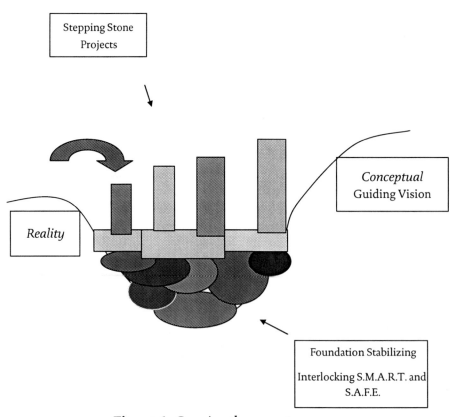

**Figure 1** *Crossing the acceptance gap*

ory-building emphasis, focus on change and learning, accommodation of researcher participation, and flexibility and responsiveness to deal with emergent issues within a complex changing system (Baskerville & Myers, 2004; Dick, 2001; Zuber-Skerritt, 2001).

The research process involved an initial conceptual stage of literature review, communication with experts, and integration of personal experience. The action research stage utilized participant observation, personal and group reflection, convergent interviews, document examination, and repeated triangulation of sources seeking disconfirming evidence (Dick, 1998; Jick, 1979). The principal author had the roles of researcher, clinical director of information services, and practicing clinician (specialist psychiatrist).

Throughout its development, action research has experienced criticism of its validity, rigor, and ethics (Hope & Waterman, 2003; Meyer, 1993; Williamson & Prosser, 2002) and these issues within the context of limitations of the methodology are explored further in an additional paper related to this project (Orr *et al.*, 2005).

## Relevant findings
### The "acceptance" or "concept–reality" gap

The action research cycles of action and critical reflection aimed to develop conceptual models (built on emergent key project issues and related issues) that may enhance the implementation of electronic health knowledge management systems at Waitemata. A central metaphor utilized throughout the project was that of crossing the "acceptance" or "concept–reality" gap (Figure 1). This originated as a visual representation of a common theme in a range of disciplines that as an individual or system faces a stressor or change, there may be an initial drop in functioning before a reorganization, improved resilience and capability, and return to baseline if not ideally improved function. This general theme is illustrated in such concepts as the reengineering curve, the death valley of change, crossing the quality chasm, moving through a grief process, and so on (Committee on Quality of Healthcare in America, 2001; Elrod & Tippett, 2002; Kelley & Tucci, 2001).

In an industrial reengineering process this initial drop in functioning may be acceptable if a change is expected to lead to greater productivity. However, in a healthcare system, any drop or perceived drop in functioning that may affect the system's capacity to maintain patient safety can lead to abandonment of the new process and return to the original trusted, if flawed, process. Failure to appreciate the magnitude of the concept–reality or "acceptance" gap, with particular relation to the complex multiple enmeshed systems characteristic of healthcare, contributes to the common, at least partial, failure of ICT implementations and health system changes in general (Glouberman & Mintzberg, 1996; Heeks *et al.*, 1999; Orr, 2000).

## Evolution of gap metaphor

The original primary message of the "acceptance" gap was that you could try to jump from reality to concept in one go. However, the health ICT literature would suggest that there was a high likelihood that if your concept involved significant system change you would crash and burn. Instead, you needed to incrementalize your conceptualized vision, break the journey down into foundation and stepping stones, and recognize that each component could be further reduced again to component parts. You needed to build firm foundations of SMART (Specific, Measurable, Acceptable, Resourced, and Timelined) and SAFE (Scalable, Affordable, Flexible, and Equitable) projects, and then perhaps try some stepping-stone projects involving some process or system change, but never attempting to change too much at once (Orr, 2000, 2004).

*"You're weaving fibres together to create a beautiful rug, you're not stacking cans in a supermarket."* (Project team member)

Reductionistic metaphors or models by their implicit nature in their attempt to clarify and simplify run the risk of losing important complexity. However, they can perform an important role in communication and act as catalysts for further individual and group understanding (Orr, 2004). A central focus of action research is to deal with the data and issues that emerge in the real system rather than be bounded by preconditions or assumptions of what those issues may be. The author had originally assumed that a major focus of the group and individual reflective sessions would be identifying a detailed technical content picture of what our conceptual vision was, our current reality, and the detailed technology stepping stones we needed to take to get there.

Instead, the focus was more on individual, group, and inter-group dynamic relationship and functioning issues, such as dealing with ambiguity, different cultures, different systems, control, competency, and connectedness. The core project team averaged only 10–12 individuals, and comprised a mixture of seconded clinicians (with various levels of project management and ICT experience) complemented by external specialist ICT contractors. However, to achieve their task the core team had to interact with and influence multiple other enmeshed systems, with the project directly affecting at least 2,500 staff in multiple teams and services, and 130 primary care practices within the district.

Simply identifying the technical content of stepping stones or a conceptual vision was not enough. Standard project management scope detailing, breakdown, and timelining aimed to fill this role and it was an important role. However, it was not just a matter of filling cans and stacking them, and the acceptance gap metaphor was repeatedly challenged with such questions as:

- What was the supporting life force, passion, or ecosystem or "agents" that were required to build and hold it altogether?
- How could you get everyone to cooperate across multiple systems with different cultures, languages, and priorities?
- How should and could the building stones link, who should design, build, or own them?
- Was there an optimal stone size or gap, should we have a three-dimensional model, could we identify all the stones and did we have to?
- Was incrementalism always right, did it not just encourage inertia?

- Was it not better sometimes just to make a leap of faith, do something radical, and force the system to change?

The reflective learning and subsequent capability development sessions helped deal with the dissonance between the simplicity of the project Gantt chart and the ambiguity, variability, and emergent issues that reflected the complexity of the system they were operating in.

### The learning curve

*"As move through learning curve, more focus on walking the boards than documentation... still on the rollercoaster but see things differently and know will cope."* (Project team member)

*"It's not what you know, its who you know."* (Project team member)

A common theme, particularly for seconded clinical team members, was an initial sense of lack of competence and lack of control, within the multiple systems they found themselves in, and a concern that they may have compensated for their perceived lack of formal technical and project management knowledge and experience with a focus on ever more detailed documentation. However, as time progressed they became more comfortable with the inherent ambiguity, and recognized that it was their intuition within, knowledge of, and ability to interact with and develop local health systems and agents that was of most value to the project. To assist people moving through this learning curve, the value of a buddy system placing people together with complementary skills was also recognized.

### "The health knowledge ecosystem"

*"It's like pebbles skipping off the water... need to understand its not real for them, not the same urgency until impacting on their world."* (Project team member)

The team also faced the challenge of how each enmeshed system and agents from technical staff to clinicians were already invariably caught up with dealing with multiple changes, pressures, and requirements within their own world.

Key components or subsystems of the health knowledge "ecosystem" that emerged were the Innovation, Innovators, Implementors (both the core team and wider technical expertise), Individuals (both clinicians, patient, and administrative users), the Invironment (used to capture the concept of the associated clinical and administrative processes and wider sociopolitical holistic environment), the Investors, Informaticians, and Integrators.

Aligning the priorities of these systems was a perpetual challenge and a focus for capability development. It was also recognized that although project funding often focused on the purchase of the Innovation or software and specialist implementers, a viable health knowledge system required sustained investment in the development of all the components (Orr *et al.*, 2005; Orr & Day, 2004).

*"The life cycle of a piece of paper... touches multiple layers."* (Project team member)

One particular illustration of the complexity of the system was the replacement of paper lab results with electronic viewing and signoff. Significant work was involved trying to map all the subsystems that the paper lab result moved through and the actions triggered at each stage, particularly the implications if the paper triggers were removed.

### Mutual empathy

In terms of capability development, reflection sessions led to the team exploring a number of areas, including the reasons health information systems fail, acceptance gaps, utility of resistance, the psychological impact of change, building networks, communication, listening, learning and linking, negotiation and dealing with difficult situations, and ambiguity.

Mutual empathy was identified as a key capability, and building on the work of Stuart and Lieberman (1993), the "empathy" mnemonic was developed to capture the key features thought important to this concept:

48

- E*motion*: How do the key stakeholders feel about an issue: their sense of control, competency, connectedness?

- M*otivation*: What drives them: values, reason, emotion, self-interest?

- P*ressures*: What are the pressures impacting on their behavior/decisions?

- A*ttachments*: What are the key attachments or networks for stakeholders?

- T*rouble*: What issues trouble each stakeholder group most?

- H*andle*: How do stakeholders cope/adapt/ learn from experience/utilize supports?

- Y*ou*: What part do you play in each stakeholder's conceptualization of an issue?

## Acceptance gap metaphor as a projective technique

One particular focus was the need to develop a shared language, understanding, significance, and hope and priority for action between often disparate in culture but interdependent systems and agents. As time progressed (and with subsequent experience), it emerged that the acceptance gap metaphor's major value was not in creating time-intense detailed content pictures of every specific step. Instead, it served better as a brief projective technique for groups, surfacing the assumptions and perceptions and values of those present as to what the concept, reality, perceived risks and benefits, and needed steps were, illustrating differences, but also setting the basis for moving toward that desired shared language, understanding, significance, and hope.

## Emergent demand and concerns

Project management creates a very important framework to drive processes along. However, within a complex system it is difficult and of limiting utility to fix scope and timelines in concrete, and not allow for the wider and enduring systemic issues, ambiguities, emergent phenomena, challenges, and opportunities that have to be dealt with as they arise. Similarly, for the implementation team, although the project had a defined scope and timeline, as they started on their journey they uncovered all sorts of emergent demands and concerns with regard

to not just how technology could facilitate the care system, but also the fundamental processes and interfaces of our systems of care. The team recognized that they were ambassadors for how ICT could empower health systems, not just for this fixed project time and scope, but for the continual process of development. They were initiating a system whereby clinicians could move from using technology on a sporadic basis for wordprocessing, email, and the internet, to integrating technology into their daily care systems and considering how it could change those systems. The team recognized the need to have clear mechanisms to capture the changes as well as processes to deal with them, but not to be sidetracked or dragged down by them.

## Catalyst projects

Each component of the project could be perceived as an opportunity to get access to and attention from fully engaged preoccupied subsystems, to understand their needs, processes, and interfaces.

With all the key agents invariably busy, if anyone, but particularly clinicians, took the time to raise concerns, rather than being perceived as resistance this could be grasped as an opportunity to harness energy and enthusiasm, develop a portal, and strengthen links into their system.

Each step, project, or engaged agent can act as a catalyst toward getting a greater understanding of the complexity, needs, and attractors of interfacing systems aligning and altering if necessary one piece at a time, to build capacity for more fundamental change.

## Discussion

This paper was neither an attempt at an ontological or epistemological critical analysis nor a formal prospective application of complexity theory (Phelan, 1999; Solem, 2003). Instead, it describes how a group with little academic knowledge of the language of systems or complexity theory utilized action research to build the capability to cope with the implementation of an electronic health knowledge management system within the complex health environment. The author describes how he began the journey by looking for content and ended it by focusing on process.

Mutual empathy emerged as a core capability to be identified and nourished, to help build a shared language, understanding, significance, and hope, and thrive within a complex environment of inherent ambiguity and variability, and issues of control, competency and connectedness.

The author as psychiatrist repeatedly questioned how much this emergent focus on dynamic and complex system issues was a function of his own selective abstraction or cognitive filters, or his influence on the group as participant observer. However, this focus can be traced to the intertwined origins of action research and group dynamics, with Kurt Lewin being considered a central originator of both, and both being born out of a central appreciation of iterative reflection, systems, and relationships and the need to deal with the emergent variability of the real world (Lewin, 1948).

With action research's enmeshed links with group dynamics, the hope is that it can get the group from "forming" to "performing" while minimizing the negative impact of "storming" and eventual "mourning" (Tuckman, 2001; Tuckman & Jensen, 1977).

The concept of a health knowledge management system utilized in this paper aims to move away from the inherent focus on technology when discussing such issues as the "electronic patient record" and highlight the essential importance of taking a wider holistic view. This is a view that recognizes complexity and the need to develop the required sustaining systems, interfaces, and empathy (between Innovators, Innovation, Implementors, Individuals, Invironment, Investors, Informaticians, and Integrators) and a culture that respects, values, and protects the creation, acquisition, and sharing of health information.

### Project management, action research, complexity, and the development of critically reflective practitioners

There is an increasing recognition within the formal project management literature of a need to re-examine some of its fundamental tenets if it is to cope and add value in an increasingly complex environment: a need to develop critical reflective practitioners with the capability to embrace complexity and emergence and thrive within an environment where all outcomes and interactions cannot be readily predicted or controlled.

Winter and Smith (2006), reporting on the UK "rethinking project management" research network, identify five key directions for future project management research. These key directions emphasize the need to recognize the complexity of projects, the inherent social process, a move in focus from product creation to value creation, a broader conceptualization of projects that recognizes and can adapt to multiple objectives or fuzzy or non-predefined emergent objectives, and a shift in practitioner development focus from one that produces trained technicians toward facilitating the development of reflective practitioners. Similarly, Jafaari (2003) concludes that project management requires further research and development of a "creative-reflective" model if it is to avoid irrelevance in an increasingly complex world. This project echoed the importance of many of these issues.

Wilson et al. (2001) suggest some principles to facilitate decision making in the "complex zone." These are using intuition, experimenting, minimum specification, chunking, using metaphors, and asking provocative questions. These principles or techniques evolved within the team as a natural consequence of the action research reflective learning process, adding some empirical support to action research's perceived synergic utility with traditional project management processes within a complex environment.

### Snowden's "three ages" of knowledge management

Snowden (2002) posits that we are entering a third age of knowledge management. The first age was correlated with the dominance of business process reengineering and focused on the computerization of key processes and the structure and flow of information to decision makers. The first age failed to value or recognize the importance of experience, apprenticeship, or collective knowledge.

The second age beginning circa 1995 was driven by the SECI (Socialization, Externalization, Combination, Internalization) model (Nonaka & Takeuchi, 1995), with a focus on converting knowledge from tacit to explicit forms. Snowden (2002) notes that the concept of tacit and explicit knowledge was not new (Polanyi, 1974), and had and continues to have value. However, Snowden (2002) argues that a major failing of the second age was a dualistic rather than dialectical interpretation of the tacit-explicit concept and in particular the SECI model. Snowden comments that Nonaka (Nonaka & Konno, 1998) later went on to attempt to clarify and emphasize the dialectic and holistic intent of the original model. However, the widespread dualistic misinterpretation saw knowledge frequently viewed as a "thing" that could and should be separated from its origin and context, codified, stored, valued, and traded; tacit and explicit as two opposites rather than integral parts of the same whole.

Stacey (2001) contends that knowledge is not a "thing" that can be stored or managed but a dynamic relational process. Snowden (2002), commenting on Stacey (2001), argues that knowledge can be perceived as a "thing" but also paradoxically as a "flow," and our understanding and knowledge are enriched by synergically exploring both perspectives.

Snowden (2002) argues that in the "third generation of KM" we need to further evolve our knowledge management capability, so that we are no longer primarily focusing on content management where knowledge is perceived as a "thing," but shift our paradigm to also appreciate knowledge as a "flow" where context and narrative are inherent.

### The "third age" value of traditional healthcare knowledge processes

Healthcare is globally considered one of the last great challenges, and increasing priorities for information and communication technology (ICT) facilitated process reengineering. ICT can certainly play a role in helping healthcare better manage knowledge to facilitate more effective integrated care. However, there is a need for ICT professionals entering the healthcare area not to make the same mistakes as other industries. They need to recognize the "third age" value of traditional healthcare knowledge processes and avoid regressing healthcare back to live through the negative aspects of Snowden's first and second ages. Context, story telling, apprenticeship, fellowship, professional ethics, community, and collective knowledge have been central to traditional models of clinical development and practice. ICT should seek to value and enhance these important traditional processes.

### A "third age" health knowledge management system

Healthcare requires critically reflective practitioners who can cope in real time with the complex ambiguity they often face. ICT can facilitate creating a context or supporting ecosystem for healthcare workers to facilitate the development and exercise of this critical reflectiveness; a context for collaboration with their stakeholder communities and connection with their supporting resources; a context that can provide timely knowledge and coordination and facilitate the self-organization and management of knowledge (Snowden, 2002).

Systems designed to facilitate the control or predictions of risk in the health environment certainly have a role. However, systems designed to control risk by controlling clinicians via the application of increasing levels of rules that do not take into account the complex time-pressured environment in which clinicians operate have frequently met with failure. As well as being switched off due to their sheer lack of utility, they can also potentially lead to increased risk due to their capacity to disempower the clinician's sense of ownership and responsibility and in-the-moment critical reflectiveness. There is a need to avoid autopilot systems that result in the driver falling asleep at the wheel or becoming deskilled to the point where they can no longer cope with the complex ambiguity inherent in their work. Systems need to synergically enhance and build on, rather than try to replace, clinicians' professional ethical training and core critical reflectiveness.

Attempting to control or predict the risk of an undesirable outcome in a complex environment by introducing ever-increasing levels of rules or barriers, based on a retrospective analysis of a past undesirable outcome, is fraught with limitations. Such an analysis may certainly assist an understanding and system improvement. However, this is with the caveat that the reviewers appreciate the role of retrospective coherence, and that although it may appear to make perfect logical sense as to what factors contributed to an adverse outcome or pattern, these factors in a complex environment may have resulted in several different outcomes or patterns (Snowden, 2005).

In a complex environment it is important to consider not just how the barriers to the conditions or patterns associated with bad outcomes can be increased, but also to enhance and develop the attractors associated with good outcomes (Snowden, 2005).

## Growing the right thing

The central focus for the systems implemented in this project were not to control clinician behavior but to create a context that enhanced the frequency of patterns known to be associated with good patient care outcomes; namely, timely access to appropriate information and communication with other caregivers. Throughout the design and implementation process there was always (and with ongoing developments there continues to be) a focus on not just how you may stop people doing undesired things, but how do you help users do the right thing.

## The primacy of the core clinician–individual patient relationship

Though there has been a shift to a population health focus that may consider an individual's needs within the context of a community's needs, and associated costs and opportunity costs, traditionally the predominant culture, values, or attractors for clinicians, from basic training to ongoing professional development, have focused on the primacy of the core clinician–individual patient relationship. There is an increasing capacity for electronic technology developments to affect that core relation-

ship via the introduction of decision support or guidelines. As noted previously, such decision support or guidance has the potential to be of significant value. Unfortunately, guidelines are often experienced as inflexible mandated protocol, a linear solution in a complex nonlinear environment that fails to recognize and accommodate complexity, variability, and emergence. Electronic health knowledge systems that seek to provide guidance need to embrace their key function of acting as potential catalysts for the wider ecosystem to review, align, and develop their associated context, processes, values, and key relationships. The technology and content can be borrowed or purchased, but will still need the associated professionalism, processes, and relationships to deal with ambiguity, and balance risks and benefits, costs and opportunity costs (Grol *et al.*, 1998; Rousseau *et al.*, 2003; Shiffmann *et al.*, 1999).

## Informing and connecting rather than controlling and changing

The project developments discussed in this paper, in keeping with the majority of developments in New Zealand to date, are focused on enhancing the core clinician–patient interface, informing and connecting rather than controlling or significantly changing traditional clinical processes or systems. These developments are designed to provide a context to network the knowledge of key stakeholders so that better questions can be formulated, rather than the focus being on providing mandated answers. This focus to date may have contributed to the relative success of clinical ICT diffusion in New Zealand, while also incrementally building the capability for more fundamental positive change. This includes the ongoing development of electronic guidelines and decision support that recognize and embrace complexity and chronicity as well as individual and group needs and values.

Health knowledge system implementation investments are typically focused on the Innovation or piece of software and the Implementors. This project and ongoing developments have highlighted that a sustainable health knowledge system requires the need to invest not just in the Innovation and Implementors, but in a long-term developmental relationship with the wider ecosystem of Innovators, Invironment, Individuals, Investors, Integrators, and Informaticians. Investments in each area can grow and interconnect and support each other, increasing the capacity for all areas to progress. For the implementation team, core ethical values of professionalism, critical reflectiveness, and mutual empathy for others, rather than fixed rules, were central to the team's capacity to operate in a complex, ambiguous environment. Similarly with ongoing developments, core values, reflectiveness, and professionalism continue to play a central role, as we strive to create an environment that respects, values, and protects health knowledge.

## References

Anderson, R. A. and McDaniel, R. R. (2000). "Managing health care organizations: Where professionalism meets complexity science," *Healthcare Management Review*, ISSN 0361-6274, 25(1): 83-92.

Ash, J. (1997). "Organizational factors that influence Information Technology diffusion in Academic Health Sciences Centers," *Journal of the American Medical Informatics Association*, ISSN 1067-5027, 4(2): 102-111.

Ash, J.A., Berg, M. and Coiera, E. (2004). "Some unintended consequences of Information Technology in health care: The nature of patient care information system-related errors," *Journal of the American Medical Informatics Association*, ISSN 1067-5027, 11(2): 104-112.

Baskerville, R. and Myers, M. (2004). "Making IS research relevant to practice," *MIS Quarterly*, ISSN 0276-7783, 28(3): 329-335.

Berger, R.G. and Kichak, J.P. (2004). "Viewpoint paper computerized physician order entry: helpful or harmful?" *Journal of the American Medical Informatics Association*, ISSN 1067-5027, 11(2): 100-103.

Bryant, J. (1998). "The importance of human and organizational factors in the implementation of computerized information systems: An emerging theme in European healthcare," The *British Journal of Healthcare Computing and Information Management*, ISSN 0266-5127, 15(4): 27-29.

Committee on Quality of Health Care in America (2001). *Crossing the Quality Chasm: A New Health System for the 21st Century*, ISBN 9780309072809.

Dick, B. (1998). "Convergent interviewing: A technique for qualitative data collection," http://www.scu.edu.au/schools/gcm/ar/arp/iview.html.

Dick, B. (2001). "Action research: Action and research," in S. Shankar, B. Dick, R. Passfield and P. Swepson (eds.), *Effective Change Management Using Action Learning and Action Research*, ISBN 9781875855551, NSW, Australia: Southern Cross University Press.

Elrod, P. and Tippet, D. (2002). "The death valley of change," *Journal of Organizational Change Management*, ISSN 1832-5912, 15(3): 273-291.

Fraser, S. W. and Greenhalgh, T. (2001). "Complexity science: Coping with complexity, educating for capability," *British Medical Journal*, ISSN 1468-5833, 323(Oct): 799-803.

Garg, A., Adhikari, N., McDonald, H., Rosas-Arellano, M., Devereaux, P., Beyene, J., Sam, J. and Haynes, B. (2005). "Effects of computerized decision support systems on practitioner performance and patient outcomes: A systematic review," *Journal of the American Medical Association*, ISSN 1067-5027, 293: 1223-1238.

Glouberman, S. and Mintzberg, H. (1996). "Managing the care of health and the cure of disease. Part 1: Differentiation," *Healthcare Management Review*, ISSN 0361-6274, 26(1): 56-59.

Goldberger, A. L. (1996). "Non-linear dynamics for clinicians: Chaos theory, fractals, and complexity at the bedside," *The Lancet*, ISSN 0140-6736, 347: 9011.

Grol, R., Dalhuijsen, J., Thomas, S., In't Veld, C., Rutten, G. and Mokkink, H. (1998). "Attributes of clinical guidelines that influence use of guidelines in general practice: Observational study," *British Medical Journal*, ISSN 0959-8138, 317(Sep): 858-861.

Heeks, R., Mundy, D. and Salazar, A. (1999). "Why health care information systems succeed or fail: Information systems for public sector management," Working Paper Series, paper no. 9, Manchester: Institute for Development Policy and Management.

Hope, K. W. and Waterman, H. A. (2003). "Praiseworthy pragmatism? Validity and action research," *Journal of Advanced Nursing*, ISSN 1365-2648, 44(2): 120-127.

Institute of Medicine (2000). *To Err Is Human: Building a Safer Health System*, ISBN 9780309068376.

Jafaari, A. (2003) "Project management in the age of complexity and change," *Project Management Journal*, ISSN 8756-9728, 34(4): 45-57.

Jick, T. D. (1979). "Mixing qualitative and quantitative methods: Triangulation in action," *Administrative Science Quarterly*, ISSN 0001-8392, 24: 602-611.

Kelley, M. A. and Tucci, J. M. (2001). "Bridging the quality chasm," *British Medical Journal*, ISSN 1468-5833, 323: 61-62.

Kurtz, C. F. and Snowden, D. J. (2003). "The new dynamics of strategy: Sense-making in a complex and complicated world," *IBM Systems Journal*, ISSN 0018-8646, 42(3).

Lemak, C. H. and Goodrick, E. (2003). "Strategy as simple rules: Understanding success in a rural clinic," *Health Care Management Review*, ISSN 0361-6274, 28(2, Apr-Jun).

Lewin, K. (1948). *Resolving Social Conflicts: Selected Papers on Group Dynamics*, Gertrude W. Lewin (ed.), ISBN 9781557984159 (1997).

McDaniel, R. R., Jordon, M. E. and Fleeman, B. F. (2003). "Surprise, surprise, surprise! A complexity science view of the unexpected," *Health Care Management Review*, ISSN 0361-6274, 28(3): 266-278.

Meyer, J. E. (1993). "New paradigm research in practice: The trials and tribulations of action research," *Journal of Advanced Nursing*, ISSN 1365-2648, 18: 1066-1072.

Nonaka, I. and Konno, N. (1998). "The concept of Ba: Building a foundation for knowledge creation," *California Management Review*, ISSN 0008-1256, 40(3): 41-53.

Nonaka, I. and Takeuchi, H. (1995). *The Knowledge-Creating Company: How Japanese Companies Create the Dynamics of Innovation*, ISBN 9780195092691.

Orr, M. (2000). "Implementation of health information systems: Background literature review for MBA dissertation," Lismore, NSW: Southern Cross University.

Orr, M. (2004). "Evolution of New Zealand's health knowledge management system," *British Journal of Healthcare Computing and Information Management*, ISSN 0266-5127, 21(10): 28-30.

Orr, M. (2005). "Privacy, security and the implementation of health knowledge management systems," in R. K. Bali (ed.), *Clinical Knowledge Management: Opportunities and Challenges*, ISBN 9781591403005, pp. 72-95.

Orr, M. and Day, K. (2004). "Knowledge and learning in successful IT projects: A case study," *Healthcare and Informatics Review Online*, ISSN 1174-4201, June.

Orr, M., Sankaran, S. and James, P. (2005). "The implementation of electronic health knowledge management systems in a District Health Board: 'Respect and Protect'," paper presented at The Fifth International Conference on Knowledge, Culture and Change in Organizations, Rhodes, Greece, July. Revised paper published in *International Journal of Knowledge, Culture and Change Management*, ISSN 1447-9575, 2005, 5(9):113-124.

Phelan, S. E. (1999). "A note on the correspondence between complexity and systems theory," *Systemic Practice and Action Research*, ISSN 1094-429X, 12(3): 237-246.

Plesk, P. E. and Greenhalgh, T. (2001). "Complexity science: The challenge of complexity in health care," *British Medical Journal*, ISSN 1468-5833, 323(Sep): 625-628.

Plesk, P. E. and Wilson, T. (2001). "Complexity science: Complexity, leadership, and management in healthcare organizations," *British Medical Journal*, ISSN 1468-5833, 323(Sep): 746-749.

Polanyi, M. (1974). *Personal Knowledge: Towards a Post-Critical Philosophy*, ISBN 9780226672885.

Price, I. F. (2004). "Complexity, complicatedness and complexity: A new science behind organizational intervention?" *Emergence: Complexity & Organization*, ISSN 1521-3250, 6(1-2): 40-48.

Protti, D. (2003). "Local clinician involvement in clinical information systems: Luxury or necessity? A review of two international experiences," *British Journal of Healthcare Computing and Information Management*, ISSN 0266-5127, 20(10): 28-30.

Reid, I. and Notcutt, W. (2002). "Complexity science: Let them eat complexity: The emperor's new toolkit," *British Medical Journal*, ISSN 1468-5833, 324(Jan): 171.

Rousseau, N., McColl, E., Newton, J., Grimshaw, J. and Eccles, M. (2003). "Practice-based, longitudinal, qualitative interview study of computerized evidence based guidelines in primary care," *British Medical Journal*, ISSN 1468-5833, 326(Feb): 314.

Shiffman, R. N., Liaw, Y., Brandt, C. and Corb, G. J. (1999). "Computer-based guideline implementation systems: A systematic review of functionality and effectiveness," *Journal of the American Medical Informatics Association*, ISSN 1067-5027, 6(2, Mar/Apr): 104-114.

Snowden, D. (2002). "Complex acts of knowing: Paradox and descriptive self awareness," *Journal of Knowledge Management*, ISSN 1367-3270, 6(2):100-111.

Snowden, D. (2005). "Striking the right balance with KM and risk," *Knowledge Management Review*, ISSN 1369-7633, 8(1): 24-27.

Solem, O. (2003). "Epistemology and logistics: A critical overview," *Systemic Practice and Action*

*Research*, ISSN 1094-429X, 16(6): 437-454.

Southon, F. C. G., Sauer, C. and Dampney, C. N. (1997). "Information technology in complex health services: Organizational impediments to successful technology transfer and diffusion," *Journal of the American Medical Informatics Association*, ISSN 1067-5027, 4(2): 112-124.

Stacey, R. (2001). *Complex Responsive Processes in Organizations: Learning and Knowledge Creation*, ISBN 9780415249195.

Standards Australia (2001). *Knowledge Management: A Framework for Succeeding in the Knowledge Era*, ISBN 9780733739033.

Standards Australia/Standards New Zealand (2001). *Information Technology: Code of Practice for Information Security Management*, ISBN 9780733738760.

Stuart, M. R. and Lieberman, J. A. (eds) (1993). *The Fifteen Minute Hour: Applied Psychotherapy for the Primary Care Physician*, ISBN 9780275944995.

Sveiby, K-E. (2001). "Knowledge management: Lessons from the pioneers," http://www.sveiby.com/Portals/0/articles/KM-lessons.doc.

Tuckman, B. (2001). "Developmental sequence in small groups," *Group Facilitation: A Research and Applications Journal*, ISSN 1534-5653, 3(Spring): 66-81.

Tuckman, B. and Jensen, M. A. (1977). "Stages of small-group development revisited," *Group and Organizational Studies*, 2: 419-427.

Williamson, G. and Prosser, S. (2002). "Action research: Politics, ethics and participation," *Journal of Advanced Nursing*, ISSN 1365-2648, 40(5): 587-593.

Wilson, T., Holt, T. and Greenhalgh, T. (2001). "Complexity science: Complexity and clinical care," *British Medical Journal*, ISSN 1468-5833, 323(Sep): 685-688.

Winter, M. and Smith, C. (2006) "Rethinking project management," EPSRC Network 2004-2006 Final report, May, http://www.mace.manchester.ac.uk/project/research/management/rethinkpm/pdf/final_report.pdf.

Wyatt, J. (2001). "Top tips on knowledge management," *Clinical Governance Bulletin*, ISSN 1470-9023, 2(3): 8.

Zuber-Skerritt. O. (2001). "Action learning and action research: Paradigm, praxis and programs," in S. Sankaran, B. Dick, R. Passfield and P. Swepson (eds.), *Effective Change Management Using Action Learning and Action Research*, ISBN 9781875855551, NSW, Australia: Southern Cross University Press.

**Martin Orr** is a psychiatrist, a doctoral student at Southern Cross University, a Senior Lecturer at Auckland University School of Population Health, and Clinical Director of Information Services for the Waitemata District Health Board (Auckland, New Zealand). Dr Orr is involved on a daily basis in the pragmatics of meeting the "opportunities and challenges" of developing health knowledge systems. His key research interests lie in working with the dedicated professionals that, through the development, implementation, and utilization of health knowledge systems, strive to "make a healthy difference" for their communities. He has an interest in change, action research, reflective practice, innovation diffusion, individual and group dynamics, and information privacy and security within the complex health sector, particularly with relationship to health knowledge management systems.

**Shankar Sankaran** is a control system engineer and project manager by background and is currently employed as a Senior Lecturer at the Faculty of Design, Architecture and Building, University of Technology, Australia. He is also the leader of the research node on project management at the Centre for Applied Built Environment Research (CABER) being set up at the Faculty. Shankar teaches project management and supervises doctoral students at Doctor of Project Management, Doctoral of Business Administration and PhD levels. Some of Shankar's doctoral students use action research and soft systems methodology in their research. Shankar has presented papers at international conferences and published refereed papers in international journals.

Practitioner

# A complexity perspective on work with offenders and victims of crime*

Victor R. D. MacGill
Freelance Researcher, NZ

Internationally, cognitive behavioral theories form the foundation of work with offenders, because they have proved to be the most effective in bringing about changes and reducing levels of reoffending. As with any theory, the original theory has been consistently modified and adapted in attempts to make it even more effective at bringing about behavioral changes in offenders. This paper first gives an overview of cognitive behavioral theory, seeing how its linear approach has cut it off from wider perspectives that might make it more effective. It also develops an understanding of criminal behavior from a complexity viewpoint. From there it examines from a complexity perspective the work of the Community Probation Service in New Zealand, which uses a cognitive behavioral approach, and the recently completed pilot of the restorative justice system, bringing offender and victim together in a mediated forum. An effective complex adaptive system has strong autonomy and efficient connectivity. If any member of a community violates the autonomy or connectivity of another, a crime is committed. Work with offenders and victims focuses on restoring the autonomy and connectivity of those involved and the whole community, better enabling the dynamics of self-organization to reemerge. Offenders are seen as developing schemas supported by cognitive distortions that allow them to bypass the barriers that keep most of us from offending. If an existing maladaptive schema can be carefully destabilized, it can enable the formation of a new, more effective schema that does not include offending behaviors.

*With the permission of the Community Probation Service of New Zealand.

## Introduction

Cognitive behavioral theories form the foundation of work with offenders internationally, because they have proved to be the most effective at bringing about changes in offenders' behavior and reducing levels of reoffending (McGuire, 2000). Cognitive behavioral theory is based on the idea that a person's thoughts and emotions determine their behavior. Therefore, if we change the thoughts and emotions, the behavior is changed. A simple model often used to explain the principles of cognitive behavioral theory to offenders is the ETC model. This simply describes behavior as the process from an event, which leads to thoughts (and feelings) about the event, which then determines the consequences. Understanding this process can help offenders realize they can have control over impulsive offending behaviors.

## Cognitive behavioral theory and complexity theory

Complexity theory has some areas in common with cognitive behavioral theory, therefore it will be useful to examine how they might complement each other to provide even more effective methods of working with offenders. For example, the ETC model process can be explained as moving from one attractor basin to another on the phase space. Having this alternative understanding might generate new techniques for using the ETC model in practice. The differences between the approaches may point to new ways of using cognitive behavior therapy that increase its effectiveness. Both recognize behavior as a recursive process.

Cognitive behavioral theory tends to sharply define the difference between thoughts and emotions. The boundary between thoughts and emotions is, however, fuzzy at best, and it may even be that thoughts and emotions are merely different aspects of the same neurological processes, as proposed in Minsky's theory of emotions (Minsky, 1998).

Cognitive behavioral theory proposes that when an event happens, we first have thoughts about the event followed by emotions, from which the response is determined. An evolutionary psychological approach would suggest that since emotions appeared earlier in our evolutionary history and are less complex neurologically than cognitive processes, it is more likely that an emotional response would appear before a cognitive response (Sagan, 1978). This is supported by the APET therapy model (Griffin & Tyrrell, 2004). This shows that emotions are elicited in the limbic system and are pre-linguistic. Messages are then sent to the cerebral cortex to be processed where thinking occurs. They are then returned to the limbic system, generating a feedback loop of further thoughts and emotions. This casts doubt on the view of cognitive behavioral therapy that behavior is best changed by addressing distorted thinking. There has already been an emotional response before thinking has begun. A wider perspective is needed that reflects the true complexity of neurological processes occurring in the brain.

A complexity perspective suggests that the brain is an autopoietic system (Maturana & Varela, 1980) with many feedback loops and connections between the various parts. It would suggest that decision making is an emergent self-organizing process and that thoughts and feelings are mutually arising, co-emergent phenomena.

Some actions, such as murder and rape, would be universally seen as offending against individuals or the community, while others such as "soft" drug use, abortion, or euthanasia are less clear and will be determined as a violation by some societies and not by others. For the purposes of this paper, an offense is defined as an action prohibited by the laws of New Zealand.

## Autonomy and connectivity in complex adaptive systems

A complex adaptive system is a nonlinear system formed by many autonomous agents intensely interacting among themselves, thereby allowing the system to maintain both strong autonomy and connectivity. Emergent properties can then appear that could not have been previously predicted. A complex adaptive system can adapt to changes in its environment to make itself more fit to operate within the environment. In other words, a complex adaptive system can learn from past experiences to make better decisions for the future (Levin, 1998; Fryer, 2005).

Human beings, like all complex adaptive systems (Capra, 1997), require effective autonomy and connectivity to operate optimally (Stacey, 1996). A strong autonomous human agent is able to make informed decisions freely within its environment without being unduly influenced by other agents. At the same time, that agent must be open to receiving information from other agents and working constructively in a wider network for the greater good of the whole. Autonomy and connectivity thus stand as complementary aspects. They are dynamically interlinked and influence each other. Enhancing connectivity can affect the autonomy of the individual agents and vice versa.

If a system is too strongly focused on the autonomy of the individual agents, then the agents lose their ability to cooperate and the whole system becomes less effective as the individual agents work against each other destructively. Alternatively, if the system focuses too strongly on its connectivity, the agents lose their individuality and diversity and the system becomes inflexible. Maintaining the correct dynamic balance between autonomy and connectivity is crucial for a complex adaptive system to maintain its internal properties.

Because of the intense interconnections between the agents in a complex adaptive system, any agent or agents that violate other agents and adversely affect their ability to maintain their autonomy or connectivity also reduce the ability of the entire system to operate effectively as a complex adaptive system. The system becomes less able to sustain itself within its boundaries and adapt to external environmental pressures.

A crime is committed whenever a person's autonomy is violated or their connectivity with others is significantly disrupted. Work with offenders and victims focuses on repairing the autonomy and connectivity of the offender and the victim so that both return to being a fully integral part of their community.

This paper assumes that the best results in working with offenders and victims are achieved when the dynamics of self-organization are supported. We must note, however, that since we can never be certain of the outcome of any particular behavior in complex systems, at times behaviors that seem to support self-organization will work against it, and seemingly destructive behaviors will unexpectedly result in positive outcomes.

Keeping this in mind, however, some broad principles can be developed, which can provide a theoretical basis for work with offenders and victims.

Like all dissipative systems, a complex adaptive system requires a flow of energy through it to survive and maintain itself (Prigogine & Stengers, 1984). The system itself defines its own boundary, which is a dynamic boundary changing according to the state of the external and internal environment. The boundary must be semi-permeable, allowing an interchange, usually of chemicals and organisms, with the outside environment or there can be no connectivity. For example, a body cell must be able to allow certain substances into the cell, while excluding others.

Other complex adaptive systems have immaterial boundaries, such as our sense of identity. Rather than chemicals and organisms, there is a flow of experiences, each of which must be incorporated into the person's sense of identity or rejected as harmful. Just as the cell will sometimes fail to detect a harmful organism, a person can unwisely incorporate harmful experiences into their sense of identity. Such invasions tend to give a short-term advantage to the invader, while being harmful for the person invaded and the community they live in. A crime is such an invasion.

Privacy is a key strategy used to protect our autonomy from violation by others. If every part of ourselves is open to influence by other agents, we are no longer autonomous. To protect autonomy, the more critical parts of the system are walled off, so that only highly trusted outsiders can gain access. We maintain areas of privacy at all levels from our individual self to wider social levels. We have private body parts, diaries, private rooms in our houses or workplaces, and private military installations in our nation. To significantly invade any of these places is a crime.

## Schemas

Human beings have a need for a sense of meaning, security, and control or we feel anxiety. Cognitive behavioral theory proposes that one way in which we meet these needs and avoid anxiety is by forming schemas (Stacey, 1996; King, 1999). A schema is an internal representation of the world, an organization of concepts and actions that can be revised by new information about the world (Answers.com, 2006). The schema acts as an attractor of beliefs and values consistent with an individual's mode of functioning.

A person's schema affects all aspects of their being, so if someone has a schema that justifies violence, then violence will be expressed in many different ways within them. Their aggression will show in their physical body, in their thoughts and emotions, in their relationships, and in their interactions with the outside world. If the underlying belief system is changed, the new behaviors tend to filter back through the whole being.

A well-balanced person with a strong sense of autonomy and vibrant connectivity will have strong, effective schemas. They will have beliefs that support themselves and their communities. A person whose sense of autonomy and connectivity is not well balanced will form distorted and maladaptive schemas (Young, 2003) that may lead to behaviors that violate the autonomy and/or connectivity of others.

Whenever a person's schema is challenged, anxiety arises. Ideally we will have the ability to adapt our schema to integrate the new event, but often we do not. Stacey (1996) talks of anxiety containment, whereby a person uses a variety of strategies to alleviate feelings of anxiety while retaining the maladaptive schema. We often choose destructive and addictive strategies such as drugs, alcohol, gambling, or adrenaline rushes to contain our anxiety rather than dealing with the cause of the anxiety. The addictions often lead to offending, which then becomes incorporated into the person's schema. Offending becomes justified, because that is easier than dealing with the addiction.

There are other theories about how we formulate our experiences into a coherent whole that might be used to understand criminal behavior in ways that open up new perspectives.

Maturana and Varela's work on autopoiesis (Maturana & Varela, 1980) and later enactive cognitive theory (McGee, 2006) examine cognitive processes from a complexity perspective. Rather than a linear approach aimed at a specific predefined outcome, autopoesis recognizes structural coupling between the different elements of cognition, so the system is cognizing the environment and the environment is responding to the cognition. An autopoietic system is one that is organized as a network in such a way that the components of the network maintain themselves and the relationships between them (University College London, 2003). McGee (2006) identifies autonomy, coupling, feedback, temporality (or maintaining its history) and downward causality (where the macro level influences the micro level) as characteristic of enactive perspectives of cognition. He also states that there is no objective history before people interact, that the whole process is interconnected through mutual arising.

The role of the observer is also seen as important in cognition, which is not recognized in cognitive behavioral theory. Enactive cognitive theory states that the observer cannot have access to the cognitive system of another person, as they live in their own world of experience. At the same time, objective reality arises from the coordinated actions of human agents.

Minsky's society of mind (Minsky, 1988), heavily influenced by his background in artificial intelligence, proposes that our mind is formed by a large number of automatically operating components somewhat like a suitcase full of many individual items, which together enable complex cognitive tasks to be undertaken. The similarity with complexity is

obvious and provides a possible extension to cognitive behavioral theory that could provide more flexibility in describing the realities of cognitive processes.

Minsky also proposed that we use frames to conceptualize our world. A frame might be "living room." The frame would not only hold information about the living room, but also information about how the frame would be used. This frame could have subframes that give meaning to part of the frame and the frame could be a subframe for a higher-level frame. Each time we go into a living room, the living room frame is activated in our mind, simplifying the act of perception. Minsky states that frames hold default assumptions formed from information gained by past experiences. The frames together therefore interact in a coherent way to enable perception that is heavily weighted by past experience.

Sterelny (2003) questions whether a theory of mind, an internal mapping system, is necessary to explain human behavior. He concludes that other apes such as chimpanzees probably do not need a mental representational system to exhibit the behavior seen, but proving this possibility for humans is more difficult. Sterelny describes some chimpanzee behavior based on imitation that is cognitively complex but would not require a theory of mind.

Work with mirror cells discovered by Rizzoatti (Buccino, *et al.*, 2004) may reveal information that sheds light on the nature of how we form a coherent understanding of our world that can influence techniques of working with offenders.

## The offender

By offending, an offender has chosen to violate the autonomy or connectivity of other agents within their community, reducing the ability of the system to self-organize to higher levels of development. As well as the negative effects for the victim, there are negative consequences for the offender. Offenders lose some of their autonomy as they hide more and more of themselves from themselves to maintain their deluded positive self-view. Their connectivity is also altered, since they have something to hide from others. Under normal circumstances such a violation would engender feelings of guilt or shame, motivating the agent to stop and avoid violating others and themselves.

An offender's schema, however, allows those feelings to be overridden. They may be swayed by short-term gains, such as money, a rush of emotion, or gaining the esteem of peers. Cognitive distortions are used to contain the anxiety generated by the conflict between the person's internal code of conduct and their actions. The following is a list of cognitive distortions that are commonly used (King, 1999):

- *Deny*: "It didn't happen at all." "I wasn't even there at the time."
- *Blame*: "He made me do it." "If you knew your job, I wouldn't be here now."
- *Minimize*: "It didn't hit him, it was just a push." "It's not as if he was unconscious."
- *Justify*: "Well, he hit me first." "They can afford it, besides they'll get insurance."

These alter the agent's perception of the events surrounding the offense, making their actions more acceptable to themselves and others. This reduces the anxiety and maintains their existing maladaptive schema.

Through habitual use, the offending schema has been canalized on the individual's phase space. To encourage the emergence of a new non-offending schema, the attachment to the existing schema must be destabilized, tipping (Gladwell, 2002) the offender toward the edge of chaos (Waldrop, 1992) so that a bifurcation can allow the emergence of new non-offending schema.

Motivational interviewing is a technique that challenges the pro-criminal schema by highlighting the cognitive distortions and incongruities of the discourse and feeding them back to the offender. This destabilizes the schema and pushes the person from their local optimum on the phase space toward the edge of chaos. The offender is supported to build a new optimum on the phase space, set on a foundation within the bounds of an attractor acceptable to the community. The worker helps the offender to build a "bridge" on the phase space between the two optima to facilitate movement from one to the other (Lucas & Milov, 1997).

## The victim

The victim is the agent who has lost some autonomy and/or connectivity because of a violation. The violation often triggers emotions such as anxiety, shame, anger, and sadness. Ideally, these feelings trigger the agent into acting to stop the violation from occurring.

The violation of the offender separates both the offender and the victim from their community. They have been cut off and need to be reintegrated back into the community. Once reintegrated, the agents can once again play their full role in building the emergence of self-organization within the community. Under the present system, the offender is often punished rather than being offered a pathway back into the community. The situation is usually worse for the victim, who is generally also the innocent party. The courts have taken over the role of ensuring that justice is dispensed, leaving the victim with no means of expressing their pain and anger. They, too, are kept from being able to reintegrate with their community again.

## The offender/victim duality

The traditional justice system, and indeed also restorative justice as discussed below, need to be able to isolate the offender, defined as the one who is responsible for the violation, from the victim, who is seen as innocent. In reality, the distinction between offender and victim is often fuzzy. Often an offense has occurred because of a conflict between people that escalated. The offender is the one who won the fight, and the victim is the one who lost.

Defining the offender and victim like this reduces the level of complexity to allow more linear processes to determine how justice will be maintained. We must ask in what ways acknowledging the fuzziness of the victim and offender might change how we would work with offenders. The main difficulty in acknowledging the fuzziness is the problem of

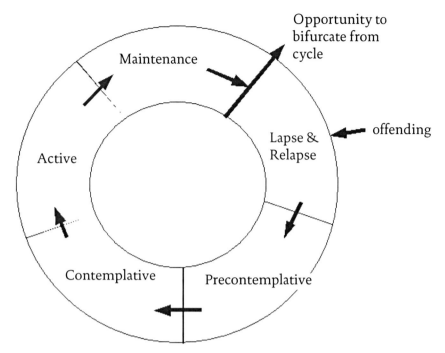

**Figure 1** *The cycle of change*
*(Adapted from the work of Prochaska and Di Clemente with permission)*

re-victimizing the victim. The victim is the one who has been violated. The offender should be the one taking responsibility for what has happened. If we do not do this, the victim, who has been violated by the crime, can then be violated again by being made responsible for the crime. The other side is that it allows the offender to avoid taking responsibility for their actions.

## Wider interactions

Because of the high level of connectivity of human societies, the actions of an individual committing a crime against another affects the whole community, just as each agent affects a whole system. Some of those affected will be friends, family, or acquaintances. All community members will feel less safe. Property may be damaged and policing and justice are significant costs to a community. Unless the violation is resolved, the whole community suffers and the overall connectivity is reduced.

## The relapse cycle

Prochaska and Di Clemente (1994) developed the cycle of change from their work on alcohol and drugs, and found it to be applicable generally in work with offenders.

The model is presented as a revolving wheel, with individuals being at one of six stages on the cycle. There are bifurcation points around the cycle that provide the opportunity to either move forward on the cycle, regress backward, or leave the cycle of offending altogether. The cycle is seen as more flexible now than originally formulated. People do not necessarily need to move through the cycle in the strict order, but can flick forward or backward to other parts of the circle and can bifurcate out from other points on the cycle.

The stages of the cycle are (see also Figure 1):

1. *Pre-contemplation*: This person has little or no awareness of their problem and no investment in making any changes. Other people are generally blamed for any problems;

2. *Contemplation*: They now realize they have a problem, but do not have the skills or motivation to make any changes by themselves;

3. *Determination*: These people have made up their mind to make changes, but still have significant negative habit patterns to overcome. They can easily regress to earlier stages in the cycle;

4. *Action stage*: Here people have committed themselves to the process of change. They have less likelihood of a return to offending, but the threat remains. They must cope with the realities of making changes, such as ridicule or rejection by their peers, and loss of (illegal) income;

5. *Maintenance*: These people have progressed and learned the skills they need to avoid reoffending, but in sufficiently adverse situations may still struggle to remain offense free;

6. *Lapse and relapse*: Those who cannot maintain the necessary changes lapse back into criminal behavior and begin the whole cycle again.

The role of the worker is to determine where the person is on the relapse cycle. Then they can utilize techniques such as motivational interviewing appropriate to that point on the cycle, to strengthen the autonomy and connectivity and to encourage the self-organization of the schema toward the next stage of development around the wheel.

If the disruption to the existing schema is too severe, the person will withdraw from the process or move into deep chaos. A standpoint of unconditional positive regard (Pescitelli, 1996) is required for the person to feel supported through the process of change. A person may stay at one point on the wheel for a very long time, or quickly progress to leave the offending cycle altogether after the maintenance phase. If they are not strong enough to canalize the new behavior, they will relapse into offending behavior.

## Power law distributions

Ormerod *et al.* (2001; see also Cook *et al.*, 2004) found power law distributions in the correspondences between the seriousness of offending and the number of offenders at each level. The authors found that the power law distribution held for people who had already offended, whereas those who had not faced court appearances did not conform to a similar pattern. The authors therefore concluded that the two groups should be dealt with differently, with the focus being on the low-risk offenders before they have a criminal record, in the hope that they would not shift into those who fitted a power law relationship.

This conclusion is certainly logical from the correspondences found; however, the standard approach to working with offenders is actually to focus on work with the higher-risk offenders for two practical reasons.

The first is that the small number of high-risk offenders causes the most harm to the community. Work with them is more likely to reduce the effects of crime on the community. This raises the question of how a complex adaptive system returns to a power law distribution after a significant perturbation. In other words, does reducing the number of high-risk offenders merely create opportunities for other, lower-risk offenders in the community to replace them?

The main reason, however, is that there is no reliable method to determine which people will actually go on to become high-risk offenders. The proportion who do is very small and the result of prioritizing first-time offenders would be a large input of resources into people who would never become high risk anyway.

In spite of these practical reasons for prioritizing high-risk offenders, a trial of the approach as suggested by Omerod may indicate the validity of a radically different approach to working with offenders.

## Ways of working with offenders

Before a particular intervention is chosen three main factors are considered (Andrews & Bonta, 2003):

- *Risk*: Since interventions are primarily aimed at high-risk offenders, assessing the level of risk is crucial;

- *Needs*: There must be an assessment of the criminogenic (crime-producing) needs of the offender. Examples are violence propensity, alcohol and drugs, and offense-related sexual arousal;

- *Responsivity*: There is a need to assess the likelihood that the person will be able to respond to an intervention. Barriers to responsivity include intellectual incapacity, alcohol or drug use, and poor motivation.

## One-to-one interviewing

Most of the work with offenders in the Community Probation Service is one-to-one work. Tipping points (Gladwell, 2002) are sometimes evident in work with offenders. If agents are progressively withdrawn from a complex adaptive system, it continues to function surprisingly well for a long time because a multitude of alternative pathways can be utilized in order to continue functioning. However, a point is suddenly reached where there are not enough alternative pathways operating for the system to maintain itself and the degeneration is very rapid. When the old schema has disintegrated, the probation officer must support the offender to form a more positive new schema or old habit patterns will form an attractor back to a maladaptive schema.

This principle can explain why a seemingly small comment at a critical point in the life of an offender can precipitate a major breakdown in that person's schema. It is important that after the schema is broken down, it is reconstituted with a more effective schema; if not, the old schema manages to reform or an even less effective schema at a lower optimum on the phase space predominates.

From an autopoietic perspective, a probation officer would be attempting to use languaging and emotioning within the consensual domain of the offender in an attempt to bring about changes (Maturana & Varela, 1980)

## Programs

Until recently, the Community Probation Service in New Zealand ran two cognitive skills-based small group programs, the Criminogenic program and the Straight Thinking program. The dynamics of group work differs significantly from one-to-one work. While in both cases the schema of the participants is disrupted toward a far-from-equilibrium position, the more complex dynamics of groups allows opens more possibilities to encourage self-organization of the schema. Participants will often challenge each other, which is generally more effective than a challenge from a facilitator. On the other hand, the risks of the

emergence of destructive dynamics and catastrophes are greater than in one-to-one work. Negative ideas can very quickly shift the entire group rather than just one individual.

Agreed groundrules are very useful in maintaining the connectivity of the group. They help to ensure that the behavior of the participants remains within the bounds of the attractor and does not move to a destructive location on the fitness landscape. Rules such as no violence or abusive language help to preserve the autonomy of participants, while rules such as honesty and listening foster connectivity.

## New developments in cognitive behavioral therapy

More recent developments in cognitive behavioral therapy better reflect the more integrated perspectives of a complexity-based viewpoint. Acceptance and AommitmentTheory (ACT; see Hayes *et al.*, 2003) uses creative hopelessness, carefully shifting the client into a creative but unstable state in a way that allows them to feel safe enough to try a new approach to their problems, rather than trying to control thoughts and feelings. We can see the similarity to complexity principles of being far from equilibrium, edge of chaos, and tipping points.

Metaphor is seen as a powerful means of inducing creative hopelessness. ACT, as a part of the "third wave" of behavior therapy, has not yet been integrated into the work of the Community Probation Service, but shows promise as a therapy, moving cognitive behavioral techniques to be even more in line with the principles of complexity.

Mindfulness-based cognitive behavior therapy (Cayoun, 2004) focuses on allowing a person to gain control over the processes that maintain incapacitating thoughts rather than trying to change the thoughts themselves. Cayoun proposes that intrusive thoughts, which maintain old habit patterns, self-organize as a part of a fourfold feedback cycle of sensory perception-evaluation-interoception-reaction. The reaction phase then feeds back into the sensory perception phase, creating a feedback cycle. If we then learn not to react to newly arising thoughts, then the self-organized entity must collapse just as a person deprived of food for long enough will collapse. This allows old memories, which are at the core of negative behavior, to reach awareness, where they can be reprocessed in a more positive way. He proposes a co-emergence model of reinforcement where internal thoughts and body sensations co-emerge during the cycle and by meditation the four components can be more effectively dynamically balanced, which brings about positive changes in a person's behavior.

These new developments in cognitive behavioral therapy are even more in line with the concepts of complexity and show more promise in the way that cognitive based theories and the principles of complexity might be used to support each other in the future.

## Restorative justice

The traditional retribution-based justice system sees the offender and victim as protagonist and antagonist. A complexity perspective allows a more realistic view of the two as dynamically complementary elements capable of co-evolving to new emergent levels of interaction (Lucas & Milov, 1997).

In the traditional court system, the victim has little part to play unless they are used as a witness in a trial. The state has largely taken over the role, so the victim has no way of finding their resolution directly. Without being able to interact positively, both offender and victim are left in limbo, unable to bifurcate toward a point of emotional healing.

The restorative justice model (Zehr, 1990) brings together the offender, the victim, and their support people to guide them through a process allowing the violation to be acknowledged and healed, and restoring the offender and victim back into their community (Umbreit, 1998). Tribal-based justice systems, such as that of the New Zealand Maori, exhibit many similarities to the restorative justice model (Consedine, 1995). In a traditional Maori community, the whole community was brought together following a transgression. The entire community would discuss the issue, and come to a joint decision that was then announced by the chief to the people.

Naturally, a restorative justice conference will not always be appropriate. Often either the offender or victim does not wish to participate, or safety issues may make proceeding unwise. Restorative justice must remain alongside the traditional justice system. It has, however, proven itself to be extremely effective and enabled significant healing between offender and victim, even in crimes such as rape (Szmania, 2004).

## Conclusion

Cognitive behavioral theory tends to be very linear in its approach, thereby missing many of the dynamics operating within an offender. Complexity theory extends our perspective on offending behaviors and has the potential to develop more effective techniques for working with offenders. Autpoiesis and enactive cognitive theory are well-developed concepts that could help extend cognitive behavioral theory. New developments such as ACT and mindfulness techniques show a closer link with complexity principles and could lead to an enhancement of work with offenders in New Zealand.

Restorative justice takes the additional step of working with the victims of crime and provides new ways of resolving the violation caused by crime. This brings all people affected back into playing their role in society in a way that is more likely to enable the emergence to new levels of functioning throughout the community.

A complexity perspective therefore offers a more holistic viewpoint, which acknowledges the unpredictability and complex nature of work with offenders and victims. Using less linear techniques that better recognize the complexity of neurological processes will help to develop more effective techniques to positively enhance the autonomy and connectivity of the offender, the victim, and the community to heal the damage caused by crime for all involved.

## References

Andrews, D. and Bonta, J. (2003). *The Psychology of Criminal Conduct*, 3rd edn, ISBN 9781593453213 (2007)

Answers.com, (2006). "Definition of 'schemea'," http://www.answers.com/schema.

Buccino, G., Vogt, S., Ritzl, A., Fink, G., Zilles, K., Freund, H. and Rizzolatti, G. (2004). "Neural circuits underlying neural imitation of hand actions, an event related fMRI study," *Neuron*, ISSN 0896-6273, 42(April): 323-334.

Capra, F. (1997). *The Web of Life: A New Scientific Understanding of Living Systems*, ISBN 9780006547518.

Cayoun, B. (2004). "A four stage model of mindfulness-based cognitive behavior therapy: A training manual for crisis intervention and relapse prevention," Dunedin, New Zealand: Otago University.

Consedine, J. (1995). *Restorative Justice, Healing the Effects of Crime*, ISBN 9780473029920.

Cook, W., Omerod, P. and Cooper, E. (2004). "Scaling behavior in the number of criminal acts committed by individuals," *Journal of Statistical Mechanics: Theory and Experiment*, ISSN 1742-5468, P07003.

Fryer, P. (2005). "What are complex adaptive systems: A brief description of complex adaptive systems and complexity theory," http://www.trojanmice.com/articles/complexadaptivesystems.htm.

Gladwell, M. (2002). *Tipping Point: How Little Things Can Make a Big Difference*, ISBN 9780349113463.

Griffin, J. and Tyrrell, I. (2004). *Human Givens: A New Approach to Emotional Health and Clear Thinking*, ISBN 9781899398317.

Hayes, S. C., Masuda, A. and De May, H. (2003). "Acceptance and commitment therapy and the third wave of behavior therapy," *Gedragstherapie*, 2, 69-96.

King, L. (1999). "The role of beliefs, cognitive processes and products in offending," New Zealand: Department of Corrections Psychological Service Violence Prevention Unit.

Levin, S. A. (1998). "Ecosystems and the biosphere as complex adaptive systems," *Ecosystems*, ISSN 1432-9840, 1: 531-546.

Lucas, C. and Milov, Y. (1997). "Conflict as emergent phenomena of complexity," Calresco Group, http://www.calresco.org/group/conflict.htm.

Maturana, H. R. and Varela, F. J. (1980). *Autopoiesis and Cognition*, ISBN 9789027710161 (2001)

McGee, K. (2006). "Enactive cognitive science - Part 2: Methods, insights, and potential," *Constructivist Foundations*, ISSN 1782-348X, 1(2): 73-82.

McGuire, J. (2000). "Cognitive-behavioral approaches: An introduction to theory and research," M. J. Furniss (ed.), London: Her Majesty's Inspectorate of Probation.

Minsky, M. (1988). *The Society of Mind*, ISBN 9780671657130.

Minsky, M. (1998). "Consciousness is a big suitcase: A talk with Marvin Minsky," *Edge*, http://www.edge.org/3rd_culture/minsky/index.html.

Omerod, P., Mountfield, C. and Smith, L. (2001). "Non-linear modeling of burglary and violent crime in the UK," London, England: Volterra Consulting Ltd.

Pescitelli, D. (1996). "An analysis of Carl Rogers' theory of personality," http://pandc.ca/?cat=carl_rogers&page=rogerian_theory.

Prigogine, I. and Stengers, I. (1984). *Order out of Chaos: Man's New Dialogue with Nature*, ISBN 9780394542041.

Prochaska, J. O. and Di Clemente, C. C. (1994). *The Transtheoretical Approach: Crossing Traditional Boundaries of Therapy*, ISBN 9780894648489.

Sagan, C. (1978). *The Dragons of Eden*, ISBN 9780340226858.

Stacey, R. (1996). *Complexity and Creativity in Organizations*, ISBN 9781881052890.

Sterelny, K. (2003). *Thought in a Hostile World: The Evolution of Human Cognition*, ISBN 9780631188872.

Szmania, S. J. (2004). "Narrative, complexity theory, and rhetorical possibility in victim-offender mediation," Austin, TX: University of Texas at Austin.

Umbreit. M. S. (1998). "Restorative justice through victim-offender mediation: A multisite assessment," *Western Criminology Review*, ISSN 1096-4886.

University College London (2003). "Literal definition of 'Autopoiesis'," http://www.cs.ucl.ac.uk/staff/t.quick/autopoiesis.html#def.

Waldrop, M. M. (1992). *Complexity: The Emerging Science at the Edge of Order and Chaos*, ISBN 9780671767891.

Young, J. (2003). "Early maladaptive schemas and schema domains," http://www.schematherapy.com/id73.htm.

Zehr, H. (1990). *Changing Lenses: A New Focus for Crime and Justice*, ISBN 9780836135121.

**Victor MacGill** attended Canterbury University, New Zealand, and completed a BA in Psychology and Maori Studies. He has worked as a probation officer for the last four years. His interest in complexity began as a result of watching a television program on fractals in 1996 and in 2002 he completed an MA in Chaos, Complexity and Creativity through the University of Western Sydney. He also gained a Diploma in Social Work through Otago University. His research interests are the various aspects of social complexity. His publications include *When the Dragon Stirs* and *Under the Eye of the Saddle Hill Taniwha*.

Practitioner

# A complexity view of three Maori tribal groups of the South Island of New Zealand and the Moriori of the Chatham Islands

Victor R. D. MacGill
Freelance Researcher, NZ

Indigenous tribal groups can operate as complex adaptive systems. Tribal members are then autonomous agents interacting intensely among themselves and with their environment. Technology, social structure, economics, education, and so on develop over time to help the tribe maintain its fitness within its environment. These developments may be due to chance discoveries, the operation of natural selection, and under certain critical conditions the intense interactions may enable the emergence of higher levels of social complexity. At times when the environment becomes less favorable for human habitation, the means of subsistence regresses to earlier forms, which necessitates a similar regression in the social structure binding the society together. This paper examines the three tribes living in the South Island of New Zealand between 1250 and 1800 AD. The three tribes were named Waitaha, Ngati Mamoe, and Kaitahu. They had to cope with changes in climate, food, and resources, as well as intra- and inter-tribal threats. Particularly during the latter stages, there was intense competition for the more productive land and sea areas. On the Chatham Islands, some 800 kilometers to the East of the South Island, the Moriori people formed their own distinctive culture, which will also be examined. The Moriori, who descended from the Maori people of New Zealand, lived in an even more harsh and isolated environment than the Maori, which significantly shaped their distinctive culture.

## Introduction

This paper investigates the three main tribal groups living in the South Island of New Zealand between 1250 and 1800 AD and the degree to which they operated as complex adaptive systems, intensely interacting with their environment and with each other. The Moriori of the Chatham Islands, who emigrated from the South Island of New Zealand, will be similarly discussed.

Just because a group of people comes together and interacts, it does not necessarily mean that they operate as a complex adaptive system. Often, for example, a community will come together and interact such that emergence enables a new level of complexity to appear within the group, but some members of the group seeking personal power then distort the community for their own gain and take the community away from being able to further self-organize.

There are a number of ways in which tribal groups change over time. A tribal member might make a chance discovery, perhaps finding a new material or a new technique, which they then teach to other tribal members. Some tribes change in the way they operate in response to an environmental change, which might be a change in the weather or an event related to a neighboring tribe. This might be part of a ratcheting effect of natural selection, with each tribal group trying to gain or maintain a dominant position on the land.

A group can also operate as a complex adaptive system, where the intense interactions between tribal members lead to self-organizing behaviors through which new levels of complex social organization emerge.

Holland (1996) defines a complex adaptive system as a dynamic network of many agents acting in parallel, constantly acting and reacting to what the other agents are doing. Control tends to be highly dispersed and decentralized. If there is to be any coherent behavior in the system, it has to arise from competition and cooperation among the agents themselves. The overall behavior of the system is the result of a huge number of decisions made every moment by many individual agents (Waldrop, 1992).

Emergence occurs within a complex adaptive system when self-organization transcends the elements from which it has developed (Letiche, 2000). A group of people can operate as a complex adaptive system in their own right, where the individual agents are human beings. The individuals act autonomously, but also cooperate to maintain the cohesion of the group. When the dynamic balance is right, a sudden leap can enable previously unpredictable levels of complexity to emerge. Through this process the group can learn and build a body of knowledge that is passed on to new group members (Capra, 2003).

Autopoietic systems (Maturana & Varela, 1991) have many similarities with complex adaptive systems. An autopoietic system is one that has a clear boundary with the outside formed by the constituents of the system and their interactions, which sustain their existence over time through those interactions (Hall, 2003). According to Maturana and Varela, an autopoieteic system must have organic agents. They would therefore deny that a tribal grouping could be an autopoietic system, even though many of the characteristics of non-organic complex adaptive systems are very similar to autopoietic sytstems.

## The traditional Maori tribes of the South Island of New Zealand

New Zealand is the last significant land mass in the entire world to have been occupied by human beings. The traditional occupation of the South Island of New Zealand by the Maori people has been divided into three time periods. The early period began around 1200-1250 AD with the first migration of the Waitaha people and continued until 1350 AD. The Waitaha people continued to occupy the South Island through the middle period (1350-1550 AD), which was characterized by more difficult living circumstances. During the late period (1550-1800 AD), Ngati Mamoe and Ngaitahu (or Kaitahu as they are known in their own dialect) joined Waitaha from the North Island (Waitangi Tribunal, 1991).

## Maori tribal groups as complex adaptive systems

Letiche states that emergence has only occurred if the system's structure has changed so substantially that old laws don't apply and a "new" world exists (Letiche, 2000). The challenge is therefore to determine when the tribes were likely to have been acting as complex adaptive systems and emergence would have been evident. An "edge of chaos" dynamic is more likely to have operated at critical points in the history of the tribe, during which they can make significant progress, then followed by a much longer time when the new change is integrated into the tribal identity.

### Self-organized criticality

Bak (1996) suggested that when systems reach critical conditions, a small, previously unpredictable change can catalyze a major change in the whole system. The harsh climate, the presence of rival tribes, and loss of access to resources could all move the tribal groups toward a point of criticality. During the earlier period, the human impact was generally less complex and did not reach critical levels in the way it did later. This is similar to a gentle flow of water, which is generally predictable with no turbulence. If the force of the water exceeds flow limits, however, the system must change form to contain the energy. Turbulent flows with fractal swirling vortices of energy emerge. Carneiro (as quoted in Goerner, 1994: 94) suggests that where the force (resource needs) and limitation on flow (environmental restriction) were critical, the emergence of hierarchical societies could follow. When critical factors reach particular levels, the system can longer maintain its existing state and must restructure itself to cope with the new realities or it may not survive.

The Waitaha, Ngati Mamoe, and Kaitahu tribes exhibited some of the qualities of complex adaptive systems. This next section explores how those qualities were made manifest and shows how those qualities worked to maintain their structure.

Complex adaptive systems sustain themselves by taking in energy from the outside environment and releasing unused energy back into the external environment (Lucas, 1997). The Maori tribal groups accessed a flow of physical, emotional, intellectual, and spiritual energies to maintain their structure. Negative feedback loops and positive feedback loops (Boje, 2006) both operate to create complex dynamics. Structural coupling (Maturana & Varela, 1991; Lucas, 2000), generated by the intense interactions between tribal members and with the external environment, enabled the formation and at times the emergence of tribal identities operating within self-generated boundaries.

The self-generated tribal boundaries were formed by the interaction of the many factors affecting the tribe, both internally and externally. These include geography, technology, food production, external threats, and internal dissention. Linear examples affecting tribal boundaries might be, for example, if the population decreases and the tribe's ability to sustain and protect themselves is reduced; they may cope by reducing the tribal area in which they live, or if a competing tribe moves further away, more territory might open up.

The Waitaha, Ngati Mamoe, and Kai Tahu tribal groups had the ability to develop strategies to optimize their functioning in their environment in a measurable way (Axelrod & Cohen, 2000). Each tribe sought to gain access to a greater share of natural resources to survive and become dominant in their environment.

As is typical of complex adaptive systems, Maori society formed into nested self-similar layers. Individuals formed into *whanau* (family) groups, which grouped to form sub-tribes (*hapu*). Hapu were collected together to form *iwi* (tribal) groups. Several *iwi* groups made up a canoe (*waka*), relating to the ancestral canoes on which the first Maori came to New Zealand. It is likely that in the South Island Maori related primarily to their *hapu* (Waitangi Tribunal, 1991).

Each *hapu* had a *rangatira* or chief (often called an *upoko* in the South Island). Elders (*kaumatua*) and shaman (*tohunga*) were highly respected. Below them were warriors, commoners, and slaves. In spite of the sharply defined roles, the interactions between all levels of the hierarchy were significant. For example,

issues were generally discussed by the whole *hapu*, after which the chief would decide on behalf of the tribe. Such inter-level interactions increase the likelihood of emergence

There is a similarity in the way tribes form into groups within groups and the systems within systems found in fractals. As in all human societies, however, there were also distortions of the fractal-like hierarchy, generally created by those at the top to enable them to maintain their position of power.

### Legitimate and shadow networks

Stacey (1996) identifies two networks within organizations operating as complex adaptive systems. The legitimate network is the control network of those in power. The shadow network is the informal network. The shadow network forms its own set of rules, which may support or conflict with the legitimate network. The shadow network is more spontaneous and fluid and can arise within an individual or in a subgroup, such as a *hapu*. It could, for example, develop from a disagreement within the tribe. If the legitimate network and shadow network become too dissonant, conflict is likely.

Emergent narratives would help create shared understandings from which the tribal structure formed, but the emergent narrative often tends to become frozen and distorted over time to create an "acceptable understanding of history" according to the needs of the tribal members. Those in positions of power tend to have a greater ability to define the discourse through the legitimate network.

### Small world networks

Small world networks can function extremely efficiently and exhibit emergent behaviors (Buchanan, 2002). They require a critical number of agents linked together before a tipping point (Gladwell, 2002) is reached and complex dynamics appear. In the earlier stages of the occupation of the South Island there was only a small population distributed over a large landmass. It was unlikely that there would have been enough interactions to generate emergent behaviors. Tribal members would have often come together for social occasions such as marriages, funerals, or to discuss important tribal issues, increasing the likelihood of self-organizing narratives emerging. In a short time a distinctly New Zealand-flavored culture developed, heavily influenced by the physical environment and climate. Emergent dynamics generated by the tribal groups operating as complex adaptive systems are likely to have played some role, and perhaps even a significant role in the development of this culture.

If a group of people acts as a small world network, but there are too many linkages between the agents, the group quickly becomes less efficient. Everybody knows each other and is too involved in the lives of the others for maximum efficiency. Maintaining relationships then takes up too much energy, because too much energy is spent maintaining those links.

## Rules

As with complex adaptive systems, individual tribal members had simple rules to obey, which generated complex behavioral outcomes for the tribe. Principles such as *tapu, noa, rahui, mana, mauri,* and *tikanga* (Irwin, 1984; Adams *et al.*, 2003) were developed by the tribal groups over time.

According to the Maori worldview, everything in the world is either *tapu* or *noa*. Anything *tapu* is separated off from everything *noa* (common) and is considered special and sacred. Sacred and traditional knowledge, death, treasured possessions, and sacred ceremonies are all *tapu*. Food and women in particular are *noa* and have the power to take away *tapu*. There are clear rules about how to act and how not to act in the presence of *tapu*. It is important not to taint something that is *tapu* by something that is *noa*. *Tapu* therefore also played a role in maintaining hygiene. Food, which is *noa*, could not be taken to a toileting area or in the presence of a dead body, which is *tapu*, thus avoiding the risk of infection. On leaving a *tapu* area it is necessary to wash one's hands. Thus, without any knowledge of bacteria, the Maori had an effective means of significantly reducing many possible health threats.

A *rahui* is a temporary restriction, which might be put in place to protect a food source that might be in danger of being over-

harvested. *Mana* is a person's authority or prestige, which clarifies their place and influence in the society. *Mauri* is the essential life force of a person, which must be protected and nurtured for all people to flourish in the tribe. *Tikanga* comes from the root word *tika*, meaning right, straight, or correct. *Tikanga* is the customary way in which certain social interactions happen. To do something according to *tikanga* is to do it the correct, socially acceptable way.

It is likely that these concepts formed from conversations around the fireside or in similar places where observations and theories were shared and discussed. At times new understanding would emerge from the narratives, and at other times concepts would slowly develop.

While these concepts may appear illogical according to a logical positivist perspective, they gave shape and meaning to the people living on the land and formed a coherent, effective means of structuring their lives to overcome threats to their wellbeing.

All these concepts formed a culturally consistent worldview and rule system, which ensured that each individual agent's behavior remained within the attractors needed to maintain hygiene, safety, and social cohesion. Values act as strange attractors (UIA, 2005), and shared values powerfully align the individual tribal members and increase their commitment to working altruistically for the good of the whole tribe.

Complex adaptive systems have the ability to adapt on the basis of new learning. In the early stages of occupation, learning would have been about observing and understanding the new environment and developing the best uses of the resources available. Existing cultural knowledge would have been adapted for the new situation. Geographical features similar to those in the original homeland often took the same name. Mythical characters and stories were often retained but repositioned into the new environment, providing a sense of continuity.

As well as informal teaching of how to gather or catch food and other practical life skills, the ancient Maori had a system of *wananga* or schools of learning for passing on tribal wisdom that grew over time (Best, 1923). Young people were carefully selected to learn specific roles to play within the tribe. This would include knowledge of their tribal history, genealogy, songs, dances, religion, arts, and mythology. This would tend to develop from the legitimate network and have a stabilizing effect on the tribes. Emergent discourse would, on occasion, destabilize the tribes and allow novelty to be introduced. Being closer to the edge of chaos would make the emergence of new structures and understandings more likely.

## Autonomy and connectivity

The tension between autonomy and connectivity is vital to the continuation of any complex adaptive system. If a system is too strongly focused on the autonomy of the individual agents, then the system loses its ability to co-operate and becomes less effective as individual agents work against each other destructively. Alternatively, if the system focuses too strongly on its connectivity, the agents lose their individuality and diversity and the system becomes inflexible. Autonomy and connectivity are not opposites, but rather complementary, something like dancing partners, continually modifying and adapting to each other in order than the joint system exhibits complex behaviors not possible by each alone. Maintaining the correct dynamic balance between autonomy and connectivity is crucial for a complex adaptive system to maintain its internal properties.

This tension was apparent in traditional Maori life. Autonomy was increased by developing unique tribal identities and decreased by the negative effects of warfare, the lack of resources, and the demands of a harsh climate. Connectivity was increased by trade, a universally comprehensible language, common genealogical links between tribes, and inter-tribal marriage. Connectivity was decreased by warfare, geographical isolation, competition for resources, a harsh climate, difficult and slow travel, and clashes over genealogical links.

## Early, middle, and late periods of Maori occupation
### Early period (Waitaha)

The 1200-1250 AD migration from the Pacific Islands must have been carefully planned, with many women and perhaps even children on board to create a sustainable population in their new land. Oral traditions indicate that they knew exactly where they were going, how to accurately navigate their way, and how to utilize their knowledge of the various tides, currents, and winds, as well as seasonal variations in the elements of nature needed for the journey (Dalley & McLean, 2005).

The first immigrants came from Pacific Islands with warm climates and plentiful crops. They also had pigs, chickens, dogs, and rats. On arriving in New Zealand, they set about creating similar societies, but especially in the colder south horticulture was unable to sustain the population (Sutton, 1994). The kumara and gourd were the only viable introduced crops, but neither would grow in the southern half of the South Island (Waitangi Tribunal, 1991). Of the animals only the dog (*kuri*) and rat (*kiore*) came to, or survived in, New Zealand.

Relatively quickly, hunting and gathering rather than horticulture became the main mode of obtaining food and the social structure accordingly reverted to one typical of hunter/gatherers with an itinerant lifestyle, smaller social groupings, and a more flat social structure. Complex adaptive systems can regress to earlier structures if that is the most efficient form to survive in a changing external environment.

The Waitaha had to adapt quickly to their new environment by ceasing to operate in ways that were effective in their small tropical island environment and find new resources and ways to use them to be effective in the South Island. This was certainly a time when as a group they were closer to the "edge of chaos." While this would have increased the likelihood of the tribes acting as effective complex adaptive systems, the low population distribution, as already discussed, worked against this.

Sutton (1994) suggests that the lack of large predators caused an overabundance of bird and marine life in the South Island. In particular was the moa, a flightless bird (*ratite*) that ranged in size from that of a turkey through to a four-meter creature towering above the humans (Anderson, 1983). With few predators it is likely that the moa, and many other species, were easy prey to the first humans.

Anderson (1990) estimated that tens of thousands of the slow-breeding moa were alive at any given time. Moa hunting would have begun as a positive feedback loop fueled by the ease of capture and a quickly expanding Maori population. Only later when moa numbers decreased significantly did negative feedback loops emerge to reduce the kill sizes. Over-reliance on the moa as a food source is likely, bypassing the tipping point for the species and making the final demise rapid. Moa hunting, and to a lesser extent deforestation by fire, rats, or dogs eating moa eggs, as well as disease most likely caused the extinction of the moa by around 1600 AD in all but a few remote areas (Anderson, 1983; Diamond, 1998). Orbell (1985) stated that a native eagle, crow, pelican, a harrier hawk, swan, geese, duck, and rail also went extinct during the same period (Worthy & Holdaway, 2002).

For several hundred years the moa probably provided around 25 percent of the dietary needs of people in Canterbury, Otago, and Southland, with 100,000–500,000 moa being killed. Anderson (1990) records 229 moa sites in the South Island and commonly around two-thirds of the birds uncovered had major parts of their meat left uneaten.

The total human population of the South Island during the period discussed probably never increased beyond 3,000, growing from an initial population perhaps as small as 100 people (Sutton, 1994). This small population on such a large landmass meant that disputes could generally be resolved by a bifurcation of the group, with one group moving to a new uninhabited area. Waitaha had no need to develop a warrior culture. Indeed, no weapons of war or fortifications have been found in Waitaha archeological sites (Duff, 1956). The social structure was also much flatter, reducing the level of societal conflict. The distribution of wealth was more even, with less stress on possessing items of value.

The Waitaha ancestor, Rakaihautu, led the initial exploration of the land (Waitangi Tribunal, 1991). Axelrod and Cohen (2000) talk of the need of complex adaptive systems to balance exploration and exploitation of the environment. At this early stage, much was to be gained by extensive exploration of the new land, but as new unexplored areas became fewer and more difficult to access, the balance shifted more toward exploitation of those areas that had already been explored. This also links with Stacey's (1996) ideas of the behavioral loop of discovery, choice, and action forming co-evolutionary feedback loops.

Anderson (1983) states that during the early period life expectancy was about 28 years for males and 30 for females. The most usual cause of death was pneumonia and other ailments caused by constant exposure to weather and water, and degenerative diseases of the neck and backbone, caused by the constant demands of carrying loads. This short lifespan would have made accruing a knowledge base through accumulated wisdom more difficult and made it harder to maintain tribal wisdom.

### Middle period (Waitaha)

During the middle period the moa and many other easy food sources became extinct. Deforestation, especially through fires, both caused by humans as well as natural causes, significantly changed the environment (Ogden *et al.*, 1998). Food became harder to acquire and coastal and marine food sources increased in significance (Anderson, 1983). The population of seals and sea elephants rapidly decreased. The human population decreased to around 2,000 and communities fragmented so that less complex social structures re-emerged. Less palatable and more labor-intensive foods such as the root of the ti tree and the fernroot became important parts of the diet (Anderson, 1983). The previous local maximum on the phase space of the effectiveness of survival of South Island Maori based on available resources dropped suddenly, so other local maxima in the form of new food sources had to be sought to ensure the survival of the tribe.

E:CO Vol. 9 Nos. 1-2 2007 pp. 67-76

In the south of the South Island in particular, life became an annual migratory cycle, moving in a rhythm with the seasonal harvesting of foods such as muttonbirds, eels and lamprey, forest birds, fish and seal, since there was no longer sufficient food for people to live just in one area. Housing construction was simpler in the south, with circular houses without piles being used (Tau, 2003).

The Waitaha people had to reform themselves to be able to operate as efficiently as possible in their given environment. That meant regressing to a less complex structure and begs the question of whether the process of emergence can result in a less complex structure.

## Late period (classical period) (Waitaha, Ngati Mamoe, and Kaitahu)

In the North Island the environment and social circumstances were quite different. The population and population densities were higher, increasing the requisite variety. Gathering wild foods still predominated, but horticulture became more central to the culture than in the south. The people developed levels of social complexity not previously observed in the South Island.

Sutton (1994) suggests that the overshoot of population compared to wild food resources led to greater levels of conflict among tribes. The greater use of horticulture in the north enabled larger, permanently occupied villages to be developed. Protection was now necessary for strategic sites, buildings, possessions, and resources. This precipitated the development of a warrior class, which could be resourced from a higher surplus (Cowan & Beck, 1996). Slavery and cannibalism became evident (Salmond, 1992).

The boundaries of complex adaptive systems are permeable, so the more rapid social developments in the north affected the South Island, which is unlikely to have developed a warrior-based society on its own. Whatumamoe led a tribe known as Ngati Mamoe down from the Napier area in the North Island (Waitangi Tribunal, 1991) in the mid-sixteenth century. They came to dominate the South Island more by strategic marriages than

warfare. In general they were peacefully absorbed into the South Island, but the structural coupling meant that the Waitaha people had to adapt to new tribal boundaries and having strangers among them.

As a tribe grows larger the boundaries it must maintain become increasingly stretched because there is more outer perimeter to defend. Often the extending boundary reaches a critical point when a seemingly insignificant incident initiates a "butterfly effect" (Gleick, 1994), leading to a bifurcation of the tribe into two groups. Polynesian history reveals a consistent pattern of stories of conflict between two brothers. Traditionally, the elder brother (*tuakana*) takes precedence, and so the younger brother (*teina*) typically takes part of the tribe and leaves in search of new lands in which to set up a new tribe (Adams *et al.*, 2003).

Stirling (1994) tells of Porourangi and Tahupotiki, two brothers living on the East Coast of the North Island about 400 years ago. Porourangi was married to Hamo-te-Rangi, but Tahupotiki secretly loved her. When this became known, Tahupotiki had to leave to live in the South Island. The tribe did not come to the South Island in one group, but came in two main separate migrations. Ngai Tuhaitara came south under Tuahuriri and Ngati Kuri under Maru Kaitatea (Tau, 2003). The new tribe was eventually named Ngai Tahu/Kai Tahu after Tahupotiki. The Waitangi Tribunal (1991) states in regard to this story, "The movement [migration] had far more general causes than the historic incident which sparked it," suggesting that other critical issues (Bak, 1996) were necessary in order that small initial changes led to system-wide changes.

By the late period, migrating meant displacing existing occupiers. Although the land and climate were not as attractive, the relative ease of conquering the more peaceful South Island tribes made it a tempting option. Those dwelling in the South Island had no choice but to adapt their own social structure to accommodate the presence of Kaitahu. As Kaitahu came from the north, Ngati Mamoe and Waitaha tended to move further south, so that to this day the influence of Ngati Mamoe and Waitaha is generally stronger as one moves further south.

After Kaitahu split from Ngati Porou, a new sense of autonomy and identity was needed. Patterns of tribal differentiation through clothing, song, dance, and a distinct dialect quickly developed. The dialect of the Kaitahu people is probably the most distinctive dialect of New Zealand Maori. Wherever one finds the letter *ng* in standard Maori it is replaced with the letter *k*. Thus, the name Kaitahu is known as Ngai Tahu in the north and the river Waitaki is the same as Waitangi in the north.

Bakhtin states that all language is dialogic and is thus infused with the values, culture, and environment of its speakers (Lye, 1998). The language of South Island Maori thus has its roots in the values, culture, and environment of those living on the land. It also carried its Pacific history, changing dynamically to meet the needs of its speakers. The *s* and *l* common to most Pacific Islanders were generally dropped when the Maori arrived in New Zealand, but are still found in many early written South Island Maori manuscripts.

Bahktin talks about monoglossic centripetal forces forcing the language to be frozen, limiting the ability of tribal members to reach beyond the conceptual restraints held in place by the nature of the language, and heteroglossic centrifugal forces freeing the language from within itself, making the language more socially distinguished. These two forces would have been operating against each other in shaping the language, while the language in turn was shaping the culture and social dynamics. Bahktin also mentions polyglossia, the contestation of languages as would have occurred when two tribal variants come in contact with each other, although in the South Island the differences in the language were relatively minor. Linguistic differences are typical of the many difficulties created as the tribes increasingly differentiated themselves from each other. An example of how they coped with the cultural divergence was the general understanding that the *kawa* (protocol of ritual) of the tribal area one is visiting is followed, even if that is totally opposite to one's own beliefs and traditions. This enabled people to move through the land without generating too much conflict.

The pattern of conquest was to kill or enslave the men and marry the women (Waitangi Tribunal, 1991). This meant that the traditions of the conquered tribes were retained through the women. Like a parasite or a virus, Waitaha and Ngati Mamoe reformed as separate complex adaptive subsystems or as shadow networks (Stacey, 1996), structurally coupled to the host, thus preserving their own traditions within Kaitahu.

## Chatham Islands

The Moriori people of the Chatham Islands originally descended from the same Polynesian people as the Maori on the mainland, probably arriving from New Zealand around the thirteenth or fourteenth century (King, 1989). Their environment was even harsher and far more isolated than the South Island. No sustainable cropping was possible and their society regressed in complexity to small family groupings with little or no social hierarchy. Tools became less advanced over time, particularly since there were no trees large enough to build canoes capable of returning to New Zealand (King, 1989).

It is even less likely that the Moriori operated as complex adaptive systems. Their society generally regressed over time, contrary to most societies that self-organize to increasing levels of complexity. The society's structure became flatter with decreasing levels of requisite variety.

There was no such thing as a stranger among the Moriori. This made resolving conflict much easier. People also knew that if disagreements were to get out of hand, the very survival of the whole population was in question. Moriori traditions state that an ancestor named Nunuku made a ruling prohibiting killing people. Disputes were settled by combat with staffs no thicker than a person's thumb. The combat ended as soon as blood was drawn (King, 1989). Rather than being a sign of spiritual development, this peaceful way of life was an environmental necessity for survival.

The Moriori of the Chatham Islands did not generate sufficient food surpluses to enable a hierarchical society to form, and castration

E:CO Vol. 9 Nos. 1-2 2007 pp. 67-76

was practiced to control population size. All the people needed to work to produce enough food. There were no resources to sustain a nonproductive higher class, and signs of rank such as tattoos disappeared. A chief's house became indistinguishable from the house of a commoner. Life expectancy was around 32 years and infant mortality rates were one third (King, 1989). Emergence springing from complex dynamics was even less likely to have been evident on the Chatham Islands than on the mainland. The flat societal structure bred a level of conformity that worked against the likelihood of emergence.

## Conclusion

The Waitaha, Ngati Mamoe, and Kaitahu in the South Island of New Zealand and the Moriori people of the Chatham Islands lived for hundreds of years and adapted to significant challenges in their environment. Complex distinctive cultures were developed in a relatively short time. While it is difficult to determine the actual extent of self-organizing dynamics within the three tribes, it is likely that the dynamics of complex adaptive systems were evident at times through their history and may have been behind major changes in the life of the people.

Emergence would have been occurring often in the individual lives of tribal members. For the three tribal groups the main critical times discussed when emergence was more likely to have occurred were when the Waitaha people first arrived, when food became scarce during the middle period, and when northern tribes migrated to the South Island. Particularly because of the isolation of the Moriori people, it is less likely that they experienced self-organization.

## References

Adams, T., Benton, R., Frame, A., Meredith, P., Benton, N. and Karena, T. (2003). "Te Matapunenga: A compendium of references to concepts of Maori customary law," Te Matahauariki Institute Occasional Paper Series No 8, University of Waikato, Hamilton, New Zealand.

Anderson, A. (1983). When All the Moa-Ovens Grew Cold: Nine Centuries of Changing Fortune for the Southern Maori, ISBN 9780959772333.

Anderson, A. (1990). Prodigious Birds, Moas and Moa Hunting in Prehistoric New Zealand, ISBN 9780521352093.

Axelrod, R. and Cohen, M. D. (2000). Harnessing Complexity: Organizational Implications of a Scientific Frontier, ISBN 9780465005505 (2001).

Bak, P. (1996). How Nature Works: The Science of Self Organized Criticality, ISBN 9780387947914.

Best, E. (1923). "The Maori school of learning, its objectives, methods and ceremonials," Wellington, New Zealand: Dominion Museum.

Boje, M. (2006). "It is time to set story free from narrative prison!" http://business.nmsu.edu/~dboje/690/papers/Narrative_Prison.pdf.

Buchanan, M. (2002). Nexus: Small World Networks and the Groundbreaking Theory of Networks, ISBN 9780393041538.

Capra, F. (2003). The Hidden Connections: A Science for Sustainable Living, ISBN 9780006551584.

Cowan, C. and Beck, D. (1996). Spiral Dynamics: Mastering Values, Leadership and Change, ISBN 9781557869401.

Dalley, B. and McLean, G. (2005). Frontier of Dreams: The Story of New Zealand, ISBN 9781869710064.

Duff, R. (1956). The Moa-Hunter Period of Maori Culture, Wellington, New Zealand: Government Printer.

Diamond, J. (1998). Guns, Germs, and Steel: The Fates of Human Societies, ISBN 9780099302780.

Gladwell, M, (2002). The Tipping Point: How Little Things Can Make a Big Difference, ISBN 9780349113463.

Gleick, J. (1994). Chaos: Making a New Science, ISBN 9780749386061 (1997).

Goerner, S. J. (1994). Chaos and the Evolving Ecological Universe, ISBN 9782881246357.

Hall. W, (2003). "Organizational autopoiesis and knowledge management," Presented, ISD '03 Twelfth International Conference on Information Systems Development - Methods & Tools, Theory & Practice, Melbourne, Australia, 25-27 August.

Holland, J. (1996). Hidden Order: How Adaptation Builds Complexity, ISBN 9780201442304.

Irwin, J. (1984). An Introduction to Maori Religion, ISBN 9780908083114.

King, M. (1989). Moriori: A People Rediscovered, ISBN 9780670826551.

Letiche, H. (2000). "Phenomenal complexity as informed by Bergson," Journal of Organizational Change Management, ISSN 0953-4814, 13(6): 545-557.

Lucas, C. (1997). "Self-organizing systems (SOS) FAQ," http://www.calresco.org/sos/sosfaq.htm.

Lucas, C. (2000). "Autopoiesis and coevolution," http://www.calresco.org/lucas/auto.htm.

Lye, J. (1998). "Mikhail Mikhailovich Bakhtin on language," http://www.brocku.ca/english/courses/4F70/bakhtin.html.

Maturana, H. and Varela, F. (1991). *Autopoiesis and Cognition: The Realization of the Living*, ISBN 9789027710161 (2001).

Ogden, J., Basher, L. and McGlone, M. (1998). "Fire, forest regeneration and links with early human habitation: Evidence from New Zealand," *Annals of Botany*, ISSN 0305-7364, 81: 787-696.

Orbell, M. (1985). *The Natural World of the Maori*, ISBN 9780911378528.

Salmond, A. (1992). *Two Worlds: First Meetings Between Maori and Europeans, 1642-1772*, ISBN 9780824814670.

Stacey, R. (1996). *Complexity and Creativity in Organizations*, ISBN 9781881052890.

Stirling, E. (1994). *Eruera: The Teachings of a Maori Elder*, A. Salmond (ed.), ISBN 9780195580709.

Sutton, D. (ed.) (1994). *The Origins of the First New Zealanders*, ISBN 9781869400989.

Tau, Rawiri Te Maire (2003). *Nga Pikituroa O Ngai Tahu: The Oral Traditions of Ngai Tahu*, ISBN 9781877276279.

UIA (Union of International Associations) (2006). "Complexity: Values as attractors," http://www.uia.org/values/valcom_bodies.php?kap=10.

Waitangi Tribunal (1991). *The Ngai Tahu Report 1991*, Wai 27, http://www.waitangi-tribunal.govt.nz/publications/published_reports.asp.

Waldrop, M. M. (1992). *Complexity: The Emerging Science at the Edge of Order and Chaos*, ISBN 9780671767891.

Worthy, T. H. and Holdaway, R. N. (2002). *The Lost World of the Moa: Prehistoric Life of New Zealand*, ISBN 9780253340344.

**Victor MacGill** attended Canterbury University, New Zealand, and completed a BA in Psychology and Maori Studies. He has worked as a probation officer for the last four years. His interest in complexity began as a result of watching a television program on fractals in 1996 and in 2002 he completed an MA in Chaos, Complexity and Creativity through the University of Western Sydney. He also gained a Diploma in Social Work through Otago University. His research interests are the various aspects of social complexity. His publications include *When the Dragon Stirs* and *Under the Eye of the Saddle Hill Taniwha*.

Transforming education
E:CO Issue Vol. 9 Nos. 1-2 2007 pp. 77-92

Practitioner

# Transforming education: Evidential support for a complex systems approach

Chris Goldspink
University of Surrey, UK

This paper documents the findings of research into a rare example of successful school-based education reform. The reform commenced within the South Australian Department of Education and Children's Services in 1999 and is ongoing. It drew explicitly on systems thinking in establishing change principles. Subsequent research into "what worked" reinforced the value of following practices consistent with loosely coupled and complex systems theory. This paper compares the approach adopted in South Australia with the more commonly adopted managerialist or so-called new public management approaches and elaborates on the relevance of complexity as a base for planning and implementing reform. The paper demonstrates that complex systems ideas have profound implications for the policy underpinning institutional change and provides evidence of their relevance and value in practice.

## Introduction

Over the past two decades the principal ideas influencing approaches to the reform of public administration are managerialism (or the "new public management") and public choice theory (Aucoin, 1990; Self, 2000). The former is an application of managerial method to public institutions and the latter is an extension of the logic of economic markets to administrative and political exchange (Stretton & Orchard, 1994; Udehn, 1996). These two sets of ideas provide the primary basis also for the reform of education in OECD countries and beyond, being described by Jones and Kettle (2003) as an international phenomenon. Australia and New Zealand have been among the more avid adopters of change informed by this thinking.

Most politically initiated educational reform in the State of South Australia had been consistent with these underpinnings. However, beginning in 1999 the South Australian Department of Education and Children's Services (DECS) introduced an innovation from within its central policy directorate that, while modest in scale, had a bold ambition: the transformation of schooling in South Australia. This reform was strikingly different, being informed by systems thinking and learning theory. A detailed account of the project design and outcomes is beyond the scope of this paper and has been documented elsewhere (see Department of Education and Children's Services, 2004; Goldspink, 2002, 2003).

This paper discusses the theory and principles that guided this reform and research findings into the outcomes. These are compared with the principles and practices of educational reform inspired by the more common "managerial" ideas. The two are demonstrated to be in stark contrast, leading to conflicting principles for practice. The paper concludes by outlining a theory base consistent with the findings into what worked in South Australia. This draws on the concept of loosely coupled systems and complex systems theory.

## Contrasting two approaches to educational reform

### Assumptions underpinning "Learning to Learn"

The South Australian school reform initiative is known as "Learning to Learn." The initiative grew out of dissatisfaction with past approaches to reform that did not assist with "The generation of new thinking and understandings about the learning process... [and] the translation of this knowledge and learning outwards to the system as a whole" (Foster, *et al.*, 2000: 5)

This project drew on the family of theories of learning that are grouped under the title of "constructivism"[1] and systems theory.

1 This was incorporated into the South Australian

Constructivism implied embracing a diversity of perspectives and valuing alternative knowledge bases. This compelled a co-developmental rather than top-down approach to change. It implied that no one knowledge base or position would or could grasp the complexity of the task of education within the diverse communities in which it was enacted. The emphasis was, therefore, on providing an environment in which all parties (administrators, teachers, parents, and children) could "learn their way forward" (Foster, 2001). Multiple stimuli that encouraged active experimentation in a context of trust were provided. The intent was to re-engage teachers' intrinsic concern for student learning in order to focus on student and social outcomes of education rather than short-term achievement.

The incorporation of systems ideas was initially somewhat eclectic. This eclectic approach was not necessarily a weakness at the inception of the idea. Loose use of systems concepts served to focus attention on relationships and connections while being nonprescriptive and avoiding a sideline debate about which approach might be "best."

The following key precepts were identified by the project manager as having informed the design of the initiative (adapted from Foster, 2001):

- Transformation rather than incremental improvement is needed;

- Meta learning skills are increasingly important to society and business as a basis for knowledge and should be a focal point for education;

- Increasingly education is expected to be future oriented;

- A catalyst or leader is needed to trigger the development of partnerships between stakeholders as a basis for achieving

Curriculum Standards and Accountability Framework (SACSA) and defined in quite general terms, vis: "The central thesis of constructivism is that the learner is active in the process of taking in information and building knowledge and understanding" (DECS, 2001: 10). Le Cornu, *et al.* (2003a, b) provide an account of what this philosophy meant in practice within the context of the initiative.

a change in how learning is approached through schooling;

- Complex problems need complex solutions and these can come from those who are confronting the problems at a local level;

- A sense of vocation constitutes a motivational resource for teachers in the context of education;

- Learning comes through trust and acceptance of risk;

- Reflection on deeply held worldviews and a questioning of identity, not just administrative change, is needed for sustainable benefit;

- Change and uncertainty are ubiquitous and form the backdrop for transformation;

- Sustainable change comes only through responsibility taken at a local level, not through imposition.

These principles guided the selection of change strategies and, equally importantly, informed the behavior of the advocates of change.

The strong emphasis on constructivism and its relativist epistemology, combined with the emphasis on human values and qualities and the assumption that transformational change was possible by changing thinking, places this initiative within the radical humanist paradigm of Burrell and Morgan (1994).

This paradigm would not normally embrace systems approaches and so it could be argued that there is a contradiction between the constructivist theory informing Learning to Learn and its appeal to systems ideas. However, as complex systems theory is being increasingly applied to the social domain, it is becoming accepted that this does compel the adoption of a relativist epistemology. This position has been argued forcefully by Cilliers (1998, 2000), is evident in an autopoietic understanding of social dynamics (Varela, *et al.*, 1992), and is supported by recent developments of connectionist models of cognition (Brooks, 1991).

As the project progressed there was increased explicit use of complex systems theory to discuss, evaluate, and design aspects of the change process. This was not championed by anyone in particular but, rather, those advocating change found that they were increasingly drawn to this set of ideas as relevant and helpful in explaining their experience. The author was asked to join the project as a resource to assist with this thinking and as a critical friend to raise questions and challenge from a complexity perspective. The author also has a strong background in public management reform and a longstanding interest in learning theory and practice.

## Assumptions underpinning new public management

The Learning to Learn project took place within a much longer-running reform process within the government sector of the State of South Australia. Past and other concurrent attempts at improving education were informed by the ideas underpinning this wider reform effort. Over the past two decades in many developed countries, including Australia (O'Brein & Down, 2002), New Zealand (Tooley, 2000), the UK (Simkins, 2000), and Canada (Hughes, 1999), the dominant thinking behind the reform of public institutions has been that of "managerialism" or the so-called new public management (NPM). NPM is an amalgam of private-sector management practices and prescriptions derived from institutional economics, including agency and public choice theories.

In terms of their philosophical assumptions and implications for practice these ideas are in stark contrast to those informing Learning to Learn. In a paradigmatic sense, NPM is quintessentially functionalist in Burrell and Morgan's schema. The functionalist paradigm rests on regulatory and objectivist assumptions and is:

*"usually committed to a philosophy of social engineering as a basis for social change and emphasises the importance of understanding order, equilibrium and stability."* (Burrell & Morgan,1994: 26)

Here the social world is viewed as comprising concrete entities and relations that can be studied using reductionist approaches in or-

der to identify underlying cause–effect relations and derive laws governing behavior. While the form of constructivism adopted by the advocates of Learning to Learn was also realist, the epistemological relativism assumed places it in contrast. As Burrell and Morgan remind us, the radical humanist paradigm and the functionalist paradigm are based on irreconcilably different and incompatible assumptions. We see this incompatibility in the systems theory adopted also.

Burrell and Morgan place most systems theory in the functionalist paradigm. One of the reasons is the common attribution of "purposefulness" to organizations as systems. They note also that much of systems theory is applied to the search for form and function; or rather, the processes by which organizations change and new social structures emerge. In other words, systems theorists tend to examine how social systems maintain stability (homeostasis) rather than how they demonstrate self–renewal and how alternative organization is generated. These observations demonstrably do not apply to complex systems approaches.

True to their functionalist roots, new public management methods are seen as value neutral, instrumental/technical approaches for improving the efficiency and effectiveness of organizations (Wilenski, 1986; Considine, 1990; Fitzsimons, 2004). Pollitt (1990: 60) argues, for example, that management represents,

*"a concentration on the immediate, concrete, controllable things which go on within one's own organization and an avoidance of entanglement with wider-value questions."*

This is echoed by Taptiklis (2005: 5), who describes managerialism as obsessed with control, seeing complexity as the enemy. He argues that managerialism,

*"assumes an artificial non-human world, and then develops models and prescribes solutions only in terms of its own artifice."*

Within government, managerial methods were seen as helpful for achieving a shift from a bureaucratic preoccupation with processes to a focus on results (Keating, 1990). However, advocates of managerial approaches value task differentiation and place great store by the efficacy of formal command-and-control mechanisms – a concern with process and method is never far away. Organizational performance is assumed to be a direct product of rational control from above. Under "managerialism," there is commonly devolution of responsibility to middle managers for budgetary and administrative functions and a change from process conformity to output delivery for accountability. Often, however, a limited range of outputs are privileged – generally those that are readily measured (such as dollars) rather than necessarily those that are most important in a policy sense.

NPM embraces a range of assumptions consistent with neoclassical economic thinking, including ideas promoted under the rubric of "public choice." This theory characterizes bureaucrats and politicians as self-seeking and budget maximizing; concerned to act for themselves rather than for citizens (Brennan, 1996; Udehn, 1996). Applied to education, advocates favor industrial de-powering and tighter accountability for teachers and argue for the creation of educational "markets."

Both "managerialism" and "public choice" have contributed to the push for public agencies to be subjected to "contestability": competition with or comparison to similar private agencies as a means to find efficiencies. An additional economics-derived theory – agency theory – has informed thinking in this area. De Laine (1997) suggests that agency theory "derives from the idea that political life can best be represented as a series of contracts between parties." From this perspective education is cast as a chain of exchanges mediated by contract between a principal (government) and agents (i.e., schools, both public and private). This facilitates a separation between the policy aspect of education ("steering not rowing" – Osborne & Gaebler, 1993) and the provision of education services. This focus on instrumental levers and formal aspects of organization has been argued to have had significant consequences in the human and informal aspects of organization. In their analysis of reform in New Zealand and Norway, for example, Christensen and Laegreid (2001: 89) argue that NPM has:

*"replaced a system based on mutual trust among civil servants on different levels, and between politicians and administrators, with a system which potentially furthers distrust. The main idea of NPM is that if only the external incentives are right, good governance is guaranteed whatever the character of the individuals. It is, however, difficult to construct workable democratic administrative institutions in a civil service where the bureaucrats are driven solely by external incentives and private benefits."*

Here, then, we see two competing approaches to reform in general and educational reform in particular. Each is based on fundamentally contradictory assumptions about the origins of and basis for organizational change and improvement. The debate about which is better has commonly been fought on ideological grounds with little empirical evidence to illuminate it. There is, however, an accumulating body of research that gives a clear indication as to what works in practice. To this body of research can now be added the experience of Learning to Learn. This has been systematically documented and is still being studied – including by the author – so a reasonable body of evidence is accumulating.

## What works?

The author commenced research into the Learning to Learn initiative in 2001. The aim of the research was to inform policy and program design by identifying what had and had not worked and by theorizing about the program. Evidence was collected using interviews, teacher narratives, case studies, and the analysis of extant documentation (such as school annual reports and departmental data). The evidence was initially analyzed in a manner consistent with grounded theory (Miller & Fredericks, 1999). There is an established history of the use of grounded theory in education research (Lyall & McNamara, 2000) and

E:CO Vol. 9 Nos. 1-2 2007 pp. 77-92

the approach was compatible with the constructivist ideas that have informed Learning to Learn. It also avoided a tendency to prejudge what might be an appropriate theory base.

### The findings from research into Learning to Learn compared to managerialist approaches

The key findings as to the basis for the success of Learning to Learn were as follows. Observations are made under each point about how that finding compares to the assumptions underpinning "managerialism."

1. *Finding: Learning to Learn aimed to "reignite the passion of teachers."* Appealing to teachers' and administrators' intrinsic motivation was found to be fundamental to what was achieved. The interview and teacher narrative data made clear that many teachers became excited by the learning orientation of the project and by the values and learning principles that informed it. Many reported being excited about teaching again for the first time in many years. Those who were reinvigorated demonstrated a willingness to self-organize to bring about substantial change in their practice.

*Comment*: From this finding it is clear that the very assumptions on which managerialism and public choice are based will interfere with the establishment of a desire to change and a willingness to commit to change by teachers. Teachers are turned off by the utilitarian assumptions and antihumanistic values intrinsic to NPM; even the language associated with it gets in the way. Where administrators operate from an assumption of risk of opportunism, and in response implement extensive and often intrusive accountability measures, based on the South Australian findings, they consolidate an existing mistrust and cynicism that dampens any enthusiasm teachers may have for self-organization around issues of concern. Similarly, imposed "solutions" that cast teachers as "the problem" will be vigorously resisted.

2. *Finding: Pursuing change with high levels of flexibility and a learning- and risk-tolerant approach to accountability leads to rigorous approaches to change and a focus on results.* The

focus on learning carries implications of allowance of experimentation, tolerance of mistakes, flexibility, and openness to alternative ideas, approaches, and means of change. The constructivism and encouragement of a pluralism of ideas reinforced this, as did the developmental opportunities offered to teachers that were diverse and rich, drawing on a wide range of ideas from leading researchers in education. There was no "one right way" prescribed from above. The interview and case studies made clear that this was also fundamental to a) gaining commitment, b) allowing learning to proceed within a school based on its distinctive challenges and the motivation and passion of those within it, c) finding ways that worked in the local context. The data revealed also that the approach encouraged a high level of personal and institutional commitment and discipline.

*Comment*: This approach to change is inconsistent with what is normally found under NPM. NPM changes are generally rolled out from the policy center with a concern for consistency and conformity. There may be consultation but little room for learning by doing, for encountering challenging local conditions and inventing approaches on the basis of local inquiry and discovery. Most significantly, the assumption that loose accountability and risk tolerance will lead to disciplined and focused approaches runs directly counter to the "malingering" and opportunistic assumptions of institutional economics.

3. *Finding: Maintaining a high level of congruence with the learning-focused principles and values informing the change was vital.* Congruence with the principles of inquiry, empowerment, and learning that informed the project proved essential to the establishment of trust. Provided trust was established both between the school and the policy area and within the school (i.e., between school leaders and teachers), deep commitment to change was often achieved. However, the evidence was that trust was hard won. Schools reported an initial deep cynicism that those initiating the project would or intended to stay true to the principles they

were espousing. The initiators reported being continually tested for congruence with these principles. In several cases this testing persisted over several years. Only when reassured that their commitment would be rewarded did they offer it. Once given, it was often substantial and unrestrained.

*Comment*: This finding is consistent with contemporary recognition within management theory of the importance of agreement on values and the need for trust. However, much contemporary practice in management is incompatible with what is needed to establish that, in particular processes of accountability that emphasize tight reporting and monitoring of processes and outputs. Managers overly concerned with a need to control will send the wrong signals, close down scope for learning (Paul, 1997), and undermine the establishment of a set of professional practices and the felt obligation and responsibility essential to education (Avis, 2003). Recalling that with Learning to Learn the necessary level of trust took, in several cases, years to establish, it is apparent that the time needed will seldom be allowed in managerial reforms, with their attendant demands for short-term, tangible results. Allowing considerable scope for independent action also conflicts with economic theories arguing that trust cannot be assumed and hence institutions should be managed on the assumption of the risk of opportunism.

4. *Finding: A "nondeficit" approach to reform (i.e., avoiding the assumption that the current system is dysfunctional because of the individuals within it) opened up possibilities for institution-wide learning and such learning grew from the local area out.* Many teachers reported being excited by the opportunity to learn and to work to improve school practice. Despite being within an ageing and cynical workforce (Commonwealth of Australia, 2000), those interviewed identified outcomes including enjoying teaching again (80 percent), greater professionalism (70 percent), feeling their experience was valued (60 percent), being challenged by different views (80 percent), ownership of change (50 percent), and being affirmed (40

percent). There was little evidence of a sense of threat or blame.

*Comment*: In government accountability is increasingly interpreted as "a process of assigning blame and punishing wrong-doing" (Canada Treasury Board, n.d.). Politicians can readily be tempted into trying to satisfy a public desire to find "who is at fault." The idea that where there is failure there must be negligence is also indicative of the functionalist/managerial assumption that complex systems are intrinsically controllable if only leaders "stay on the ball." This assumption commonly draws managers into an attempt to "lock down" or systematize practices (as often seen in contemporary quality management) in the hope that this will avoid error, thus preventing the one strategy that can address error in complex systems – learning and flexibility (Stacey, 1996, 2001). Searching for "who is at fault" drives out learning and diminishes capacity building within organizations; most of all, it fosters resistance.

5. *Finding: Evaluation pursued as an opportunity for learning rather than to attribute fault or blame maintained a focus on outcomes and added substantial value to the policy development process, ensuring practice could be improved in complex and unpredictable environments.* The concern of education and educators is with the wellbeing, both short and long term, of students and the wider society (see for example Delors, 2000: 69). This is often challenging and subject to a wide range of influences, both social and economic. It was apparent from our data as well as from earlier studies that teachers resent having to focus on short-term (and often politically expedient) outputs at the expense of these wider values-linked concerns. When the interests of children and community became the focus for learning, teachers proved willing to engage and to adopt their own evaluation practices. The case studies revealed that some schools had invented elaborate and sophisticated, quantitative and qualitative methods for collecting evidence about how well they were doing. They were likely, however, to comment unfavorably on

what they regarded as the "busywork" institutional evaluation frameworks.

*Comment*: While the managerial reforms of the 1980s placed a clear emphasis on outcomes, the increased influence of economic approaches and in particular the use of purchaser/provider and contractual links has shifted the focus to outputs: "tangible intermediate deliverables," in NPM speak (Department of Treasury and Finance, 1997). Arguably, this reintroduced a potential for goal displacement (Bohte & Meier, 2000) or working to the measure. It certainly should have if the utility-maximizing and opportunism assumptions of institutional economics were correct. Significantly, the Learning to Learn evidence supports what others have found (see for example O'Brein & Down, 2002), that the output focus and a concern with what was readily measurable were in conflict with teachers' sense of commitment to students' long-term interests. Evidence suggests that when confronted with such a conflict teachers passively or actively resist.

6. *Finding: Within Learning to Learn, tight hierarchical/administrative control was not necessary to achieve a very high level of strategic coherence.* Indeed, emergent insights into possibilities for strategic improvement arose where diversity and pluralism of perspective were encouraged and supported. The project advocated the need to "learn our way forward" (Foster, 2001), recognizing that the challenges needing to be addressed could not be readily identified in advance. The adoption of a "best practice" orientation, with its attendant belief that models drawn from elsewhere, or identified in advance based on reductive analysis, can lead to effective change, was explicitly rejected. Contracts struck between the policy center and sites were based on establishing principles and relationships, not specifying outputs or mandating process.

*Comment*: Such an approach is consistent with Tsoukas's view (Tsoukas & Chia, 2002) that "Change programs 'work' insofar as they are fine-tuned and adjusted by actors in particular contexts – that is, insofar as they are further

changed on an ongoing basis." This is in direct conflict with managerial assumptions and the emphasis on the need for hierarchies of plans and consistent policies propagated from the center out or top down, and the assumption that the major issues can be identified in advance and accommodated in the plan (Stacey, 2000, 2001; Taptiklis, 2005). The finding is also consistent with research into what constitute effective institutional responses to "wicked" policy problems. The long-term goals of education set out by peak bodies such as UNESCO and indeed by the Australian Government (www.aspa.asn.au/natgoals.htm) qualify as "wicked' (Conklin, 2005), embracing as they do wide aspirations for the long-term outcomes for students, economies, and societies from investments in education. It is increasingly being realized that conventional tight hierarchical management does not lead to effective responses to such problems (Kernick, 2005).

7. *Finding: Reciprocal obligations based around trust were effective in maintaining a high level of compliance to principles and in protecting and balancing stakeholder interests.* Far from leading to opportunistic behavior, the change process generated considerable commitment to a felt common purpose. This purpose focused on the interests of children but grew in some sites to embrace wider sections of the school community. There was no evidence of schools fighting for a greater share of resources or opportunity and a great willingness was shown by teachers and school leaders to put in additional time and to share learning within and across sites.

*Comment*: This finding can conflict with managerialist assumptions about the need for formal structures and mechanisms (rules and material incentives) to maintain compliance and does conflict with economic, and particularly public choice advocates', assumptions about the likelihood of opportunistic or self-serving behavior arising in the absence of such rules and incentives.

In short, what the research revealed as the basis for success in South Australia can be seen to conflict in almost all respects with what has been done where managerial and economic principles have been used as the theoretical base for designing and implementing educational reform.

NPM, as with management theory in general, is somewhat of an eclectic melange of ideas, albeit derived from common (functionalist) assumptions. Learning to Learn to a large degree eschewed this body of theory in favor of an alternative – that of learning and systems theories, in particular complex systems theory. Having found the theory adopted by advocates of NPM wanting in terms of its capacity to provide an effective basis for the design and implementation of effective change in education, do these other theories offer a more effective alternative? More importantly, can they offer a coherent and internally consistent foundation for such change, or is it the case that they too offer only a fragmented and partial base from which one can draw selectively to justify what is in reality being pursued for different (perhaps ideological) reasons?

## Towards an alternative theory base: Educational organizations as complex systems

In the earlier section of this paper it was argued that complex systems theory was compatible with a constructivist philosophy. In this section this idea will be pursued. A case is put for adopting a theory of organization that is based in two interlinked theoretical positions. These are a constructivist theory of knowledge and learning – in particular that furnished by the theory of autopoietic systems – and complex systems. These two sets of ideas have been suggested as a basis for an internally consistent theory of sociality and organization (Goldspink & Kay, 2003, 2004). Here this theory is combined with Karl Weick's proposition that educational systems are best viewed as "loosely coupled" systems. Paradoxically, under the influence of "managerialism" and institutional economics, many government and private services are now being delivered less by tightly coupled hierarchies and more by distributed networks. While management theory concentrates on

how to make these tractable (generally by tightening the coupling), the ideas presented here may suggest an alternative – a means of better capitalizing on the intrinsic benefits of loose coupling. The argument therefore has potentially wider application than just in education.

Loose coupling within education systems has been variously interpreted (Orton & Weick, 1990). However, the critical insight is that systems organized loosely do not lend themselves to formal or bureaucratic control; rather, they need a different form of management if their distinctive advantages are to be realized. Loose coupling suggests a rich, multidimensional coupling between the many "agents" that make up a system but with no single locus of control. Weick expressly identifies such systems as more capable of remaining viable in complex and uncertain environments. Benefits include "persistence," "buffering," "adaptability," "satisfaction," and "effectiveness" (Orton & Weick, 1990: 217). Loose coupling does not require coherence between different parts of the system for it to remain viable.

While loosely coupled systems deal with local challenges well, they imply a slow diffusion of central initiatives. As a consequence, Weick (1982: 675) argues that,

*"the administrator has to start projects earlier, start more projects, start projects in a greater variety of places, talk more frequently about those projects that have been started, and articulate a general direction in terms of which individual members of the system can make their own improvisations."*

Learning to Learn provides an example of this approach in practice, with its emphasis on learning as the change framework; provision of multiple stimuli at multiple points throughout the system; encouraging active experimentation in a context of trust; maintaining a focus on outcomes and core values as a central target and integration point; tightening and providing richly connected structures around pedagogy; and loosening structures of compliance and administration. However, the more we looked at the evidence, the more we questioned how far this perspective could take us.

## Who or what is loosely coupled?

For Weick, it is institutions that are loosely coupled. He does not delve too deeply into the mechanisms by which institutions form nor the mechanisms by which they organize into networks.

Managerialists and institutional economists assume that institutions can readily be designed to perform specific functions: that institution forming is a rational process.

In drawing on constructivist theories of knowledge and on complexity theory, the initiators of the Learning to Learn initiative did not accept this assumption and did not act as if it were true.

The appeal of complexity theory was that it directly challenged the functionalist assumptions on which contemporary management is based (Stacey, 1996, 2001; Marion, 1999; Cilliers, 2000). Complex systems can display high levels of both order and disorder. Importantly, order in complex systems is usually a result of microstructuring processes that provide for robust self-organization. This form of order is not dependent on hierarchical control, is distributed and local in its operation, but can lead to macro or system-wide stability (or instability!). Importantly, rational control is seen as only one source of order within complex systems (McKelvey, 1997).

What this means is that no actor, neither the janitor nor the CEO, gets to "choose" the form of "organization" in which he/she is just one agent. The pattern, which an observer might call "the organization," "the school," the "department of state," is emergent. It is capable of a wide range of dynamics and even though some actors may be able to exert considerable influence on important subprocesses, the consequences of their choices may be manifold and often unanticipated. Viewed from this perspective, the functionalist assumption of the possibility of command and control is a fantasy.

## Implications

While we are only beginning to explore the degree to which the implications of this theory align with what we commonly observe in organizations, some insights applied to education are explored below. Connections are made to some of the most important empirical observations made in the case of Learning to Learn.

### Initiating change: Implications for leadership

From this theoretical perspective the role of a policy unit within a Department of Education, for example, would need to be thought about quite differently than we generally observe through a functionalist lens. An advocate of a policy change who wants to maximize his/her chance of making a difference will try to locate the patterns that shape the existing dynamics within the system. In the case of education, these will almost certainly spill out beyond "the department" or "the school," to include the wider community. The policy advocate will attempt to use available resources to act as a catalyst and will also be positioned as an agent provocateur, seeking to amplify those elements that are generating dynamics that can be helpful and disrupt or disturb those judged unhelpful. Note that the judgment about what is helpful or unhelpful and what is contributing to it is highly observer dependent and, as it is never possible to really understand "the system" (as the observer only interacts with his/her successive construction of it), implies the need to "learn one's way forward" and a great deal of critical self-reflection. The advocate needs a well-developed capacity to hold many possible interpretations simultaneously and to question the assumptions on which they are based: to learn epistemically.

At this juncture it is perhaps worth reflecting on the selection criteria commonly found for senior managers in contemporary organizations. We are likely to see great value placed on confidence and a clear sense of direction. A level of modesty and circumspection and a capacity to question one's own deepest assumptions are unlikely to feature, but based on the argument being presented here, would seem more what is called for.

Leadership then becomes a process of inviting others to participate in critical inquiry involving a lot of active experimentation. It requires a willingness to acknowledge that "we don't know how!" As more observers enter the process (as commitment is generated and gained) then ways of maintaining this critical reflection across wider networks become a priority for those wanting to advance change. Within Learning to Learn, those in leadership positions frequently reported feeling torn between acting as they felt they were expected to in their formal (functionalist) role – as controllers – or as the supporters of their own and others' learning, which meant acknowledging that "they did not know how." They reported becoming more effective as they managed this personal change.

### Finding the points of integration

Accepting that it is not possible to determine specific outcomes implies that beginning with highly specific goals is of little value, as are detailed plans. What is needed is some insight into the underlying dynamics of the system: a sense, even if only tentative, of what keeps it as it is and where there are tensions and points of divergence.

Applied to education, there are many systemic influences that conspire to keep teaching the same. These include the expectations of the wider community and of teachers themselves about what school "is" and how it should work. These expectations are often conservative, and are based on how school was experienced by the stakeholders when they were young. These conservative "forces" have conspired to undermine many central initiatives for change (Sarason, 1990).

Another integrating factor in school education is the well-documented intrinsic concern teachers have for student learning (Dinham & Scott, 2000). Teachers resist anything that in their view runs counter to the interests of students. Typically, "what is in the interest of students" will be conservative assumptions about how school has operated in the past and should continue to operate. What was significant in the case of Learning to Learn was the change triggered at the level of teach-

ers' own critical reflections on their practice and the induction of a deep questioning and willingness to revisit and rethink what they had traditionally done. Arguably, picking and disrupting this conservative dynamic, and in so doing reframing teachers' sense of what was in students' interests, was the most significant contributor to the change that was achieved. Once this reframing was underway, this intrinsic concern of teachers began to work for the change rather than against it. Importantly, it also converged with the interests of other stakeholders.

### Initiate creative disruption

The evidence suggests that it was the introduction of constructivist learning principles that was the most disruptive aspect of the Learning to Learn initiative from the perspective of teaching practice. This may seem surprising, as constructivist theories of learning have been around for a long time. In the case of South Australia, the curriculum framework, which had been released some years before the Learning to Learn initiative, was based on constructivist principles. There was evidence, however, that this had been largely ignored or its implications for teaching practice not appreciated by most teachers (Foster, 2001). Had the change to constructivism been demanded by central dictate, it would most probably have been resisted (both actively and passively). Learning to Learn approached the introduction of constructivist thinking in an "invitational" way. There was something that worked about inviting teachers to renew their waning enthusiasm for teaching by learning more about learning, focusing this around constructivism, and hence inviting teachers to begin to reflect on their assumptions about knowledge and linking this to their intrinsic concern for children.

The adoption of a constructivist learning framework was, for many, a major shift. It was a shift at the level of epistemological assumptions and implied the need not only to question their day-to-day teaching practice but in many cases their way of seeing the world. The evidence suggested (Goldspink, 2002) that another important ingredient in achieving this shift was the establishment of a challenging yet safe environment that genuinely supported and valued teachers' own learning. That it was genuine was communicated most powerfully by the behavior of those advocating the change and in the invitational stance adopted: In essence teachers reported perceiving a high level of congruence between the espoused principles and the practice. Interestingly, this level of congruence also acted as a significant perturbation of the system (teachers reported assuming that the policy advocates' actions would be inconsistent with their espoused values and were surprised when they were consistent!).

### Meaning changes practice and practice changes meaning

From the perspective of the theoretical lens being adopted here, once whatever kept the system as it was has been disrupted and some new dynamic has started to emerge, change can become autocatalytic: It can proceed very rapidly but in directions that cannot be anticipated by individual players. The more agents actively reflect on the relationship between the macro outcomes and their own judgments about what is valued, and as they use their personal agency to perturb the system, there is a simultaneous shift in many system parameters and not only will its dynamics change, but the range and type of dynamic of which it is capable change also. What is happening can be tracked to some degree by mapping the narratives emerging from those domains (the way those involved attribute meaning to the experiences they are participating in and contributing to). As the underlying coupling and intersection of networks are maintained primarily in and through language, patterns in language provide a useful marker about the unfolding dynamics and points of convergence and divergence within the network. Many of the resulting dynamics will not be expected and will be alternatively construed from the perspective of different observers.

To maintain the progress of the desired change the cycle of reflection and action needs to continue: A focus on maintaining the learning and generating more active experimentation around a set of (also evolving) principles becomes important. As change accelerates and

moves in unanticipated ways, there may be a loss of stability around short-term outputs, so focusing on long-term outcomes or orienting principles or values becomes more critical. Paradoxically, as new domains of shared meaning emerge, out-groups may form. This is a valuable process, as too much convergence re-stabilizes the network – potentially around dynamics that harm what is being sought in terms of outcomes. The focus of "managing the change" becomes a process of maintaining a balance of turbulence and coalescence of pattern, again attempting to converge desired patterns and disturb undesired patterns.

Within the early stages of Learning to Learn, constructivism, while connecting to teachers' concern that the focus of change be about children and their learning needs, had little or no felt meaning. As a set of ideas it had limited potential to influence practice. Only relatively few teachers appreciated what the epistemic shift implied. These teachers used the introduction to modify their practice. The evidence shows clearly how this became autocatalytic, inspiring other teachers, eliciting support from leaders and community as the changes were seen to be effective (Goldspink, 2002). As a consequence, it was possible also to trace the shift in thinking and practice, first within relatively isolated pockets, then within schools, and subsequently through networks of schools.

### Measure what is valued

Managerialism and economic approaches suggest that performance should be evaluated in terms of tangible results (outputs). However, goal displacement inevitably arises when these are substituted for the desired longer-term social and individual benefits that are the focus of policy and the concern of the stakeholders of education. The output approach is based on the assumption that what is needed and how to achieve it can be unambiguously identified in advance by competent managers: that the problem is tame rather than wicked. However, where performance (and associated rewards) hang on the achievement of tangibles within specified timeframes, the complex and the challenging will be avoided. This implies that individuals or groups that are rewarded on the basis of short-term tangible outputs may maximize performance in ways that reduce the system's capacity to deliver against longer-term outcomes. As Lumley notes,

*"rewarding only quantitative results tends to drive the system back towards the 'fabricative' pole and suppress both creativity and organizational learning."* (1997: 19)

As a result, adopting such approaches can erode the longer-term adaptive capacity and hence viability of educational institutions. In contrast to the data-driven "managerialist" approach to evaluation common within the wider department, the Learning to Learn approach focused on collecting rich (qualitative and quantitative) evidence to inform learning toward long-term goals. At the same time, a strong emphasis was placed on encouraging and focusing teachers' intrinsic commitment to students' wellbeing. An environment was co-constructed that was both provocative and supportive. Teachers were provided with access to a wide range of ideas and thinkers in many areas of education; these included specialists in the cognitive sciences, educational administration, and pedagogy. There were few mandatory requirements that this be accessed and teachers were invited into exploring different ways of making sense of teaching and learning. Local research was encouraged promoting critical reflection at the local level, often with support from leading academics: Teachers felt valued and empowered to inquire and to question. The few mandatory "deliverables" were also oriented to learning. Many teachers stated that being expected to present the story of their own site's learning to other sites at practicums and an annual expo was the most threatening yet rewarding experience of the change process.

### No trust – no capacity to Influence (for the better)

Kelly and Allison (1998) argue that high-command, low-trust systems generate self-organization that works to the detriment of the organization. They emphasize the need to concentrate on the more informal aspects of organization to effect self-organization that is

advantageous. This includes facilitating self-reinforcing cycles based on deep commitment, open learning, responsible action, and trust. Again we see evidence of this in practice with Learning to Learn, and the research makes clear that this "informal" and "high-touch" orientation was central to the success of the project.

There was clear evidence that the ageing workforce in South Australia had become fatigued by previous change and was cynical of centrally driven attempts to improve schooling.[2] Many staff are in the latter stage of their career and had little real incentive to change – yet change they did. But they did not do so immediately and only proceeded with caution. The evidence suggests that the critical factor affecting the willingness to engage was the existence of the alignment of values around children's interests and learning, and, after repeated testing for congruence, that this value orientation could be trusted.

To clearly identify trust as essential is also to go only partway toward an explanation. Trust is often talked of as important within the management literature; it is, however, elusive in practice. Significantly, the values being espoused by Learning to Learn were at odds with those reflected not so much in the "management speak" of the wider organization, but certainly in the power-focused culture. The achievement of trust within the context of Learning to Learn can be partly attributed to the individuals involved in promoting and managing the project and to their integrity. To focus on this, however, would cast the other stakeholders in too passive a role. What is clear is that, at least within education and despite the recent adoption of the language of learning, the assumptions on which managerialism rests and the practices to which it gives rise are all too often in direct contradiction to what is required to open up the possibility of genuine inquiry and learning at the institutional level. In the case of NPM, with its explicit use of agency theory and other economics-derived ideas, the conflict is explicit.

---

2 A managerial reform being pursued at the same time was vigorously resisted.

## Conclusions

Educational systems demonstrate considerable robustness and resilience in the face of both environmental and intended change. Despite many attempts to reform educational systems to make them more effective and efficient, little change has been realized in over a century. Classical bureaucratic, managerial, and economics-based approaches to reform have proven to be limited in effect. In part this is attributable to inappropriate assumptions about the nature and origins of order in educational systems.

Empirical insights into "what works" in educational reform derived from the South Australian Learning to Learn project lend support to the adoption of a complex systems perspective as a basis for the design and implementation of school change.

In contrast to the managerialist approaches currently enjoying wide favor, this approach advocates working with and harnessing the robust self-organization possible in such systems, while also revealing the basis for strategic intervention and change. This includes having those involved find ways to build intrinsic motivation and innovate at a local level to find solutions to wider institutional problems. A key to this is a focus on relationships and the building of congruent behavior based around trust. Such a theory base is also compatible with recent postmodern influences on, and advances to, our understanding of learning. In this way it is more intrinsically compatible with contemporary learning practices than are either conventional management approaches and/or economics-derived theory bases.

Much of the management literature works from the assumption of the need for change to begin from the top. This is argued as a lesson of history, but is more likely a truism; that is, it is true within the organizational environments that result from adoption of this view. Lewin, *et al.* (1998: 37) note, "managers have learned that change does not happen simply because they plan or mandate it." This is only too evident in education reform, where real change has been identified as difficult to achieve despite significant top-down effort (Sarason, 1990; Fullan, 1994; Spillane, 1999; Evans, 2001).

If change is to be grown from the inside out, the role of the policy center in initiating or supporting the diffusion of system-wide change is to act as a catalyst and to encourage and support a search for loci of change, and to encourage or orchestrate intervention at multiple local points to trigger change. It must do so, however, with integrity and ethics and in a context of trust. There is a role also to monitor for the inevitable unintended consequences and to use this to refine interventions to maximize the positive and minimize the negative. They may also have a role in collecting rich information about macro outcomes of local action to feed back to local levels to help inform local decisions about what works and why.

Shaw (1997), drawing on a complex systems perspective, notes that the emphasis for intervention needs to shift from formal systems to informal and from macro-level intervention to micro. This reinforces Weick's observation and the lessons from Learning to Learn, that multiple simultaneous interventions at multiple points throughout the system are necessary and effective at influencing change in loosely coupled systems. Importantly, these interventions will tap into and influence the deep seams of discourse – those that are important and may not be explicit in orientating what people value and what they act on. It will bypass or avoid or perhaps disrupt those domains of discourse that integrate behavior inconsistent with that which is desired. This can only be done if those inventing the interventions are sufficiently located within those domains to understand their subtleties yet can separate themselves by inventing and participating in a viable meta-discourse of inquiry into them.

## References

Aucoin, P. (1990). "Administrative reform in public management: Paradigms, principles, paradoxes and pendulums," *Governance*, ISSN 0952-1895, 3(2): 115-137.

Avis, J. (2003). "Rethinking trust in a performative culture: The case of education," *Journal of Educational Policy*, ISSN 0268-0939, 18(3): 315-332.

Bohte, J. and Meier, K. J. (2000). "Goal displacement:

Assessing the motivation for organizational cheating," *Public Administration Review*, ISSN 1540-6210, 60: 173-182.

Brennan, D. (1996). "Reinventing government: Circumventing citizenship?" in A. Farrar and J. Inglis (eds.), *Keeping It Together*, ISBN 9781864030303.

Brooks, R. A. (1991). "Intelligence without representation," *Artificial Intelligence*, ISSN 0004-3702, 47: 139-159.

Burrell, G. and Morgan, G. (1994). *Sociological Paradigms and Organizational Analysis*, ISBN 9781857421149.

Canada Treasury Board (n.d.). Modernizing Accountability Practices in the Public Sector, Treasury Board of Canada Secretariat, http://www.tbs-sct.gc.ca/rma/account/oagtbs-PR_e.asp?printable=True.

Christensen, T. and Laegreid, P. (2001). "New Public Management: The effects of contractualism and devolution on political control," *Public Management Review*, ISSN 1471-9037, 3(1): 73-94.

Cilliers, P. (1998). *Complexity and Postmodernism: Understanding Complex Systems*, ISBN 9780415152877.

Cilliers, P. (2000). "Knowledge, complexity, and understanding," *Emergence*, ISSN 1521-3250, 2(4): 7-13.

Commonwealth of Australia (2000). A Class Act. Canberra: Senate Employment, Workplace Relations, Small Business and Education Committee, http://www.aph.gov.au/SENATE/committee/EET_CTTE/completed_inquiries/1996-99/teachers/report/contents.htm.

Conklin, J. (2005) "Wicked problems and social complexity," http://www.cognexus.org/wpf/wickedproblems.pdf.

Considine, M. (1990). "Managerialism strikes out," in M. Considine and M. Painter (eds), *Managerialism: The Great Debate*, ISBN 9780522847598.

de Laine, M. (1997). "International themes in public service reform," Department of the Parliamentary Library, www.aph.gov.au/library/pubs/bp/1997-98/98bp03.htm.

Delors, J. (2000). *Learning: The Treasure Within - Report for UNESCO*, http://www.teacherswithoutborders.org/pdf/Delors.pdf.

DECS (Department of Education and Children's Services) (2001). *South Australian Curriculum Standards and Accountability Framework*.

Department of Education and Children's Services (2004). "Assessing the impact of Phases I and II Learning to Learn 1999-2004," Adelaide: Department of Education and Children's Services: 31.

Department of Treasury and Finance (1997). "Output specification and performance measurement," Melbourne: Department of Treasury and Finance.

Dinham, S. and Scott, C. (2000). "Enhancing teacher professionalism: The need to engage with the third domain," presented to the Australian Council for Educational Administration, Annual Conference, Hobart, 9-12 September.

Evans, R. (2001). *The Human Side of School Change*, ISBN 9780787956110.

Fitzsimons, P. (2004). "Managerialism and education," http://www.ffst.hr/ENCYCLOPAEDIA/managerialism.htm.

Foster, M. (2001). "Learning our way forward," Department of Education, Training and Employment, Government of South Australia.

Foster, M., Le Cornu, R. and Peters, J. (2000). "Leadership for Learning," Australian Association for Research in Education Conference, Sydney.

Fullan, M. J. (1994). "Coordinating top-down and bottom-up strategies for educational reform," http://www.ed.gov/ZipDocs/SysReforms.zip.

Goldspink, C. (2002). "Learning to Learn: A foundation for school engagement," report prepared for the Department of Education and Children's Services, Government of South Australia, http://www.learningtolearn.sa.edu.au/Colleagues/files/links/FoundationSchoolEngagement.doc.

Goldspink, C. (2003). "Outcomes of Learning to Learn: An account of the results of learner centred educational reform in South Australian Public Education," report prepared for the Department of Education and Children's Services, Government of South Australia.

Goldspink, C. and Kay, R. (2003). "Organizations as self-organizing and sustaining systems: A complex and autopoietic systems perspective," *International Journal of General Systems*, ISSN 0308-1079, 32(5): 459-474.

Goldspink, C. and Kay, R. (2004). "Bridging the micro-macro divide: A new basis for social science," *Human Relations*, ISSN 0018-7267, 57(5): 597-618.

Hughes, N. (1999). "School reforms in Ontario: The marketisation of education and the resulting silence on equity," *Alberta Journal of Educational Research*, ISSN 0002-4805, 45(2).

Jones, L. R. and Kettle, D. F. (2003). "Assessing public management reform in an international context," *International Public Management Review*, ISSN 1471-9047, 4(1).

Keating, M. (1990). "Managing for results in the public interest," in M. Considine and M. Painter (eds), *Managerialism: The Great Debate*, ISBN 9780522847598.

Kelly, S. and Allison, M. A. (1998). *The Complexity Advantage*, ISBN 9780070014008.

Kernick, D. P. (2005). "Facilitating resource decision making in public organizations drawing upon insights from complexity theory," *Emergence: Complexity and Organization*, ISSN 1521-3250, 7(1): 23-2.

Le Cornu, R., Peters, J. and Collins, J. (2003a). "Constructing relationships for learning," NZARE/AARE Joint Conference, Auckland, New Zealand, http://www.aare.edu.au/03pap/pet03355.pdf.

Le Cornu, R., Peters, J. and Collins, J. (2003b). "What are the characteristics of constructivist learning cultures?" British Educational Research Association Conference, Edinburgh, http://www.learningtolearn.sa.edu.au/Colleagues/files/links/Constructivist_Learning_C_1.pdf.

Lewin, R., Parker, T. and Regine, B. (1998). "Complexity theory and the organization: Beyond the metaphor," *Complexity*, ISSN 1076-2787, 3(4): 36-40.

Lumley, T. (1997). "Complexity and the learning organization," *Complexity*, ISSN 1076-2787, 2(5): 14-22.

Lyall, R. and McNamara, S. (2000). "Influences on the orientations to learning of distance education students in Australia," *Open Learning*, ISSN 0268-0513, 15(2): 107-122.

Marion, R. (1999). *The Edge of Organization: Chaos and Complexity Theories of Formal Social Systems*, ISBN 9780761912668.

McKelvey, B. (1997). "Quasi-natural organization science," *Organization Science*, ISSN 1047-7039, 8: 351-380.

Miller, S. I. and Fredericks, M. (1999). "How does grounded theory explain?" *Qualitative Health Research*, ISSN 1049-7323, 9(4): 538-552.

O'Brein, P. and Down, B. (2002). "What are teachers saying about new managerialism?" *Journal of Educational Enquiry*, ISSN 1444-5530, 3(1): 111-133.

Orton, D. J. and Weick, K. E. (1990). "Loosely coupled systems: A reconceptualization," *Academy of Management Review*, ISSN 0363-7425, 15(2): 203-223.

Osborne, D. and Gaebler, T. (1993). *Reinventing Government: How the Entrepreneurial Spirit Is Transforming the Public Sector*, ISBN 9780452269422.

Paul, M. (1997). "Moving from blame to accountability," *The Systems Thinker*, ISSN 1050-2726, 8(1).

Pollitt, C. (1990). *Managerialism and the Public Service: The Anglo-American Experience*, ISBN 9780199257935.

Sarason, S. B. (1990). *The Predictable Failure of Educational Reform*, ISBN 9781555426231.

Self, P. (2000). *Rolling Back the Market*, ISBN 9780312226527.

Shaw, P. (1997). "Intervening in the shadow systems of organizations: Consulting from a complexity perspective," *Journal of Organizational Change Management*, ISSN 0953-4814, 10(3): 235-250.

Simkins, T. (2000). "Educational reform and managerialism: Comparing the experience of schools and colleges," *Education Policy*, ISSN 0268-0939, 15(3): 317-332.

Spillane, J. P. (1999). "External reform initiatives and teachers' efforts to reconstruct their practice: The mediating role of teachers' zones of enactment," *Curriculum Studies*, ISSN 0022-0272, 31(2): 143-175.

Stacey, R. D. (1996). *Complexity and Creativity in Organizations*, ISBN 9781881052890.

Stacey, R. D. (2000). *Strategic Management and Organization Dynamics: the Challenge of Complexity*, ISBN 9780273613756.

Stacey, R. (2001). *Complex Responsive Processes in Organizations: Learning and Knowledge Creation*, ISBN 9780415249195.

Stretton, H. and Orchard, L. (1994). *Public Goods, Public Enterprise, Public Choice: Theoretical Foundations of the Contemporary Attack on Government*, ISBN 9780333607244.

Taptiklis, T. (2005). "After managerialism," *Emergence: Complexity and Organization*, ISSN 1521-3250, 7(3-4): 2-14.

Tooley, S. (2000). "School-based management: Some observations on the imposition of 'New Public Management' within New Zealand's State Education System," Sydney, Australia: International Public Management Network, http://www.inpuma.net/research/papers/sydney/stuarttooley.html.

Tsoukas, H. and Chia, R. (2002). "On organizational becoming: Rethinking organizational change," *Organization Science*, ISSN 1047-7039, 13(5): 567-582.

Udehn, L. (1996). *The Limits of Public Choice: A Sociological Critique of the Economic Theory of Politics*, ISBN 9780415125123.

Varela, F., Thompson, E. and Rosch, E. (1992). *The Embodied Mind*, ISBN 9780262720212.

Weick, K. E. (1982). "Administering education in loosely coupled schools," *Phi Delta Kappan*, ISSN 0031-7217, June: 673-676.

Wilenski, P. (1986). *Public Power and Public Administration*, ISBN 9780868062662.

**Chris Goldspink** has 15 years experience as an internal and external consultant in organization and management improvement. His background includes experience with information technology, education, organizational management, and public-sector reform. He has senior and middle management experience and maintains an interest in practical management in both the public and private sectors, teaching and consulting in both. His research interests include the applicability of complex systems theory to social and organizational analysis, computer simulation of social phenomena, and issues in cross-cultural education. He is also currently assisting the South Australian Education Department to conduct research directed at improving school education. Chris resides permanently in New Zealand but is currently based in England as a research fellow at the University of Surrey. He has a PhD from the University of Western Sydney.

Philosophy

# Complexity and Philosophy

# Complexity theory applied to itself

Robin J. Nunn
Institute for the History and Philosophy of Science and Technology, University of Toronto, CAN

This paper describes how complexity theory can be applied to itself at a metaphorical level to generate ideas about complexity, including proposals for modeling the evolution of complexity theory and treating computer modeling as a part of complexity theory, not just a medium of its expression. Proposals for more rigorous application of complexity theory to itself include studying the fitness of ideas within complexity theory, using various proxies for measuring those ideas, studying the autocatalysis of ideas, estimating the fractal geometry, and developing general computer models of complexity theory.

## Introduction

Complexity theory is everywhere. It occupies a substantial academic niche with its own courses, programs, departments, and extensive lists of publications, including journals devoted exclusively to complexity. By nature interdisciplinary, complexity theory has been applied across disciplines as diverse as meteorology, biology, geology, mathematics, physics, medicine, history, sociology, economics, education, business management, and political science, to name a few (see for example the range of disciplines in the references provided at the end of this paper). Or perhaps listing the disciplines not yet under the influence of complexity theory would be the shorter way to describe the explosion of complexity theorizing. Still, there is a significant gap. In this paper, I extend the list by sketching the application of complexity theory

to yet another subject, itself, and offer specific proposals for further research.

What is the purpose of applying complexity theory to itself? This paper has no room for a full treatment of the importance and implications of notions such as self-reference, reflexivity, recursion, and paradox (see for example Luhmann, 1990; Bartlett, 1992). Several observations will have to serve as placeholders for a longer discussion. It is simply interesting and fun to apply a pattern to itself and see where it leads. It is also likely to lead to something useful, since recursive procedures can be very expressive and efficient. To describe something by reference to itself is to abbreviate the description. So self-reference can simplify. Also, parts of complexity theory are already expressed reflexively, so it seems sensible to ask whether the whole thing is reflexive. We might try to construct complexity theory from complexity theories all the way down.

Applying theory to itself joins theory and practice: The theory has to put its money where its mouth is, as they say. For instance, Cilliers (2005: 261) has asked whether the statement that we can never have complete knowledge of complex systems is trapped in a performative contradiction, between the absolute statement itself and the incompleteness in its claim. This is a logical analog of the ideal that no one, or in this case no concept, is above the law, so complexity theory should not hover in the air above its own rules. Any theory can be challenged by showing its hypocrisy, that it does not fit into its own description of the world, but this discussion is not just about logical consistency, or self-referential consistency, as much as it is concerned with the ways in which complexity theory can provide insight into itself. Complexity theory would be more persuasive if it could parse itself, by analogy to the way a new computer language can be used to write a parser to process and test the new language itself.

Piecemeal hints at applying complexity theory to itself appear in the literature. Allen (2001), for example, describes complexity science in the nested expression "knowledge of the limits to knowledge." Luhmann (1990) offers a theory of social systems as recursively closed systems with respect to communications. Beyond these and other similar hints, however, I am not aware of any project specifically proposing to apply complexity theory to itself.

As these are just early steps, I address only some of the most basic questions, such as asking what is complexity and what is emergence. But from these basics, surprising issues appear, such as whether computer source code forms a part of complexity theory and literature. I hope not only to clarify issues within complexity theory and inspire more ideas, but also to provide the satisfaction of entering if not closing the circle of self-reference that is one of the hallmarks of complex systems.

The promise of complexity theory, implicit in its name, is to explain complex phenomena. What could be more exciting to a scientist than revealing the great mysteries of our complex world, maybe even the origin of life? Yet it is natural to be wary of the heart-racing promises made in the mysterious, and sometimes mystical, apparently self-organizing realm of complexity theory, with its breathless exuberance for everything that can be characterized by a well-worn cluster of terms such as nonlinear dynamics, chaos, self-organization, criticality, autocatalysis, emergence, phase transition, random boolean networks, fitness landscapes, fractals, and so on. These collected notions may be inspiring, but they are also dreamlike in their pageantry.

Complexity theory seeks simple rules for complex phenomena. But that is the essence of all science and all theorizing. Science is also skeptical, seeking replication, confirmation, and falsification, but with complexity theory there is something uncomfortable that inspires extra caution. It is not just the inevitability that scientific theories of every era, including ours, will eventually turn out to be false. It is not just that similar overarching theories such as general systems theory and catastrophe theory have come and gone, and so one day we may also awaken from the complexity dream. It is partly the refusal to be pinned down, the very all-inclusiveness that lets complexity theory be applied to virtually any phenomena, not only the physical but all levels from the subatomic to the social. Complexity theorists are on firm ground when discussing observed data from dissipative physical systems, but when they venture far afield their persuasiveness wanes, as they reach to explain how a market economy and democracy are pinnacles of evolution (explanations that can only be validated, if at all, in retrospect and in any event cannot help us understand a future that is sensitive to initial conditions). For instance, while complexity theory may suggest that democracy has evolved by analogy to the processes that created life, and purport to explain why the former Soviet Union dissolved by analogy to avalanches and extinctions, the same theory has curiously little to say about the growing power of Communist China or even the continued existence of Cuba (see for example Kauffman, 1995: 245). The dream of finding simple physics-like laws governing all complexity seems as simplistic as the dream of world peace. Complexity theorizing floats on its own plane, not down on earth in the tangible grit of science, but hovering in the air like smog over Los Angeles, with the promising but ghostly apparition of something beautiful hidden behind an obscuring layer. The question comes to mind whether there is any *there* there.

But let us not dwell on the negative side. On the positive side, complexity theory is also full of inspiring metaphors that spark other metaphors: butterfly wings that trigger tornadoes, avalanches that change the world, automatons that organize themselves, bacteria that know their world. Complexity theorists are most persuasive in their metaphorical musings about nonlinear patterns. Following that tradition, this metaphorical, imprecise, and non-technical essay is an attempt to turn the spotlight of complexity theory inward to illuminate its own complexity.

This project of applying complexity theory to itself "emerged" from what seem to be casual references made to the emergence of complexity theory. For instance, Waldrop (1992) enshrined the emergence of complexity theory in the title of his book about the emergence of the Santa Fe Institute, *Complexity: The Emerging Science at the Edge of Order and Chaos*. From the continental side, Emmece (1997: 43) writes,

*"I leave it to others to speculate on the possibility that the emergence of the "sciences of complexity" is a reflection of the changing social situation for the scientific subsystem in a postmodern and hyper-differentiated world."*

In a similar vein, when discussing the properties of complex systems Kauffman (1995: 19) states, "The search for such properties is emerging as a fundamental research strategy, one I shall make much use of in this book." Kauffman is probably not literally describing emergence twice removed, the search for properties emerging from some unstated meta-complexity composed of properties including the property called emergence. Instead, these writers may be using the term emergence in the colloquial sense, as a top-of-the-mind concept, or as a clever literary device. But these and other similar references prompt me to wonder: What if complexity theory were indeed an emergent, self-similar, nonlinear phenomenon, as those terms are applied to any other so-called complex system?

I should also note that I use the term complexity theory, not complexity science. While there is no general debate that theories about complex systems help us to understand our complex world, on the other hand, there is no general agreement that there is a separate science of complexity or even that it is science. Even its proponents cannot offer more than generalities about complexity science such as calling it "a subject that's still so new and wide-ranging that nobody quite knows how to define it, or even where its boundaries lie" (Waldrop 1992: 9). The subject called complexity science shifts, like a pseudo-science that refuses to be refuted, as the subjects studied under the complexity view change. Emmece (1997), for example, set out four descriptions of complex systems and a fifth, "quite separate" notion, for social systems.

If I am wrong and complexity theory does not itself exhibit the very features that are the objects of complexity theory, then what features properly describe it? Is complexity theory linear? Is complexity theory an emergent whole or can it be reduced to a composite of its parts?

## Undefined but complex theory

To apply a theory to something, we could begin by defining the theory so that we know exactly what we are applying and to what we are applying it. In the present case, we might want to know what complexity theory is and how complex something must be for it to become an object of the theory. When applying complexity theory to itself, we might think that we could solve both problems at once, scoping both the theory and the objects; that is, the parts of complexity theory that we are theorizing about. But defining complexity theory is elusive. Kauffman, for instance, uses the word complexity in various contexts, and tells us how fundamental complexity is to our very existence, but he avoids telling us exactly what complexity is. He writes confident statements, such as "Laws of complexity spontaneously generate much of the order of the natural world" (Kauffman, 1995: 8). From such assertions we are led to believe not only that complexity is something real and fundamental, but also that it has laws and other definite features.

Like many others, Kauffman champions complexity theory in association with chaos theory. Neither of these frequently paired notions is easily captured. One critic, merging them into the discordant term "chaoplexity," says,

*"Each term, and chaos in particular, has been defined in specific, distinct ways by specific*

*individuals. But each has also been defined in so many overlapping ways by so many different scientists and journalists that the terms have become virtually synonymous, if not meaningless."* (Horgan, 1996: 192)

A more charitable view is that definitions are not always easy:

*"Scientific terms may be roughly divided into two categories: those that are introduced by means of a precise and even formal definition (which is the case for many of the more recent mathematical terms) and those that are drawn from everyday language and which have further to travel before they attain the status of an unequivocal definition. The word complexity (from the Latin* complecti, *grasp, comprehend, embrace) belongs to the second category and is particularly resistant to precise definition."* (Israel, 2005: 479)

In any event, there is no generally accepted statement of what complexity theory is or how complex something must be to come within the ambit of complexity theory.

Without defining the boundaries of complexity theory, we could be left with the task of applying a theory of everything to itself. Does complexity theory explain the most complex phenomena and therefore everything included in that complexity? Exemplars of complex phenomena cited in the literature vary in their scale of complexity from simple one-line equations, such as the logistic function, to the entire workings of the human brain. Complex entities studied under the umbrella of complexity theory range from the microscopic to the global. Kauffman, for example, claims that complexity theory implies that the bacterium *E. coli* and the multinational corporation IBM "know their worlds in much the same way" (Kauffman, 1993: 388, 404). Cilliers (2001: 6) refers to "accepting the complexity of the boundaries of complex systems." In so doing, he implicitly supports this project of applying complexity theory to itself, as we try to understand the complex boundaries in order to sort out the complexities of the systems delimited by those complex boundaries.

A definition of complexity theory is not essential. We do not need to be so formal about definitions that we become exhausted with the effort before getting to the meat of the matter. Lacking the structure, or stricture, of definitions, we are free to debate and create our own ideas. If we cannot define complexity theory, however, then we may not gain much from attempting to define its parts. Or despite lacking a definition, something might emerge from its parts.

If a scientific theory is something that simplifies, unifies, and explains the apparent complexity of our world, then perhaps complexity theory may never be defined because it is an oxymoron. Complexity may be one thing and a tractable theory something else. As Arthur C. Clarke states in his widely quoted third law, "Any sufficiently advanced technology is indistinguishable from magic" (Clarke, 1962). The same may be said of sufficiently complex systems and theory. If we know the simple laws, if we see the sleight of hand for what it really is, then we are not mesmerized by the complex system. If it is no longer magic then it is no longer complex. Chaos theory may also be an oxymoron if a scientific theory finds order in apparent disorder. Perhaps then complexity and chaos theory do not simplify, unify, explain, and provide order. Or perhaps chaos and complexity theory properly converge on complexity from both the simple and the not-simple.

We will return to the difficulties of nomenclature when we come to the concept of emergence. For now, let us continue to apply complexity theory to itself.

### Self-similar

One part of complexity theory is the concept of nested self-similarity. Complex systems can be composed of other complex systems. An ecology, for example, is composed of organisms that are composed of internal systems including individual cells, and each of those levels of organization is a complex system. Complexity theory itself is composed of other complex parts, including notions such as nonlinearity and self-organization, each of which has further complex components. So here we have one way in which complexity theory exhibits self-similarity, and thereby recurses into itself consistently with its own theory. Self-similarity may be considered to be a complex phenomenon within the cluster of facets comprising complexity theory. This concept, and others in the set of complexity-theoretical ideas, is unlikely to be exactly self-similar, but is more likely to be quasi-self-similar, as is typical of fractal recursion relations.

Fractals quantify the geometry of self-similar entities. They also represent another example of simple rules that generate complex results. If complexity theory is composed of self-similar features, a project for the future would be to calculate various estimates of the fractional dimensionality of complexity theory and its components.

As a coevolving group of ideas, each influencing the other, the facets of complexity theory could be considered to exhibit complexity all the way down to single statements such as "complexity theory is defined as..." or "self-organized criticality is..." Each of these statements is, metaphorically speaking, like an individual logistic map (discussed in more detail elsewhere in this paper). If not pushed too far, the statements are at equilibrium and not interesting, while if pushed too far they become incomprehensible, no better than random signals, mere noise. On the edge of incomprehensibility, however, they become interesting ideas.

To the extent that complexity theory is a separate unifying theory, it dissolves the boundaries separating its parts, and so must involve various disciplines that divide and view the parts differently. Understanding complexity theory also demands an understanding of its origins in physics, chemistry, biology, economics, mathematics, and so on. Every complexity theorist must join an expedition that ventures from sandpiles to tornadoes, fractals to boolean networks, bacteria to humans to multinational corporations, while feasting on a primordial complexity soup of ideas. Viewed through the lens of complexity theory applied to itself, the parts of complexity theory appear to be interdisciplinary complexities in their own right.

## Self-organizing

Self-organization is another part of complexity theory, and like other parts this notion stands for simple rules generating complex results. What are the reasons for the order we see in a thermodynamically disordering world? What rules explain why complex systems that could exist in many different states seem to be attracted only to comparatively few states? Commonly cited examples of self-organization include everyday phenomena such as crystallization, magnetization, and turbulence, as well as more exotic phenomena such as Belousov-Zhabotinsky chemical reactions, the persistent red spot on the planet Jupiter, and the origin of life. An algorithmic example of self-organization is the flocking of birds that can be modeled with simple rules (Flake, 1998). Like complexity theory itself, the contained notion of self-organization has been applied to many objects in many disciplines, from substances in physics to organisms in biology to human social activity including economics and politics. As with complexity theory, the question might be asked: Does the theory of self-organizing entities apply to itself? What if complexity theory were self-organizing?

Building on a century-old idea of autocatalytic enzymes (Fry, 2000: 74), Kauffman (1993: 309) proposes that life originated from self-organizing, autocatalytic sets of molecules. He offers various estimates of the number of polymers needed, in terms such as these: "for a probability of catalysis of only $10^{-9}$, a mere 18,000 to 19,000 polymers should achieve the critical minimum complexity for collective autocatalysis!" (Kauffman, 1993: 311). A critical mass of ideas could also be said to generate a synergy of self-catalyzing ideas; rub a sufficient diversity of interdisciplinary notions together, and then like molecules and nuclear reactors, they may go supracritical, exploding into new ideas. We may have reached this metaphorical autocatalysis, as complexity reactions have been bursting forth in every discipline, and as everyone who is paid to think important thoughts now asks whether complexity theory can be applied to understand each discipline's underlying order.

Under the umbrella of self-organization, another part of complexity theory is the notion of self-organized criticality. When systems are in ordered states, a small change affects only local events, while in the disordered chaotic realm a small change can change everything. Self-organized criticality refers to states between order and disorder. On the critical edge, a small change has the optimum effect to maintain the system. Bak *et al.* (1987: 382) used the image of a sandpile to explain the idea:

*"In order to visualize a physical system expected to exhibit self-organized criticality, consider a pile of sand. If the slope is too large, the pile is far from equilibrium, and the pile will collapse until the average slope reaches a critical value where the system is barely stable with respect to small perturbations."*

Bak's sandpile model has yielded sub-metaphors, including the image of periodic avalanches caused by events as small as the addition of a single grain of sand. The sandpile model is a visible expression of nonlinearity and sensitivity to initial conditions. Other indicia of self-organized criticality include various mathematical relationships such as 1/f laws, power laws, scale invariance, and, of course, complexity.

In a trivial sense, every theory could be the consequence of the self-organizing mind, as Bak (1996: 175), among others, has argued that the mind is in a self-organized critical state. In a practical sense, every text, including this one, begins as a completely ordered blank page that may become a disordered set of notes that eventually settle around the attractor that is the thesis of the text. In that way, order and disorder become organized puzzle solving. More specifically, the ideas within complexity theory could be envisioned as poised at the edge of chaos, at the leading edge of understanding.

The avalanche metaphor may also be applied to complexity theory. Kauffman (1995: 129) uses the image in reference to biological systems, saying for instance, "Like the sandpile grains of sand, where each may unleash a small or large avalanche, the poised ecosystems will create small and large bursts of molecular novelty." Substitute the word "theory" for "ecosystems," and it could be said that the various theories within complexity theory will create bursts of theoretical activity, avalanches of ideas sparked by notions as small as grains of sand. If the avalanche is significant enough, it may eventually qualify as a new scientific paradigm.

Unlike physical systems such as sandpiles, the more complex category of live self-organizing systems, including individual organisms, ecologies, and social systems, adapt to their environments. Adaptive systems invite metaphors from biological adaptation with its notions such as fitness, competition, survival, and evolution. Applied to complexity theory, we could think of the Darwinian marketplace of ideas. When considering how fit are the ideas of fitness landscapes and other aspects of complexity theory, we could measure the ideas not only in the general marketplace but also within the organism we are calling complexity theory, by analogy to the way fitness depends on interactions among genes (see for example Kauffman 1995: 170). If there is an adaptation in the theory of fitness landscapes or of self-similarity that affects the survival of those ideas, for example, then related ideas will also be influenced.

Because ideas cannot readily be measured in the abstract, we could use scientometrics, citations of authors and publications, or frequency of word usage, or prevalence of complexity course syllabi, conferences, and workshops, as proxies for fitness. We could build computer models to represent these idea networks and compare the models to actual citations, conferences, and so on (see for example Price, 1965). We could create fitness landscapes with peaks and valleys (all we need is to represent something, anything at all, as having a height and a distance from something else, with a measure of success in competition, such as rate of reproduction, attached to the something being represented). In the context of the present discussion, the rate of reproduction could be of growth in number of ideas, frequency of publications and of cited papers and authors, courses offered in higher education institutions, number and size of research grants. These and other measures could provide models of the evolution of complexity theory.

## Nonlinear

The great hope of complexity theory is to find simple rules underlying the complexity of our world. Of course, this could be said of all science, indeed of all knowledge: that we seek order in the buzzing confusion. Simple rules are the legends of science. Archimedes discovered a simple rule about buoyancy, apparently while sitting in his bathtub. Newton discovered many simple rules, but probably not while sitting under an apple tree. Einstein gave us the most famous of all one-line rules of nature, $E=mc^2$. But these examples are from physics. The promise of complexity theory is to find simple physics-like rules in other disciplines (critics have used the term "physics envy," attributed to various sources, to describe this reductionist goal).

A single physics-like equation is insufficient to cover all of complexity theory. But a large part of complexity theory can be stated in only four words: sensitivity to initial conditions. This is a compact way of saying that complex systems are nonlinear, inherently unpredictable, and dependent on history. Data describing a complex system cannot be infinitely exact, so as errors multiply, the noise overwhelms the signal. But is this not just a description of chaos theory? Chaos theory, nonlinear dynamics, and complexity theory all cover overlapping or the same territory, but again precise definitions are elusive. Lorenz (1993: 8), one of the leading figures in complexity and chaos theory, defines chaos as sensitive dependence on initial conditions, although he also devotes the whole of the first chapter and much of the rest of his book to refinements of the definition. Chaos is deterministic behavior (not random but governed by laws) that does not appear to be deterministic. Lorenz also addresses complexity, explaining,

*"complexity is sometimes used to indicate sensitive dependency and everything that goes with it... Sometimes a distinction is made between "chaos" and "complexity," with the former*

*term referring to irregularity in time, and the latter implying irregularity in space. The two types of irregularity are often found together, as, for example, in turbulent fluids. Complexity is frequently used in a rather different sense, to indicate the length of a set of instructions that one would have to follow to depict or construct a system."* (Lorenz, 1993: 167)

One way of using the theme of nonlinearity to examine complexity theory itself can be seen in the observation of bifurcation in complex phenomena. Bifurcation is the sudden branching seen in complex systems near the edge of chaos. A frequently observed bifurcation is period doubling (with a specific ratio of steps in doubling known as the Feigenbaum constant). Finite difference equations such as the logistic equation are often used to illustrate these concepts; one version is $x_{x+1} = rx_n(1-x_n)$. This equation, which describes dynamic systems such as the evolution of animal populations, shows many features of nonlinear systems, from order to bifurcation to chaotic, apparent randomness (for diagrams see Glass & Mackey, 1988: 26ff). Applying these ideas to complexity theory at the metaphorical level, bifurcation could be a divergence of opinions and viewpoints. Only the simplest notions would have a unity of views. Multiple splits in viewpoint could be a measure of complexity. At a higher level, bifurcations could be seen as a split between disciplines and their approach to complexity studies, as they each head in their own direction but in a self-similar way, like the paths of a bifurcating graph. In yet a different way to slice the concepts, bifurcation could be a metaphor representing the cycling of paradigms over time. For example, at various times aspects of complexity theory have been gathered as systems theory, as cybernetics, and as complexity theory, each overlapping the other but not covering exactly the same ideas and not engaging the same minds.

There is also a historical theme of complexity within complexity theory. Lorenz concludes his book, while still fleshing out the definition of chaos, with a chapter titled "What else is chaos?" There while explaining what fractals have to do with chaos, he makes a retrospective prediction about the theory that describes the unpredictable:

*"It was near the close of the seventies that 'chaos' was rapidly becoming established as a standard term for phenomena exhibiting sensitive dependence. It was also at just about this time that new strange attractors were rapidly being encountered and these attractors with their fractal structure, rather than the absence of periodicity or the presence of sensitive dependence, were the features that some specialists were finding most appealing. Temporarily, at least, they were becoming the principal subject of chaos theory. It was but a short step for "chaos" to extend its domain to fractals of all kinds, and even to more general shapes that had not become familiar objects of study before the advent of computers. In retrospect, it would be hard to imagine that the original meaning of "chaos" could more appropriately have been extended to one of these categories of shapes than another. There is little question but that "chaos" like "strange attractor" is an appealing term – the kind that tends to establish itself. I have often speculated as to how well James Gleick's best-seller would have fared at the bookstores if it had borne a title like* Sensitive Dependence: Making a New Science.*"* (Lorenz, 1993: 177)

Or if finding simple rules for complex phenomena had been called simplicity theory, it might have died quickly, for who would want to be known as an expert in simplicity? Who would fund research into what sounds like a mere restatement of science, or simply an updated Ockham's Razor? Much more fulfilling for the ego to be an expert in complexity. Not only is complexity theory dependent on its history, but so are its constituent parts, including its terminology. Had there been a slight adjustment to the initial historical conditions, we could now be discussing sensitive-dependence theory, parsing the notions of sensitivity and dependence instead of chaos and complexity. Just as we cannot change history, however, we cannot avoid it. Cilliers (2001: 1) refers to the Santa Fe approach, which he calls the most popular, as "lots of chaos theory and mathematics." We cannot ignore these origins of

complexity theory in chaos theory, mathematics, and computers, no matter how complexity theory has evolved or continues to evolve, any more than we can ignore our own human evolution. Reflexively speaking, this is one reason why this paper relies heavily on those historical origins of complexity and chaos theory (see also the discussion in this paper of Bak preferring computer models to "grandiose philosophical claims").

Of all possible states in which nonlinear dynamical systems could exist, they are attracted to a relatively small set. If complexity theory itself is considered to be such a system, possible attractors could be the set of concepts, including self-organization, nonlinearity, and so on, with ideas in complexity orbiting around these central concepts. Other metaphorical attractors are the set of authors and their publications concerned with complexity theory.

At a global level, in the stable equilibrium region, with too little complexity, not much interesting happens. In the chaotic region, where nobody agrees on anything, nothing productive happens. At the edge of chaos, complexity research thrives.

And for one more example of the application of nonlinear dynamics and sensitive-dependence theory to itself: Nobody predicted that theories of a meteorologist trying to predict weather would develop into theories of the organization of bacteria and large corporations.

## Networks

Networks are another feature common to complex systems. Draw connections between the parts, consider the parts to be the nodes of a connected graph, and suddenly a network exists. The network metaphor is so pervasive in our computer-networked, broadcast-networked, socially networked vocabulary that it seems more substantial than a mere metaphor. At times the notion of a network is used as a synonym for a complex system. So when applying complexity theory to its own parts, it will come as no surprise that networks are easy to find. The interlinked notions of complexity, chaos, nonlinearity, and so on form a network of notions. Other ways to slice the network concept include networks of authors, publications, research institutions, graduate programs, and courses devoted to complexity research.

The many parts and groups of parts comprising complex systems interact in combinatorial explosions of complex phenomena. Consider for instance a simple 10 by 10 square, like a crossword puzzle, with either 1 or 0 in each box. Those 100 boxes might represent networked nodes in a computer model that could be in $2^{100}$ different states. To tame that kind of explosion, random boolean networks can serve as idealized, frictionless models of complexity. In biology, for instance, genes can be idealized as present or absent, active or inactive, and their interactions modeled accordingly (Kauffman, 1993: 444). In particular, the models can demonstrate how a complex system can be attracted to comparatively few of its billions and billions of possible states. These computer models are a boolean analog of the logistic equation, showing a range of results from ordered to chaotic, depending on how the experimenter tunes the computer code. Summarizing adaptation in complex systems, Kauffman states,

*"Random NK Boolean networks with K = 2 inputs to each of 100 000 binary elements yield systems which typically localize behavior to attractors with about 317 states among $2^{100\,000}$ possible alternative states of activity. Whatever else you may mark to note and remember in this book, note and remember that our intuitions about the requirements for order in very complex systems have been wrong. Vast order abounds for selection's further use. Having marked to note that complex systems exhibit spontaneous order, mark a second, bold and fundamental possibility: Adaptive evolution achieves the kind of complex systems which are able to adapt. The lawful property of such systems may well be that they abide on the edge of chaos. This possibility appears to me to be terribly important."* (Kauffman, 1993: 235) [Italics in the original text]

The notion of idealizing complexity as networked nodes, which are attracted to rela-

tively few ordered states, has been pushed to the limit in theories based on *infinite* boolean networks of symbols. All interactions within any computer model can be considered to be symbol strings. Those abstract symbols can be interpreted as any phenomena. They can, for instance, be deemed to be chemical reactions of strings representing polymers catalyzing combinations and splits in other strings. The chemical reactions in turn can be interpreted as precursors of the replication of RNA and DNA in living organisms. Interactions of strings can also be considered as grammars for transforming strings to other strings. All of this, as ever, is in aid of finding patterns that explain the world, including possibly explaining complexity theory itself. In proposing the study of infinite boolean networks and random grammars for mapping strings to other strings, Kauffman stated the aim this way:

*"Random grammars and the resulting systems of interacting strings will hopefully become useful models of functionally integrated, functionally interacting molecular, biological, neural, psychological, technological, and cultural systems. The central image is that a string represents a polymer, a good or service, an element in a conceptual system, or a role in a cultural system. Polymers acting on polymers produce polymers; goods acting on goods produce goods; ideas acting on ideas produce ideas. The aim is to develop a new class of models in which the underlying grammar implicitly yields the ways in which strings act on strings to produce strings, to interpret such production as functional couplings, and to study the emergent behaviors of string systems in these contexts."* (Kauffman, 1993: 387)

As yet we have no such grammar or string representation for the conceptual system known as complexity theory.

When extending the boolean network model to infinite boolean networks represented by strings of 1s and 0s, the experimenter can decide everything that goes in and comes out, numbering each possible string and combination of strings, and deciding how one string transforms another or inhibits transformation, where new strings come from, whether they are born from nothing or recombined from other strings, and whether they stay in the system or vanish in an arbitrary string death. These logical systems are not constrained as physical systems are.

*"Obviously, finiteness in physical systems is also controlled - by thermodynamics in chemical systems, for instance, and by costs of production, aggregate demand, and budget constraints in economics. However, in the worlds of ideas, myths, scientific creations, cultural transformations, and so on, no such bound may occur. Thus it is of interest to see how such algorithmic string systems can control their own exploration of their possible composition set of dynamic control over the processes they undergo."* (Kauffman, 1993: 382)

Kauffman is not referring to complexity theory, but by analogy string systems could be used to explore complexity theory and generate data that can illuminate the theory of the theory. How closely coupled are the parts of complexity theory? What parts are most important? What is missing? This brings us to another proposal for future research: to develop a computer model of the parts and interactions within the network of related ideas gathered under the term complexity theory.

## Computer models

Computer models have not been considered to be features of complexity theory, but only the medium through which the theory is expressed. But it is worth noting that complexity theory depends so heavily on computers that without them the necessary calculations would be impracticable. In theory, clever people could rely on the computing power of their brains and maybe a pencil and paper. In practice, however, complexity theory has only emerged with the advent of powerful computer technology. So in that sense computers and the phenomena they exhibit are part of the theory.

All of the phase transitions and other patterns found in random boolean networks are not data from the observed physical world but are merely representations, abstractions, meta-

phors, imagery. The abstractions can represent anything or nothing. Kauffman's proposal to study random strings acting on random strings inside a computer illustrates how far removed from the natural world the phenomena underlying complexity theory can become. Yet if computers are a vital part of the theory, then we cannot understand the theory without understanding how those abstractions behave in the world of the computer, quite apart from the metaphorical relationship, if any, of computer models to the natural world.

Still, it would be easy to dismiss computer models altogether as mere games, just automated abstractions that teach us only about computers and nothing outside them. Compared to the natural world, computer models may simply be too simple. Bak (1996: 138) discusses algorithms in his models of simulated evolution:

*"The programs were so simple that the programming for each version would take no more than ten minutes, and the computer would take a few seconds to arrive at some rough results... In summary the model was probably simpler than any model that anybody had ever written for anything. Random numbers are arranged in a circle. At each time step, the lowest number, and the numbers at its two neighbors, are each replaced by new random numbers. That's all! This step is repeated again and again. What could be simpler than replacing some random numbers with some other random numbers? Who says complexity cannot be simple? This simple scheme leads to rich behavior beyond what we could imagine. The complexity of its behavior sharply contrasts with its simple definition."* [Italics in the original text]

Leaving aside the exclamations and overzealous generalization about "anybody" and "anything," how is it possible that flipping random numbers should tell us anything about the complexity of our world, let alone fundamental realities in it like the evolution of life? Bak (1996: 161) explains,

*"The main reason for dealing with grossly oversimplified toy models is that we can study*

*them not only with computer simulations but also with mathematical models. This puts our results on a firmer ground, so that we are not confined to general grandiose, philosophical claims."*

The models have to be simple enough to be understood as mathematical models. Computer models, essential as they are, nevertheless are not entirely trustworthy unless they are simple.

Another source of distrust is in the failure of complexity researchers to publish source code. In the early days of computers, computer source code was mostly secret, like the secret discoveries of alchemists and early scientists. Today source code for entire operating systems and applications has been widely published. Open source frameworks are also available specifically for developing models used in researching complex systems. So it is puzzling that researchers like Bak, Kauffman, and others, who base their arguments on computer simulations, publish only their results without source code, while in the traditionally secret corporate world, rivals like Microsoft, Sun, and IBM are now publishing some of their commercial source code.

From a textual description, we do not know exactly how computer models are constructed. When discussing physical systems constructed to carry out computations, Kauffman writes,

*"We know that some computations cannot be described in a more compact form than carrying out the computation and observing its unfolding. Thus, we could not, in principle, have general laws, shorter more compact descriptions, of such behavior. Thus we could not have general laws about the behavior of arbitrary, far-from-equilibrium systems. This argument, however, contains a vital premise. It is we who construct the non-equilibrium system in some arbitrary way. Having specified its structure and logic, we find the system capable of arbitrary behavior"* (Kauffman, 1993: 387) [Italics in original text].

Without source code, other researchers can still try to reproduce the same output using different code on different systems. It could be argued that such independent "experimentation" is essential for verification of any results and therefore makes publishing source code unnecessary. But this is not a matter of verification of scientific observations of the world available to anyone outside the computer. Source code is needed to verify the inputs and logic used to create those particular arbitrary worlds inside the computer from which analogies to the world outside the computer are derived.

We cannot understand complexity theory without understanding the medium of its expression. Computer code is as significant to the literature as are the equations and graphs resulting from computer models. That is, computer code itself is the literature relevant to any explanation of phenomena observed in computer simulations. Consistent with the scientometric study I have proposed for the *natural language text* of complexity theory, a higher-order study of the complexity of the *computer language text* of complexity theory could be done using common source code complexity metrics. Further to the proposal to develop computer models of complexity theory, then, is this proposal: that source code be published, not just a description of the models and a summary of the output. With the source code, particularly the kind discussed by Bak that can be written in ten minutes, we may find that complexity theory, like complex phenomena, is built on very simple rules indeed.

## Levels with indeterminate boundaries

The parts of complex systems can be considered at different levels. The levels of a living organism, for example, include the whole individual, the various internal systems, the cells, the parts making up the cells, and so on from macroscopic down through microscopic to subatomic levels. The levels are not exact but have indeterminate boundaries. So that opens the question of how to describe where the boundaries are. We can debate what exactly are the genes and other separate components of a cell. Complexity theory also has levels with indeterminate boundaries.

One way of slicing the levels is within the theory itself. Is emergence, for example, a part of complexity theory, or such an essential feature of complexity that it is at the same level, a peer of the whole emergent theory? Another way of slicing the levels is between the theoretical and other levels, such as the non-technical metaphorical level of this discussion, the technical level expressed in mathematical terms, the experimental and observation levels, the computer simulation level, and the ever-present shadow of any theoretical discussion, the practical level. A third possible slicing of the levels of complexity theory can be found within computer simulations themselves. Computer models range in complexity from simple equations in a few lines of code to massive internetworked systems. The notion of levels brings us to the emergence of those levels.

## Emergence

Complexity theory may be hard to pin down in a definition as something greater than, or at least different from, its parts. Here is another recursive opportunity, a self-similarity emerging from the notion of emergence, one of the principal features of complexity theory. Is complexity theory just a cluster of related ideas or something more?

Examples of emergent phenomena are everywhere. How do the properties of water emerge from the combination of hydrogen and oxygen atoms? How do ant colonies emerge from individual ants? How does a mind emerge from neurons? Yet despite its ubiquity, emergence has eluded precise definition by philosophers from before Aristotle to the present day. It would be impossible here to address the full range of definitions, some of which hinge on slippery concepts such as supervenience and downward causation. Nor will I address the holist-reductionist conundrum of seeing emergence in the *reduction* of complexity to simple, so-called holistic laws. Instead, I will use the statement of Holland (1998: 1), who explains emergence in only three or four words: much coming from little, or simply, much from little. His definition leaves room for the skepti-

cal theme in this paper; that is, the suspicion that much *there* may have been made of little *there*. The definition also is readily applied to complexity theory itself without requiring an exact analogy to physical systems. By contrast, narrower definitions rely on multiple identical or similar entities acting autonomously, such as water molecules, ants, and neurons. There is no need, however, to suggest that the component parts of complexity theory are anything like billions of identical water molecules, or that the parts of complexity theory are autonomous agents, in order to suggest that much comes from little.

Let us metaphorically overlap parts of complexity theory like polymers in an autocatalytic soup. Consider the parts we are calling emergence, networks, systems, and nonlinearity. Parts of linear systems can be added or multiplied, but a linear system does not exceed the sum of its parts. We know from basic Euclidean geometry and elementary algebra that the whole can be entirely expressed in simple linear relations among its composite parts, such as $x(a+b) = xa + xb$. What results is only that, a resultant, like the term used for the addition of vectors. By contrast, a nonlinear system may be said to exceed the sum of its describing equations. Does the concept of emergence say anything more than the concept of nonlinearity? It could be argued that emergence is merely some variety of nonlinear geometry, expressed in nonlinear equations, not more than its parts, just a nonlinear composite. If this is so, then complexity, emergence, and nonlinearity are virtually interchangeable ways of explaining much coming from little. Or complexity theory, if it has an independent existence beyond its constituent parts, is a system, a group of ideas forming a whole. Complexity theory could be construed as an emergent whole, and emergence itself an emergent property of this whole set of ideas that have become known as complexity theory. Like other parts of complexity theory, such as networks and nonlinear dynamics, emergence can appear to be part of complexity theory or a synonym for complexity; if we suspect that a system is complex, even before having analyzed it, then what we are calling the system must be some kind of

E:CO Vol. 9 Nos. 1-2 2007 pp. 93-106

whole. Whether we can explain the system as emergent is another question.

On the other hand, patterns emerge from parts everywhere. Humans are pattern perceivers. It is what we do. We do not see only scattered stars in the sky, we also see constellations. If seeing patterns in 1s and 0s of a random boolean network is evidence of emergence, what patterns are not emergent? This is one of the lessons from Thomas Kuhn's analysis of science in which observations from normal puzzle-solving science are slotted into the prevailing paradigm (Kuhn, 1962). Having decided that there is a pattern, then scientists play the game of finding evidence to support the pattern. Patterns within (emerging from?) complexity theory include not only emergence but also nonlinearity, networks, self-similarity, power laws, periodic avalanches, and so on. Likewise, this project of applying complexity theory to itself could be described as slotting patterns into patterns. Complexity theory promises that we can find comparatively simple rules, possibly reducible to individual equations, that explain the apparently improbable living organism or brain or other complexities in the universe. But the perception of patterns, including complexity theory itself, does not necessarily entail whole new entities emerging from their parts.

A concept linked to emergence and networks is that of a phase change, another notion borrowed from the physical sciences. The change from a liquid to a solid – that is, freezing – is one of the more common examples of phase change. To demonstrate phase change in relation to complex systems, Kauffman (1995: 54) uses the image of buttons connected by threads in a random graph. As the number of connections is increased, the connectedness of the graph does not increase linearly but instead suddenly becomes a clump of connected buttons, a composite, something other than the separate parts. Similarly, according to the theme of this paper, as networks of concepts become interlinked, does a phase change happen and complexity theory suddenly emerge? The networked parts of complexity theory are tightly coupled. Each concept leads to other concepts. There is no obvious beginning or end point.

This paper, for example, could equally have started with emergence or nonlinearity or networks. No single concept can be discussed without adding a see-also link to a related concept: complexity theory, see also chaos theory, see also catastrophe theory, see also general systems theory, see also cybernetics, see also nonlinear dynamics, see also emergence, and so on. Or starting with the geometry of complexity theory, see also fractal, see also self-similarity, see also recursion, and so on all the way around the network of ideas. With no obvious direction, and no linear progression from concept to concept, we get the composite of all threads bundled, or buttoned, into complexity theory, just as the theory itself suggests.

## Conclusion

The template may not be a perfect fit, but I have tried to show briefly how complexity theory can be applied to itself at a metaphorical level to generate ideas about complexity. For most of the discussion I have considered basic issues such as defining the parts of complexity theory. I have taken a middle ground between gushing and derisive accounts of complexity theory, preferring a skeptical but positive view of its potential. In doing so I have teased out various approaches, including proposals for modeling the evolution of complexity theory and treating computer modeling as a part of complexity theory, not just a medium of its expression. Because computers in my view are peers, not subordinates, in complexity theory, I have also advocated the release of computer source code as scientific literature supporting any models. In addition, I have made suggestions for moving from the metaphorical to the mathematical. Proposals for more rigorous application of complexity theory to complexity theory include exploring the mathematical relationships, such as power laws, within complexity theory; studying the fitness of ideas within complexity theory; using various proxies for measuring those ideas; studying the autocatalysis of ideas; estimating the fractal geometry; and developing general computer models of complexity theory.

## References

Allen, P. (2001). "*What is complexity science: Knowledge of the limits to knowledge*," Emergence, ISSN 1521-3250, 3(1): 24-42.

Bak, P. (1996). *How Nature Works: The Science of Self-Organized Criticality*, ISBN 9780387947914.

Bak, P., Tang C. and Wiesenfeld, K. (1987). "Self-organized criticality: An explanation of the 1/f noise," *Physical Review Letters*, ISSN 0031-9007, 59 (4): 382-384.

Bartlett, S. J. (1992). *Reflexivity: A Source-Book in Self-Reference*, ISBN 9780444890924.

Cilliers, P. (2001). "Boundaries, hierarchies and networks in complex systems," *International Journal of Innovation Management*, ISSN 1363-9196, 5(2): 135-147.

Cilliers, P. (2005). "Complexity, deconstruction and relativism," *Theory Culture and Society*, ISSN 0263-2764, 22(5): 255-267.

Clarke, A. C. (1962) "Hazards of prophecy: The failure of imagination," in A. C. Clarke, *Profiles of the Future: An Inquiry into the Limits of the Possible*, ISBN 9780060107925 (1973).

Emmeche, C. (1997). "Aspects of complexity in life and science," *Philosophica*, ISSN 0379-8402, 59: 41-68.

Flake, G. W. (1998). *The Computational Beauty of Nature: Computer Explorations of Fractals, Chaos, Complex Systems, and Adaptation*, ISBN 9780262062008.

Fry, I. (2000). *The Emergence of Life on Earth: A Historical and Scientific Overview*, ISBN 9781853434815.

Glass, L. and Mackey M. C. (1988). *From Clocks to Chaos*, ISBN 9780691084954.

Holland, J. H. (1998). *Emergence: From Chaos to Order*, ISBN 9780198504092.

Horgan, J. (1996). *The End of Science*, ISBN 9780349109268 (1998).

Israel, G. (2005). "The science of complexity: Epistemological problems and perspectives," *Science in Context*, ISSN 0269-8897, 18(3): 479-509.

Kauffman, S. (1993). *The Origins of Order: Self-Organization and Selection in Evolution*, ISBN 9780195058116.

Kauffman, S. (1995). *At Home in the Universe: The Search for the Laws of Self-Organization and Complexity*, ISBN 9780195111309.

Kuhn, T. S. (1962). *The Structure of Scientific Revolutions*, ISBN 9780226458083 (1996).

Lorenz, E. N. (1993). The Essence of Chaos, ISBN 9780295972701.

Luhmann, N. (1990). *Essays on Self-Reference*, ISBN 9780231063685 (1993).

Price, D. J. D. (1965). "Networks of scientific papers," *Science*, ISSN 0036-8075, 149(3683): 510-515.

Waldrop, M. M. (1992). *Complexity: The Emerging Science at the Edge of Order and Chaos*, ISBN 9780671767891.

**Robin Nunn** is a computer systems consultant, helping a wide variety of corporations, government agencies and educational institutions to understand and benefit from new technology. With research interests in self-aware and evolutionary systems and related technologies for managing complexity, Robin is also a scholar at the University of Toronto. Comments on this paper can be sent to complexity@arjana.com.

Philosophy

# Ecology is not rocket science

Dale R. Lockwood
Department of Mathematics, Colorado State University, US

Ecology is the foundation of the methods used in conservation, pest, rangeland, forest and fisheries management. A theme among many ecologists is the need to justify the science as a rigorous discipline. Coupled with this is the notion that physics represents an ideal model of a rigorous science. To that end recent discussions in the literature have placed emphasis on identifying Laws of ecology. In particular, Malthusian growth has been identified as a prime candidate for an ecological law, and much has been written favorably comparing the expression to Newton's laws of motion. Malthusian growth is shown here to be a poor example of a potential ecological law, largely due its numerous *ceteris paribus* conditions and lack of universality. In fact, as a simple linear model, Malthusian growth fails to adequately address the nonlinear complexities that make ecology such a rich and fascinating discipline. Ecological theory would do well to ignore comparisons to other sciences and focus on explaining the complex dynamics within ecology.

## Introduction

The management of systems exhibiting complexity is not more apparent or important than in natural ecosystems. With the world's fisheries in global decline, rangeland desertification spreading and the IUCN red list growing annually there is no doubt about the importance of understanding management with regards to environmental issues. Issues such as the spread of new diseases (think West Nile Virus, Chronic Wasting Disease, avian influenza, to name a few), invasive species, and multiple resistance bacteria it is clear that there is a substantial ecological component to problems facing the medicine, agriculture, city planning, recreation, public health and a myriad other organizations.

The management of natural systems, either through conservation, restoration, integrated pest management, fisheries regulations or other means is based scientifically on ecological results. Good management practices require some level of confidence that an action taking will result in a specific outcome. Causality in ecology has proven difficult and generalizations of results are even more challenging for the science. Ecology requires a firm philosophical foundation that will allow a framework of theoretical results to inform empirical studies which can be utilized by managers to implement policy decisions. Ultimately, understanding ecology is critical to organizing our societies for a sustainable future.

The sciences that are most directly associated with the notion of complexity are also those sciences in which the debate about laws governing them still holds sway (Fodor, 1989; McIntyre, 1998; Mikulecky, 2000; Carroll, 2003; Hausman, 2003; Lyman & O'Brien, 2004). Consider the role of laws in ecology. Although much attention has been given to this question recently, the most frequently suggested laws are plagued with problems that raise doubt about their validity. Ecologists frequently compare their science to physics, and particularly Newtonian mechanics which is often taken as an ideal formulation of science. Recently proposed ecological laws have been equated – or at least favorably compared – to Newton's Laws of Motion. Unfortunately, there appears to be much confusion about the nature and structure of Newton's Laws of Motion that casts doubt on the usefulness or validity of such comparisons. Such comparisons, even if invalid, do not obviate the proposed laws from lawhood, but further examination demonstrates that for one of the most common of the proposed ecological laws, there can be little support for it. Even if the suggested laws are not sufficiently law-like, there may be other suitable candidates, so a formulation of ecology in the mold of classical mechanics might be conceivable. However, before such a venture is seriously pursued a more important question remains: what is – or should be – the theoretical structure of ecology? As we shall see, laws, and in particular physical laws, carry with them a certain concept that the processes they describe are either simply expressions of the laws or additive assemblages of the laws. Ecological processes are strongly resistant to the development of additive functions that adequately describe such processes. Ecological processes are complex and as such aggregative laws are likely unsuitable as a theoretical foundation to underpin the science.

## The role of Law

The notion of a law of science is problematic (Armstrong, 1983; Cartwright, 1983; Van Fraassen, 1989; Carroll, 1990; Lange, 1993; Lewis, 1994; Giere,1999; Maturana, 2000; Murray, 2000) and with respect to ecological laws several approaches are used. A general working definition for such a law is a factual truth (as opposed to a logical truth) that is spatio-temporally universal, supports counterfactuals and has a high level of necessity (or resilience as per Cooper, 2003). This definition precludes simple patterns unless such patterns demonstrate a high level of necessity. Berryman (2003) argues for principles rather than laws in defining governing equations. Berryman's use of principle derives from general definitions of laws and principles and is quite different from a more scientifically oriented definition (Parker, 1989). Lawton (1999) divides laws into general and universal and argues that the idea of a general law is more appropriate for ecology. Lange (2005) discounts both Berryman and Lawton claiming that both give a definition of a law that is simply a general truth. Murray (2000) argues for the existence of universal ecological laws. In each case some aspect of ecology has been nominated as a law (Table 1). Ecology is a broad science and any likely law will be with respect to a narrow subdiscipline. I will restrict my further consideration of ecological laws to population dynamics. This subdiscipline provides an exemplary case, being one of the most highly quantified and seemingly physics-like aspects of ecology. Population ecology, is of course, importantly tied to organizational structures as it is coupled with economic theory for man-

agement of natural resources and is the foundation of understanding disease dynamics to which public health systems must respond.

The need for laws in a science is something that is not universally agreed upon (van Fraasen, 1989; Giere, 1999; Shrader-Frechette & McCoy, 1993), but a consistent theoretical framework for a science does appear to be necessary. Theoretical ecology is founded on the concept of the "model" which is taken here to be a mathematical, or more broadly, algorithmic construction that reproduces a quantitative (or qualitative) dynamic observed in nature. The model is, by necessity, a restricted image of reality. Models vary in their intended descriptions of nature, with some describing a process that has occurred or is only repeatable in a qualitative sense, while other models attempt to provide a predictive capability for systems that operate on scales too large to experimentally manipulate or for systems where experimental manipulations have the potential for irreversible change (e.g,. conservation of endangered species). It could be argued that models that are well supported for specific species or populations would be laws where the universality is defined over the population or species. Most ecologists would argue that universality at such a small scale is not very useful for ecology and would simply be defining away the issue that universality is difficult to observe in ecological theory. Thus many ecological models are ill suited for consideration as laws.

A theoretical framework provides coherence for the collected body of facts, models and relations among them. More broadly, the theory of a discipline is viewed as an overarching interpretation of a body of knowledge and is intimately linked to the principle of falsifiability. Although many argue against the need for a strict Popperian falsifiability in ecology or science in general (Murray, 2000), without a method for determining the validity of a theoretical construct, there appears to be little hope in determining which of two or more competing models is more correct. In the absence of a consistent theoretical framework ecology is a body of numerous models that are used to only describe particular systems

| Law | Specification | Source |
|---|---|---|
| First Law of Population Dynamics | A population with constant age-specific rates of survival and initial size of cohorts maintains a steady state. | Murray, 1979 |
| Second Law of Population Dynamics | In the absence of changes in age-specific birth and death rates, a population will eventually establish a stable age distribution | Murray, 1979 |
| First Law of Evolution | Genotypes and phenotypes with the greatest Malthusian parameter increase more rapidly than those with smaller Malthusian parameters. | Murray, 2000 |
| Second Law of Evolution | In the absence of changes in selection forces, a population will reach and remain in an evolutionary steady state. | Murray, 2000 |
| Third Law of Evolution | Selection favors those females that lay as few eggs or bear as few young as are consistent with re-placement because they have the highest probability of surviving to breed again, their young have the highest probability of surviving to breed, or both. | Murray, 2000 |
| First Law of Population Dynamics – Exponential Growth | A population will grow (or decline) exponentially as long as the environment experienced by all individuals in the population remains constant. | Turchin, 2001 |
| Second Principle – Self Limitation | There has to be some upper bound beyond which population density cannot increase. | Turchin, 2001 |
| Law of Consumer-Resource Oscillations | A pure resource-consumer system will inevitably exhibit unstable oscillations. | Turchin, 2001 |
| First Principle – Geometric Growth | All populations grow at a constant logarithmic rate unless affected by other forces in their environment. | Berryman, 2003 |
| Second Principle – Cooperation | There is a positive relationship between individual fitness and the numbers or density of conspecifics. | Berryman, 2003 |
| Third Principle – Competition | The per-capita growth rate of a population is limited directly by its own density via competition. | Berryman, 2003 |
| Fourth Principle – Interacting Species | When populations are involved in a negative feedback with other species or components of the environment, oscillating population dynamics occur. | Berryman, 2003 |
| Fifth Principle – Limiting Factors | Of all the biotic and abiotic factors that influence a population, one must be limiting. | Berryman, 2003 |
| Kleiber Allometry | Basal metabolism rate is proportional to a ¾ power of body weight | Colyvan & Ginzburg, 2003 |

**Table 1** *Proposed laws of ecology*

or kinds of systems. And ecologists have realized that as the models increase their generality, their applicability decreases via the loss of accuracy in predictions and increasing number of parameters necessary to extend the models. These models, in and of themselves, provide valuable insights, particularly with respect to our prediction and manipulation of the systems. But if each ecological system requires its own unique model, then theoretical ecology is nothing more than a form of quantitative natural history. While natural history is the backbone of ecology and fundamental to the science, this descriptive methodology does not yield broad theoretical constructs. As Watt (1971) points out, without theoretical underpinnings ecology will "all be washed out to sea in an immense tide of unrelated information." So, are there then no generalizations to be made about ecological processes? If so, it would seem that ecological theory becomes so much quantitative stamp collecting. Ironically, the notion of quantitative stamp collecting might apply to physics as it is composed of a collection of laws, theories and models that are not intimately or explicitly connected across scales and systems.

Ecology is fundamentally different from much of the physical sciences (Ulanowicz, 1999) in that it is both contingent (historically dominated) and mechanistic. Mikkelson (2003) describes ecology more broadly as caught in tension between the idiographic and the nomothetic. The interplay between the historical processes and mechanical processes are at the heart of the theory of ecology. The laws proposed for ecology are almost exclusively mechanistic in nature and ignore contingency and mathematical frameworks in which contingency can operate. Any attempt at a formulation of a law in ecology currently may best be restricted to a verbal rather than mathematical structure, owing to the diversity of mathematical formulations that describe the same overall dynamic with entirely different processes.

## Newtonian mechanics and Malthusian growth

The difference between physical and ecological processes becomes clear when considering the strenuous effort to compare Newtonian mechanics to population dynamics. Comparisons are often made between Newton's First Law of Motion and Malthusian growth with the intention of showing a favorable relationship between the conceptualizations of Malthus and Newton. In fact, there is little in the two conceptualizations to indicate any commonality. To get to the root of these comparisons and their shortcomings we must understand the laws being compared.

Consider Newton's First Law, which states that, an object's center of mass remains at rest or moves in a straight line (at a constant velocity, $\vec{v}$), unless acted upon by a net outside force. This can be expressed mathematically using Newton's Second Law of Motion as,

$$\vec{F} = m\frac{d\vec{v}}{dt}$$

The equation is made with a vector notation. This is important for our discussion of Newton's First Law because an object remains at rest or moving in a straight line when the net (sum of the vectors) forces are zero. The equation describes the First Law precisely when,

$$d\vec{v}/dt = 0,$$

which implies that an object will remain at constant velocity in the absence of a net force, whether that velocity is 0 or some vector quantity.

While the equation would imply that Newton's First Law is simply a special case of the Second Law, it is more than that. Newton's First Law defines the inertial frame of reference for which the other two laws are valid. This also will be an important distinction between Newton's and Malthus's expressions.

Newton's Laws of Motion describe an ideal system completely, acknowledging the provisos that the objects, velocities, and distances are not too big or too small (where too big or too small would require Relativity or Quantum Theory, respectively). The state of an object in this framework is composed of its location, velocity and acceleration. If I kick a soccer ball it will roll according to these rules. The force I apply to the ball is added to the force of friction as the ball travels across a surface and from these an estimate of the ball's trajectory can be derived. I can create arbitrarily more detailed models of the motion by including more details about the shape of the ball and texture of the surface, but increasing details such as these just means adding or refining vectors of force. Claims regarding the failure of Newton's First Law are based on two concepts; the first is the misperception that the law must operate in isolation and that in and of itself it does not predict the motion of objects. Rather it always functions in an aggregative manner with the other laws, again with the proviso that the object is not too big or too small and the velocities are not too fast. The forces acting on any body are elegantly additive, with the important feature that force is always expressed in the same units (or convertible to the same units). The second is that the law (coupled with the other laws of motion) do not account for all of the interactions between the ball and my foot and the surface it is rolling across. This is true enough but electromagnetic forces and the loss of heat energy really do not affect the general predictive quality of Newton's laws under the majority of instances when it is invoked. Reality is wildly complex, but in this case the laws give an approximation that is more than satisfactory. This, of course, is the distinction between scientific laws and natural laws at the heart of Cartwright's (1983) claim that all scientific laws are false.

Turning to Malthusian growth, the difference between ecology and physics becomes evident. Malthus's basic assumption is that each individual reproduces on average at a constant rate and given that level of reproduction a population will grow or decline exponentially. This implies that the environment remains constant – there is no effect of increasing density (hence space and spatial heterogeneity are absent), change in resources, interactions with other species, or changes in abiotic influences. That said, Malthusian growth can be expressed as,

$$N_t = N_0 e^t$$

Malthusian growth has been compared favorably to Newton's Law of Inertia based on several criteria. However, these criteria are insufficient to support the notion that exponential growth represents an ecological law. Consider the argument that both laws are not directly observable in real-life situations. The only time Malthusian growth might occur in a natural setting is with the introduction of new species to certain environments, but such growth is limited to a very few generations. In a mere 40 generations starting with two univoltine individuals the discrete form of Malthusian growth predicts more than one trillion individuals if the growth rate is 2. Malthusian growth predicts that at about 175 generations there would be more individuals than there are atoms in the earth. It is equally clear that not all introduced or invasive species demonstrate Malthusian growth or even an approximation of such growth. If we consider highly controlled environments, the closest we might come to such a system would be a chemostat, but the density of the organisms increases rapidly with the physical limitations of the chemostat volume placing a hard bound on population growth so that exponential growth occurs only for a very limited number of generations. The universality of Malthus's equation is directly limited by its formulation. The equation predicts all populations with an average growth rate greater than zero will increase unboundedly. A further argument against the use of Malthusian growth is presented by Elgin and Sober (2002) who argue that forward-directed dynamical laws do not provide covering-law causal explanations.

On the other hand, instances of Newton's First Law are observable in numerous forms. Note that all the objects resting on a desk are in fact at rest. This of course, is only one end of the law, but the law with constant non-zero velocity is easily achieved by any object falling to earth and reaching terminal velocity. Terminal velocity is exactly the situation when the net forces acting on the object are zero. The force of gravity is equal in magnitude to air resistance and each have opposite directions. Although there are clearly other forces working on the bodies, the overwhelmingly large effects of the forces of drag and gravity dominate the system and allow both description of the process and prediction of the process with sufficient accuracy. Here, one can argue that the gravitational force by itself is insufficient to explain the interaction of two or more masses under all conditions, as Cartwright (1980) does. A fundamental question then, is the discrepancy in the predicted movements of the masses unaccounted for or can it be explained by the addition of other laws, such as Coulomb's Law? If the net forces can be described by the additive effects of more than one law, then each law can be seen as valid under a simple proviso.

Often, ecologists' efforts to show that Newton's Law can be favorably compared to ecology are based on incomplete statements of the physical law. Berryman (2003) states that "all inanimate bodies move with uniform motion in a straight line unless affected by external forces" and Turchin contends that inertia describes the motion of a body in the absence of forces exerted on it. Colvan and Ginsberg (2003) state that Newton's Law describes a system where "there are no mechanical forces." None of these statements fully addresses Newton's First Law. Inertia does not only describe motion in the absence of external forces (which is likely an impossibility in our universe), but it describes motion when the net forces are zero within the given inertial frame of reference (which occurs relatively frequently in our universe). As such, these comparisons fail to account for the fundamental interaction between Newton's First Law (which define the frame of reference for the system) and other laws of physics. For example, a person bouncing a ball in the aisle of an airliner will see the ball fall in a straight line and bounce back up. The inertial frame of reference of the observer and the ball are within the aircraft traveling 500 mph. In rare cases, Malthusian growth might appear to provide a similar frame of reference but even then the framework is not aggregative or additive.

Malthusian growth is ontologically dissimilar from Newtonian mechanics, but this in and of itself does not disqualify it as a law. But now consider the conditions stated earlier for lawhood. A law must be factually true. The for-

mulation of the law by its very nature simply precludes this condition. Malthusian growth allows for any population to increase without bounds. Such a statement necessarily contradicts the physical law that no two objects can occupy the same space at the same time. Since any unbounded population of organisms must necessarily be bounded by that region of the earth's biosphere capable of supporting the species, unbounded growth in a finite space is impossible. It has been suggested that Malthusian growth may occur during some initial invasions but no data definitively shows exponential growth for more than a few generations. Likewise many invasive species do not exhibit such growth. Clearly Malthusian growth is not spatially and temporally universal. The failure of many species to recover from overexploitation indicates a failure to support counterfactuals. "In the absence of overharvesting, populations will increase exponentially" is the simple form of a counterfactual that is implied by the Malthusian growth formulation. Unfortunately, many species do not spring back. It might be argued that the population would spring back if given release from predation, disease, etc. and given no space or food restrictions and thus Malthusian growth would support the counterfactual. The problem is that for just about all species, we are unable to construct an experiment meeting the idealized conditions and thus cannot confirm the statement. Here, Malthusian growth might be a law but one so far removed from reality as to be useless. It might also be argued that the rate of growth is now unity for the population thus leveling the total population. Again, no natural population has ever been demonstrated to have a growth rate of 1. While an average value of one would result in a bounded time series, we would have little predictability for the next time step unless we understand the causes of the perturbations.

## Ecological mechanics?

When adding to ecological laws to develop a coherent system it is unclear where to turn next. Unlike Newtonian mechanics, the processes that operate on a population are not vectors, do not function in the same manner, and are not necessarily additive. Population dynamics operates on a scalar value and we have numerous models that differ from each other by fundamental processes. Any additions to the Malthusian growth replace the constant $r$ by a function and in most cases a nonlinear function.

Consider the proposed law of self limitation (Turchin, 2001). A host of functions have been suggested to describe the nature of negative density dependence (e.g., the logistic, Allee, Beverton-Holt, and Ricker, among many others). While self limitation appears to be a common process, the form of the process remains undetermined and there is as yet no evidence that a single function governs a substantial proportion of populations. Although each of the recent works proposing population laws refers to the notion of "forces" acting on populations, this appropriation of a Newtonian term lends an air of similarity without substance. Self limitation can take the form of cannibalism, physiological changes, strict competition for resources, or other processes including a host of indirect interactions. The point is that each of these processes functions in a different manner and the notion that each is a force, somehow equivalent at some fundamental level, only confounds the complexity by which populations operate.

In fact, in each of the basic population laws proposed, multiple functions can accomplish the stated process. In the case of the Berryman's (2003) Limiting Factors, that one biotic or abiotic factor regulates the population, it is unclear that this statement is necessarily complete as stated. For example, Lockwood and Lockwood (1989, 1991) demonstrate that population limitation may be associated with the combination of multiple abiotic factors and that while a single factor is sufficient to limit the population, limitation is achieved with the interplay of multiple factors prior to the limit imposed by any single factor. In fact, self organization can also explain a population dynamic in which no limiting factor can be ascribed and the population's current value is highly contingent upon its past spatial configuration (Adami, 1995; Lockwood & Lockwood, 1997). Other research on spatially explicit chaotic dynamics

indicates that long term transients can persist in a population resulting in highly unstable dynamics (Hastings, 1997). These transients are not revealed if the population is allowed to equilibrate after many generations.

One problem with assigning mechanistic functions as laws is the inherent duplicative nature of the mechanisms in ecology. Since more than one mechanism may describe a process, both counterfactuals and universality are called into question.

## Contingent and complex

The basic ecological models often appearing in ecology texts (e.g., single species dynamics, consumer-resource dynamics, competition and the like) are mechanistic and do not lend themselves to the notion of history. The consideration of contingency is important in ecology. Metapopulation ecology, invasion ecology and biodiversity are but three ecological disciplines that are greatly influenced by contingent factors. Evolution informs population dynamics as well as community dynamics and at its heart evolution relies on contingencies: genetic drift, mutation and environmental variability in time and space all significantly shape evolution, and in turn ecological dynamics. Much of physics is profoundly ahistorical, with the exceptions of cosmology and some of astronomy. For example, Newton's laws describe the motion of an object by its instantaneous position and forces, not by its past motions. In fact, physics strongly embraces the uniformity principle that all processes and properties are constant throughout space and time (excepting the short duration following the Big Bang). Ecology is rife with entirely new properties and processes – predators were not the first life forms and photosynthesis evolved millions of years after the origin of life. New species with novel capacities have occurred throughout the history of life, and will no doubt continue to form in the future.

How do we describe ecological processes? More than ever, *complex* is the term used to capture the fullness of ecological dynamics (Milne, 1998). Many now refer to populations and communities as complex adaptive systems (Levin, 1998, Bissonette & Storch, 2002; Sole, *et al.*, 2002; Grimm, *et al.*, 2005; Levin, 2005). Adaptive implies functional change to contingencies. If a population did not experience a changing environment, as with the idealized Malthusian population, then adaptation would be unnecessary.

Complex systems, particularly ecological systems are considered to have self-organizing dynamics (Pascual & Guichard, 2005). Generally the system is metastable and responses to external changes result in a reordering of the state to a new metastable state with scale invariance describing the overall dynamics. This is similar to the concept of autocatalysis in which the product of a reaction catalyzes the reaction which has also been put forth as an operational property of ecosystems (Ulanowicz, 2002). When combined with the radical contingencies of complex, ecological systems, such an approach would seem to have considerable promise for powerful models without bogging down in the terminology of laws.

Definitions of complexity are, like definitions of scientific laws, problematic (Chu, *et al.*, 2003). But consider the relationship given by Wimsatt (1997) describing system properties as aggregative or emergent. He defines emergent properties as non-aggregative and a property of a system is aggregative if it: 1) allows for the intersubstitution of parts, 2) maintains qualitative similarity with the addition or subtraction of parts, 3) is unchanged when the parts are reaggregated, and 4) exhibits no cooperative or inhibitory relations among the parts.

Wimsatt does not explicitly refer to complexity but the logical coupling of emergence and complexity seems to allow the use of this definition of emergent properties to be, at the least, a surrogate for complexity. Under this definition of complexity, there is no strict separation between the complex and the aggregate but a relative scale of complexity. Properties can be more complex compared to other properties, but no single property can be said to be strictly complex, although a property can be said to be purely aggregative.

Wimsatt points out that the archetypal cases of aggregativity are Newton's laws. And it is evident that population dynamics for a single, isolated, ideal Malthusian population is an aggregative property. But just as clearly, no actual population or any other proposed law for population ecology when combined with Malthusian dynamics fits the definition of aggregative (the fourth property – the absence of cooperation and inhibition among parts – is applicable only for idealized populations free of intraspecific behavioral responses). In fact, most populations and communities would not be considered to have any of the four conditions, except under rare and limited situations. Thus the complex nature of ecology removes from consideration the notion of physics-like aggregative laws.

## All other things being equal...

Scientific laws are not well or discretely defined, and perhaps a statement's law-likeness is a continuous property of our ability to model a natural phenomenon. A model becomes more law-like the fewer the *ceteris paribus* conditions it contains (*ceteris paribus* is the caveat of "all other things being equal" which is a standard assumption in the development of scientific laws meant to rule out an unspecified set of relevant – but less important – factors in the phenomenon of interest). Malthusian growth has so many *ceteris paribus* conditions that no natural population can ever be considered to obey the law for more than a few generations. While it is argued that all laws require associated *ceteris paribus* conditions, there is a clear distinction in the practical application of Newton's Laws and Malthusian growth or even Hardy-Weinberg equilibrium. The ceteris paribus conditions of Newton's Laws over the scale of universality are such that other forces can be considered negligible. For those physical systems where other forces such as electromagnetic forces are too large to be negligible, the laws are additive in effect. Malthusian growth to be applied for an arbitrary time interval (or more precisely, number of generations) requires the population to have unlimited space and resources. The population must not have any interactions with other populations that would result in nonlinearities in the dynamics. These conditions are so extreme ecologically that they can never be met.

The result is that the Malthusian Law has no real instances. Laws regarding complex processes should not be given a pass on the direct applicability of the law to the natural world.

## Complexity in ecology

Models from complexity science are applied to many population ecology problems. Catastrophe theory has been applied to plankton (Kemph, *et al.*, 1984; Greve, 1995), insects (Lockwood & Lockwood, 1989, 1991) forest dynamics (Frelich & Reich, 1999), fisheries (Jones & Walters, 1976) and livestock (Loehle, 1985) ; self organized criticality to insect outbreaks (Lockwood & Lockwood, 1997), bird populations (Milne, 1997) and rainforest community dynamics (Solé & Manrubia, 1995); and chaos has been applied to a wide range of systems including insects, marine fish, microorganisms and .

The discussion has been restricted to population ecology, but there are proposed laws of ecology that exist outside the level of population. Most notable are allometric relationships (West, *et al.*, 1997; West, *et al.*, 1999; Gillooly, *et al.*, 2001; Brown, *et al.*, 2004). Generally applied at the ecosystem scale, this work, labeled the Metabolic Theory of Ecology, indicates that universal fractal scaling of metabolic processes exists. While this work has spurred important advances in ecology, its broad application is not without criticism (Darveau, *et al.*, 2002; Cottingham & Zens, 2004; Clarke, 2004; Cyr & Walker, 2004; Marquet, *et al.*, 2004; Glazier, 2005; Makarieva, *et al.*, 2005; Nee, *et al.*, 2005; Niven & Scharlemann, 2005; Clarke, 2006) some of which has direct applicability to considering the overall results candidates for lawhood. In particular, the universality and necessity (from a philosophical perspective) are called into question. This is not to say that the results are not without tremendous merit, but rather it highlights the difficulties in finding laws in ecology.

## Conclusions

In the absence of a consistent, reliable definition of a law, the question regarding laws in ecology would appear to yield a relative answer at best. Ecological theory does not interact with empirical ecology in the same manner as is found in physics and it should be clear that ecologists should not attempt to ape the physical sciences in an effort to validate or ground their science.

The scales in ecology are such that empirical studies are all but impossible for many *in situ* populations and communities. For example, to determine the efficacy of marine protected areas as a means of fishery management requires empirical studies to extend to decades as the life spans of many of the species are extremely long, if they are known at all. As such, the theoretical models of marine reserves do not necessarily generate predictive hypotheses that can then be tested, but rather provide insight into the long-term dynamics. As such the models must be robust to a range of parameter variations and confidence is gained if qualitatively similar results are arrived at from different theoretical approaches. This methodology is far removed from the manner in which physics has developed. It also implies that the universality of many ecological models will remain unknown for a considerable period of time.

It is important to note that the only purely aggregative properties in the natural world are the conservation laws (mass, energy, momentum and net charge) in physics (Wimsatt, 1997). Vulgar reductionism (sensu Wimsatt, 1997) will never explain ecological processes in terms of these four laws alone. Understanding complex phenomena cannot occur without understanding the parts, the interactions of the parts comprising the system, and the history of the parts and the system. While ecology is complex, there is no reason to consider ecological systems as necessarily devoid of laws. However, the framework of an aggregative set of laws clearly is inappropriate, and a different concept of laws will be required if the desire remains to place ecology within such a framework. And it should be noted that there is yet to be a convincing argument that such a framework is the only or best approach to ecological science. Other approaches such as the one proposed by Ulanowicz (1999, 2002) suggest that substantial progress can be made while avoiding the issues surrounding laws.

The laws presented to date are largely dynamical in nature and take into consideration the processes that operate in the absence of historical context. In fact, much of ecological theory has been constructed around this underlying concept that the dynamics operate in a machine-like fashion and that variation is added on top of the mechanics as an extra error term. Physics is grounded by the ideal of Platonic forms. As examples, all electrons carry equal charge and variation in the speed of light is attributable only to measurement error. Ecology is generally absent such notions, as there is not an ideal population of wolves and no ideal desert in which variation is due to observational error alone, yet the theoretical constructs reduce the rich biological realism down to an atomistic individual approach. Elsasser (1981) addresses the notion of heterogeneous classes of objects in biology and suggests that "mathematical" laws are to be replaced by a more set-theoretical notion of organization. While addressing the metaphysics of biology, this approach does not appear to have generated an explicit solution to the question of laws in ecology. Of course, we are limited in expressing contingency in theory as either: we do not have enough detailed data to model the variation from all the possible sources, or we are faced with the pressing human need to provide a predictive statement for an unpredictable future. Some complexity models account for the historical nature of the process, namely chaos and self-organized criticality. Importantly, both demonstrate that we can place in context the overall dynamics but are not able to offer precise predictions based on the model. Uncertainly is inherent in the system, and such complexity (along with quantum probabilities) may apply to physical systems as well, further undermining the simplistic perception of physics that seems to captivate ecologists. Indeed, modern physics might be said to be maturing towards a more complex and contingent understanding of abiotic properties, forces, and entities as ecology is avidly pursuing an increasingly antiquated version of pre-20th century physics.

Some may argue that ecologists are aware of the contingency and non-reductive nature of ecology when compared to physics, but the direct comparison of proposed ecological laws to physical laws implies that that understanding does not fully translate into the philosophy of ecologists. Accepting the complexity of ecology and the weakness of models such as Malthusian growth and the logistic (see Hall (1988) for a critique of this construct) is belied by the fact that the standard population dynamics and ecology texts all use these equations as first principles for laying the ground work of ecological theory (MacArthur & Connell, 1966; Ehrlich & Roughgarden, 1987; Edelstein-Keshet, 1988; Murray, 1989; Gotelli, 1995; Hastings, 1996).

A practical distinction between the laws of physics and those proposed in ecology is the demonstrability of the physical laws. Ignoring the important philosophical considerations regarding the truth or validity of the laws, simply put, Newton's laws are robust, testable and are of practical necessity for a range of processes that can best be described as operating on a human scale. The proposed laws of ecology have limited empirical support at this point, with limited tests and only a limited practical necessity. As such, the use of these laws to draw conclusions for human systems, such as sustainable development, conservation and agriculture is fraught with risk.

At this point, the proposed laws of population ecology are insufficient to be considered highly law-like due either to their lack of universality or their abstractions (or overwhelming *ceteris paribus* conditions) that take them too far from real ecological systems to provide any useful information. Rather than nominating previously stated models for lawhood, ecological theorists should be attempting to mathematically describe the general empirical patterns that have been identified. In one important comparison to physics, the catholic need for "mechanistic" models in ecology should be tempered by the fact that much of physical law is predictive but not mechanical. The law of gravity describes what happens and predicts what happens – but does nothing to elucidate the mechanics of what is happening.

E:CO Vol. 9 Nos. 1-2 2007 pp. 107-119

## Acknowledgements

I thank Jeffrey Lockwood and Franz-Peter Griesmaier for useful comments and discussions. This work is partially supported by the National Science Foundation through grant DGE-0221595.

## References

Adami, C. (1995). "Self-organized criticality in living systems," *Physics Letters A*, ISSN 0375-9601, 203: 29-32.

Armstrong, D. (1983). *What is a Law of Nature?*, ISBN 9780521314817 (1985).

Berryman, A.A. (2003). "On principles, laws and theory in population ecology," *Oikos*, ISSN 0030-1299, 103: 695-701.

Bissonette, J. A. and Storch, I. (2002). "Fragmentation: Is the message clear?" *Conservation Ecology*, ISSN 1195-5449, 6.

Brown, J.H., Gillooly, J.F., Allen, A.P., Savage, V.M. and West, G.B. (2004). "Toward a metabolic theory of ecology," *Ecology*, ISSN 0012-9658, 85: 1771-1789.

Carroll, J. (1990). *Laws of Nature*, ISBN 9780521433341 (2003).

Carroll, J. W. (2003). "Laws of nature," E. N. Zalta (ed.), *The Stanford Encyclopedia of Philosophy*.

Cartwright, N. (1980). "Do the laws of physics state the facts?" *Pacific Philosophical Quarterly*, ISSN 0279-0750, 61: 75-84.

Cartwright, N. (1983). *How the Laws of Physics Lie*, ISBN 9780198247043 (2002).

Chu, D., Strand, R. and Fjelland, R. (2003). "Theories of complexity," *Complexity*, ISSN 1076-2787, 8: 19-30.

Clarke, A. (2004). "Is there a universal temperature dependence of metabolism? *Functional Ecology*, ISSN 0269-8463, 18: 252-256.

Clarke, A. (2006). "Temperature and the metabolic theory of ecology," *Functional Ecology*, ISSN 0269-8463, 20:405-412.

Colyvan, M., and Ginzburg, L.R. (2003). "Laws of nature and laws of ecology," *Oikos*, ISSN 0030-1299, 101: 649-653.

Cooper, G. J. (2003). *The Science of the Struggle for Existence: On the Foundations of Ecology,* ISBN 9780521804325.

Cottingham, K.L. and Zens, M.S. (2004). "Metabolic rate opens a grand vista on ecology," *Ecology*, ISSN 0012-9658, 85: 1805-1807.

Cyr, H. and Walker, S.C. (2004). "An illusion of mechanistic understanding," *Ecology*, ISSN 0012-9658, 85: 1802-1804.

Darveau, C.-A., Suarez, R.K., Andrews, R.D. and

Hochachka, P.W. (2002). "Allometric cascade as a unifying principle of body mass effects on metabolism," *Nature*, ISSN 0028-0836, 417: 166-170.

Edelstein-Keshet, L. (1988). *Mathematical Models in Biology*, ISBN 9780898715545 (2005).

Ehrlich, P.R. and Roughgarden, J. (1987). *The Science of Ecology*, ISBN 9780023317002.

Elgin, M. and Sober, E. (2002). "Cartwright on explanation and idealization," *Erkenntnis,* ISSN 1572-8420, 57: 441-50.

Elsasser, W.M. (1981). "A form of logic suited for biology," in R. Rosen (ed.), *Progress in Theoretical Biology*, Volume 6, ISBN 9780125431064, pp. 23-62. Reproduced in Richardson, K.A. and Goldstein, J.A. (eds.) (2007). *Classic Complexity: From the Abstract to the Concrete*, ISBN 9780979168833, pp. 60-107.

Fodor, J., (1989). "Making mind matter more," *Philosophical Topics*, ISSN 0276-2080, 17: 59-79.

Frelich, L.E. and Reich, P.B. (1999). "Neighborhood effects, disturbance severity, and community stability in forests," *Ecosystems*, ISSN 1432-9840, 2:151-166.

Giere, R. (1999). *Science Without Law*, ISBN 9780226292083.

Gillooly, J.F., Brown, J.H., West, G.B., Savage, V.M. and Charnov, E.L. (2001). "Effects of size and temperature on metabolic rate," *Science*, ISSN 0036-8075, 293: 2248-2251.

Glazier, D.S. (2005). "Beyond the '3/4-power law': Variation in the intra- and interspecific scaling of metabolic rate in animals," *Biological reviews of the Cambridge Philosophical Society*, ISSN 1464-7931, 80: 611-612.

Gotelli, N. J. (1995). *A Primer of Ecology*, ISBN 9780878932733 (2001).

Greve, W. (1995). "Mutual predation causes bifurcations in pelagic ecosystems: The simulation model PLITCH (PLanktonic switch), experimental tests, and theory," *ICES Journal of Marine Science*, ISSN 1054-3139, 52: 505-510.

Grimm, V., Revilla, E., Berger, U., Jeltsch, F., Mooij, W. M., Railsback, S. F., Thulke, H., Weiner, J., Wiegand, T. and DeAngelis, D. L. (2005). "Pattern-oriented modeling of agent-based complex systems: Lessons from Ecology," *Science*, ISSN 0036-8075, 310: 987-991.

Hall, C.A.S. (1988). "An assessment of several of the historically most influential theoretical models used in ecology and of the data provided in their support," *Ecological Modeling*, ISSN 0304-3800, 43: 5-31.

Hastings, A. (1996). *Population Biology: Concepts and Models*, ISBN 9780387948539.

Hastings, A. (1997). "Transients in spatial ecological models," in J. Bascompte and R. V. Solé (eds.), *Modeling Spatiotemporal Dynamics in Ecology*, ISBN 9783540634492, pp. 185-194.

Hausman, D.M. (2003). "Philosophy of economics," in E. N. Zalta, *The Stanford Encyclopedia of Philosophy*.

Jones, D.D. and Walters, C.J. (1976). "Catastrophe theory and fisheries regulation," *Journal of the Fisheries Research Board of Canada*, ISSN 0015-296X, 33: 2829-2833.

Kempf, J., Duckstein, L., Casti, J. (1984). "Relaxation oscillations and other non-michaelian behavior in a slow-fast phytoplankton growth model," *Ecological Modeling*, ISSN 0304-3800, 23: 67-90.

Lange, M. (1993). *Natural Laws in Scientific Practice*, ISBN 9780195131482 (2002).

Lange, M. (2005). "Ecological laws: What would they be and why would they matter?" *Oikos*, ISSN 0030-1299, 110(2): 394-403.

Lawton, J. H. (1999). "Are there general laws in ecology?" *Oikos*, ISSN 0030-1299, 84: 177-192.

Levin, S. A. (1998). "Ecosystems and the biosphere as complex adaptive systems," *Ecosystems*, ISSN 1435-0629, 1: 431-436.

Levin, S. A. (2005). "Self-organization and the emergence of complexity in ecological systems," *BioScience*, ISSN 0006-3568, 55: 1075-1079.

Lewis, D. (1994). "Humean supervenience debugged," *Mind*, ISSN 0026-4423, 103: 473-390.

Lockwood, D.R., and Lockwood, J.A. (1989). "Application of catastrophe theory to population dynamics of rangeland grasshoppers," in L.L. McDonald, B.F. Manly, J.A. Lockwood, and J. Logan (eds.), *Estimation and Analysis of Insect Populations*, ISBN 9780387969985, pp. 268-277.

Lockwood, D.R., and Lockwood, J.A. (1997). "Evidence of self organized criticality in insect populations," *Complexity*, ISSN 1076-2787, 2: 49-58.

Lockwood, J.A., and Lockwood, D.R. (1991). "Rangeland grasshopper (Orthoptera, Acrididae) population-dynamics: Insights from catastrophe-theory," *Environmental Entomology*, ISSN 0046-225X, 20: 970-980.

Loehle, C. (1985). "Optimal stocking for semi-desert range: a catastrophe theory model," *Ecological Modeling*, ISSN 0304-3800, 27: 285-297.

Lyman, R.L. and O'Brien, M. J. (2004). "Nomothetic science and idiographic history in twentieth-century Americanist anthropology," *Journal of the History of the Behavioral Sciences*, ISSN 0022-5061, 40(1): 77-96.

MacArthur, R. and Connell, J. (1966). *The Biology of Populations*, ISBN 9780471559740.

Makarieva, A.M., Gorshkov, V.G. and Li, B.-L. (2005). "Biochemical universality of living matter and its metabolic implications," *Functional Ecology*, ISSN 0269-8463, 19: 547-557.

Marquet, P.A., Labra, F.A. and Maurer, B.A. (2004). "Metabolic ecology: Linking individuals to ecosystems," *Ecology*, ISSN 0012-9658, 85: 1794-1796.

Maturana, H. R. (2000). "The nature of the laws of nature," *Systems Research and Behavioral Science*, ISSN 1092-7026, 17: 459-468.

McIntyre, L. (1998). "Complexity: A philosopher's reflections," *Complexity*, ISSN 1076-2787, 3(6):26-32.

Mikkelson, G.M. (2003). "Ecological kinds and ecological laws," *Philosophy of Science*, ISSN 0031-8248, 70:1390-1400.

Mikulecky, D.C. (2000). "Robert Rosen: The well posed question and its answer: Why are organisms different from machines?" *Systems Research and Behavioral Science*, ISSN 1092-7026, 17: 419-432.

Milne, B. T. (1998). "Motivation and benefits of complex systems approaches in ecology," *Ecosystems*, ISSN 1435-0629, 1: 449-456.

Milne, B.T. (1997). "Applications of fractal geometry in wildlife biology," in J.A. Bossonette (ed.), *Wildlife and Landscape Ecology: Effects of Pattern and Scale*, ISBN 9780387947891, pp. 32-69.

Murray Jr., B.G. (1979). *Population Dynamics: Alternative Models*, ISBN 9780125117500 (1980).

Murray Jr., B.G. (2000). "Universal laws and predictive theory in ecology and evolution," *Oikos*, ISSN 0030-1299, 89: 403-408.

Murray, J.D. (1989). *Mathematical Biology*, ISBN 9780387952239 (2005).

Nee, S., Colegrave, N., West, S.A., and Grafen, A. (2005). "The Illusion of invariant quantities in life histories," *Science*, ISSN 0036-8075, 309: 1236-1239.

Niven, J.E. and Scharlemann, J.P.W. (2005). "Do insect metabolic rates at rest and during flight scale with body mass?" *Biology Letters*, ISSN 1744-9561, 1 (Suppl.): 346-349.

Parker, S.P. (1989). *McGraw-Hill Dictionary of Scientific and Technical Terms*, 4th Edition, ISBN 9780070423138 (2002).

Pascual, M. and Guichard, F. (2005). "Criticality and disturbance in spatial ecological systems," *Trends in Ecology and Evolution*, ISSN 0169-5347, 20(2): 88-95.

Shrader-Frechette, K.S. and McCoy, E.D. (1993). *Method in Ecology*, ISBN 9780521446938 (2003).

Solé, R. V. and Manrubia, S. C. (1995). "Are rainforests self-organized in a critical state?" *Journal of Theoretical Biology*, ISSN 0022-5193, 173: 31-40.

Solé, R. V., Alonso, D. and McKane, A. (2002). "Self-organized instability in complex ecosystems," *Philosophical Transactions of the Royal Society B*, ISSN 0962-8436, 357: 667-681.

Turchin, P. (2001). "Does population ecology have general laws?" *Oikos*, ISSN 0030-1299, 94: 17-26.

Ulanowicz, R. E. (1999). "Life after Newton: An ecological metaphysic," BioSystems, ISSN 0303-2647, 50: 127-142.

Ulanowicz, R. E. (2002). "Ecology, a dialog between the quick and the dead," *Emergence*, ISSN 1521-3250, 4(1-2): 34-52.

Watt, K.E.F. (1971). "Dynamics of populations: A synthesis," in P.J. den Boer and G.R. Gradwell (eds.), *Dynamics of populations: Proceedings of the Advanced Study Institute on Dynamics of numbers in populations*, ISBN 9789022003558, pp. 568-580.

West, G.B., Brown, J.H. and Enquist, B.J. (1997). "A general model for the origin of allometric scaling laws in biology," Science, ISSN 0036-8075, 276: 122-126.

West, G.B., Brown, J.H. and Enquist, B.J. (1999). "A general model for the structure and allometry of plant vascular systems," Nature, ISSN 0028-0836, 400: 664-667.

Wimsatt, W.C. (1997). "Aggregativity: Reductive heuristics for finding emergence," *Philosophy of Science*, ISSN 0031-8248, 64(Proceedings): S372-S384.

**Dale R. Lockwood** is a postdoctoral fellow with the Program for Interdisciplinary Mathematics, Ecology and Statistics at Colorado State University working with the USDA National Center for Genetic Resources Preservation. His research interests include analysis of loss of genetic diversity in ex situ storage, strategies for sampling from populations to maximize diversity, the theory of marine protected areas and applying self-organized criticality and catastrophe theory to the population dynamics of rangeland grasshoppers. He is also chair of the Larimer County Environmental Advisory Board. Dale R. Lockwood received his B.S. (Computer Science and Mathematics) from New Mexico State University, a M.S. (Applied Mathematics) from the University of Arizona and a M.S. and Ph.D. (Population Biology) from the University of California, Davis.

Philosophy

# Emergence and computability

Fabio Boschetti & Randall Gray
CSIRO Marine and Atmospheric Research, AUS

This paper presents a discussion of the possible influence of incomputability and the incompleteness of mathematics as a source of apparent emergence in complex systems. The suggestion is made that the analysis of complex systems as a specific instance of a complex process may be subject to inaccessible 'emergence'. We discuss models of computation associated with transcending the limits of traditional Turing systems, and suggest that inquiry into complex systems in the light of the potential limitations of incomputability and incompleteness may be worthwhile.

## Introduction

We suggest that what we intuitively define as (strongly) emergent systems may include processes which are not computable in a classical sense. We ask how incomputable processes would appear to an observer and, via a thought experiment, show that they would display features normally defined as 'emergent'.

If this conjecture is correct, then two important corollaries follow: first, some emergent phenomena can neither be studied nor modelled via classical computer simulations and second, there may be classes of emergent phenomena which cannot be detected via standard physical measurements unless the process of measurement exhibits super-Turing properties in its own right. Borrowing from recent literature in computer science we then show that tools which enable us to break the classical computational barrier are already available and suggest some directions for a novel approach to the problem.

## Emergence

Implicit in most approaches to the study of emergence are 3 concepts:

1. *Multiple levels of representation*: there are classes of natural phenomena which, when observed at different levels or resolution, display behaviors which appear fundamentally different (Shazili, 2001; Crutchfield, 1994a, 1994b; Rabinowitz, 2005; Laughlin, 2005; Laughlin & Pines, 2000; Goldstein, 2002);

2. *Novelty*: for most complex systems, while we *expect* the properties of higher levels to causally arise from lower levels of representation, how this happens appears somehow inexplicable (Bickhard, 2000; Bedau, 1997; Darley, 1994; Rosen, 1985; Heylighen, 1991; Anderson, 1972);

3. *Inherent causality*: while we *expect* causality to arise solely from lower levels, for most complex systems the higher levels also appear to possess inherent and independent causal power (Bickhard, 2000; Campbell, 1974; see also Pattee, 1997; Goldstein, 2002; Rabinowitz, 2005; and Laughlin, 2005 for a discussion of the role of causation in complex systems).

The dilemma which has kept scientists and philosophers busy for decades is whether this novelty and inherent causality are real physical phenomena or merely lie in the eyes of the observer; said differently, whether reductionism is the only tool we need to understand Nature.

## The limits of mathematics

The most efficient language we possess to study Nature is Mathematics. This is used not only to describe processes but also, by using mathematical transformations rules, to deduce, extrapolate and manipulate novel processes. It is thus crucial to be sure that the mathematical machinery we use is consistent and correct. It is also important that it is as exhaustive as possible, since the more mathematical rules (theorems) we discover, the more options are available to us to interpret and manipulate Nature's workings. These needs motivated mathematicians at the end of the 19th century who dreamt of devising a set of axioms and transformation rules from which all other mathematical truths could be deduced as theorems. In Hilbert's dream, this would be achieved simply by mechanical manipulation of symbols devoid of external meaning (Chaitin, 1993, 1997: 1-5). Basically, Hilbert was seeking a consistent and complete formal system which would guarantee that all theorems of Mathematics could be proved. The dream was famously shattered by the work of Gödel (1931) who proved that no formal system in which we are able to do integer arithmetic can be both complete and consistent. For the sake of our discussion, Gödel's Incompleteness theorems can be summarized as follows (see Gensler (1984) for a simplified explanation of the theorem and its proof). In a formal logical system:

1. Given a set of axioms, and;
2. A set of transformation rules of sufficient complexity[1];
3. There exist statements which are either true but not provable, or false and provable. In the first case the system is incomplete, in the second it is inconsistent.

Here we focus on systems which are incomplete, that is, systems which can contain statements which are true, but not provable. Saying that a true statement, $T$, is not provable in system $S$ means that, by following the transformation rules of $S$, we cannot derive $T$ from the axioms of $S$. Importantly, Gödel's theorem applies to any mathematical system which incorporates basic number theory[2]. A related result was subsequently demonstrated and generalized by Turing (1931) (the famous Halting problem). Turing showed that there exist processes and numbers which are not computable, where 'computable' means that it can be calculated via a mechanical procedure

(an algorithm) given a certain input. Here, it is important to notice the relation between a formal system as described above and Turing machines. They both start from some initial conditions (axioms and input data), they both carry out a finite number of predetermined 'mechanical' operations (mathematical/logical rules and algorithmic instructions), they both produce results (theorems and outputs), and they both lead to inherently undecidable statements (unprovable statements which are true and incomputable numbers). This is reflected by a formal equivalence between computation and formal logic (as described in Penrose, 1994: 64-66). In the rest of the discussion we will use the words unprovable and incomputable interchangeably.

## The science of complex systems

There is quite a body of work which discusses the philosophical basis and nature of complex systems science. Seeking a deeper understanding of the science of complex systems, alternatives to the traditional scientific–reductionist approach are proposed and explored (Mitchell, 2004; McKenzie & James, 2004). Several papers have gone so far as to address the *complexity* of complex systems science. In these papers, the processes of modelling and studying complex systems are examined by either explicitly or implicitly treating these processes as complex systems in their own right (Medd, 2001; Price, 2004; Cooksey 2001). In many ways, this analysis of complex science parallels the (meta-)mathematical exploration of the foundations of mathematics and, as in meta-mathematical work, we must keep clear the distinction between the system being studied and the means of study. Clearly, advances along this line of inquiry have the potential to put complex systems approaches on a more robust footing, broaden the applicability of techniques, and conceivably make the analysis of such systems more straightforward.

There is a self-referential discourse in our attempts to understand how to "do" the science of complex systems which is maddeningly appealing. While using the structure and language of complex systems science (or something logically equivalent) is probably inescap-

1 In Gödel's original work, basic number theory (arithmetic) was used and the results can be extended to more complex axioms and rule sets.
2 For any arbitrary string, $t$ in $S$, which is unprovable in $S$, we can extend the system $S$ to some system in which $t$ is provable, but this new system will have its own set of unprovable string … and thus, it would seem, there is no escape!

able, it gives rise to a self-referential element which seems suspiciously analogous to the approach metamathematics takes with mathematics. This sort of approach opens the possibility that some Gödelization of the science of complex systems is lurking in the shadows even as we attempt to understand and classify these systems. Far from signalling a flaw in our reasoning, this may implicitly be one of the hallmarks of a complex system, and an indicator that we must be ready and willing to extend our systems.

Cilliers (2001), perhaps, comes closest to addressing the fundamental issue in his paper "Why We Cannot Know Complex Things Completely". He ties the process of *using* the science of complex systems to the fact that the construction of the meanings associated with the endeavour is itself a complex system. He then suggests that the systems we deal with operate within boundaries and limits and that since a system "can only make representation in terms of its own resources [...] it is difficult to see how any intervention in the dynamics of the system can take place." He goes on to discuss the notion of a limit to knowledge as a means of avoiding what seems an inescapable determinism in the "knowledge" in the system which must be constructed from within. This is precisely the goal of the mathematical constructionists in the late nineteenth century, and to them it seemed that a *true* statement must inescapably be derived from the axioms. If we take the position that the systems which we consider (either complex systems, or indeed the science of complex systems) possess at least the properties of simple number theory (as nearly every mathematical model will), then we have proof that there will be elements in the system which are true, but can never be reached while staying within the bounds of formal manipulation. It may seem a very tenuous connection to make between Gödel's theorem and philosophical statements about the nature of the science of complex systems, but recall that Gödel's ingenious proof rested on just such a bridge between the language of mathematical logic and numbers. The symmetry between the study of the basic structure of mathematics in the language of mathematics and the study of complex systems science in the language of complex systems is striking.

## When we say emergent, could we actually mean incomputable?

Here we carry out a thought experiment. Suppose we have a mathematical/ physical system which is consistent: we can assume that some physical relationships are robust enough that we may include them in our mathematical structure as axioms (that is we take them to be true[3]) and that these rules do not undermine the consistency of the system. Now suppose we imagine some physical process which we (magically) know to be incomputable within this system. Our purpose here is not to actually present such a process (or even to assert that such processes must exist), rather to tease out some of its consequences.

We form an extended mathematical system which takes the physical law as an axiom of the or fundamental mathematical/ physical system. There is an important point here: Gödel says that our system cannot be both complete and consistent - if our law is inconsistent with the underlying system, then we cannot necessarily make assertions about what must be present (apart from the obvious inconsistencies). For the sake of the thought experiment, we will suppose that we have chosen our physical law carefully and that it is consistent with the rest of the system.

We take this extended system to represent our 'physics', that is to say our scientific apparatus; as Gödel's theorems indicate, the system may exhibit physical laws which are true but not provable, that is, true, but not deducible from the basic 'physics' we employed. We cannot necessarily say that a given system will exhibit statements (laws) which are directly related to the new axiom or axioms, or even that it will exhibit physical manifestations of these statements but Gödel provides an avenue by which such properties may appear.

How would this system as a whole (in-

---

3 Clearly, the 'truth' values of a mathematical axiom and of experimentally defined physical laws are very different. Here we take the pragmatic view that this choice is the best available in our scientific enquiry and that it is indeed the way (physical) science is carried out. See also footnote 12, below.

E:CO Vol. 9 Nos. 1-2 2007 pp. 120-130

cluding its true but not provable physical laws) look to us?

1. We would recognise different *levels of representations*, one including the very basic axioms and others containing increasingly more complex statements resulting from the application of the transformation rules;

2. We would not be able to understand how some derived physical laws originate from the initial 'physics' (because they are not provable), and even less to predict their existence. These physical rules would look *novel* to us;

3. Since they are physical laws, these statements would carry apparent *causal power*; they would look causal to us, and since we cannot see how they originate from the basic 'physics', their causality would appear inherent and autonomous. In fact, this causality results from the basic 'physics' (which is indeed enough to determine all higher levels' features) but in ways we cannot unravel.

Basically, these physical laws would look 'emergent' to us, since they satisfy the characterizations commonly used in defining emergence. They would appear to transcend reduction because we are unable to comprehend their formal link to the basic axiomatic physical laws. However, this (like their causal power) is merely apparent. Their properties are inherent in the basic 'physics' we started from, but in ways which are not deducible/computable in our formal system.

The traditional way to address emergent processes is to study and describe the different levels separately and, most of the time, independently, by looking for laws which best describe the dynamics of the different levels in isolation. In this way, quantum mechanics describe sub-particle physics, chemistry describes molecular processes, Newton's mechanics describes macroscopic physics and so on to biology, ecology, sociology, geology, up to relativity theory and cosmology. We 'know'[4]

that these systems are nested in a Russian doll fashion, and we can describe each doll separately, but not their nesting. Along these lines, Shalizi (2001) and Rabinowitz (2005) propose information theoretic definitions of emergent levels of representation. These are, in our opinion and to our knowledge, the most developed approaches to this problem. Shalizi and Shalizi (2004) in particular gives a numerical recipe to find the most efficient level to study an emergent system based on a measure of system predictability and complexity. The most important limitation of these approaches is that they cannot discriminate between causality[5] and correlation. This would make little difference if we merely wanted to observe and describe a phenomenon, say in the fashion of natural historians of the 19th century. If we wish to manipulate or even engineer for emergence, then we need to better understand causal relations in order to exert control over it. The obvious question is whether we can describe how the emergent levels arise.

### Does incomputability exist in Nature?

Since Galileo claimed that the "language of Nature's book is mathematics"[6], it has been assumed that natural processes (physical laws) are computable[7]. More recently,

environment at different level of complexity and different levels of representation.

4 Crutchfield (1994a) gives a beautiful description of how agents discover structures and laws in their

5 In the information theoretical language used by Shalizi (2001), the word 'causal' is used frequently, but in the sense of automata in Shalizi and Shalizi (2004). Here we use it as Pattee (1997a) does in the sense that would allow an observer to intervene on the causal process and consequently exert control on its future behavior.

6 "Philosophy is written in this grand book, the universe, which stands continually open to our gaze. But the book cannot be understood unless one first learns to comprehend the language and read the characters in which it is written. It is written in the language of mathematics, and its characters are triangles, circles, and other geometric figures without which it is humanly impossible to understand a single word of it; without these one is wandering in a dark labyrinth" (Galileo, 1623).

7 It is often remarked that all known physical laws are computable. This statement carries an underlying tautology, since our current understanding and use of physics relies on and implies computability.

an increasing body of literature started to question this statement (Kauffman, 2000; Penrose, 1994; Calude, *et al.*, 1995; Cooper & Oddifreddi, 2003; Moore, 1990, 2000; Rosen, 2001). Here it is useful to discriminate among different kinds of incomputability. Fundamental limits to our ability to understand and model Nature arise from a number of sources which are well known to both the scientific and non-scientific community, among which we include sensitivity to initial conditions (which leads to chaos), inherent randomness of quantum processes, and measurement limitations due to Heisenberg's principle. Closely related to these is the incomputability discussed by Kauffman in Investigations, namely our inability to pre-state the initial conditions of certain problems[8]. As Penrose points out there is a fundamental difference between these kinds of incomputability and that derived from Gödel's theorem[9] (see also Moore, 1990). In the formal system scenario described above, there are no dynamics (not even a concept of time!), no missing information, no undetermined initial conditions, no inaccuracy in the description of the transformation rules. Does this sort of incomputability exist in Nature? Penrose, Calude *et al.* and Kellet suggest it does, but the issue is surely still open to debate[10]. Unfortunately, this question is often disregarded as irrelevant in applied science (Cooper & Oddi-

freddi, 2003), and we follow Aronson (2005) in the belief that more attention is deserved, since the potential for scientific breakthroughs could be enormous. In the following, we discuss some potential consequences on the conjecture we proposed above, namely that there may be emergence which arises from incomputability inherent in the system we are modelling.

## Some corollaries

It is interesting to discuss some consequences which would arise if our conjecture is correct:

1. *Reduction is Nature's only currency, but it is unable to fully explain Nature to us.* There are physical laws which are indeed merely the consequences of basic axioms, but these basic axioms are not sufficient for us to understand the laws themselves[11];

2. *There may be (emergent) behavior which cannot be studied via classical computer simulation,* since it is not accessible to classic computation tools; this contradicts a large portion of literature on emergence;

3. *Standard scientific experimental procedures may not be able to detect emergent processes.*

The first two statements are straightforward. The third one requires some clarification. The scientific method requires that experiments be reproducible. This implies that an experiment needs to follow a quite detailed and rigorous procedure in order to be replicated by different observers under inevitably slightly different experimental settings. Basically, an experiment is reduced to an algorithm (Stannett, 2003) and consequently scientific experimentation suffers the very same limitation of formal logic and computer systems, and thus is, by itself, unable to detect truly emergent processes unless it has access to super-Turing input. It seems that the very strength of the scientific method, that is,

---

8 Kauffman (2000) refers explicitly to the impossibility to define 'a priori' the state space of the biosphere and consequently our inability to compute its evolution. This is closely related to the fundamental incompressibility of the initial conditions on chaotic processes (p. 117) which results in apparent randomness when a finite precision is imposed upon it (see Crutchfield & Feldman, 2003, for a discussion of the effect on observations induced by sub-optimal modelling).

9 A very simple approximation of Penrose's argument might be "a chaotic system can be coded on a computer, so it must be computable". Despite the fact that the result of the computation will inevitably be imprecise, the statistics of the result will still represent a 'typical' possible outcome.

10 Interestingly, this is closely related to the similarly open debate on why Mathematics is so efficient at describing Nature and the philosophical dilemma of whether it is a 'natural' language we discover or an 'artificial' language we develop.

11 Notice the difference between this claim and the common two sides of the standard debate on reduction: a) reduction can explain all working of Nature and one day we will confirm this, and; b) reduction can not explain all workings of Nature and another concept is needed.

E:CO Vol. 9 Nos. 1-2 2007 pp. 120-130

its unique ability to define objective, reproducible and rigorous statements, by following precise measurement and logical procedures, backfires on its very purpose, by denying access to some members of the class of processes which we instinctively define as emergent. An important question which arises in this regard is "Under what conditions is our own involvement in an experiment sufficient to raise its *computational power* to a level which deals with this problem?". How much *does* it take to make our experiments super-Turing or super-Gödelian (Wiedermann & Leeuwen, 2002)?

## Breaking the computational barrier

There are models of computation which are not necessarily equivalent to Turing machines. The basic notion of how "powerful" a machine (or model of computation) might be is based on the size of the set of languages which can be accepted by the machine. Thus some systems may be beyond the representational ability of a particular model of computation, but not beyond that of another. These alternatives may make models of many systems more accessible, but they still cannot resolve the fundamental uncertainty raised by Gödel's Theorem: they still contain the basic number theory which gives rise to Gödel's result.

Graça and Costa (2003), explore the nature of general purpose analogue computers (GPACs) which are the continuous analogues to the Turing machine. They propose a continous-time GPAC which, while sacrificing some of the generality of Shannon's original machine in order to exclude undesirable configurations, maintains the significant properties of Shannon's original machine. The notion of an analog computer has a great deal of appeal since so much of what we model is inherently continuous in its nature. The basic conceptual components of a GPAC map quite readily into the usual toolbox of an analytic modeler. MacLennan (2004) takes the approach to its logical extent and derives a mathematical representation of a model of continuous computation on a state-space which is continuous in all its ordinates (including time). This paper presents a mathematical treatment of a model of computation which is quite different from traditional Turing machines and substantially different from the GPAC of Graça and Costa.

Fuzzy Turing machines (Wiedermann, 2000, 2004), for example, provide super-Turing computational power: machines can be constructed which accept a larger class of languages than a traditional Turing machine is capable of accepting. These less traditional approaches to computation may make accessible some of those emergent systems which are inaccessible to ordinary algorithmic computation. However, we are still left considering the possibility that there are complex systems which arise from Gödelian truths, and can only be studied by stepping outside the system.

Turing never claimed that his definition of computation encompasses all systems in which computation may occur. He imagined an abstract machine which, under restricted conditions, can access superior computational power (in the form on an 'Oracle') when faced with specific parts of computation it cannot perform. Surely, following Penrose's argument (Penrose, 1994), the very fact that Nature displays super-computational power (as he admits), while it highlights the limits of formal logic and classic computability, also in principle shows that processes to surpass those limits may be available, though it should be noted that these arguments may have more appeal by analogy than by robustness (Feferman, 1996). The obvious questions are what these processes might look like and whether we can employ them productively[12].

In Turing's (1931) seminal work, the computer he discussed was an abstract concept, not an actual physical machine. Similarly,

---

12 It is interesting to notice that Gödel believed in a strong analogy between mathematics and natural science. Mathematics should be studied similarly to how scientists study Nature and the choice of the fundamental mathematical axioms should be based not only on their intuitive appeal but also on the benefit they provided to the development of a theory (Chaitin, 2000: 89-94). Somehow similarly, Chaitin (1997) supports 'Experimental Mathematics' (pp. 22-26, 29, 30) according to which mathematicians should approach mathematics the same way physicists approach physics, via experimentation and statistical inference.

several authors have contemplated ideal abstract machines (hyper-machines) which could in principle break classic computational barriers (Ord, 2002; Aronson, 2005). As for today, none of these machines has been built, nor does it seem likely that any will be built anytime soon. More down-to-earth approaches, however, look more promising. In a series of papers (Verbaan, et al., 2004; Leeuwen & Wiedermann, 2003, 2001a, 2001b, 2000), van Leeuwen, Wiedermann and Verbaan show formally that agents interacting with their environment have computational capabilities comparable to Turing computers with 'advice', a milder form of Oracle. There are a number of reasons why interacting agents can cross the classic computational barrier: they run indefinitely (as long as the agent is alive), they continuously receive input from a (potentially infinite) environment and from other agents (unlike a classic machine for which the input is determined and fixed at the beginning of the calculations), they can use the local environment to store and retrieve data and can adapt to the environment. None of these features in isolation can provide super Turing computability, but, taken together, they confer a computability power superior to a classical machine. In particular, the agents' adaptivity to their environment means that the 'algorithm' within the agents (their program) can be updated constantly and, in Leeuwen and Wiedermann's paper of 2003, it is shown how super computability can arise from the very evolution of the agents. Also, the traditional distinction between data, memory and algorithm does not apply in an interactive machine with the result that the computational outcomes are more dynamic and less easily predicted (Milner, 1993). Finally, a number of conjectures have been proposed in the last decades over the possible super computational power of the human brain (Kellett, 2005; Penrose, 1989) and Gödel himself conjectured about this later in his life (Tieszen, 2006). Could a human interacting with a classic computer provide some sort of Oracle behavior? Could these systems, possessing super Turing computability, be used to model, if not understand, incomputable emergence? Could this be the way forward to understand emergence more generally? *Intriguingly, could systems like these potentially already sit on our desks?*

Today, human-computer interactions are standard in a large number of applications. These are usually seen as enhancing human capabilities by providing the fast computation resources available to electronic machines. Should we see the interaction in the opposite direction, as humans enhancing the computational capabilities of electronic machines? Leeuwen and Wiedermann (2000) speculate that personal computers, connected via the web to thousands of machines world wide, receiving inputs via various sensors and on-line instructions from users, are already beyond classic computers. Sensors now monitor many aspects of the environment routinely and are routinely installed on animals in the wilderness (Simonite, 2005). Can we envisage a network computing system, in which agents (computers) interact with the environment via analog sensors, receive data from living beings, and instructions from humans to deal with unexpected situations?

## Further considerations

The purpose of this discussion is *not* to propose a new definition of emergence nor a taxonomy of complex systems. Despite the fact that the subject we address is fairly theoretical, our aim is pragmatic. We are not interested in defining what emergence 'is'. Rather, we suggest a new direction of research to address a class of processes which may be normally labelled as emergent and which so far have evaded formal analysis. This is not the first time the concepts of emergence and incomputability are jointly discussed (Cooper & Oddifreddi, 2003; Penrose, 1994; Kauffman, 2000; Darley, 1994; Goldstein, 2002), but to our knowledge a clear relation and a possible direct approach has not been proposed. It is reasonable to ask why we should show any optimism or even a pragmatic interest in tackling a problem which is, by definition, logically and computationally intractable. Our first reason lies in the apparent ease with which incomputability arises. As discussed above, interaction with an unpredictable environment and adaptability seem to be enough to evolve super computability in simple agents with classic computational capabilities and this process seems to be further enhanced by agents' interaction and information exchange (Leeuwen & Wiedermann, 2003). Second, this seems to confirm the conjecture that the human brain does have super-Turing capabilities. Third, viewed within the perspective of Gödel's theorem, incomputability and computability seem to come together, in an inseparable fashion[13]. Designing a set of axioms of sufficient complexity and transformation rules carries incomputability as a natural consequence, that is, it *implies* incomputability. In other words, it seems impossible to conceive computation without incomputability. Finally, it has also been noticed (Bickhard, 2000; Laughlin, 2005; Atay & Josty, 2003) that emergent process are *robust*. Despite the fact that they depend on properties of lower levels, emergent processes are robust to small variations and errors at such levels[14]. This has led to the suggestion that ultimate causal power does not belong to causal laws, but to the organisation of matter (Laughlin, 2005) and processes (Bickhard, 2000). This robustness seems at odds with the 'other' kinds of incomputability which may be responsible for chaotic and unstable processes: namely incomplete descriptions of the system, and sensitivity to initial conditions. *If emergence is such a robust process, could it itself be harnessed as a means of furthering our computation?*

So, what does all of this mean for the study of emergence and complex systems in general? We happily pursue models of all sorts of systems, relatively comfortable with the knowledge that we are approximating a system. As long as we can control the size of the error in our approximations, we remain relatively content. This is the practical side of the analysis of complex systems. As participants

in a very large complex system we hope to be able to predict, or at least understand, our interactions with other component systems and as much of the aggregate system as we can. There is a very real survival value in being able to foresee the state of the system. However, in the way that the abstract consideration of non-Euclidian geometry opened the door to a number of different approaches in physics and improved our models of the way the universe may work, so the abstract, impractical side of complex systems science needs to address some basic problems to smooth the path of the practical models. It seems likely that there are systems which exhibit properties which we are unable to model well either because the properties they evince are mathematically inaccessible; the system is algorithmically impossible; or because we are unable to apprehend the true state of the system even though the dynamics of the system are understood. Systems which fall into the first category will remain difficult to model until our mathematics is capable of dealing with them: in this context, the ball is firmly in the metamathematician's court. The second category is a limitation based on our model of computation, and there are alternative models which may be helpful. Practically, it suggests that we should pursue alternatives to traditional digital computers and the traditional model of computation as an adjunct in our attempts to model and understand systems. The third category is almost certainly the largest. Strictly speaking, it isn't more "incomputable" or "inaccessible" to us than it is impossible to find the needle in a haystack. Practically, we are still looking for a strong enough magnet.

We conclude with a note about randomness, which further justifies the need for deep enquiry into these problems. Chaitin (1993) shows that incomputability also carries complete randomness. As before, this sort of randomness is not linked to incomplete information and, like formal incomputability, seems to have a more fundamental nature. Since we currently read Nature via a computable language (and experiment with a computable means), we are left to wonder how much of what we assume to be intrinsic randomness actually arises from the limitations of the lan-

---

13 As incomputable real numbers seem to arise naturally from computable ones via Cantor diagonalization arguments (see Chaitin, 1997: 9-11).

14 Small atomic imperfections do not change the rigidity of metal bar macroscopic state; the actions of a New Yorker only very rarely noticeably affects New York's everyday life; our cells are completely replaced every few days, without changing our personality, appearance and metabolism.

guage we use. Could an exploration of these meta-mathematical enquiries to the physical world have the potential to change the way we perceive several Natural processes?

## Acknowledgements

We would like to thank our reviewers whose comments contributed greatly to this work and directed us to many useful sources, particularly Torkel Franzen's book which we hope has steered us away from the worst of the logical mires, or as Franzen puts it (with respect to eating hotdogs anyway) "... [from] making a disgusting spectacle of ourselves" (Franzen 2005).

This research was carried out as a part of the CSIRO Emergence Interaction Task, http://www.per.marine.csiro.au/staff/Fabio.Boschetti/CSS emergence.htm

## References

Anderson P.B., Emmeche, C. Finnemann, N.O. and Christiansen, P.V. (eds.) (2000). *Downward Causation: Minds, Bodies and Matter*, ISBN 9788772888149.

Aronson, S. (2005). "NP-complete problems and physical reality," http://arxiv.org/abs/quant-ph/0502072.

Atay, F. and Josty, J. (2004). "On the emergence of complex systems on the basis of the coordination of complex behaviors of their elements," Working Paper 04-02-005, Santa Fe Institute, Santa Fe, http://www.santafe.edu/research/publications/wpabstract/200402005.

Bedau, M. (1998). "Weak Emergence," in J. Tomberlin (ed.), *Mind, Causation and World*, ISBN 9780631207931, pp. 375-399.

Bickhard, M.H. (2000). "Emergence," in P. B. Andersen, C. Emmeche, N. O. Finnemann and P. V. Christiansen (eds.), *Downward Causation: Minds, Bodies and Matter*, ISBN 9788772888149, pp. 322-348.

Boden, M. (1994). *Dimensions of Creativity*, ISBN 9780262023689.

Borwein, J. and Bailey, D. (2004). *Mathematics by Experiment: Plausible Reasoning in the 21st Century*, ISBN 9781568812113. Also Experimental Mathematics Website, http://www.experimentalmath.info.

Calude, C., Campbell, D.I., Svozil, K. and Stefanescu, D. (1995). "Strong determinism vs. computability," in W. Depauli-Schimanovich, E. Koehle and F. Stadler (eds.), *The Foundational Debate: Complexity and Constructivity in Mathematics and Physics*, ISBN 9780792337379, pp.115-131.

Campbell, D.T. (1974). "Downward causation in hierarchically organized biological systems," in F.J. Ayala and T. Dobzhansky (eds.), *Studies in the Philosophy of Biology*, ISBN 9780520026490, pp. 179-186.

Chaitin, G. (1993). "Randomness in arithmetic and the decline and fall of reductionism in pure mathematics," *Bulletin of the European Association for Theoretical Computer Science*, ISSN 0252-9742, 50: 314-328.

Chaitin, G. (1997). *The Limits of Mathematics: A Course on Information Theory and Limits of Formal Reasoning*, ISBN 9789813083592.

Chaitin, G. (2000). "A century of controversy over the foundations of mathematics," in C. Calude and G. Paun (eds.), Finite Versus Infinite: Contributions to an Eternal Dilemma, ISBN 9781852332518, pp. 75-100.

Cilliers, P. (2002). "Why we cannot know complex things completely," *Emergence*, ISSN 1521-3250, 4(1/2): 77-84.

Cooksey, R.W. (2001). "What is complexity science? A contextually grounded tapestry of systemic dynamism, paradigm, diversity, theoretical eclecticism and organizational learning," *Emergence*, ISSN 1521-3250, 3(1): 77-103.

Cooper, S.B. and Odifreddi, P. (2003). "Incomputability in nature," in S. B. Cooper and S. Goncharov (eds.), *Computability and Models: Perspectives East and West*, ISBN 9780306474002, pp.137-160.

Crutchfield, J. (1994b). "Is anything ever new? Considering emergence," in G. Cowan, D. Pines and D. Melzner (eds.), *Complexity: Metaphors, Models and Reality*, ISBN 9780738202327, pp. 479-497.

Crutchfield, J. and Feldman, D. (2003). "Regularities unseen, randomness observed: Levels of entropy convergence," *Chaos*, ISSN 1054-1500, 13(1) 25-54.

Crutchfield, J. P. (1994a). "The calculi of emergence: Computation, dynamics and induction," *Physica D*, ISSN 0167-2789, 75: 11-54.

Darley, V. (1994). "Emergent phenomena and complexity," in R. Brooks and P. Maes (eds.), *Artificial Life IV: Proceedings of the Fourth International Workshop on the Synthesis and Simulation of Living Systems*, ISBN 9780262521901, pp. 411-416.

Emmeche, C., Koppe, S. and Stjernfelt, F. (2000). "Levels, emergence and three versions of downward causation", in P. B. Andersen, C. Emmeche, N. O. Finnemann and P. V. Christiansen (eds.), *Downward Causation: Minds, Bodies and Matter*, ISBN 9788772888149, pp. 322-348.

Feferman, S. (1996). "Penrose's Gödelian argument," *PSYCHE: An Interdisciplinary Journal of Research on Consciousness*, ISSN 1039-723X, 2(7), http://psyche.cs.monash.edu.au/v2/psyche-2-07-feferman.html.

Franzen, T. (2005). *Gödel's Theorem: An Incomplete Guide to Its Use and Abuse*, ISBN 9781568812380.

Galilei, G. (1623) Il saggiatore (The Assayer) Accademia dei Lincei, Rome.

Gensler, H. J. (1984). *Gödel's theorem simplified*, ISBN 9780819138699.

Gödel, K. (1931). *On Formally Undecidable Propositions of Principia Mathematica and Related Systems*, ISBN 9780486669809 (1992).

Goldberg, D.E. (1989). *Genetic Algorithms in Search, Optimization, and Machine Learning*, ISBN 9780201157673.

Goldstein, J. (2002). "The singular nature of emergent levels: Suggestions for a theory of emergence," Nonlinear Dynamics, Psychology and Life Sciences, ISSN 1090-0578, 6(4): 293-309.

Graça, D.S. and Costa, J.F. (2003). "Analog computers and recursive functions over the reals," *Journal of Complexity*, ISSN 0885-064X, 19: 644-664.

Heylighen, F. (1991). "Modeling Emergence," *World Futures: Journal of General Evolution*, ISSN 0260-4027, 31: 89-104.

Holland, J. (1998). *Emergence: From Chaos to Order*, ISBN 9780738201429 (1999).

JPL-NASA (2006). Mars Rover Website, http://marsrovers.jpl.nasa.gov/home/index.html.

Kauffman, S. (2000). *Investigations*, ISBN 9780195121056.

Kellet, O. (2005). *A Multifaceted Attack On the Busy Beaver Problem*, Masters Thesis, Rensselaer Polytechnic Institute, Troy, New York, http://www.cs.rpi.edu/~kelleo/busybeaver/downloads/OwenThesis.pdf.

Laughlin, R. (2005). *A Different Universe: Reinventing Physics from the Bottom Down*, ISBN 9780465038282.

Laughlin, R. and Pines, D. (2000). "The theory of everything," *Proc of the National Academy of Science*, ISSN 0027-8424, 97(1): 28-31.

Leeuwen, J. van and Wiedermann, J. (2000). "The Turing machine paradigm in contemporary computing," in B. Engquist and W. Schmid (eds.), *Mathematics Unlimited - 2001 and Beyond*, ISBN 9783540670995, pp. 1139-1156.

Leeuwen, J. van and Wiedermann, J. (2001a). "A computational model of interaction in embedded systems," Technical Report UU-CS-2001-02, Institute of Information and Computing Sciences, Utrecht University.

Leeuwen, J. van and Wiedermann, J. (2001b). "Beyond the Turing limit: Evolving interactive systems," in L. Pacholski and P. Ruzicka (eds.), *SOFSEM 2001 - Theory and Practice of Informatics*, ISBN 9783540429128, pp. 90-109.

Leeuwen, J. van and Wiedermann, J. (2003). "The emergent computational potential of evolving artificial living systems," *AI Communications*, ISSN 0921-7126, 15: 205-215.

MacLennan, B. (2004). "Natural computation and non-Turing models of computation," *Theoretical Computer Science*, ISSN 0304-3975, 317: 115-145.

Maddy, P. (1997). *Naturalism in Mathematics*, ISBN 9780198235736 (2002).

McKenzie, C. and James, K. (2004). "Aesthetics as an aid to understanding complex systems and decision judgment in operating complex systems," *Emergence: Complexity & Organization*, ISSN 1521-3250, 6(1-2): 32-39.

Medd, W. (2001). "What is complexity science? Toward an 'ecology of ignorance'," *Emergence: Complexity & Organization*, ISSN 1521-3250, 3(1): 43-60.

Milner, R. (1993). "Elements of Interaction: Turing Award Lecture," *Communications of the ACM*, ISSN 0001-0782, 36(1): 78-90.

Mitchell, S. (2004). "Why integrative pluralism?" *Emergence: Complexity & Organization*, ISSN 1521-3250, 6(1,2): 81-91.

Moore, C. (1990). "Unpredictability and undecidability in dynamical systems," *Physical Review Letters*, ISSN 0031-9007, 64, 2354

Ord, T. (2002). "Hypercomputation: Computing more than the Turing machine," http://arxiv.org/pdf/math.LO/0209332.

Pattee, H. (1995). "Evolving self-reference: Matter, symbols and semantic closure," *Communications in Cognition-Artificial Intelligence*, ISSN 0773-4182, 12: 9-27.

Pattee, H.H. (1997a). "Causation, control and the evolution of complexity" in P. B. Andersen, C. Emmeche, N. O. Finnemann and P. V. Christiansen (eds.), *Downward Causation: Minds, Bodies and Matter*, ISBN 9788772888149, pp. 322-348.

Pattee, H.H. (1997b). "The physics of symbols and the evolution of semiotic control," *Proceedings of the Workshop on Control Mechanisms for Complex Systems: Issues of Measurement and Semiotic Analysis*, Las Cruces, New Mexico, Dec. 8-12, 1996.

Penrose, R. (1989). *The Emperor's New Mind: Concerning Computers, Minds and the Laws of Physics*, ISBN 9780192861986 (2002).

Penrose, R. (1994). *Shadows of the Mind: A Search*

*for the Missing Science of Consciousness*, ISBN 9780195106466 (1996).

Price, I. (2004). "Complexity, complicatedness and complexity: A new science behind organizational intervention?" *Emergence: Complexity & Organization*, ISSN 1521-3250, 6(1,2): 40-48.

Rabinowitz, N. (2005). *Emergence: An Algorithmic Formulation*, Honours Thesis, University of Western Australia, Perth.

Rosen, R. (1985). "Organisms as causal systems which are not mechanisms: An essay into the nature of complexity," in R. Rosen (ed.), *Theoretical Biology and Complexity: Three Essays on the Natural Philosophy of Complex Systems*, ISBN 9780125972802, pp. 165-203.

Rosen, R. (2000). *Essays on Life Itself*, ISBN 9780231105118.

Rosen, R. (2001). *Life Itself: A Comprehensive Inquiry into the Nature, Origin and Fabrication of Life*, ISBN 9780231075657 (2005).

Shalizi, C. (2001). *Causal Architecture, Complexity and Self-Organization in Time Series and Cellular Automata*, PhD Thesis, http://www.cscs.umich.edu/~crshalizi/thesis/.

Shalizi, C.R. and Shalizi, K.L. (2004). "Blind construction of optimal nonlinear recursive predictors for discrete sequences," in M. Chickering and J. Halpern (eds.), *Uncertainty in Artificial Intelligence: Proceedings of the Twentieth Conference*, ISBN 9780974903903, pp. 504-511.

Simonite, T. (2005). "Seals net data from cold seas," *Nature*, ISSN 0028-0836, 438: 402-403.

Stannett, M. (2003). "Computation and hypercomputation," *Minds and Machines*, ISSN 0924-6495, 13(1): 115-153.

Tieszen, R. (2006). "After Gödel: Mechanism, Reason and Realism in the Philosophy of Mathematics," *Philosophia Mathematic*, ISSN 0031-8019, 14(2): 229-254.

Turing, MA (1936). "On Computable Numbers, with an Application to the Entscheidungsproblem," *Proceedings of the London Mathematical Society*, ISSN 0024-6115, s2-42: 230-265.

Verbaan, P.R.A., van Leeuwen, J. and Wiedermann, J. (2004). "Lineages of automata: A model for evolving interactive systems," in J. Karhumäki, H. Maurer, G. Paun and G. Rozenberg (eds.), *Theory is Forever*, ISBN 9783540223931, pp. 268-281.

Wiedermann J. and van Leeuwen, J. (2002). "The emergent computational potential of evolving artificial living systems," *AI Communications*, ISSN 0921-7126, 15(4): 205-215.

Wiedermann, J. (2000). "Fuzzy computations are more powerful than crisp ones," Technical Report V-828, Institute of Computer Science, Academy of Sciences of the Czech Republic.

Wiedermann, J. (2004). "Characterizing super-Turing computing power and efficiency of classical fuzzy Turing machines," *Electronic Notes in Theoretical Computer Science*, ISSN 1571-0661, 317: 61-69.

**Fabio Boschetti** describes himself as an applied mathematician. For many years his work focused on geo-scientific applications. More recently he started to be interested in Complex System Science and to apply his past experience to ecological modelling with a view to improve our understanding of how ecosystems and their interaction with human activities can be best modelled. He has an extensive list of publications in geosciences, and the application of genetic algorithms to inversion problems.

**Randall Gray** is a modeler with the CSIRO Division of Marine and Atmospheric Research. He has been designing and implementing agent-based models of human - ecosystem interactions since 1992, and has been focussing on the integration of analytical and agent-/ individual-based models for the last fifteen years. His research interests are in the generalization of agent-based modelling as a means of integrating traditional modelling techniques and agent- or individual-based approaches.

Classical

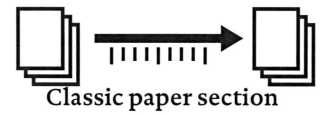

# Classic paper section

# The pretence of knowledge

Friedrich A. von Hayek (with an introduction by Rodrigo Zeidan, UNIGRANRIO, Rio de Janeiro, BRA)

Originally published in Hayek, F. A. (1975). "The pretence of knowledge," *Swedish Journal of Economics*, ISBN 0039-7318, 77(4): 433-442. Reproduced by kind permission.

Hayek was a rare breed of economist, a kind that has become extinct in the specialized, publish-or-perish world of academia. He was a political economist whose job was to develop new ideas and foster advanced thinking in social sciences. He was one of the most important economists of the 20th century, alongside Keynes, Schumpeter, and Friedman. His kind was responsible for some of the most important economic transformations of the last century, their ideas novel, their political influence far-reaching. And more importantly, none of the above contain any overstatement to Hayek's place in the economics history of the 20th century.

As every important influential figure, Hayek is immersed in controversy, since his ideological bias comes as opposed to socialism, with a stalwart defensive support of free-market capitalism. This is best illustrated in his work *The Road of Serfdom* (1944) - the historical debate is summarized in Caldwell (1997), and the work revisited in Vol. 21, issue 4 of the *European Journal of Political Economy* (2005). Hayek's book *New Studies in Philosophy, Politics, Economics and the History of Ideas* (1978) is the best example of the scope of his work, an economist that dwelt in philosophy, psychology, jurisprudence, and who expressed his ideas freely and unabashedly.

His lecture on the Pretence of Knowledge is the culmination of many methodological issues raised in earlier work and a preoccupation with the epistemology of social sciences vis-á-vis hard science. This preoccupation is part of an historical debate that is modern in the sense that Hayek's position, in a pragmatic and simplistic way, lost, and the academic economic world that prevails is the opposite of what Hayek surmises as the correct way to do science. On methodology Hayek's work dialogues with the likes of Popper and Lakatos in philosophy, and Friedman and Arrow in economics. There are many sources for Hayek's debates on methodology, (Caldwell, 2004 and White, 1984 are among the best) but in the grand tradition of Nietzsche's *Ecce Homo*, the best one is Hayek's own words in his *Autobiographical Dialogue* (1994).

In the Pretence of Knowledge, Hayek makes indirect references to his theory of complex events. It is important to give a brief review of Hayek's theory of complex events insofar as it is directly related and serves as a background to the issues raised in the lecture.

Hayek's theory of complex events is not a complexity theory *per se*, even if he names it so, since Hayek is writing in an era when complexity was not a formed body. It was a way to criticize most economic simplistic models, and firmly ground social sciences methodology. His argument evolved through time, with a direct line beginning in 'Scientism and the Study of Society (1942)', passing through 'Degrees of Explanation (1955)', and finishing with the appex in "The Theory of Complex Phenomena" (1964). His first argument, a naive one, is that problems arise in social sciences because social phenomena presents too many explanatory variables: "The number of separate variables which in any particular social phenomenon will determinate the result of a given change will as a rule be far too large for any human mind to master and manipulate them effectively" (Hayek, 1942: 290). In this case social sciences are not complex, but complicated. Dealing with a multitude of variables is, in the age information technology, a simple task and Hayek's first argument loses its power to it. However, the argument evolves over time, and is transformed into the more powerful version present in his later works.

The later argument is more well-rounded and approaches the current concept of complexity. Hayek defines complexity as "the minimum number of elements of which an instance of the pattern must consist in order to exhibit all the characteristic attributes of the class of patterns in question" (Hayek, 1964). It also acknowledges the importance of interconnectivity in building this complexity. In this sense Hayek's definition of complexity is very close to that of Herbert Simon in The Architecture of Complexity" - 1962, published in the Proceedings of American Philosophical Association.

The complexity concept that Hayek develops is to build his methodological arguments. Alongside it Hayek analyzes the shortcomings of statistics as a way to analyze social systems. Armed with it, he proceeds to deconstruct social sciences methodology to argue for practical limitations on theoretical reductionism.

Paradoxically, when arguing that economics scientific rigour is unscientific, since the economists' tools are unsuitable for the job of analyzing complex phenomena, Hayek strives for more rigour, for theories that would acknowledge its limitations: "But if it is true that in subjects of great complexity we must rely to a large extent on such mere explanations of the principle, we must not overlook some disadvantages connected with this technique. Because such theories are difficult to disprove, the elimination of inferior rival theories will be a slow affair, bound up closely with the argumentative skill and persuasiveness of those who employ them. There will be opportunities for grave abuses: possibilities for pretentious, over-elaborate theories which no simple test but only the good sense of those equally com-

petent in the field can refute. There will be no safeguards even against sheer quackery... It is not because of a failure to follow better counsel, but because of the refractory nature of certain subjects that these difficulties arise. There is no basis for the contention that they are due to the immaturity of the sciences concerned. It would be a complete misunderstanding... to think that [it is a] provisional and transitory state of the progress of those sciences which they are bound to overcome sooner or later." (Hayek, 1955)

As observed before, The Pretence of Knowledge is the culmination of his earlier works in epistemology and the methodology of social sciences. It should be read as an important historical piece that deals with the most profound epistemological implications of recognizing complexity as part of social systems. That this discussion was presented in the beginning of our understanding of complex phenomena should be testament to the intellectual prowess of Friedrich August Von Hayek, one of the sharpest minds of the 20th century. He recognized the relevance of complexity and was able to translate it into the powerful discourse presented in The Pretence of Knowledge. And for that, read on.

**References.**

Caldwell, B. (1997). "Hayek and Socialism," *Journal of Economic Literature*, ISSN 0022-0515, 35(4): 1856-1890.

Caldwell, B. (2004). *Hayek's Challenge: An Intellectual Biography of F. A. Hayek*, ISBN 9780226091914 (2003).

Hayek, F. A. (1942). "Scientism and the study of society," *Economica*, ISSN 0013-0427, 9(35): 267-291.

Hayek, F. A. (1955). "Degrees of explanation," *The British Journal for the Philosophy of Science*, ISSN 0007-0882, 6(23): 209-225.

Hayek, F. A. (1964). "The theory of complex phenomena," in M. Bunge (ed.), *The Critical Approach to Science and Philosophy*, ISBN 9780029049204.

Hayek, F. A. (1994). *Hayek on Hayek: An Autobiographical Dialogue*, edited by S. Kresge and L. Wenar, ISBN 9780226320625.

White, L. H. (1984). *Methodology of the Austrian School Economists*, Auburn, Ala.: Ludwig von Mises Institute.

# THE PRETENCE OF KNOWLEDGE*

*Friedrich August von Hayek*

Salzburg, Austria

The particular occasion of this lecture, combined with the chief practical problem which economists have to face today, have made the choice of its topic almost inevitable. On the one hand the still recent establishment of the Nobel Memorial Prize in Economic Science marks a significant step in the process by which, in the opinion of the general public, economics has been conceded some of the dignity and prestige of the physical sciences. On the other hand, the economists are at this moment called upon to say how to extricate the free world from the serious threat of accelerating inflation which, it must be admitted, has been brought about by policies which the majority of economists recommended and even urged governments to pursue. We have indeed at the moment little cause for pride: as a profession we have made a mess of things.

It seems to me that this failure of the economists to guide policy more successfully is closely connected with their propensity to imitate as closely as possible the procedures of the brilliantly successful physical sciences—an attempt which in our field may lead to outright error. It is an approach which has come to be described as the "scientistic" attitude—an attitude which, as I defined it some thirty years ago, "is decidedly unscientific in the true sense of the word, since it involves a mechanical and uncritical application of habits of thought to fields different from those in which they have been formed".[1] I want today to begin by explaining how some of the gravest errors of recent economic policy are a direct consequence of this scientistic error.

The theory which has been guiding monetary and financial policy during the last thirty years, and which I contend is largely the product of such a mistaken conception of the proper scientific procedure, consists in the assertion that there exists a simple positive correlation between total employment and the size of the aggregate demand for goods and services; it leads to the belief that we can permanently assure full employment by maintaining total money expenditure at an appropriate level. Among the various theories advanced to account for extensive unemployment, this is probably the only one in support of

---

* Nobel Memorial Lecture held December 11, 1974. © The Nobel Foundation, 1975.
[1] "Scientism and the Study of Society", *Economica*, vol. IX, no. 35, August 1942, reprinted in *The Counter-Revolution of Science*, Glencoe, Ill., 1952, p. 15 of this reprint.

which strong quantitative evidence can be adduced. I nevertheless regard it as fundamentally false, and to act upon it, as we now experience, as very harmful.

This brings me to the crucial issue. Unlike the position that exists in the physical sciences, in economics and other disciplines that deal with essentially complex phenomena, the aspects of the events to be accounted for about which we can get quantitative data are necessarily limited and may not include the important ones. While in the physical sciences it is generally assumed, probably with good reason, that any important factor which determines the observed events will itself be directly observable and measurable, in the study of such complex phenomena as the market, which depend on the actions of many individuals, all the circumstances which will determine the outcome of a process, for reasons which I shall explain later, will hardly ever be fully known or measurable. And while in the physical sciences the investigator will be able to measure what, on the basis of a *prima facie* theory, he thinks important, in the social sciences often that is treated as important which happens to be accessible to measurement. This is sometimes carried to the point where it is demanded that our theories must be formulated in such terms that they refer only to measurable magnitudes.

It can hardly be denied that such a demand quite arbitrarily limits the facts which are to be admitted as possible causes of the events which occur in the real world. This view, which is often quite naively accepted as required by scientific procedure, has some rather paradoxical consequences. We know, of course, with regard to the market and similar social structures, a great many facts which we cannot measure and on which indeed we have only some very imprecise and general information. And because the effects of these facts in any particular instance cannot be confirmed by quantitative evidence, they are simply disregarded by those sworn to admit only what they regard as scientific evidence: they thereupon happily proceed on the fiction that the factors which they can measure are the only ones that are relevant.

The correlation between aggregate demand and total employment, for instance, may only be approximate, but as it is the *only* one on which we have quantitative data, it is accepted as the only causal connection that counts. On this standard there may thus well exist better "scientific" evidence for a false theory, which will be accepted because it is more "scientific", than for a valid explanation, which is rejected because there is no sufficient quantitative evidence for it.

Let me illustrate this by a brief sketch of what I regard as the chief actual cause of extensive unemployment—an account which will also explain why such unemployment cannot be lastingly cured by the inflationary policies recommended by the now fashionable theory. This correct explanation appears to me to be the existence of discrepancies between the distribution of demand among the different goods and services and the allocation of labour and other resources among the production of those outputs. We possess a fairly good "qualitative" knowledge of the forces by which a correspondence between demand and supply in the different sectors of the economic system is brought about, of the conditions under which it will be achieved, and of the factors likely to prevent such an adjustment. The separate steps in the account of this process rely on facts of everyday experience, and few who take the trouble to follow the argument will question the validity of the factual assumptions, or the logical correctness of the conclusions drawn from them. We have indeed good reason to believe that unemployment indicates that the structure of relative prices and wages has been distorted (usually by monopolistic or governmental price fixing), and that to restore equality between the demand and the supply of labour in all sectors changes of relative prices and some transfers of labour will be necessary.

But when we are asked for quantitative evidence for the particular structure of prices and wages that would be required in order to assure a smooth continuous sale of the products and services offered, we must admit that we have no such information. We know, in other words, the general conditions in which what we call, somewhat misleadingly, an equilibrium will establish itself: but we never know what the particular prices or wages are which would exist if the market were to bring about such an equilibrium. We can merely say what the conditions are in which we can expect the market to establish prices and wages at which demand will equal supply. But we can never produce statistical information which would show how much the prevailing prices and wages *deviate* from those which would secure a continuous sale of the current supply of labour. Though this account of the causes of unemployment is an empirical theory, in the sense that it might be proved false, e.g. if, with a constant money supply, a general increase of wages did not lead to unemployment, it is certainly not the kind of theory which we could use to obtain specific numerical predictions concerning the rates of wages, or the distribution of labour, to be expected.

Why should we, however, in economics, have to plead ignorance of the sort of facts on which, in the case of a physical theory, a scientist would certainly be expected to give precise information? It is probably not surprising that those impressed by the example of the physical sciences should find this position very unsatisfactory and should insist on the standards of proof which they find there. The reason for this state of affairs is the fact, to which I have already briefly referred, that the social sciences, like much of biology but unlike most fields of the physical sciences, have to deal with structures of *essential* complexity, i.e. with structures whose characteristic properties can be exhibited only by models made up of relatively large numbers of variables. Competition, for instance, is a process which will produce certain results only if it proceeds among a fairly large number of acting persons.

In some fields, particularly where problems of a similar kind arise in the

*Swed. J. of Economics* 1975

physical sciences, the difficulties can be overcome by using, instead of specific information about the individual elements, data about the relative frequency, or the probability, of the occurrence of the various distinctive properties of the elements. But this is true only where we have to deal with what has been called by Dr Warren Weaver (formerly of the Rockefeller Foundation), with a distinction which ought to be much more widely understood, "phenomena of unorganized complexity", in contrast to those "phenomena of organized complexity" with which we have to deal in the social sciences.[1] Organized complexity here means that the character of the structures showing it depends not only on the properties of the individual elements of which they are composed, and the relative frequency with which they occur, but also on the manner in which the individual elements are connected with each other. In the explanation of the working of such structures we can for this reason not replace the information about the individual elements by statistical information, but require full information about each element if from our theory we are to derive specific predictions about individual events. Without such specific information about the individual elements we shall be confined to what on another occasion I have called mere pattern predictions—predictions of some of the general attributes of the structures that will form themselves, but not containing specific statements about the individual elements of which the structures will be made up.[2]

This is particularly true of our theories accounting for the determination of the systems of relative prices and wages that will form themselves on a well-functioning market. Into the determination of these prices and wages there will enter the effects of particular information possessed by every one of the participants in the market process—a sum of facts which in their totality cannot be known to the scientific observer, or to any other single brain. It is indeed the source of the superiority of the market order, and the reason why, when it is not suppressed by the powers of government, it regularly displaces other types of order, that in the resulting allocation of resources more of the knowledge of particular facts will be utilized which exists only dispersed among uncounted persons, than any one person can possess. But because we, the observing scientists, can thus never know all the determinants of such an order, and in consequence also cannot know at which particular structure of prices and wages demand would everywhere equal supply, we also cannot measure the deviations from that order; nor can we statistically test our theory that it is the deviations from that "equilibrium" system of prices and wages

---

[1] Warren Weaver, "A Quarter Century in the Natural Sciences", *The Rockefeller Foundation Annual Report 1958*, chapter I, "Science and Complexity".
[2] See my essay "The Theory of Complex Phenomena" in *The Critical Approach to Science and Philosophy. Essays in Honor of K. R. Popper*, ed. M. Bunge, New York 1964, and reprinted (with additions) in my *Studies in Philosophy, Politics and Economics*, London and Chicago 1967.

*Swed. J. of Economics* 1975

which make it impossible to sell some of the products and services at the prices at which they are offered.

Before I continue with my immediate concern, the effects of all this on the employment policies currently pursued, allow me to define more specifically the inherent limitations of our numerical knowledge which are so often overlooked. I want to do this to avoid giving the impression that I generally reject the mathematical method in economics. I regard it in fact as the great advantage of the mathematical technique that it allows us to describe, by means of algebraic equations, the general character of a pattern even where we are ignorant of the numerical values which will determine its particular manifestation. We could scarcely have achieved that comprehensive picture of the mutual interdependencies of the different events in a market without this algebraic technique. It has led to the illusion, however, that we can use this technique for the determination and prediction of the numerical values of those magnitudes; and this has led to a vain search for quantitative or numerical constants. This happened in spite of the fact that the modern founders of mathematical economics had no such illusions. It is true that their systems of equations describing the pattern of a market equilibrium are so framed that *if* we were able to fill in the blanks of the abstract formulae, i.e. *if* we knew all the parameters of these equations, we could calculate the prices and quantities of all commodities and services sold. But, as Vilfredo Pareto, one of the founders of this theory, clearly stated, its purpose cannot be "to arrive at a numerical calculation of prices", because, as he said, it would be "absurd" to assume that we could ascertain all the data.[1] Indeed, the cief point was already seen by those remarkable anticipators of modern economics, the Spanish schoolmen of the sixteenth century, who emphasized that what they called *pretium mathematicum*, the mathematical price, depended on so many particular circumstances that it could never be known to man but was known only to God.[2] I sometimes wish that our mathematical economists would take this to heart. I must confess that I still doubt whether their search for measurable magnitudes has made significant contributions to our *theoretical* understanding of economic phenomena—as distinct from their value as a description of particular situations. Nor am I prepared to accept the excuse that this branch of research is still very young: Sir William Petty, the founder of econometrics, was after all a somewhat senior colleague of Sir Isaac Newton in the Royal Society!

There may be few instances in which the superstition that only measurable magnitudes can be important has done positive harm in the economic field: but the present inflation and employment problems are a very serious one. Its

---

[1] V. Pareto, *Manuel d'économie politique*, 2nd ed., Paris 1927, pp. 223–4.
[2] See, e.g., Luis Molina, *De iustitia et iure*, Cologne 1596–1600, tom. II, disp. 347, no. 3, and particularly Johannes de Lugo, *Disputationum de iustitia et iure tomus secundus*, Lyon 1642, disp. 26, sect. 4, no. 40.

effect has been that what is probably the true cause of extensive unemployment has been disregarded by the scientistically minded majority of economists, because its operation could not be confirmed by directly observable relations between measurable magnitudes, and that an almost exclusive concentration on quantitatively measurable surface phenomena has produced a policy which has made matters worse.

It has, of course, to be readily admitted that the kind of theory which I regard as the true explanation of unemployment is a theory of somewhat limited content because it allows us to make only very general predictions of the *kind* of events which we must expect in a given situation. But the effects on policy of the more ambitious constructions have not been very fortunate and I confess that I prefer true but imperfect knowledge, even if it leaves much indetermined and unpredictable, to a pretence of exact knowledge that is likely to be false. The credit which the apparent conformity with recognized scientific standards can gain for seemingly simple but false theories may, as the present instance shows, have grave consequences.

In fact, in the case discussed, the very measures which the dominant "macroeconomic" theory has recommended as a remedy for unemployment, namely the increase of aggregate demand, have become a cause of a very extensive misallocation of resources which is likely to make later large-scale unemployment inevitable. The continuous injection of additional amounts of money at points of the economic system where it creates a temporary demand which must cease when the increase of the quantity of money stops or slows down, together with the expectation of a continuing rise of prices, draws labour and other resources into employments which can last only so long as the increase of the quantity of money continues at the same rate—or perhaps even only so long as it continues to accelerate at a given rate. What this policy has produced is not so much a level of employment that could not have been brought about in other ways, as a distribution of employment which cannot be indefinitely maintained and which after some time can be maintained only by a rate of inflation which would rapidly lead to a disorganisation of all economic activity. The fact is that by a mistaken theoretical view we have been led into a precarious position in which we cannot prevent substantial unemployment from re-appearing; not because, as this view is sometimes misrepresented, this unemployment is deliberately brought about as a means to combat inflation, but because it is now bound to occur as a deeply regrettable but inescapable consequence of the mistaken policies of the past as soon as inflation ceases to accelerate.

I must, however, now leave these problems of immediate practical importance which I have introduced chiefly as an illustration of the momentous consequences that may follow from errors concerning abstract problems of the philosophy of science. There is as much reason to be apprehensive about the long run dangers created in a much wider field by the uncritical acceptance

*Swed. J. of Economics* 1975

of assertions which have the *appearance* of being scientific as there is with regard to the problems I have just discussed. What I mainly wanted to bring out by the topical illustration is that certainly in my field, but I believe also generally in the sciences of man, what looks superficially like the most scientific procedure is often the most unscientific, and, beyond this, that in these fields there are definite limits to what we can expect science to achieve. This means that to entrust to science—or to deliberate control according to scientific principles—more than scientific method can achieve may have deplorable effects. The progress of the natural sciences in modern times has of course so much exceeded all expectations that any suggestion that there may be some limits to it is bound to arouse suspicion. Especially all those will resist such an insight who have hoped that our increasing power of prediction and control, generally regarded as the characteristic result of scientific advance, applied to the process of society, would soon enable us to mould society entirely to our liking. It is indeed true that, in contrast to the exhilaration which the discoveries of the physical sciences tend to produce, the insights which we gain from the study of society more often have a dampening effect on our aspirations; and it is perhaps not surprising that the more impetuous younger members of our profession are not always prepared to accept this. Yet the confidence in the unlimited power of science is only too often based on a false belief that the scientific method consists in the application of a ready-made technique, or in imitating the form rather than the substance of scientific procedure, as if one needed only to follow some cooking recipes to solve all social problems. It sometimes almost seems as if the techniques of science were more easily learnt than the thinking that shows us what the problems are and how to approach them.

The conflict between what in its present mood the public expects science to achieve in satisfaction of popular hopes and what is really in its power is a serious matter because, even if the true scientists should all recognize the limitations of what they can do in the field of human affairs, so long as the public expects more there will always be some who will pretend, and perhaps honestly believe, that they can do more to meet popular demands than is really in their power. It is often difficult enough for the expert, and certainly in many instances impossible for the layman, to distinguish between legitimate and illegitimate claims advanced in the name of science. The enormous publicity recently given by the media to a report pronouncing in the name of science on *The Limits to Growth*, and the silence of the same media about the devastating criticism this report has received from the competent experts,[1] must make one feel somewhat apprehensive about the use to which the prestige

---

[1] See *The Limits to Growth: A Report of the Club of Rome's Project on the Predicament of Mankind*, New York 1972; for a systematic examination of this by a competent economist cf. Wilfred Beckerman, *In Defence of Economic Growth*, London 1974, and, for a list of earlier criticisms by experts, Gottfried Haberler, *Economic Growth and Stability*, Los Angeles 1974, who rightly calls their effect "devastating".

*Swed. J. of Economics* 1975

of science can be put. But it is by no means only in the field of economics that far-reaching claims are made on behalf of a more scientific direction of all human activities and the desirability of replacing spontaneous processes by "conscious human control". If I am not mistaken, psychology, psychiatry and some branches of sociology, not to speak about the so-called philosophy of history, are even more affected by what I have called the scientistic prejudice, and by specious claims of what science can achieve.[1]

If we are to safeguard the reputation of science, and to prevent the arrogation of knowledge based on a superficial similarity of procedure with that of the physical sciences, much effort will have to be directed toward debunking such arrogations, some of which have by now become the vested interests of established university departments. We cannot be grateful enough to such modern philosophers of science as Sir Karl Popper for giving us a test by which we can distinguish between what we may accept as scientific and what not—a test which I am sure some doctrines now widely accepted as scientific would not pass. There are some special problems, however, in connection with those essentially complex phenomena of which social structures are so important an instance, which make me wish to restate in conclusion in more general terms the reasons why in these fields not only are there absolute obstacles to the prediction of specific events, but why to act as if we possessed scientific knowledge enabling us to transcend them may itself become a serious obstacle to the advance of the human intellect.

The chief point we must remember is that the great and rapid advance of the physical sciences took place in fields where it proved that explanation and prediction could be based on laws which accounted for the observed phenomena as functions of comparatively few variables—either particular facts or relative frequencies of events. This may even be the ultimate reason why we single out these realms as "physical" in contrast to those more highly organized structures which I have here called essentially complex phenomena. There is no reason why the position must be the same in the latter as in the former fields. The difficulties which we encounter in the latter are not, as one might at first suspect, difficulties about formulating theories for the explanation of the observed events—although they cause also special difficulties about testing proposed explanations and therefore about eliminating bad theories. They are due to the chief problem which arises when we apply our theories to any particular situation in the real world. A theory of essentially complex phenomena must refer to a large number of particular facts; and to derive a prediction from it, or to test, it, we have to ascertain all these particular facts. Once we succeeded in this there should be no particular difficulty

---

[1] I have given some illustrations of these tendencies in other fields in my inaugural lecture as Visiting Professor at the University of Salzburg, *Die Irrtümer des Konstruktivismus und die Grundlagen legitimer Kritik gesellschaftlicher Gebilde*, Munich 1970, now re-issued for the Walter Eucken Institute, at Freiburg i.Brg. by J. C. B. Mohr, Tübingen 1975.

*Swed. J. of Economics* 1975

E:CO Vol. 9 Nos. 1-2 2007 pp. 131-142

about deriving testable predictions—with the help of modern computers it should be easy enough to insert these data into the appropriate blanks of the theoretical formulae and to derive a prediction. The real difficulty, to the solution of which science has little to contribute, and which is sometimes indeed insoluble, consists in the ascertainment of the particular facts.

A simple example will show the nature of this difficulty. Consider some ball game played by a few people of approximately equal skill. If we knew a few particular facts in addition to our general knowledge of the ability of the individual players, such as their state of attention, their perceptions and the state of their hearts, lungs, muscles etc. at each moment of the game, we could probably predict the outcome. Indeed, if we were familiar both with the game and the teams we should probably have a fairly shrewd idea on what the outcome will depend. But we shall of course not be able to ascertain those facts and in consequence the result of the game will be outside the range of the scientifically predictable, however well we may know what effects particular events would have on the result of the game. This does not mean that we can make no predictions at all about the course of such a game. If we know the rules of the different games we shall, in watching one, very soon know which game is being played and what kinds of actions we can expect and what kind not. But our capacity to predict will be confined to such general characteristics of the events to be expected and not include the capacity of predicting particular individual events.

This corresponds to what I have called earlier the mere pattern predictions to which we are increasingly confined as we penetrate from the realm in which relatively simple laws prevail into the range of phenomena where organized complexity rules. As we advance we find more and more frequently that we can in fact ascertain only some but not all the particular circumstances which determine the outcome of a given process; and in consequence we are able to predict only some but not all the properties of the result we have to expect. Often all that we shall be able to predict will be some abstract characteristic of the pattern that will appear—relations between kinds of elements about which individually we know very little. Yet, as I am anxious to repeat, we will still achieve predictions which can be falsified and which therefore are of empirical significance.

Of course, compared with the precise predictions we have learnt to expect in the physical sciences, this sort of mere pattern predictions is a second best with which one does not like to have to be content. Yet the danger of which I want to warn is precisely the belief that in order to have a claim to be accepted as scientific it is necessary to achieve more. This way lies charlatanism and worse. To act on the belief that we possess the knowledge and the power which enable us to shape the processes of society entirely to our liking, knowledge which in fact we do *not* possess, is likely to make us do much harm. In the physical sciences there may be little objection to trying to do the impos-

*Swed. J. of Economics* 1975

sible; one might even feel that one ought not to discourage the over-confident because their experiments may after all produce some new insights. But in the social field the erroneous belief that the exercise of some power would have beneficial consequences is likely to lead to a new power to coerce other men being confered on some authority. Even if such power is not in itself bad, its exercise is likely to impede the functioning of those spontaneous ordering forces by which, without understanding them, man is in fact so largely assisted in the pursuit of his aims. We are only beginning to understand on how subtle a communication system the functioning of an advanced industrial society is based—a communications system which we call the market and which turns out to be a more efficient mechanism for digesting dispersed information than any that man has deliberately designed.

If man is not to do more harm than good in his efforts to improve the social order, he will have to learn that in this, as in all other fields where essential complexity of an organized kind prevails, he cannot acquire the full knowledge which would make mastery of the events possible. He will therefore have to use what knowledge he can achieve, not to shape the results as the craftsman shapes his handiwork, but rather to cultivate a growth by providing the appropriate environment, in the manner in which the gardener does this for his plants. There is danger in the exuberant feeling of ever growing power which the advance of the physical sciences has engendered and which tempts man to try, "dizzy with success", to use a characteristic phrase of early communism, to subject not only our natural but also our human environment to the control of a human will. The recognition of the insuperable limits to his knowledge ought indeed to teach the student of society a lesson of humility which should guard him against becoming an accomplice in men's fatal striving to control society—a striving which makes him not only a tyrant over his fellows, but which may well make him the destroyer of a civilization which no brain has designed but which has grown from the free efforts of millions of individuals.

*Swed. J. of Economics* 1975

# The theory of complex phenomena

Friedrich A. von Hayek (with an introduction by Mihnea Moldoveanu, Rotman School of Management, University of Toronto, CAN)

Originally published in Hayek, F. A. (1967). *Studies in Philosophy, Politics and Economics*, London, UK: Routledge & Kegan Paul, pp. 22-42. Reproduced by kind permission.

## Hayek's *The Theory of Complex Phenomena*: A Precocious Play on the Epistemology of Complexity

Friedrich Hayek's *The Theory of Complex Phenomena* (Hayek, 1964) is a precocious and far-sighted attempt to illuminate a topic that has loomed increasingly important in the 53 years since the printing of the paper: the epistemology of complexity. It posits a tension between real insight into complex phenomena and a narrow – but, common – interpretation of a Popperian falsificationism, and suggests that we make a 'hard choice' – one that subsequent research and philosophical forays into complexity science can be usefully understood as having implicitly made on numerous occasions.

Popper suggested *actual* falsifiability of hypotheses derived from a theory as a criterion of demarcation between scientific and 'metaphysical' or 'pseudo-scientific' theories and of choice among alternative empirical theories (Popper, 1959). Thus, the 'theory' which states that 'the orbit of planet Z has the form of a circle, i.e, $x^2 + y^2 = R^2$' is to be preferred (before testing) to a theory which states that 'the orbit of planet Z has the form of an ellipse, i.e., $a^2x^2 + b^2y^2 = c^2$ because it takes fewer points – or, measurements (namely, 3) to disconfirm the former theory than it takes (4) to disconfirm the latter. Popper capitalizes on the example to make the point that the (normative) emphasis placed by some philosophers of science on simplicity as a criterion for theory choice *follows from* (and is therefore not independent of) a commitment to actual falsifiability.

This is precisely the point that Hayek focuses on, in reference to 'complex phenomena'. He sees that the astute researcher of complexity faces a hard choice between the 'point-wise' testability that Popper takes for granted on the one hand, and insight or understanding on the other – and advocates that the constraints which testability places on theory choice be loosened in favor of allowing for more complicated nomological relationships among independent variables, which, in turn, will orient the empiricist away from attempting to predict point events and towards predicting 'patterns' or dynamical regimes. This is a precocious and far sighted insight, and here is a case in point: Apparently unbeknownst to Hayek (plausibly so: Hayek finished the paper in 1961, two years before the Lorenz paper that kicked off 'chaos theory' was published), chaos theory got off the ground approximately at the same time Hayek was writing his paper, starting from (Edward) Lorenz's startling realization that some dynamical systems (such as that made up by the coupling between the system of nonlinear ordinary differential equations he was trying to solve numerically and the finite-precision arithmetic operations that his computer instantiated) exhibit highly sensitive dependence of their long-run dynamics on their initial conditions, such that two points in the phase space of the system that start out arbitrarily close together will – in the course of the system's evolution and after an only finite amount of time – end up very far apart. 'Chaos theory', then, touches reality not by making predictions about point events, but, rather, by specifying dynamical systems and regimes or regions of their parameter spaces that exhibit 'transition to chaos' (Ott, 2002) – that is, by making predictions about *patterns* of behavior rather than about highly localized space-time hyper-volumes ('points') of behavior.

But, is the development of an empirical chaos theory really a validation of Hayek's claim that strict falsificationism must be relaxed in order to make progress on a science of complexity? Note, in this regard, that formal languages used for representing dynamical systems (such as those exhibiting chaotic behavior) come equipped with highly efficacious state space contraction devices and maneuvers, which collapse half-planes into lines and lines into points. It is, then, possible – by the application of such devices – to render predictions about macroscopic patterns and dynamical regimes of behavior into predictions about the 'rate of transition to chaos and boundaries between ordered and disordered behavior, which make possible precisely the kind of subsequent 'point-wise testing' that Popper is often interpreted as having had in mind. Doing so, however, will presuppose a flexibility on the part of the researcher at a level which most social scientists in general and economists trained in the neoclassical tradition in particular have to date had little consideration for: the ontological one – a flexibility about the objects in-terms-of-which discourse proceeds. This is something that Hayek glimpses and points the way to his paper, without fully calling out: 'statistics' – he argues – cannot be used to teach us much about a population of computers, unless we also have access to the code that runs on them (Hayek, 1961, *ibid.*). Knowledge of the code used to design the computers will not only give us a radically different number and set of hypotheses that 'statistics' can be used to test, but also, perhaps more importantly, a different conceptualization of the 'computer' in terms of 'intentional' terms ('algorithms') rather than in terms of causal entities ('electrons and holes'). And this may be a far more penetrating insight of Hayek's paper than is the exhortation to loosen the epistemological constraints that we place on 'complexity science' – and one which complexity researchers may do well to heed. Should they choose to do so, the black box of human decision making (mind → brain → behavior) – neatly bracketed in economic analyses by rational choice models and linear demand functions – could be made to yield much illuminating insight under the gaze of new conceptual toolkits.

## References

Hayek, F. (1961). "The theory of complex phenomena," in M. Bunge (ed.), *The Critical Approach to Science and Philosophy*, ISBN 9780029049204.

Lorenz, E. (1963). "Deterministic non-periodic flow," *Journal of Atmospheric Sciences*, ISSN 0022-4928, 20: 130-141.

Ott, E. (2002). *Chaos in Dynamical Systems*, ISBN 9780521010849.

Popper, K. R. (1959). *The Logic of Scientific Discovery*, ISBN 9780415278447 (2002).

CHAPTER TWO

# *The Theory of Complex Phenomena**

## 1. *Pattern Recognition and Pattern Prediction*

Man has been impelled to scientific inquiry by wonder and by need. Of these wonder has been incomparably more fertile. There are good reasons for this. Where we wonder we have already a question to ask. But however urgently we may want to find our way in what appears just chaotic, so long as we do not know what to look for, even the most attentive and persistent observation of the bare facts is not likely to make them more intelligible. Intimate acquaintance with the facts is certainly important; but systematic observation can start only after problems have arisen. Until we have definite questions to ask we cannot employ our intellect; and questions presuppose that we have formed some provisional hypothesis or theory about the events.[1]

* Reprinted from *The Critical Approach to Science and Philosophy. Essays in Honor of* K. R. *Popper*, ed. M. Bunge, New York (The Free Press), 1964. The article was there printed (apart from a few stylistic emendations by the editor) in the form in which I had completed the manuscript in December 1961 and without my ever having seen proofs. I have now availed myself of this opportunity to insert some references I had intended to add in the proofs.

[1] See already Aristotle, *Metaphysics,* I, II, 9, 9826b (Loeb ed. p. 13): 'It is through wonder that men now begin and originally began to philosophize . . . it is obvious that they pursued science for the sake of knowledge, and not for any practical utility'; also Adam Smith, 'The Principles which Lead and Direct Philosophical Inquiries, as Illustrated by the History of Astronomy', in *Essays*, London, 1869, p. 340: 'Wonder, therefore, and not any expectation of advantage from its discoveries, is the first principle which prompts mankind to the study of philosophy, that science which pretends to lay open the concealed connections that unite the various appearances of nature; and they pursue this study for its own sake, as an original pleasure or good in itself, without regarding its tendency to procure them the means of many other pleasures.' Is there really any evidence for the now popular contrary view that, e.g., 'hunger in the Nile Valley led to the development of geometry' (as Gardner Murphy in the *Handbook of Social Psychology*, ed. by Gardner Lindzey, 1954, Vol. II, p. 616, tells us)? Surely the fact that the discovery of geometry turned out to be useful does not prove that it was discovered because of its usefulness. On the fact that economics

Questions will arise at first only after our senses have discerned some recurring pattern or order in the events. It is a re-cognition of some regularity (or recurring pattern, or order), of some similar feature in otherwise different circumstances, which makes us wonder and ask 'why?'[2] Our minds are so made that when we notice such regularity in diversity we suspect the presence of the same agent and become curious to detect it. It is to this trait of our minds that we owe whatever understanding and mastery of our environment we have achieved.

Many such regularities of nature are recognized 'intuitively' by our senses. We see and hear patterns as much as individual events without having to resort to intellectual operations. In many instances these patterns are of course so much part of the environment which we take for granted that they do not cause questions. But where our senses show us new patterns, this causes surprise and questioning. To such curiosity we owe the beginning of science.

Marvellous, however, as the intuitive capacity of our senses for pattern recognition is, it is still limited.[3] Only certain kinds of regular arrangements (not necessarily the simplest) obtrude themselves on our senses. Many of the patterns of nature we can discover only *after* they have been constructed by our mind. The systematic construction of such new patterns is the business of mathematics.[4] The role which geometry plays in this respect with regard to some visual patterns is merely the most familiar instance of this. The great strength of mathe-

---

[2] See K. R. Popper, *The Poverty of Historicism*, London, 1957, p. 121: 'Science . . . cannot start with observations, or with the "collection of data", as some students of method believe. Before we can collect data, our interest in *data of a certain kind* must be aroused: the *problem* always comes first.' Also in his *The Logic of Scientific Discovery*, London, 1959, p. 59: 'observation is always *observation in the light of theories*.'

[3] Although in some respects the capacity of our senses for pattern recognition clearly also exceeds the capacity of our mind for specifying these patterns. The question of the extent to which this capacity of our senses is the result of another kind of (pre-sensory) experience is another matter. See, on this and on the general point that all perception involves a theory or hypothesis, my book *The Sensory Order*, London and Chicago, 1952, esp. para. 7.37. Cf. also the remarkable thought expressed by Adam Ferguson (and probably derived from George Berkeley) in *The History of Civil Society*, London, 1767, p. 39, that 'the inferences of thought are sometimes not to be distinguished from the perception of sense'; as well as H. von Helmholtz's theory of the 'unconscious inferences' involved in most perceptions. For a recent revival of these ideas see N. R. Hanson, *Patterns of Discovery*, Cambridge University Press, 1958, esp. p. 19, and the views on the role of 'hypotheses' in perception as developed in recent 'cognition theory' by J. S. Bruner, L. Postman and others.

[4] Cf. G. H. Hardy, *Mathematician's Apology*, Cambridge University Press, 1941, p. 24: 'A mathematician, like a painter or poet, is a maker of patterns.'

---

has in some degree been an exception to the general rule and has suffered by being guided more by need than by detached curiosity, see my lecture on 'The Trend of Economic Thinking' in *Economica*, 1933.

[ 23 ]

c

matics is that it enables us to describe abstract patterns which cannot be perceived by our senses, and to state the common properties of hierarchies or classes of patterns of a highly abstract character. Every algebraic equation or set of such equations defines in this sense a class of patterns, with the individual manifestation of this kind of pattern being particularized as we substitute definite values for the variables.

It is probably the capacity of our senses spontaneously to recognize certain kinds of patterns that has led to the erroneous belief that if we look only long enough, or at a sufficient number of instances of natural events, a pattern will always reveal itself. That this often is so means merely that in those cases the theorizing has been done already by our senses. Where, however, we have to deal with patterns for the development of which there has been no biological reason, we shall first have to invent the pattern before we can discover its presence in the phenomena —or before we shall be able to test its applicability to what we observe. A theory will always define only a kind (or class) of patterns, and the particular manifestation of the pattern to be expected will depend on the particular circumstances (the 'initial and marginal conditions' to which, for the purposes of this article, we shall refer as 'data'). How much in fact we shall be able to predict will depend on how many of those data we can ascertain.

The description of the pattern which the theory provides is commonly regarded merely as a tool which will enable us to predict the particular manifestations of the pattern that will appear in specific circumstances. But the prediction that in certain general conditions a pattern of a certain kind will appear is also a significant (and falsifiable) prediction. If I tell somebody that if he goes to my study he will find there a rug with a pattern made up of diamonds and meanders, he will have no difficulty in deciding 'whether that prediction was verified or falsified by the result',[5] even though I have said nothing about the arrangement, size, colour, etc., of the elements from which the pattern of the rug is formed.

The distinction between a prediction of the appearance of a pattern of a certain class and a prediction of the appearance of a particular instance of this class is sometimes important even in the physical sciences. The mineralogist who states that the crystals of a certain mineral are hexagonal, or the astronomer who assumes that the course of a celestial body in the field of gravity of another will correspond to one of the conic sections, make significant predictions which can be refuted. But in general the physical sciences tend to assume that it will in principle

[5] Charles Dickens, *David Copperfield*, p. 1.

[ 24 ]

always be possible to specify their predictions to any degree desired.[6] The distinction assumes, however, much greater importance when we turn from the relatively simple phenomena with which the natural sciences deal, to the more complex phenomena of life, of mind, and of society, where such specifications may not always be possible.[7]

### 2. *Degrees of Complexity*

The distinction between simplicity and complexity raises considerable philosophical difficulties when applied to statements. But there seems to exist a fairly easy and adequate way to measure the degree of complexity of different kinds of abstract patterns. The minimum number of elements of which an instance of the pattern must consist in order to exhibit all the characteristic attributes of the class of patterns in question appears to provide an unambiguous criterion.

It has occasionally been questioned whether the phenomena of life, of mind, and of society are really more complex than those of the physical world.[8] This seems to be largely due to a confusion between the degree

[6] Though it may be permissible to doubt whether it is in fact possible to predict, e.g., the precise pattern which the vibrations of an airplane will at a particular moment produce in the standing wave on the surface of the coffee in my cup.

[7] Cf. Michael Scriven, 'A Possible Distinction between Traditional Scientific Disciplines and the Study of Human Behavior', *Minnesota Studies in the Philosophy of Science*, I, 1956, p. 332: 'The difference between the scientific study of behavior and that of physical phenomena is thus partly due to the relatively greater complexity of the simplest phenomena we are concerned to account for in a behavioral theory.'

[8] Ernest Nagel, *The Structure of Science*, New York, 1961, p. 505: 'though social phenomena may indeed be complex, it is by no means certain that they are in general more complex than physical and biological phenomena.' See, however, Johann von Neumann, 'The General and Logical Theory of Automata', *Cerebral Mechanism in Behavior*. The Hixon Symposium, New York, 1951, p. 24: 'we are dealing here with parts of logic with which we have practically no experience. The order of complexity is out of all proportion to anything we have ever known.' It may be useful to give here a few illustrations of the orders of magnitude with which biology and neurology have to deal. While the total number of electrons in the Universe has been estimated at $10^{79}$ and the number of electrons and protons at $10^{100}$, there are in chromosomes with 1,000 locations [genes] with 10 allelomorphs $10^{1000}$ possible combinations; and the number of possible proteins is estimated at $10^{2700}$ (L. von Bertalanffy, *Problems of Life*, New York, 1952, p. 103). C. Judson Herrick (*Brains of Rats and Men*, New York), suggests that 'during a few minutes of intense cortical activity the number of interneuronic connections actually made (counting also those that are actuated more than once in different associational patterns) may well be as great as the total number of atoms in the solar system' (i.e. $10^{56}$); and Ralph W. Gerard (*Scientific American*, September 1953, p. 118) has estimated that in the course of seventy years a man may accumulate $15 \times 10^{12}$ units of information ('bits'), which is more than 1,000 times larger than the number of nerve cells. The further complications which social relations superimpose upon this are, of course, relatively insignificant. But the point is that if we wanted to 'reduce' social phenomena to physical events, they would constitute an additional complication, superimposed upon that of the physiological processes determining mental events.

[ 25 ]

of complexity characteristic of a peculiar *kind* of phenomenon and the degree of complexity to which, by a combination of elements, any kind of phenomenon can be built up. Of course, in this manner physical phenomena may achieve any degree of complexity. Yet when we consider the question from the angle of the minimum number of distinct variables a formula or model must possess in order to reproduce the characteristic patterns of structures of different fields (or to exhibit the general laws which these structures obey), the increasing complexity as we proceed from the inanimate to the ('more highly organized') animate and social phenomena becomes fairly obvious.

It is, indeed, surprising how simple in these terms, i.e., in terms of the number of distinct variables, appear all the laws of physics, and particularly of mechanics, when we look through a collection of formulae expressing them.[9] On the other hand, even such relatively simple constituents of biological phenomena as feedback (or cybernetic) systems, in which a certain combination of physical structures produces an overall structure possessing distinct characteristic properties, require for their description something much more elaborate than anything describing the general laws of mechanics. In fact, when we ask ourselves by what criteria we single out certain phenomena as 'mechanical' or 'physical', we shall probably find that these laws are simple in the sense defined. Non-physical phenomena are more complex because we call physical what can be described by relatively simple formulae.

The 'emergence' of 'new' patterns as a result of the increase in the number of elements between which simple relations exist, means that this larger structure as a whole will possess certain general or abstract features which will recur independently of the particular values of the individual data, so long as the general structure (as described, e.g., by an algebraic equation) is preserved.[10] Such 'wholes', defined in terms of certain general properties of their structure, will constitute distinctive objects of explanation for a theory, even though such a theory may be merely a particular way of fitting together statements about the relations between the individual elements.

[9] Cf. Warren Weaver, 'A Quarter Century in the Natural Sciences', *The Rockefeller Foundation Annual Report*, 1958, Chapter I, 'Science and Complexity', which, when writing this, I knew only in the abbreviated version which appeared in the *American Scientist*, XXXVI, 1948.

[10] Lloyd Morgan's conception of 'emergence' derives, *via* G. H. Lewes (*Problems of Life and Mind*, 1st series, Vol. II, problem V, Ch. III, section headed 'Resultants and Emergents', American ed., Boston, 1891, p. 368), from John Stuart Mill's distinction of the 'heteropathic' laws of chemistry and other complex phenomena from the ordinary 'composition of causes' in mechanics, etc. See his *System of Logic*, London, 1843, Bk. III, Ch. 6, in Vol. I, p. 431 of the first edition, and C. Lloyd Morgan, *The Emergence of Novelty*, London, 1933, p. 12.

[ 26 ]

It is somewhat misleading to approach this task mainly from the angle of whether such structures are 'open' or 'closed' systems. There are, strictly speaking, no closed systems within the universe. All we can ask is whether in the particular instance the points of contact through which the rest of the universe acts upon the system we try to single out (and which for the theory become the data) are few or many. These data, or variables, which determine the particular form which the pattern described by the theory will assume in the given circumstances, will be more numerous in the case of complex wholes and much more difficult to ascertain and control than in the case of simple phenomena.

What we single out as wholes, or where we draw the 'partition boundary',[11] will be determined by the consideration whether we can thus isolate recurrent patterns of coherent structures of a distinct kind which we do in fact encounter in the world in which we live. Many complex patterns which are conceivable and might recur we shall not find it worthwhile to construct. Whether it will be useful to elaborate and study a pattern of a particular kind will depend on whether the structure it describes is persistent or merely accidental. The coherent structures in which we are mainly interested are those in which a complex pattern has produced properties which make self-maintaining the structure showing it.

### 3. *Pattern Prediction with Incomplete Data*

The multiplicity of even the minimum of distinct elements required to produce (and therefore also of the minimum number of data required to explain) a complex phenomenon of a certain kind creates problems which dominate the disciplines concerned with such phenomena and gives them an appearance very different from that of those concerned with simpler phenomena. The chief difficulty in the former becomes one of in fact ascertaining all the data determining a particular manifestation of the phenomenon in question, a difficulty which is often insurmountable in practice and sometimes even an absolute one.[12] Those mainly concerned with simple phenomena are often inclined to think that where this is the case a theory is useless and that scientific procedure demands that we should find a theory of sufficient simplicity to enable us to derive from it predictions of particular events. To them the theory, the knowledge of the pattern, is merely a tool whose usefulness depends

---

11 Lewis White Beck, 'The "Natural Science Ideal" in the Social Sciences', *The Scientific Monthly*, LXVIII, June 1949, p. 388.

12 Cf. F. A. Hayek, *The Sensory Order*, paras. 8.66–8.86.

[ 27 ]

entirely on our capacity to translate it into a representation of the circumstances producing a particular event. Of the theories of simple phenomena this is largely true.[13]

There is, however, no justification for the belief that it must always be possible to discover such simple regularities and that physics is more advanced because it has succeeded in doing this while other sciences have not yet done so. It is rather the other way round: physics has succeeded because it deals with phenomena which, in our sense, are simple. But a simple theory of phenomena which are in their nature complex (or one which, if that expression be preferred, has to deal with more highly organized phenomena) is probably merely of necessity false—at least without a specified *ceteris paribus* assumption, after the full statement of which the theory would no longer be simple.

We are, however, interested not only in individual events, and it is also not only predictions of individual events which can be empirically tested. We are equally interested in the recurrence of abstract patterns as such; and the prediction that a pattern of a certain kind will appear in defined circumstances is a falsifiable (and therefore empirical) statement. Knowledge of the conditions in which a pattern of a certain kind will appear, and of what depends on its preservation, may be of great practical importance. The circumstances or conditions in which the pattern described by the theory will appear are defined by the range of values which may be inserted for the variables of the formula. All we need to know in order to make such a theory applicable to a situation is, therefore, that the data possess certain general properties (or belong to the class defined by the scope of the variables). Beyond this we need to know nothing about their individual attributes so long as we are content to derive merely the sort of pattern that will appear and not its particular manifestation.

Such a theory destined to remain 'algebraic',[14] because we are in fact unable to substitute particular values for the variables, ceases then to be a mere tool and becomes the final result of our theoretical efforts. Such a theory will, of course, in Popper's terms,[15] be one of small empirical content, because it enables us to predict or explain only certain general

[13] Cf. Ernest Nagel, 'Problems of Concept and Theory Formation in the Social Sciences', in *Science, Language and Human Rights* (American Philosophical Association, Eastern Division, Vol. 1), University of Pennsylvania Press, 1952, p. 620: 'In many cases we are ignorant of the appropriate initial and boundary conditions, and cannot make precise forecasts even though available theory is adequate for that purpose.'
[14] The useful term 'algebraic theories' was suggested to me by J. W. N. Watkins.
[15] K. R. Popper, *The Logic of Scientific Discovery*, London, 1959, p. 113.

[ 28 ]

features of a situation which may be compatible with a great many particular circumstances. It will perhaps enable us to make only what M. Scriven has called 'hypothetical predictions',[16] i.e., predictions dependent on yet unknown future events; in any case the range of phenomena compatible with it will be wide and the possibility of falsifying it correspondingly small. But as in many fields this will be for the present, or perhaps forever, all the theoretical knowledge we can achieve, it will nevertheless extend the range of the possible advance of scientific knowledge.

The advance of science will thus have to proceed in two different directions: while it is certainly desirable to make our theories as falsifiable as possible, we must also push forward into fields where, as we advance, the degree of falsifiability necessarily decreases. This is the price we have to pay for an advance into the field of complex phenomena.

### 4. *Statistics Impotent to Deal with Pattern Complexity*

Before we further illustrate the use of those mere 'explanations of the principle'[17] provided by 'algebraic' theories which describe only the general character of higher-level generalities, and before we consider the important conclusions which follow from the insight into the boundaries of possible knowledge which our distinction provides, it is necessary to turn aside and consider the method which is often, but erroneously, believed to give us access to the understanding of complex phenomena: statistics. Because statistics is designed to deal with large numbers it is often thought that the difficulty arising from the large number of elements of which complex structures consist can be overcome by recourse to statistical techniques.

Statistics, however, deals with the problem of large numbers essentially by eliminating complexity and deliberately treating the individual elements which it counts as if they were not systematically connected. It avoids the problem of complexity by substituting for the information on the individual elements information on the frequency with which their different properties occur in classes of such elements, and it deliberately disregards the fact that the relative position of the different elements in a structure may matter. In other words, it proceeds

---

[16] M. Scriven, 'Explanation and Prediction in Evolutionary Theory', *Science*, August 28, 1959, p. 478 and cf. K. R. Popper, 'Prediction and Prophecy in the Social Sciences' (1949), reprinted in his *Conjectures and Refutations*, London, 1963, especially pp. 339 *et seqq.*
[17] Cf. F. A. Hayek, 'Degrees of Explanation', *The British Journal for the Philosophy of Science*, VI, No. 23, 1955, now reprinted as the first essay of the present collection.

[ 29 ]

on the assumption that information on the numerical frequencies of the different elements of a collective is enough to explain the phenomena and that no information is required on the manner in which the elements are related. The statistical method is therefore of use only where we either deliberately ignore, or are ignorant of, the relations between the individual elements with different attributes, i.e., where we ignore or are ignorant of any structure into which they are organized. Statistics in such situations enables us to regain simplicity and to make the task manageable by substituting a single attribute for the unascertainable individual attributes in the collective. It is, however, for this reason irrelevant to the solution of problems in which it is the relations between individual elements with different attributes which matters.

Statistics might assist us where we had information about many complex structures of the same kind, that is, where the complex phenomena and not the elements of which they consist could be made the elements of the statistical collective. It may provide us, e.g., with information on the relative frequency with which particular properties of the complex structures, say of the members of a species of organisms, occur together; but it presupposes that we have an independent criterion for identifying structures of the kind in question. Where we have such statistics about the properties of many individuals belonging to a class of animals, or languages, or economic systems, this may indeed be scientifically significant information.[18]

How little statistics can contribute, however, even in such cases, to the explanation of complex phenomena is clearly seen if we imagine that computers were natural objects which we found in sufficiently large numbers and whose behaviour we wanted to predict. It is clear that we should never succeed in this unless we possessed the mathematical knowledge built into the computers, that is, unless we knew the theory determining their structure. No amount of statistical information on the correlation between input and output would get us any nearer our aim. Yet the efforts which are currently made on a large scale with regard to the much more complex structures which we call organisms are of the same kind. The belief that it must be possible in this manner to discover by observation regularities in the relations between input and output without the possession of an appropriate theory in this case appears even more futile and naïve than it would be in the case of the computers.[19]

While statistics can successfully deal with complex phenomena where

[18] See F. A. Hayek, *The Counter-Revolution of Science*, Glencoe, Ill., 1952, pp. 60–63.
[19] Cf. J. G. Taylor, 'Experimental Design: A Cloak for Intellectual Sterility', *The British Journal of Psychology*, 49, 1958, esp. pp. 107–8.

[ 30 ]

these are the elements of the population on which we have information, it can tell us nothing about the structure of these elements. It treats them, in the fashionable phrase, as 'black boxes' which are presumed to be of the same kind but about whose identifying characteristics it has nothing to say. Nobody would probably seriously contend that statistics can elucidate even the comparatively not very complex structures of organic molecules, and few would argue that it can help us to explain the functioning of organisms. Yet when it comes to accounting for the functioning of social structures, that belief is widely held. It is here of course largely the product of a misconception about what the aim of a theory of social phenomena is, which is another story.

### 5. *The Theory of Evolution as an Instance of Pattern Prediction*

Probably the best illustration of a theory of complex phenomena which is of great value, although it describes merely a general pattern whose detail we can never fill in, is the Darwinian theory of evolution by natural selection. It is significant that this theory has always been something of a stumbling block for the dominant conception of scientific method. It certainly does not fit the orthodox criteria of 'prediction and control' as the hallmarks of scientific method.[20] Yet it cannot be denied that it has become the successful foundation of a great part of modern biology.

Before we examine its character we must clear out of the way a widely held misconception as to its content. It is often represented as if it consisted of an assertion about the succession of particular species of organisms which gradually changed into each other. This, however, is not the theory of evolution but an application of the theory to the particular events which took place on Earth during the last two billion years or so.[21] Most of the misapplications of evolutionary theory (parti-

---

[20] Cf., e.g., Stephen Toulmin, *Foresight and Prediction*, London, 1961, p. 24: 'No scientist has ever used this theory to foretell the coming into existence of creatures of a novel species, still less verified his forecast.'

[21] Even Professor Popper seems to imply this interpretation when he writes (*Poverty of Historicism*, p. 107) that 'the evolutionary hypothesis is not a universal law of nature but a particular (or, more precisely, singular) historical statement about the ancestry of a number of terrestrial plants and animals'. If this means that the essence of the theory of evolution is the assertion that particular species had common ancestors, or that the similarity of structure always means a common ancestry (which was the hypothesis from which the theory of evolution was derived), this is emphatically not the main content of the present theory of evolution. There is, incidentally, some contradiction between Popper's treatment of the concept of 'mammals' as a universal (*Logic*, p. 65) and the denial that the evolutionary hypothesis describes a universal law of nature. The same process might have produced mammals on other planets.

[ 31 ]

cularly in anthropology and the other social sciences) and its various abuses (e.g., in ethics) are due to this erroneous interpretation of its content.

The theory of evolution by natural selection describes a kind of process (or mechanism) which is independent of the particular circumstances in which it has taken place on Earth, which is equally applicable to a course of events in very different circumstances, and which might result in the production of an entirely different set of organisms. The basic conception of the theory is exceedingly simple and it is only in its application to the concrete circumstances that its extraordinary fertility and the range of phenomena for which it can account manifests itself.[22] The basic proposition which has this far-reaching implication is that a mechanism of reduplication with transmittable variations and competitive selection of those which prove to have a better chance of survival will in the course of time produce a great variety of structures adapted to continuous adjustment to the environment and to each other. The validity of this general proposition is not dependent on the truth of the particular applications which were first made of it: if, for example, it should have turned out that, in spite of their structural similarity, man and ape were not joint descendants from a comparatively near common ancestor but were the product of two convergent strands starting from ancestors which differed much more from each other (such as is true of the externally very similar types of marsupial and placental carnivores), this would not have refuted Darwin's general theory of evolution but only the manner of its application to the particular case.

The theory as such, as is true of all theories, describes merely a range of possibilities. In doing this it excludes other conceivable courses of events and thus can be falsified. Its empirical content consists in what it forbids.[23] If a sequence of events should be observed which cannot be fitted into its pattern, such as, e.g., that horses suddenly should begin to give birth to young with wings, or that the cutting off of a hind-paw in successive generations of dogs should result in dogs being born without that hind-paw, we should regard the theory as refuted.[24]

The range of what is permitted by the theory is undeniably wide. Yet one could also argue that it is only the limitation of our imagination which prevents us from being more aware of how much greater is the

[22] Charles Darwin himself well knew, as he once wrote to Lyell, that 'all the labour consists in the application of the theory' (quoted by C. C. Gillispie, *The Edge of Objectivity*, Princeton, 1960, p. 314).

[23] K. R. Popper, *Logic*, p. 41.

[24] Cf. Morton Beckner, *The Biological Way of Thought*, Columbia University Press, 1954, p. 241.

[ 32 ]

range of the prohibited—how infinite is the variety of conceivable forms of organisms which, thanks to the theory of evolution, we know will not in the foreseeable future appear on Earth. Commonsense may have told us before not to expect anything widely different from what we already knew. But exactly what kinds of variations are within the range of possibility and what kinds are not, only the theory of evolution can tell us. Though we may not be able to write down an exhaustive list of the possibilities, any specific question we shall, in principle, be able to answer.

For our present purposes we may disregard the fact that in one respect the theory of evolution is still incomplete because we still know only little about the mechanism of mutation. But let us assume that we knew precisely the circumstances in which (or at least the probability that in given conditions) a particular mutation will appear, and that we similarly knew also the precise advantages which any such mutation would in any particular kind of environment confer upon an individual of a specific constitution. This would not enable us to explain why the existing species or organisms have the particular structures which they possess, nor to predict what new forms will spring from them.

The reason for this is the actual impossibility of ascertaining the particular circumstances which, in the course of two billion years, have decided the emergence of the existing forms, or even those which, during the next few hundred years, will determine the selection of the types which will survive. Even if we tried to apply our explanatory scheme to a single species consisting of a known number of individuals each of which we were able to observe, and assuming that we were able to ascertain and record every single relevant fact, their sheer number would be such that we should never be able to manipulate them, i.e., to insert these data into the appropriate blanks of our theoretical formula and then to solve the 'statement equations' thus determined.[25]

What we have said about the theory of evolution applies to most of the rest of biology. The theoretical understanding of the growth and functioning of organisms can only in the rarest of instances be turned into specific predictions of what will happen in a particular case, because we can hardly ever ascertain all the facts which will contribute to determine the outcome. Hence, 'prediction and control, usually regarded as essential criteria of science, are less reliable in biology'.[26] It deals with pattern-building forces, the knowledge of which is useful for creating

[25] K. R. Popper, *Logic*, p. 73.
[26] Ralph S. Lillie, 'Some Aspects of Theoretical Biology', *Philosophy of Science*, XV, 2, 1948, p. 119.

[ 33 ]

conditions favourable to the production of certain kinds of results, while it will only in comparatively few cases be possible to control all the relevant circumstances.

## 6. *Theories of Social Structures*

It should not be difficult now to recognize the similar limitations applying to theoretical explanations of the phenomena of mind and society. One of the chief results so far achieved by theoretical work in these fields seems to me to be the demonstration that here individual events regularly depend on so many concrete circumstances that we shall never in fact be in a position to ascertain them all; and that in consequence not only the ideal of prediction and control must largely remain beyond our reach, but also the hope remain illusory that we can discover by observation regular connections between the individual events. The very insight which theory provides, for example, that almost any event in the course of a man's life may have some effect on almost any of his future actions, makes it impossible that we translate our theoretical knowledge into predictions of specific events. There is no justification for the dogmatic belief that such translation must be possible if a science of these subjects is to be achieved, and that workers in these sciences have merely not yet succeeded in what physics has done, namely to discover simple relations between a few observables. If the theories which we have yet achieved tell us anything, it is that no such simple regularities are to be expected.

I will not consider here the fact that in the case of mind attempting to explain the detail of the working of another mind of the same order of complexity, there seems to exist, in addition to the merely 'practical' yet nevertheless unsurmountable obstacles, also an absolute impossibility: because the conception of a mind fully explaining itself involves a logical contradiction. This I have discussed elsewhere.[27] It is not relevant here because the practical limits determined by the impossibility of ascertaining all the relevant data lie so far inside the logical limits that the latter have little relevance to what in fact we can do.

In the field of social phenomena only economics and linguistics[28]

[27] See *The Sensory Order*, 8.66–8.86, also *The Counter-Revolution of Science*, Glencoe, I, 22 1952, p. 48, and the following essay in the present volume.

[28] See particularly Noam Chomsky, *Syntactic Structures*, 'sGravenhage, 1957, who characteristically seems to succeed in building up such a theory after frankly abandoning the striving after an inductivist 'discovery procedure' and substituting for it the search after an 'evaluation procedure' which enables him to eliminate false theories of grammars and where these grammars may be arrived at 'by intuition, guess-work, all sorts of partial methodological hints, reliance on past experience, etc.' (p. 56).

[ 34 ]

seem to have succeeded in building up a coherent body of theory. I shall confine myself here to illustrating the general thesis with reference to economic theory, though most of what I have to say would appear to apply equally to linguistic theory.

Schumpeter well described the task of economic theory when he wrote that 'the economic life of a non-socialist society consists of millions of relations or flows between individual firms and households. We can establish certain theorems about them, but we can never observe them all.'[29] To this must be added that most of the phenomena in which we are interested, such as competition, could not occur at all unless the number of distinct elements involved were fairly large, and that the overall pattern that will form itself is determined by the significantly different behaviour of the different individuals so that the obstacle of obtaining the relevant data cannot be overcome by treating them as members of a statistical collective.

For this reason economic theory is confined to describing kinds of patterns which will appear if certain general conditions are satisfied, but can rarely if ever derive from this knowledge any predictions of specific phenomena. This is seen most clearly if we consider those systems of simultaneous equations which since Léon Walras have been widely used to represent the general relations between the prices and the quantities of all commodities bought and sold. They are so framed that *if* we were able to fill in all the blanks, i.e., *if* we knew all the parameters of these equations, we could calculate the prices and quantities of all the commodities. But, as at least the founders of this theory clearly understood, its purpose is not 'to arrive at a numerical calculation of prices', because it would be 'absurd' to assume that we can ascertain all the data.[30]

The prediction of the formation of this general kind of pattern rests on certain very general factual assumptions (such as that most people engage in trade in order to earn an income, that they prefer a larger income to a smaller one, that they are not prevented from entering whatever trade they wish, etc.,—assumptions which determine the scope of the variables but not their particular values); it is, however, not dependent on the knowledge of the more particular circumstances which we would have to know in order to be able to predict prices or quantities of particular commodities. No economist has yet succeeded in making a fortune by buying or selling commodities on the basis of his scientific prediction of future prices (even though some may have done so by selling such predictions).

[29] J. A. Schumpeter, *History of Economic Analysis*, Oxford University Press, 1954, p. 241.
[30] V. Pareto, *Manuel d'économie politique*, 2nd ed., Paris, 1927, pp. 223-4.

[ 35 ]

To the physicist it often seems puzzling why the economist should bother to formulate those equations although admittedly he sees no chance of determining the numerical values of the parameters which would enable him to derive from them the values of the individual magnitudes. Even many economists seem loath to admit that those systems of equations are not a step towards specific predictions of individual events but the final results of their theoretical efforts, a description merely of the general character of the order we shall find under specifiable conditions which, however, can never be translated into a prediction of its particular manifestations.

Predictions of a pattern are nevertheless both testable and valuable. Since the theory tells us under which general conditions a pattern of this sort will form itself, it will enable us to create such conditions and to observe whether a pattern of the kind predicted will appear. And since the theory tells us that this pattern assures a maximization of output in a certain sense, it also enables us to create the general conditions which will assure such a maximization, though we are ignorant of many of the particular circumstances which will determine the pattern that will appear.

It is not really surprising that the explanation of merely a sort of pattern may be highly significant in the field of complex phenomena but of little interest in the field of simple phenomena, such as those of mechanics. The fact is that in studies of complex phenomena the general patterns are all that is characteristic of those persistent wholes which are the main object of our interest, because a number of enduring structures have this general pattern in common and nothing else.[31]


## 7. *The Ambiguity of the Claims of Determinism*

The insight that we will sometimes be able to say that data of a certain class (or of certain classes) will bring about a pattern of a certain kind, but will not be able to ascertain the attributes of the individual elements which decide which particular form the pattern will assume, has consequences of considerable importance. It means, in the first instance, that when we assert that we know how something is determined, this state-

---

[31] A characteristic instance of the misunderstanding of this point (quoted by E. Nagel, l.c., p. 61) occurs in Charles A. Beard, *The Nature of the Social Sciences*, New York, 1934, p. 29, where it is contended that if a science of society 'were a true science, like that of astronomy, it would enable us to predict the essential movements of human affairs for the immediate and the indefinite future, to give pictures of society in the year 2000 or the year 2500 just as astronomers can map the appearances of the heavens at fixed points of time in the future.'

[ 36 ]

ment is ambiguous. It may mean that we merely know what class of circumstances determines a certain kind of phenomena, without being able to specify the particular circumstances which decide which member of the predicted class of patterns will appear; or it may mean that we can also explain the latter. Thus we can reasonably claim that a certain phenomenon is determined by known natural forces and at the same time admit that we do not know precisely how it has been produced. Nor is the claim invalidated that we can explain the principle on which a certain mechanism operates if it is pointed out that we cannot say precisely what it will do at a particular place and time. From the fact that we do know that a phenomenon is determined by certain kinds of circumstances it does not follow that we must be able to know even in one particular instance all the circumstances which have determined all its attributes.

There may well be valid and more grave philosophical objections to the claim that science can demonstrate a universal determinism; but for all practical purposes the limits created by the impossibility of ascertaining all the particular data required to derive detailed conclusions from our theories are probably much narrower. Even if the assertion of a universal determinism were meaningful, scarcely any of the conclusions usually derived from it would therefore follow. In the first of the two senses we have distinguished we may, for instance, well be able to establish that every single action of a human being is the necessary result of the inherited structure of his body (particularly of its nervous system) and of all the external influences which have acted upon it since birth. We might even be able to go further and assert that if the most important of these factors were in a particular case very much the same as with most other individuals, a particular class of influences will have a certain kind of effect. But this would be an empirical generalization based on a *ceteris paribus* assumption which we could not verify in the particular instance. The chief fact would continue to be, in spite of our knowledge of the principle on which the human mind works, that we should not be able to state the full set of particular facts which brought it about that the individual did a particular thing at a particular time. The individual personality would remain for us as much a unique and unaccountable phenomenon which we might hope to influence in a desirable direction by such empirically developed practices as praise and blame, but whose specific actions we could generally not predict or control, because we could not obtain the information on all the particular facts which determined it.

[ 37 ]

## 8. *The Ambiguity of Relativism*

The same sort of misconception underlies the conclusions derived from the various kinds of 'relativism'. In most instances these relativistic positions on questions of history, culture, or ethics are derived from the erroneous interpretations of the theory of evolution which we have already considered. But the basic conclusion that the whole of our civilization and all human values are the result of a long process of evolution in the course of which values, as the aims of human activity appeared, continue to change, seems inescapable in the light of our present knowledge. We are probably also entitled to conclude that our present values exist only as the elements of a particular cultural tradition and are significant only for some more or less long phase of evolution—whether this phase includes some of our pre-human ancestors or is confined to certain periods of human civilization. We have no more ground to ascribe to them eternal existence than to the human race itself. There is thus one possible sense in which we may legitimately regard human values as relative and speak of the probability of their further evolution.

But it is a far cry from this general insight to the claims of the ethical, cultural, or historical relativists or of evolutionary ethics. To put it crudely: while we know that all those values are relative to something, we do not know to what they are relative. We may be able to indicate the general class of circumstances which have made them what they are, but we do not know the particular conditions to which the values we hold are due, or what our values would be if those circumstances had been different. Most of the illegitimate conclusions are the result of the erroneous interpretation of the theory of evolution as the empirical establishment of a trend. Once we recognize that it gives us no more than a scheme of explanation which might be sufficient to explain particular phenomena *if* we knew all the facts which have operated in the course of history, it becomes evident that the claims of the various kinds of relativism (and of evolutionary ethics) are unfounded. Though we may meaningfully say that our values are determined by a class of circumstances definable in general terms, so long as we cannot state which particular circumstances have produced the existing values, or what our values would be under any specific set of other circumstances, no significant conclusions follow from the assertion.

It deserves brief notice in passing how radically opposed are the practical conclusions which are derived from the same evolutionary approach according as it is assumed that we can or cannot in fact

[ 38 ]

know enough about the circumstances to derive specific conclusions from our theory. While the assumption of a sufficient knowledge of the concrete facts generally produces a sort of intellectual hubris which deludes itself that reason can judge all values, the insight into the impossibility of such full knowledge induces an attitude of humility and reverence towards that experience of mankind as a whole that has been precipitated in the values and institutions of existing society.

A few observations ought to be added here about the obvious significance of our conclusions for assessing the various kinds of 'reductionism'. In the sense of the first of the distinctions which we have repeatedly made—in the sense of general description—the assertion that biological or mental phenomena are 'nothing but' certain complexes of physical events, or that they are certain classes of structures of such events, these claims are probably defensible. But in the second sense—specific prediction—which alone would justify the more ambitious claims made for reductionism, they are completely unjustified. A full reduction would be achieved only if we were able to substitute for a description of events in biological or mental terms a description in physical terms which included an exhaustive enumeration of all the physical circumstances which constitute a necessary and sufficient condition of the biological or mental phenomena in question. In fact such attempts always consist—and can consist only—in the illustrative enumeration of classes of events, usually with an added 'etc.', which might produce the phenomenon in question. Such 'etc.-reductions' are not reductions which enable us to dispense with the biological or mental entities, or to substitute for them a statement of physical events, but are mere explanations of the general character of the kind of order or pattern whose specific manifestations we know only through our concrete experience of them.[32]

### 9. *The Importance of Our Ignorance*

Perhaps it is only natural that in the exuberance generated by the successful advances of science the circumstances which limit our factual knowledge, and the consequent boundaries imposed upon the applicability of theoretical knowledge, have been rather disregarded. It is high time, however, that we take our ignorance more seriously. As Popper and others have pointed out, 'the more we learn about the world, and the deeper our learning, the more conscious, specific, and articulate will be

---

[32] Cf. My *Counter-Revolution of Science*, pp. 48 *et seqq.*, and William Craig, 'Replacement of Auxiliary Expressions', *The Philosophical Review*, 65, 1956.

[ 39 ]

our knowledge of what we do not know, our knowledge of our ignorance'.[33] We have indeed in many fields learnt enough to know that we cannot know all that we would have to know for a full explanation of the phenomena.

These boundaries may not be absolute. Though we may never know as much about certain complex phenomena as we can know about simple phenomena, we may partly pierce the boundary by deliberately cultivating a technique which aims at more limited objectives—the explanation not of individual events but merely of the appearance of certain patterns or orders. Whether we call these mere explanations of the principle or mere pattern predictions or higher-level theories does not matter. Once we explicitly recognize that the understanding of the general mechanism which produces patterns of a certain kind is not merely a tool for specific predictions but important in its own right, and that it may provide important guides to action (or sometimes indications of the desirability of no action), we may indeed find that this limited knowledge is most valuable.

What we must get rid of is the naïve superstition that the world must be so organized that it is possible by direct observation to discover simple regularities between all phenomena and that this is a necessary presupposition for the application of the scientific method. What we have by now discovered about the organization of many complex structures should be sufficient to teach us that there is no reason to expect this, and that if we want to get ahead in these fields our aims will have to be somewhat different from what they are in the fields of simple phenomena.

10. *A Postscript on the Role of 'Laws' in the Theory of Complex Phenomena*[34]

Perhaps it deserves to be added that the preceding considerations throw some doubt on the widely held view that the aim of theoretical science is to establish 'laws'—at least if the word 'law' is used as com-

---

[33] K. R. Popper, 'On the Sources of Knowledge and Ignorance', *Proceedings of the British Academy*, 46, 1960, p. 69. See also Warren Weaver, 'A Scientist Ponders Faith', *Saturday Review*, January 3, 1959: 'Is science really gaining in its assault on the totality of the unsolved? As science learns one answer, it is characteristically true that it also learns several new questions. It is as though science were working in a great forest of ignorance, making an ever larger circular clearing within which, not to insist on the pun, things are clear. . . . But, as that circle becomes larger and larger, the circumference of contact with ignorance also gets longer and longer. Science learns more and more. But there is an ultimate sense in which it does not gain; for the volume of the appreciated but not understood keeps getting larger. We keep, in science, getting a more and more sophisticated view of our ignorance.'

[34] This last section of this essay was not contained in the version originally published and has been added to this reprint.

[ 40 ]

## The Theory of Complex Phenomena

monly understood. Most people would probably accept some such definition of 'law' as that 'a scientific law is the rule by which two phenomena are connected with each other according to the principle of causality, that is to say, as cause and effect.'[35] And no less an authority than Max Planck is reported to have insisted that a true scientific law must be expressible in a single equation.[36]

Now the statement that a certain structure can assume only one of the (still infinite) number of states defined by a system of many simultaneous equations is still a perfectly good scientific (theoretical and falsifiable) statement.[37] We might still call, of course, such a statement a 'law', if we so wish (though some people might rightly feel that this would do violence to language); but the adoption of such a terminology would be likely to make us neglectful of an important distinction: for to say that such a statement describes, like an ordinary law, a relation between cause and effect would be highly misleading. It would seem, therefore, that the conception of law in the usual sense has little application to the theory of complex phenomena, and that therefore also the description of scientific theories as 'nomologic' or 'nomothetic' (or by the German term *Gesetzeswissenschaften*) is appropriate only to those two-variable or perhaps three-variable problems to which the theory of simple phenomena can be reduced, but not to the theory of phenomena which appear only above a certain level of complexity. If we assume that all the other parameters of such a system of equations describing a complex structure are constant, we can of course still call the dependence of one of the latter on the other a 'law' and describe a change in the one as 'the cause' and the change in the other as 'the effect'. But such a 'law' would be valid only for one particular set of values of all the other parameters and would change with every change in any one of them. This would evidently not be a very useful conception

[35] The particular wording which I happened to come across while drafting this is taken from H. Kelsen, 'The Natural Law Doctrine Before the Tribunal of Science' (1949), reprinted in *What is Justice?*, University of California Press, 1960, p. 139. It seems to express well a widely held view.

[36] Sir Karl Popper comments on this that it seems extremely doubtful whether any *single* one of Maxwell's equations could be said to express anything of real significance if we knew none of the others; in fact, it seems that the repeated occurrence of the symbols in the various equations is needed to secure that these symbols have the intended meanings.

[37] Cf. K. R. Popper, *Logic of Scientific Discovery*, § 17, p. 73: 'Even if the system of equations does not suffice for a unique solution, it does not allow every conceivable combination of values to be substituted for the "unknowns" (variables). Rather, the system of equations characterizes certain combinations of values or value systems as admissible, and others as inadmissible; it distinguishes the class of admissible value systems from the class of inadmissible value systems.' Note also the application of this in the following passages to 'statement equations'.

[ 41 ]

of a 'law', and the only generally valid statement about the regularities of the structure in question is the whole set of simultaneous equations from which, if the values of the parameters are continuously variable, an infinite number of particular laws, showing the dependence of one variable upon another, could be derived.

In this sense we may well have achieved a very elaborate and quite useful theory about some kind of complex phenomenon and yet have to admit that we do not know of a single law, in the ordinary sense of the word, which this kind of phenomenon obeys. I believe this to be in a great measure true of social phenomena: though we possess theories of social structures, I rather doubt whether we know of any 'laws' which social phenomena obey. It would then appear that the search for the discovery of laws is not an appropriate hall-mark of scientific procedure but merely a characteristic of the theories of simple phenomena as we have defined these earlier; and that in the field of complex phenomena the term 'law' as well as the concepts of cause and effect are not applicable without such modification as to deprive them of their ordinary meaning·

In some respect the prevalent stress on 'laws', i.e., on the discovery of regularities in two-variable relations, is probably a result of inductivism, because only such simple co-variation of two magnitudes is likely to strike the senses before an explicit theory or hypothesis has been formed. In the case of more complex phenomena it is more obvious that we must have our theory first before we can ascertain whether the things do in fact behave according to this theory. It would probably have saved much confusion if theoretical science had not in this manner come to be identified with the search for laws in the sense of a simple dependence of one magnitude upon another. It would have prevented such misconception as that, e.g., the biological theory of evolution proposed some definite 'law of evolution' such as a law of the necessary sequence of certain stages or forms. It has of course done nothing of the kind and all attempts to do this rest on a misunderstanding of Darwin's great achievement. And the prejudice that in order to be scientific one must produce laws may yet prove to be one of the most harmful of methodological conceptions. It may have been useful to some extent for the reason given by Popper, that 'simple statements . . . are to be prized more highly'[38] in all fields where simple statements are significant. But it seems to me that there will always be fields where it can be shown that all such simple statements must be false and where in consequence also the prejudice in favour of 'laws' must be harmful.

[38] *Ibid.*, p. 142.

[ 42 ]

# Forum

# Systems theory and complexity: Part 4
# The evolution of systems thinking

Kurt A. Richardson
ISCE Research, US

## Introduction

The focus throughout this series has been the consideration of general systems ideas from a complex systems perspective. This task in itself is hopefully useful to complexity thinkers and general systems thinkers alike. However, as has already been mentioned in previous installments, systems thinking has evolved considerably since the early days of General Systems Theory (GST). The developmental pathways that systems thinking has trodden during the past quarter of a century contain lessons that may facilitate, both directly and indirectly, the future development of *complex* systems thinking. It wasn't so long ago that complexity thinking was synonymous with bottom-up computer simulation. However, in the past 5-10 years we have seen other threads emerge from this mathematically focused starting point that acknowledge the profound philosophical implications of complexity (implications that are not too dissimilar to those that triggered the soft systems movement in the last 70s, early 80s), and the value of qualitative methods and methodologies to the understanding of complex problems (sometimes labeled 'messy', or 'wicked', in the systems literature). The path from abstract mathematics to critical pluralism bears such a resemblance to the path from GST to systemic intervention (for example) that it is difficult to ignore the lessons that complexity thinkers may glean from a study of the modern systems literature and its recent evolution. Given the deep similarities it is strange indeed that these two bodies of literature currently co-exist almost independently from each other.

As advertised in part 3 of this series (Richardson, 2005), this final installment is concerned with the recent evolution of systems theory/thinking. Since part 3 was published, ISCE Events organized the 1st International Workshop on Complexity and Policy Analysis that was hosted by the Department of Government University College Cork, Ireland which ran from 22-24 June, 2005 (an edited book of papers is due to appear later this summer, Dennard, et al., 2007). On day three of this event the participants listened to a presentation that not only briefly summarized the recent history of systems theory/thinking, but also looked at some of the connections with complexity theory and provided some short examples of modern systems practice. The focus of this lecture, titled "Systems thinking for community involvement in policy analysis" given by Gerald Midgley of ESR in New Zealand, matched so closely the originally plan for the final installment of this series that it was decided to base this installment on the edited transcript of Gerald's presentation. So here it is...

## References

Dennard, L., Richardson, K. A. and Goktug, M. (2007). *Complexity and Policy Analysis*, Mansfield, MA: ISCE Publishing, forthcoming.

Richardson, K. A. (2005). "Systems theory and complexity: Part 3," *Emergence: Complexity & Organization*, ISSN 1521-3250, 7(2): 104-114.

Forum

# Systems Thinking for Community Involvement in Policy Analysis

Gerald Midgley[1] & Kurt A. Richardson[2] (ed.)
[1]Institute of Environmental Science and Research (ESR), NZ
[2]ISCE Research, US

This paper is the text of a presentation to the 1st International Workshop on Complexity and Policy Analysis delivered by Gerald Midgley and transcribed and edited by Kurt Richardson. It charts the development of systems thinking since the 1960s, identifying a number of different systems paradigms. These are then compared with paradigms in complexity research, and significant parallels are identified. It is argued that there are several interacting research communities (including those writing about complexity, systems thinking and cybernetics) that have the potential to learn from one another. A research program on systemic intervention is then presented, focusing on the need to think critically about boundaries and values as a means of dealing with the inevitable lack of comprehensiveness in systemic interventions. A rationale for methodological pluralism is also given. All through the paper, the theoretical and methodological ideas are illustrated with practical examples.

## Introduction

I would like to start by thanking you for inviting me. I feel quite privileged to be invited to a complexity conference, given that I haven't made much of a contribution to complexity thinking at all, being primarily engaged with the systems community. But my hope is that there can be learning across these two communities, and that's one of the things I want to talk about today.

My talk is called "Systems Thinking for Community Involvement in Policy Analysis", and over the years I have talked with numerous audiences, particularly in the areas of management and community development. Some approaches that I've used are adaptable across domains, so I'm hoping that what I say will have some relevance to policy.

I want to start by acknowledging some of the history of policy analysis because, as I understand it, in the 1960s policy analysis and systems analysis were considered virtually synonymous – most policy people were using systems analysis in some way. That approach came into disrepute in the late 60s and early 70s. In this presentation I want to touch on what happened with systems analysis, in case there are people out there who are skeptical about why somebody would even bother to talk about systems thinking again. I also want to give some information about where systems thinking has moved to, because it has entered a space that has a lot of commonalities with complexity thinking. I would also like to talk about the relationship between systems thinking and complexity science before going onto my own work, which is about *systemic intervention*.

When I talk about 'systemic intervention', I am making an assumption that I think all systems thinking and complexity approaches make: that everything in the universe is directly or indirectly connected with everything else. However, you can't have a God's eye view of that interconnectedness, so there are inevitable limits to understanding, and it is those limits that we call *boundaries*. So, systemic intervention is fundamentally about how to explore those boundaries, and how to take account of the inevitable lack of comprehensiveness and begin to deal with it. This will lead me onto talk about something that I've called *boundary critique*. And by this I mean being critical of boundaries, rethinking them, considering the different meanings they invoke and the values associated with those meanings.

The discussion of boundary critique will take me onto the need for theoretical and methodological pluralism, drawing upon mixed methods, and evolving methodology on an ongoing basis. Throughout this talk I will give you some practical examples, as I think

- The death of the 'super model'

- The limits of 'rational planning'

- The limits of the 'engineering' metaphor

- The limits of 'expertise'

- The limits of 'optimisation'

- The inability to deal adequately with conflicting values, viewpoints, policy preferences, ideologies & power relations

- The self-justifying ideology of systems science as comprehensive analysis

**Slide 1** *The critique of systems analysis ('60s and '70s)*

it is quite important to ground these ideas in practice to give them deeper meaning.

## The critique of systems analysis (1960s and 1970s) (slide 1)

Let us start with what happened to system analysis in the early days. People may be aware that there were lots of large scale modeling projects in the 1950s and 1960s. The ones that seemed to come into most disrepute were the ones where giant models were built, especially in California (the Californian experience seems to be the typical one that other authors have written about), where local government offices were recruiting consultants to build models of whole cities with no particular purpose in mind. The belief was that a policymaker could go to the modeler and say, "Well, can you now answer this question for me given all the wonderful data that you have?" Of course, by building models without purposes you end up with such huge complexity that the results are largely unreliable and meaningless. In the 1960s, millions of dollars were invested in giant models of this nature, with limited practical results. I call this phenomenon *the death of the super model.*

People also began to realize the limits of conventional *rational planning.* And the example that I like to give (it's not really an example from systems thinking actually – it's an example from operations research in the UK) is the planning of Stansted airport. Here, they spent a lot of money commissioning an analysis of the best option for building a new London airport. They evaluated a number of alternatives, taking account of environmental and social impacts, etc., and then said, "This is the best one." The politicians promptly replied, "Well, that's no good. It doesn't take into account our political realities, and we'll choose this one instead." This example is widely regarded in the OR community as illustrating the decline of rational planning. Actually to me it's an example of *irrational* planning. It's irrational because it did not take into account the perspectives (or the rationali*ties* – plural) of those people who needed to take the decision. That doesn't mean that you just agree with political perspectives, regardless of the assumptions they are based upon, but it does mean that you have to work with them in order to be able to get something that's going to be useful.

Interestingly, these issues were not only encountered by systems analysts. There was also a major *systems engineering* movement that spread across the world in the 1950s and 1960s. With the term 'engineering', of course, come all the connotations of being able to command and control social systems, as if people with their own self-consciousness didn't actually sometimes say, "I want to resist those kinds of improvements." So, the engineering metaphor began to die away.

E:CO Vol. 9 Nos. 1-2 2007 pp. 167-183

- Model for particular purposes, and *explore* those purposes rather than take them for granted

- Accept the relevance of multiple rationali*ties* instead of generating 'objectively rational policy'

- Abandon 'engineering' in favour of engaging with self-conscious actors

- Democratise 'expertise'

- Confine 'optimisation' approaches to limited spheres of application

- Account for conflicting values, viewpoints, policy preferences, etc.

- Accept that systems thinking is about dealing with the inevitable *lack* of comprehensiveness, and is not the means to *achieve* comprehensiveness

**Slide 2** *More recent systems thinking principles*

The notion of 'expertise' also came under scrutiny, i.e., the idea that modelers and scientists always know best. People began to realize that other kinds of expertise (e.g., the expertise of the people on the receiving end of some of these policies), were actually important.

People also began to appreciate the limits of optimization approaches. It is simply the case that what is optimal from one perspective may, given a different value set and a different perspective, be completely unacceptable. So, simply talking about optimization as the only thing that we do is not enough.

With the inability to deal adequately with conflicting values, viewpoints, policy preferences, ideologies, power relations, etc., the limitations of some of the 'engineering', 'rational' and 'optimization' approaches began to show through. People began to realize that, if you simply start with the goal of one stakeholder and assume that this is unproblematic, then all kinds of side effects can emerge.

Finally, on Slide 1, I have said that, in the 1960s, the 'self-justifying ideology' of systems science was one of *comprehensive analysis*. What often happened is that if a model failed (i.e., if people were not satisfied with the results), the modelers simply said "we weren't comprehensive enough so we need more systems analysis." If that kind of reply is given often enough, people will eventually declare,

"the Emperor has no clothes."

So that's what was happening in the 1960s and 1970s, with the backlash against systems analysis, and it really took systems thinking a good decade to recover its credibility. In that process of recovery, some quite dramatic shifts in systems thinking happened. I'll talk very generally about what those shifts involved. Of course you will always be able to find exceptions to these generalizations, and there are dimensions to the shift that I will not cover, but here I am only able to provide an overview.

## More recent systems thinking principles (slide 2)

Instead of producing massive super models, modeling for particular purposes (rather than all purposes) became more usual. Much more focused modeling was undertaken that didn't necessarily pretend to be comprehensive, but actually thought about what is involved in making a model fit for purpose. Also, modelers *explored* those purposes instead of just taking them for granted. So, now people began to embed that modeling in a social process, as opposed to simply producing a mathematical model and thinking that it will produce the answers on its own.

Part of the new socially-embedded modeling process was accepting the relevance of multiple rationalities, instead of generating

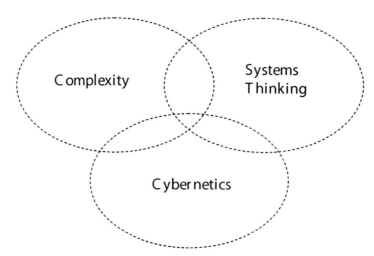

**Slide 3** *Systems thinking and complexity science*

a so-called objective rational policy. We began to realize of course that, if there are different perspectives out there, it's going to matter whether our modeling is meaningful or not to those different perspectives.

The engineering metaphor was largely abandoned in favor of engaging with self-conscious actors, although it is still around in a few places. For example, in the military domain, people still talk about systems engineering. It's also still prominent in China where there's an institute for systems engineering (which has over 600 researchers) that is as important as the institutes for physics, biology and chemistry. In Colombia, there are still systems engineering degrees, but what they teach is actually the whole breadth of systems thinking, so the term has changed its meaning.

The democratization of expertise has also taken place. Instead of assuming that the necessary expertise is simply scientific, modeling or policy expertise, many other possible types of expertise are recognized, including perspectives from people in the community. From my own point of view, it is really important to preserve the notion of expertise because, although there have been some people arguing that we should just get rid of the term, it's quite dangerous to pretend that the systems thinker, or the intervener, is 'just another participant'. They actually play quite a pivotal role in constructing events, and by labeling it as a particular kind of expertise, you can make them accountable. If you lose the notion of expertise altogether, there is a risk that you lose

accountability for the exercise of power.

The value of optimization approaches has not been entirely undermined, but there is a growing acceptance that such approaches have limited spheres of application. I like something that somebody said yesterday about *islands of tractability*, as it is an idea that has really come into favor. The idea is that there *are*, of course, valid applications for optimization techniques. You want the trains to run on time. You want to be able to get to a conference like this on time. Of course we need optimization techniques, but they have *limited domains of application*. We also need approaches that account for conflicting values, viewpoints, policy preferences, etc.

Ultimately, the contemporary systems view urges us to accept that *systems thinking is about dealing with the inevitable lack of comprehensiveness, and is not the means to achieve comprehensiveness.* This is a really crucial shift in how systems thinking has developed.

## Systems thinking and complexity science (slide 3)

In terms of the relationship between complexity and systems (why I'm here basically, in terms of learning from complexity people and hopefully the learning being two-way), I see systems thinking as a discourse that has a community of people who are engaged within it, with fuzzy boundaries at the edges. I think that complexity is quite similar in that respect. There's a community of complexity researchers, and both communities overlap

| Complexity | Systems |
|---|---|
| Complexity Science (e.g., Gell-Mann) | General System Theory (e.g., Von Bertalanffy) |
| Agent-Based Modeling (e.g., Allen) | Hard Systems Thinking (e.g., Hall) |
| Interpretive Complexity / Social Interactionism (e.g., Stacey) | Soft Systems Thinking (e.g., Checkland) |
| Critical Complexity (e.g., Cilliers) | Critical Systems Thinking (e.g., Ulrich) |

**Slide 4** *Multiple paradigms of systems and complexity*

with one another. I can see people around this room that I encounter in both communities. There are other communities that interact with systems and complexity as well: for example, the cybernetics community. I just put a third one (cybernetics) on the overhead as an example of a research community that both systems thinking and complexity science is connected with, but there are others. I think that this is a much more fruitful way of thinking about the interrelationships between these various communities than to try to say, "well, actually systems thinking is the thing that encompasses all these communities, and complexity is a sub-approach", or "complexity encompasses everything and we'll fit systems thinking within it." There are differences in the agendas, so the separate identities are worth preserving (and there will be different views about what those differences are), but there is sufficient similarity to make mutual respect and learning across community boundaries worthwhile.

## Multiple paradigms of systems and complexity (slide 4)

And yet neither complexity nor systems thinking are easy to define. We saw that in our first day here. It was quite clear that people are using the words in different ways. However, it is not necessarily productive to try to define them exactly. Arguably

a more constructive approach, that gives room for different perspectives but also gives us an overview, is to look at the main paradigms within a research area. I therefore want to give some examples of paradigms in both complexity and systems thinking. I've done this in Slide 4.

It seems to me that the same set of paradigms has emerged in both perspectives: you have the basic scientific theories; the modeling approaches; the interpretive and social interaction approaches; and the critical approaches (which are really about values and ethics). Of course this is just a story that I've created to reduce the complexity, and there is also a lot of variety that is not represented in Slide 4, but I find these similarities quite interesting.

## The meaning of 'systemic intervention' (slide 5)

I have presented the previous material primarily to situate where I'm coming from, and why I'm here. I next want to give you a little bit of background to my own work. The systemic intervention research program that I've been developing is something that I've been working on over the last twenty-or-so years, mostly in the UK, but now in New Zealand. It's a program that has been continually building theory and practice that mutually inform one another, so I've been engaged in a lot

*Intervention*:

## Purposeful Action by an Agent to Create Change

*Systemic Intervention*:

## Purposeful Action by an Agent to Create Change *in Relation to Reflection upon Boundaries*

**Slide 5** *The meaning of 'systemic intervention'*

of multi-agency and community development work around social and environmental issues.

I want to start by defining what I mean by 'intervention', knowing that this definition will raise more questions than it gives answers. I want you to ride with this because, as the talk unfolds, you'll see where I'm going with it. I want to define intervention as *purposeful action by an agent to create change*. Now, that doesn't mean completely pre-planned, or based on flawless prediction, or any of those sorts of things, but I think you can talk about action being *purposeful*. It doesn't mean that the purpose is necessarily coming from outside, as if you're manipulating a system. Whether you're coming from inside an organization or whether you're brought in from outside (like a consultant), you become part of the organization as soon as you engage with it. Once action starts, it is always action from inside.

And what I mean by *systemic* intervention – going back to what I said right at the very beginning – is that because we can't know the interconnectedness of reality, the full interconnectedness of everything (i.e., we cannot have that God's eye view), we necessarily have boundaries. Whether you're aware of them or not, in your understanding of anything there are boundaries involved. So, systemic intervention for me means purposeful action by an agent to create change *in relation to reflection on those boundaries*. So that's the basic concept I like to use to begin to think about how you deal with the impossibility of knowing everything.

### Some ideas about boundaries

What I want to do next is go very briefly through the history of some of the ideas about boundaries in the systems community that I think might be relevant to the complexity community as well. I want to start with the basic boundary idea that was introduced by Churchman in the 1960s, because he made a radical departure from the previous systems ideas where people just assumed that boundaries are reflections of reality: real markers of the edge of a system (e.g., the skin of my body being a boundary). What Churchman did was to say that boundaries could be conceptual or social constructs. They mark the inclusion or exclusion of stakeholders, people and issues. They demarcate what is relevant to an analysis. A boundary may coincide with a physical edge or not, depending on the purposes of the person looking at the system.

The ellipse in Slide 6 represents a boundary which marks who's included, who's excluded, what issues are in the analysis, and what issues are out. The peak represents the values that are associated with that particular boundary. Churchman's key insight was that value judgments always drive boundary judgments, and so it is impossible to have a situation where you have a bounded understanding without having some values lying behind that. So, the idea of absolutely objective analysis is problematic. You might be able to reconstruct the notion of objectivity, but you have to acknowledge that there are values involved in any boundary judgment. But, at the same time, because we don't come to a situation completely from the outside with pre-given values,

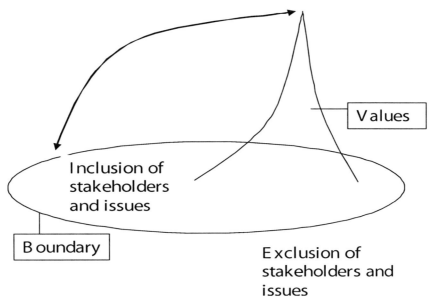

Slide 6 *The boundary idea*

those values actually emerge from the systems that we are already embedded in. So the given boundary judgments that are made in institutions and in human communities already constrain the kinds of values that can possibly emerge. There is therefore an intimate, two-way relationship between boundaries and values, and to explore that kind of relationship is a useful starting point for systemic intervention.

In terms of my own experience of facilitating systemic interventions, if you start to talk about boundaries, people often get stuck with thinking about current, familiar boundaries, and they tend to be constrained in their thinking. If you actually start with values, people are often less used to thinking that way, and it opens up considerations more easily. Thus, my starting point tends to be around values, moving onto the boundaries that these imply.

Churchman was working in the 1960s, and his mission was to create an ethical systems practice. He believed that, because boundaries constrain values, the most ethical systems practice is one that pushes out the boundaries of analysis widely, to be inclusive of as many different value perspectives as possible – but without going to the extreme of over-inclusion so that action is paralyzed. He basically said that you should push out the boundaries as widely as possible, within the limits of the human capacity to process information. How-

ever, in the early 1980s, one of his students, Werner Ulrich, was quite critical of this. He said, "Well, that's all very well in theory, but in practice there are a lot of constraints that stop you pushing out the boundaries as widely as possible. And, it's not necessarily irrational to live with those constraints when you have to take practical actions." He wanted to think about how you rationally justify boundary judgments, given that you can't be as comprehensive as you would want to be a lot of the time.

In order to answer that question, "how can you rationally justify system boundaries?", he had to ask a deeper question, which is, "what is rationality?" I'm sure nobody has come to this policy analysis workshop to answer the question "what is rationality?", but Ulrich actually had to address this in order to deal with the problem of boundary setting, and he came to the conclusion that any argument concerned with the justification of a boundary is always expressed in language. Language is something that is socially shared with other people: it's not something that is a purely private affair. That doesn't mean we always completely agree on the meanings of words and signs, but they are nevertheless socially shared. So he came out with the principal that to say something is *rationally justified* means that it has to be *agreed with all those involved in, and affected by, the thing that we're looking at.* Of course,

Ulrich recognized that this is a high standard of rationality to achieve in many practical situations and said, "Yes, but it is something you try to *move towards*; you try to secure an agreement between those involved in planning *and* those affected by it, even if you know that you will not always succeed."

To make this idea practical, he developed a set of '*critical systems heuristics*' questions that both planners and ordinary people could use in debate to think through issues. These questions were about what the situation currently *is* and what it *ought* to be. The twelve questions he developed focus on four areas, namely:

- *Motivation* – why would you want to be planning this system in the first place?

- *Control* – who should have decision-making power? What should people have some say over, and what shouldn't they have a say over?

- *Expertise* – what forms of knowledge are necessary, and from what sources?

- *Legitimacy* – what are the values this is based on? Are you creating an oppressive system and, if so, what should you do about it (if anything)?

So there are twelve questions, three for each of these four areas, and I've used them myself in a number of different studies: for example, with children living on the streets; with people with mental health problems in prison; and with older people in residential care. I think Ulrich is quite right to claim that these are questions that ordinary people with no experience of planning can engage with. I have found that ordinary people can produce outputs that are at least as comprehensive as those generated by professional planners, providing that the questions are translated into everyday language (Ulrich's original questions contain some academic jargon, so you have to rephrase them).

When I came into this research area in the mid-to-late 1980s, I was interested in what Ulrich had done, but I was also interested in what happened when different value and boundary judgments come into conflict, i.e., when you have a situation where people make different boundary judgments and have different values, and they get into entrenched conflicts that begin to stabilize. I wanted to both try to explain that phenomenon, and see if I could identify some methods to do something about it. So, I developed the idea that in most situations there isn't just one boundary judgment going on, but multiple judgments (as depicted in Slide 7). The inner ellipse represents a boundary judgment that might be made by one group, and the next ellipse is a boundary judgment that might be made by a second group. The area in between these two boundaries is referred to as the *marginal* area. There are things that are of core interest to everybody,

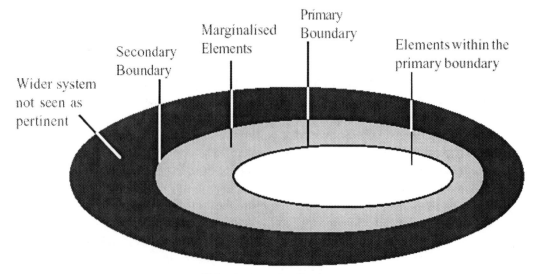

**Slide 7** *Marginalization*

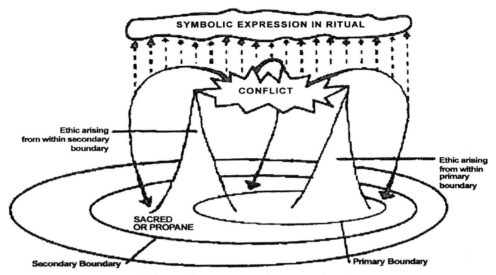

**Slide 8** *The process of marginalization*

and things that only interest some groups.

To give an example, consider unemployment. An industrial organization may have ethical owners and managers who are concerned with the welfare of their employees: they are concerned with paying them a decent wage, but are not interested in giving money to people who are unemployed in the local community. This community is outside their sphere of concern. As is quite common and understandable, they are concerned with the health of their own organization, with their own employees. On the other hand, you may have activists in the community who are very interested in people who are unemployed, and who believe that the industry has some responsibility to deal with unemployment. So you begin to get conflict.

Now Slide 8. This might look horrific at first, but I'll talk you through it. First, you see the same boundaries here as in Slide 7. In the center is a narrow boundary judgment. Let us say that this is the one made by the industrial organization, which claims that it only needs to be interested in the welfare of its own employees. The next (middle) boundary represents the one made by the community activists who say that the industrial organization should also be interested in dealing with unemployment. The two peaks represent the values that are associated with each boundary judgment, and these values come into conflict (represented by the 'explosion' between the two values).

I realized through practical experiences in a number of projects that these kinds of situations are not necessarily always resolved. There is a tendency to assume that when you've got a conflict, somehow the conflict gets resolved and everything's nice in the end. However, a lot of conflicts are not easily resolved: they stabilize, and they perpetuate for weeks, months, years, or even generations, and there is something going on that creates this situation. In my research I began to look at what is happening to the things in the margins, and I realized that they have a role in stabilizing conflict situations. I noticed that the things in the margins are attributed the status of being *sacred* or *profane*, and I use such strong words to emphasize the power of these kinds of judgments. If the things in the margins are viewed as profane, then it justifies only looking at the narrow boundary. So people who are unemployed, for example, begin to be looked on as scroungers who are wasting taxpayers' money, thereby justifying people in the organization saying, "It's not a concern of ours; these are wasters; and it's not our responsibility." Or they get viewed as sacred, so the community activists begin to say, "If we could only harness the energy of the unemployed, they'll be the vanguard for a new political movement." I can certainly identify with this sentiment personally: in my early 20s I was involved in a political party, and I stood outside employment exchanges (where unemployed people register for welfare) handing out leaflets seeking to recruit people. In retrospect, I can now see that I was making the unemployed people sacred. My perspective on this was just part of a wider system that included those who saw the same people as profane.

Interestingly, there's rarely a consensus around whether things in the margins – whether issues or people – are sacred or profane, and this is critical to the perpetuation of conflict. The stabilization eventually happens through the *institutionalization of ritual*, and either the sacred or profane attribution is made dominant. To give an example of ritual, I was unemployed for three years in the early 1980s (the early Reagan/Thatcher years), and I had to sign a register once a week to declare that I was eligible for work. That particular ritual had a function: it allowed the people working in the employment exchange to know that I was available for work. However, it was also an exercise in ritual humiliation that basically expressed the view that unemployed people are 'profane'.

So, this is the kind of process that I believe is going on, and it happens at all sorts of levels. I've seen it going on in small groups; within organizations; between organizations; across communities; and in international relations. Some processes are easier to shift than others. Some are very, very difficult to shift indeed. I was at a conference a few years ago, and when I reached this part of the talk a woman in the audience asked me an absolute bummer of a question. She said, "I'm from Israel, and this model really explains the Palestinian/Israeli conflict. *What would you do about it?*" I said, "Well, some problems are easier to diagnosis than they are to solve!" What is actually going on in some really, really entrenched situations is that this whole process of marginalization is given life, and made very resistant to change, by conflicting discourses that are embedded in institutions across societies.

I can illustrate with the example of unemployment again. The marginal status of the unemployed is extremely difficult to change. The reason I see for this relates to the conflict that goes on in our institutions between the discourses of capitalism and liberalism. Al-though these two discourses are mutually supportive in many situations (for instance, liberalism promotes the ideal of individual choice and capitalism allows the manufacture of a variety of goods to choose between), in relation to unemployment they are not. In capitalist societies, you need organizations to be responsible for their own employees, but they mustn't be responsible for others in the community. If organizations had to be responsible for all the people in their local communities (which the liberal ideal of equal citizenship might suggest would be a good thing) then they could not have any influence over their own competitiveness and the capitalist system as we know it would collapse. At the same time, if you actually said that it is legitimate for unemployed people to be completely neglected, to starve on the streets, then the liberal ideal of equal citizenship would collapse instead. The only way to preserve both things at the same time is to have unemployed people neither totally inside nor totally outside. They have to be kept in that marginal position.

Of course, like any model, Slide 8 is an oversimplification. In real situations there are lots of dynamic processes like this interacting. I should also note that my interest in this is not purely sociological. My main interest is to ask, "What meaning can this have for intervention? What can you actually learn from this? How can you reflect on these kinds of processes and do something about them?"

### An example: Developing services for young people (under 16) living on the streets

To give you a practical example to ground these ideas a little better, I want to very briefly talk about a project, which was about developing services for young people under sixteen living on the streets. This is a project I worked on in Manchester (UK) in partnership with two colleagues, Alan Boyd and Mandy Brown. Three voluntary organizations commissioned this project because they were aware that there were lots of homeless children living on the streets, and they were falling through the net of all the agencies. No agency had a statutory responsibility to deal with the situation: these particular children were not in

**To deal with this marginalisation we:**

- **Sought the views of young people before involving professionals so the voices of the former were not crowded out**

- **Communicated *their* words (not just ours) to professionals, to convey the emotional experience of being on the streets, thereby securing multi-agency commitments to change**

- **Used the same design methods with young people as with professionals to ensure we did not reproduce the perception that young people are less 'rational'**

**Slide 9** *Developing services for young people (under 16) living on the streets 2*

school, so the schools did not have to deal with them; and state housing is for people over sixteen, so the housing authority didn't have to deal with them. You could go from one agency to another, and each would argue that child homelessness is not their responsibility. The voluntary organizations wanted us to work with the young people themselves, as well as with the agencies, to try to get some commitment to actually do something about the situation, even though it was not anyone's statutory responsibility.

I'd like to give you the whole story, but here I'll just focus on one aspect of marginalization. It was really important to us to involve young people centrally in this project. We noticed that, in terms of Slide 8, there were two kinds of marginalization going on. First of all, young people in general are marginalized in the sense that they're regarded as less rational, and less able to make informed decisions about their own lives, than adults. As such, they can only vote when they're eighteen; they can only buy alcohol at a certain age; there's an age of consent for sex; etc. Various things mark out young people as different in relation to their decision making ability. Secondly, these particular children were living on the streets. We're talking about something like 2,000 children in the one year living on the streets of Manchester. I thought this was a problem in Brazil. I didn't think it was a problem that existed in

the UK. So it was a shock to me, as a UK researcher, that this sort of thing was going on. It was really a hidden problem. If they want to stay on the streets for any length of time, these children can only survive through petty crime or prostitution. They are children who could easily be classified as 'troubled teenagers' and be marginalized in that way.

How did we go about getting broad involvement (Slide 9)? First of all, we sought the views of young people before approaching professionals: the voices of the young people were actually the foundation upon which the professionals could build commitment. Going to young people first was effective in harnessing multi-agency involvement because their voices were very, very powerful. It was really strong, emotional material that we generated through interviews with children on the streets. This basically made it emotionally impossible for the agencies to say that they were not going to get involved. We communicated the *young people's* words, not just ours, to professionals. This was really important, partly because of the need for emotional engagement, and partly because we had a situation where, as we were interviewing young people on the streets, a number of them were making quite strong allegations about how the police were behaving towards them; that they'd been abused by the police in various ways. We had a workshop with the police, and we decided that, ethically, we couldn't just set this aside and pretend that it wasn't happening. So we produced quotations – all of the quotations, whether they were positive or negative about the police, filling three pages in total – and gave them out at the workshop. Initially there was silence in the room. I was sitting there thinking, "This could just explode in any direction". It was a huge risk. But the very first person who spoke put their head up and said, "I know who did this one!" And people spontaneously started to say, "Yes, we have to deal with it." Within an hour, they produced five different ideas for how they could actually correct the situation. I enjoyed working with the police: I found it to be a really proactive agency.

When we actually got onto designing the services for homeless children, we used the same design methods with the young people as with professionals. We actually had a disagreement in our team over this. One member of the team suggested that we ought to use a 'playful' approach that would allow children to represent their concerns in a play or using art techniques. My feeling was that, if we took a playful approach, it would have been very easy for the professionals to have said, "Oh yes, that's very nice, we'll take it into account, but here's the *proper* plan that we have produced." To avoid that, I thought we needed to use the same process with the young people as with the professionals. So, in separate workshops with children and agency representatives, we used the principles of *interactive planning* developed by Russ Ackoff.

There are three principles of design in interactive planning:

- Plans have to be *technologically feasible.* So there are no magic solutions to housing problems, like little fold-up houses in your pocket.

- What is produced has to be *viable.* It has to be sustainable in social, ecological, economic, and cultural terms. For the purposes of design you can disregard start-up costs, but a new development has to be sustainable by the agencies that are going to run it.

- It has to be *adaptable.* You mustn't produce some kind of super bureaucracy that is impossible to change when circumstances change around it.

These principles are designed to promote creativity and the development of ambitious proposals for change, while preventing people from fixing on completely unrealistic ideas. We also used the critical systems heuristics questions that I mentioned before (about motivation, control, expertise and legitimacy) to guide the debate. This made sure that questions of governance and young people's involvement were considered as part of the process. The young people actually produced much more detailed designs than the professionals. They dealt with things in a really sophisticated way. For example, they were talking about building a refuge for young people in the center of the city, and they discussed the drugs policy that would be needed in that refuge. There was one girl who said, "You need a 'three strikes and you're out' policy, because drugs create violence in a refuge like this, and the last thing we want is violence when people are already in a vulnerable situation." Another girl then turned around to her and said, "How can you say that? You take drugs every day." And she replied, "What I do and what is necessary for the refuge are two different things." So there was a level of awareness and responsibility amongst the children that was really striking for the professionals, and allowed the professionals to have confidence to take these ideas forward.

### Theoretical pluralism (Slide 10)

I've already talked about the notion of boundaries, and the idea that it is possible to explore different boundary judgments and the values associated with these. This legitimizes *theoretical pluralism*: drawing upon multiple theories depending on our purposes, rather than seeking one single 'grand' theory. Different theories assume different boundaries of analysis. For example, Maturana and Varela's theory of autopoiesis is about the biological nature of human beings, and it tends to put its primary emphasis on the boundary of the

E:CO Vol. 9 Nos. 1-2 2007 pp. 167-183

- Different theories assume different boundaries for analysis
- If we can decide between a wide range of possible boundaries, we can also draw upon a wide variety of theories

**Slide 10** *Theoretical pluralism*

- Different methodologies and methods make different theoretical assumptions
- Therefore, if theoretical pluralism is possible, so is methodological pluralism

**Slide 11** *Methodological pluralism*

individual organism. In contrast, Luhmann's theory of *social* autopoiesis emphasizes institutions as communicative systems, and it places biology outside its boundary of concern.

So, different theories assume different boundaries. Logically then, if it's reasonable to choose between different boundaries, it's also reasonable to choose between different theories. Whether or not you have to harmonize those theories in an intervention depends entirely on your purposes. If you're supporting the development of new policy to deal with a social issue, and draw upon several different theories to understand the human relationships unfolding through your intervention, maybe you don't actually need to harmonize the different assumptions of those theories, even if they are commonly seen as incommensurable. That might be an unnecessary exercise because the primary purpose is to support the

emergence of a new policy. But if what you're trying to do is produce a new theory of human relationships to enhance our understanding of the policy making process, then harmonizing any contributory theories would be important to making the final theoretical product coherent. It entirely depends on your purposes and audience.

### Methodological pluralism (Slide 11)

Now I want to move on from *theoretical* pluralism to *methodological* pluralism. Different methodologies and methods make different theoretical assumptions, so if you can have theoretical pluralism, you can certainly have methodological pluralism. This is the theoretical rationale for methodological pluralism, but the most important reason for embracing it is practical. There is no method, as far as I can see, that can do everything. It is

1. Learning from other methodologies to inform one's own
2. Drawing upon and mixing methods from other methodologies, which come to be seen through the 'lens' of one's own methodology

**Slide 12** *Two kinds of methodological pluralism*

- Interviews to consider boundaries and values, and to determine the main focus of the evaluation

- Soft systems methodology for planning the work of the team and establishing the focus of a database

- SSADM and database design

- Participant observation, interviews and collection of individual case study data

- Quantification and statistical analysis of client group characteristics and diversion rates

- Triangulation of the quantitative and qualitative data

- Critical Systems Heuristics and Interactive Planning to propose change in the wider criminal justice and mental health systems

*Slide 13 Evaluating a diversion from custody service for mentally disordered offenders (SSADM: Structured Systems Analysis and Design Method)*

therefore a good idea to draw upon multiple methods for different purposes.

Before continuing, I want to make a distinction between *methodology* and *method*:

- *Method* is a set of techniques to achieve some purpose, and;

- *Methodologies* are the theories and ideas that enable one to understand why particular methods are appropriate.

There are two kinds of methodological pluralism (Slide 12): there is learning from other methodologies to inform your own, and there is mixing methods from different methodological sources. First let us look at learning from other methodologies:

You can build a methodology in an ongoing way, learning from other people. I have built my understanding of methodology over a period of approximately twenty one years. In order to be credible, you have to have some coherence within the set of ideas you work with. But to have learning from other perspectives, you also need to welcome disjunctions at the same time. You have to be able to tolerate a certain amount of discord in your thinking in order to be able to take in ideas from others. In my own work, I go through periods of opening up to other ideas followed by periods of consolidation. I tend to think of developing a methodology as producing a *fragmentary*

*whole*, which is a deliberately contradictory concept: there is sufficient coherence to be able to observe some consistency in the argumentation, but new ideas can still be embraced, and integration is not necessarily immediate. What this allows you to do in an academic or practitioner community is avoid the situation that communities often get into where people build their methodologies like castles. Then they go up to the ramparts and start firing at all the other people who try to knock their castles down. If we can accept that somebody else having a good idea doesn't have to undermine our own thinking, because we can tolerate some disjunctions as we take in ideas from others, then this enables much more productive relationships and learning opportunities in our academic and practitioner communities.

Then there is the other form of methodological pluralism: mixing methods from different methodological sources.

### An example: Evaluating a diversion from custody service for mentally disordered offenders (Slide 13)

To give you an example of what I mean when I talk about methodological pluralism at the level of methods, I'll briefly discuss a project that I undertook with a colleague, Claire Cohen, when we were asked to evaluate a diversion from custody service for mentally disorder offenders (people with mental health problems who inappropriately end up in prison). Instead of getting treatment, these people have been incarcerated for a crime, or they're in custody in a police cell awaiting charge or trial, and they're not getting any help. The service brought together a social worker, a probation officer and a psychiatric nurse who were going around police cells to identify people with mental health problems. They were trying to work with the police and with the prison service to get mentally disordered offenders out of prison and find them alternatives to custody. When we were offered this evaluation, I could see straight away that they were responding to an existing situation instead of proactively trying to prevent it. So I suggested, "Instead of being a responsive service, don't you want to use your staff to try to change the system so that people with mental health problems don't actually get into prison in the first place?" And the woman I was talking with said, "No, no, no. Don't go there. We've got the funding for a responsive service, and this is all we can do right now." So I struck a deal with her that we would do what she wanted, and we would spend a year gathering data about the effectiveness of the existing service, but we agreed that if this data showed that they were only 'mopping up' (that they were an ambulance at the bottom of the cliff), they would revisit the issue of being more proactive.

We utilized multiple methods for this evaluation. These included methods drawn from Checkland's *soft systems methodology*, which is a process for engaging people in debate about the current situation and the human activities that are needed to improve it. That was useful in supporting the diversion team's planning, and also to inform the design of a database for data collection. We used participant observation and interviews; case study information on individual clients with mental health problems; and statistical analysis of client group characteristics and diversion rates. We triangulated the qualitative and quantitative data. I have suggested previously that quantitative and qualitative information are both useful for different purposes.

This project was a good example of where quantitative data was absolutely neces-

sary because the team had a view of their project as failing. I asked them to estimate what percentage of their cases involved a successful diversion from custody, and they thought they had maybe a 30-40% success rate. What our statistics showed was that they had an 85% success rate overall, and that for minor crimes this rose to 100%. However, because it might have taken five attempts before the police released someone, the four unsuccessful attempts appeared to outweigh the one successful one in their minds. Despite their subjective experience of failure, the team was actually very successful in getting people out of custody.

What we also found when we triangulated the quantitative data and the qualitative case studies, was that a small, hard core of individuals were going in and out of prison on a regular basis. There were twelve individuals in our sample who in one year alone had been in prison over twenty times each. Essentially, these people were stuck in a revolving door, and it is because of this we went back to the management of the service and said, "You really *do* need to look at the whole issue of how you design the system to prevent this from happening in the first place." They agreed. Unfortunately we had very little money left, and very little time, so we did the only thing we could with the remaining resources. We held the same kind of workshops that we did with the children on the streets that I was talking about earlier, both with professionals and with people with mental health problems who had recently been released from prison. The aim was to look at what the properties of the mental health and criminal justice systems ought to be if they were to prevent people from getting into this situation in the first place. The thing that really surprised both the professionals and the people with mental health problems was that they agreed on about 90% of what should be done. And even the areas of disagreement were not fundamental: all parties accepted that they could work on resolving them.

When we first contacted the group of mentally disordered offenders, they had no idea that there were others with similar problems. They found it enormously helpful to realize that they had common experiences. As a

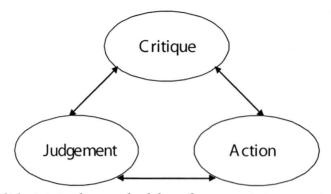

**Slide 14** *Outline methodology for systemic intervention*

- **Boundary critique enhances reflection on issues of inclusion/exclusion, marginalisation and the design of methods**

- **Methodological pluralism enables a more flexible and responsive intervention practice than adherence to an approach that only provides a limited range of methods**

- *Systemic intervention* **– involving a synergy of boundary critique and methodological pluralism – gives added value compared with either in isolation**

**Slide 15** *Conclusions about systemic intervention*

result of our intervention, they decided to form a user group, and said that they would become part of the process of dealing with the problem from that point on. So we stepped out, leaving the service with ideas to take forward for changing the system.

### Outline methodology for systemic intervention

If I could be really silly, and try to sum up everything I've written in the last twenty one years in a single overhead, it would be Slide 14. You need a minimum of three things in a systemic intervention process. First, you need a process of *critique* – i.e., thinking critically about boundaries and values. Second, you need *judgment* about what kinds of methods are going to be appropriate, and you need a creative synthesis between different approaches. It's not just about picking methods off the shelf, because most situations are com-

plex enough to actually require quite creative design processes. I often find myself inventing new methods rather than just copying something from off the shelf. Finally, you need *action*, which is about implementing the products of the interactive process of critique and judgment.

These three elements are not steps in a methodology where you simply go from one to another in a linear manner. Rather, they are lenses through which you look at a situation to make sure that you've covered the three aspects that are necessary for systemic intervention.

### Conclusions about systemic intervention (Slide 15)

The first two conclusions shown in Slide 15 are not new, but I hope the third one is. The first one is that *boundary critique enhances reflection on issues of inclusion and exclusion, marginalization and the design of methods.* I.e., boundary critique is a useful idea! People have been developing the systems theory of boundaries since the 1960s. The second conclusion, about the value of methodological pluralism, is not new either. Numerous authors over the past twenty years have explained how it allows a more flexible and responsive intervention practice than adherence to a limited approach that has just a narrow range of methods, and methodological pluralism has become a mainstream idea in the systems community. However, there are still a lot of people out there in the operations research and other communities who champion just one approach as the answer to every kind of problem, so that's why I think it's necessary to continue to talk about this.

My own contribution is to bring these two things (boundary critique and methodological pluralism) together. There is a danger in just doing boundary critique alone: you can have good sociological analyses of situations, but you do not necessarily get any action to change them at the end of the day. Similarly, by just having methodological pluralism alone, you can end up with quite a superficial analysis based on the word of a couple of managers you have spoken to, and then you pick a range of methods that you think are going to be appropriate for the situation. This superficial approach can have quite dramatic side effects when you fail to take into account other perspectives that could be impacting upon the situation. So boundary critique helps deepen analysis to allow you to make methodological choices in a more informed way. The *synergy* of the two is where I believe my own contribution to systems methodology lies.

Given the similarities between the various systems and complexity paradigms noted earlier, I hope that some of this systems research has relevance for the complexity community too.

## Acknowledgement

The research reported in this paper has been partially funded by the Foundation for Research, Science and Technology (contract C03X0304).

Forum

# "Don't dis' the ants, man!" Acknowledging the place of ants, termites, birds, and bees*

Carol Webb[1], Fiona Lettice[2] & Ip-Shing Fan[1]
[1]School of Applied Sciences, Cranfield University, UK
[2]Norwich Business School, University of East Anglia, UK

Complexity science literature abounds with anecdotes from the life sciences. Ants, termites, birds, and bees have been a popular choice of metaphor and provided inspiration in the development of simulations beneficial to learning and technological development. Recently, however, references like these seem to have dwindled. Perhaps through the overuse of anecdotes regarding such social insects, ants and termites have lost their impact and appeal, become clichéd, and, for some, even the subject of derision. But is their possible fall from grace fair? Recent research suggests not. This paper argues in favor of ants, termites, birds, and bees, presenting findings from a year-long study engaging 13 participants in interviews and the writing of qualitative diaries, showing that ants, among other species, do have a place. That place is wrapped up in the emotional and intellectual experience of individuals' learning about and developing an interest in complexity science.

## Introduction

Complexity science is understood to provide metaphors and analogies that give meaning to observed, experienced, and simulated reality (Fuller, 1999; Fuller & Moran, 2000; Lissack, 1999; Stacey, 2001, 2003a; Price, 1999). The language and metaphor of complexity science have been recognized for their potential in enabling people to revisualize their world (McMillan, 2004), by means of developing new ways of speaking and thinking about it, and in turn enabling new thinking to lead to new behavior. McMillan draws on the work of Morgan (1986) in this context and

suggests that of his eight metaphors describing organizations, the metaphor of the organization as an organism, with links to biology and biological thinking, appears most relevant to the pursuit of linking metaphors and analogies from the complexity science domain to organizations and work, and the experience of the individual and groups in that context. This correlates strongly, for example, with the description of bee hives, ant hills, termite mounds, and bird formations as used to explain the theory of complex adaptive systems.

The theory of complex adaptive systems and their emergent properties (for example self-organization and emergence) are often presented through metaphors and analogies from the natural sciences, in particular those of bee hives, ant and termite colonies, and birds in flight (Bentley, 2001; Bonabeau & Meyer, 2001; Johnson, 2001; Kelly, 1994; Lewin & Regine, 2001; McMillan, 2004; Resnick, 1997; Sole & Goodwin, 2000; Stacey, 1996, 2003b; Waldrop, 1992). In the literature, colorful descriptions abound. For example, Resnick (1997: 3-4) writes of birds, and of ants, traffic, and economic markets:

*"A flock of birds sweeps across the sky. Like a well-choreographed dance troupe, the birds veer to the left in unison. Then, suddenly, they all dart to the right and swoop down toward the group. Each movement seems perfectly coordinated. The flock as a whole is graceful – maybe more graceful – than any of the birds within it. How do birds keep their movements so orderly, so synchronised? Most people assume that birds play a game of follow-the-leader: the bird at the front of the flock leads, and the others follow. But that's not so. In fact, most bird flocks don't have leaders at all. There is no special "leader bird". Rather, the flock is an example of what some people call "self-organization". Each bird in the flock follows a set of simple rules, reacting to the movements of the*

*Acknowledgments of assistance go to the anonymous research participants who made the findings presented in this paper possible.

*birds nearby it. Orderly flock patterns arise from these simple, local interactions. None of the birds has a sense of the overall flock pattern. The bird in front just happens to end up there. The flock is organized without an organiser, coordinated without a coordinator. Bird flocks are not the only things that work that way. Ant colonies, highway traffic, market economies, immune systems – in all of these systems, patterns are determined not by some centralised authority but by local interactions among decentralised components. As ants forage for food, their trail patterns are determined not by the dictates of the queen ant, but by local interactions among thousands of worker ants. Patterns of traffic arise from local interactions among individual cars. Macroeconomic patterns arise from local interactions among millions of buyers and sellers. In immune systems, armies of antibodies seek out bacteria in a systematic coordinated attack – without any "generals" organizing the overall battle plan."*

Likewise, Bonabeau & Meyer (2001: 108) use ants as an analogy to convey the meaning and potential of self-organization in order to solve business problems, and go on to describe the way researchers at Hewlett-Packard's laboratories in the UK had developed a computer program based on such ant-foraging principles in order to route telephone calls efficiently. The authors also report other organizations taking this approach, such as France Telecom, British Telecom, and MCI World-Com. Metaphors and analogies based on ants have therefore had practical value by means of which new computer programs have been inspired and developed. Subsequently these have had an impact on the improvement of other technological processes. Other examples of computer programs similarly inspired and designed more specifically to study complex adaptive systems include genetic algorithms, as developed by John Holland of the Santa Fe Institute (Holland, 1992); the Boids simulation, developed by Reynolds (1987) to simulate the flocking behavior of birds; the Vants simulation, developed by Langton (1996) to simulate the trail-laying behavior of ants; and the Tierra simulation, developed by Ray (1992) using the

analogy of biological evolution to evolve computer programs.

In addition, ants, termites, bees, and wasps have stimulated fascination and interest at a more general level, whereby individuals have come to learn about complexity science because of their interest in the collective behavior of these species:

*"Social insects display some of the best examples of what we call emergent behavior. It is difficult not to become fascinated by the abundance of patterns shown by the work of ants, termites, bees, and social wasps. The huge nests of termites and raid patterns of army ants travelling through the rain forests are just two examples. We are fascinated by the collective behavior, but also by their ecological success: the dry weight of ants and termites in some rainforests is about four times that of all the other land animals. In some ecosystems ants compete successfully with rodents and other vertebrates. We find them all around the world, from deserts to the jungle, and they are strong competitors. Some authors even propose that this strong competitive ability leads to a well-defined partition of habitats, with ants and termites playing a central role and solitary insects having much less ecological relevance. But while colonies of social insects behave in complex ways, the capacities of individuals are relatively limited... generally speaking, single ants behave in a simple way... but then how do social insects reach such remarkable goals? The answer... comes to a large extent from self-organization: insect societies share basic dynamic properties with other complex systems... individual units do not gather, store and process information by themselves, instead they interact with each other in such a way that information is manipulated by the collective."* (Sole & Goodwin, 2000: 147–149)

However, in spite of the obvious appeal of ants, termites, birds, and bees, other work suggests that theoretically, a complex adaptive system view is not necessarily the most appropriate perspective to understand the way humans interact in organizations from the perspective of the individual in interactions with others. Stacey (2003b) offers a critical perspective on both the use of ants, birds, and bees, and so on as metaphors in general, and the theory of complex adaptive systems and simulations based on this in particular. In reference to metaphors such as that provided by the Boids simulation, Stacey argues that these cannot provide a source domain for analogies with human behavior, because the abstract relationships in such systems are relationships between cybernetic entities defined as deterministic, simple rules. Such simulations, he says, can only ever provide metaphors that may or may not provoke thinking about human interaction (Stacey, 2003b: 305).

Stacey does, however, support using complexity science analogies that resonate strongly with human experience, and also stresses the importance of acknowledging the importance of feelings, the importance of reflection-in-action, and the importance of abstract thinking (Stacey, 2001). In tandem with this is the possibility to explore how complexity science analogies could be used to make sense of complex responsive processes of relating. Therefore, it is the personal resonance with complexity science that individuals encounter that becomes important, and, increasingly so it seems, in the business world. Lewin (1999) validates this thought:

*"In our conversations with business people we saw that there was powerful resonance between their thinking about their organizations and what is known about the world of biology. This interest in applying a complexity perspective to business organizations is growing... After all, most of us work in organizations of one sort or another, and so the world of business represents the most immediate experience of complex systems on a day-to-day basis."* (Lewin, 1999: xi)

While Lewin talks of applying a complexity perspective to business, however, Stacey's position remains clear:

*"The complexity sciences can never be simply applied to human action: they can only serve as a source domain for analogies with it."* (Stacey, 2003a: 53)

However, Lissack (1997) reported on the initial results of research carried out within a division of a biotech company with many thousands of employees and within a start-up Internet content provider with fewer than 40 full-time employees. The research focused on the use of complexity science metaphors and language by managers. From his research, Lissack referenced the use of eight metaphorical concepts taken from the complexity science domain. These included the fitness landscape, attractors, simulated annealing, patches, Tau, generative relationships, increasing returns, and sensitive dependence to initial conditions. The objective of Lissack's research, carried out initially by means of semiotic analysis, was to differentiate domains in which certain types of metaphors were more appropriate and to identify action items stemming from those metaphors. Through this approach Lissack explored how the organizations he researched would benefit from learning about complexity science metaphorical concepts for specific tasks.

The research underpinning *this* paper, however, took a step back from this point of interest and sought to take into account what stimulated interest in and learning about complexity science in the first place, and how this could be seen to change over time. The study reported on in this paper deployed one main path of research, loosely inspired by the survey approach, and utilized data-collection methods commonly associated with surveys; that is, interviews and diaries. A hybrid interview style was adopted, in which elements of the different styles of semi-structured, unstructured, ethnographic, depth, intensive, and creative interviews were applied. Diaries were utilized in an open-ended format and an interactive style of ongoing research. This engaged the participation of 13 individuals in the writing of qualitative, weekly, work-focused diaries. The diarists wrote their diaries for between one and fifteen months (with an average of six months' diary writing). Participants were also emailed text-based extracts on management theory relating to the subject of complexity science and were asked to make comments concerning these in their diary. Prior to embarking on the diary-writing exercise, participants were asked to take part in interviews, to establish the context of their own personal background in addition to their interests and motivations for taking part, any prior knowledge regarding complexity science, and how they had been stimulated to learn more about it.

## Findings

The research interviews conducted with research participants prior to their embarking on the diary-writing study revealed that four of the participants had been explicitly stimulated to find out more about complexity science because of a combination of having their curiosity aroused by the natural sciences in addition to experiencing some kind of emotional connection with the subject.

Personal interest in the natural sciences therefore played a key role. Two research participants referred to their own environmental awareness as being a stepping stone into complexity science, in terms of their understanding of nature and bio-ethics. Analogies from the animal kingdom had attracted and drawn two participants further into an understanding of complexity science. Specifically mentioned were ants, bats, bees, birds, and termites. The following extracts reveal the context surrounding this.

Research Participant 1: *"If I had time at the moment, then I would definitely be looking at genetics [...] Part of what for me came out of that phase of looking at chaos theory was then also looking at this whole emotion of how do we come to be here, who we are and that linked me in with the nature/nurture thing which links in with this whole genetics thrust that there is and the whole of bio ethics ... At the moment there's also been a bit of a thread of work which I've been doing around bio ethics ... So at the moment my interest is in that field."*

Research Participant 2: *"If you take it to the ant example for instance, I like animals, I love animals, I really do. I do a yearly charity thing for Save the Rhino, which is a charity that helps save Rhino's basically, because it's what you call an indicator species – a measurement for how an ecology is working. And I like animals, I love*

*Africa, and these sort of places, this is what I do [...] Humans are not ants. Ant models are lovely to think about certain things, but they are not human beings. All these lovely programmes that have been created that describe ants and flocks of animals, describe only that. They don't explain why I fall in love or…., you know. I think they are very, very limited in their thinking. And I also think that animals are much richer than we give them credit for [...] I think humans are animals in some form, but they are different types of animals… we think as humans and therefore we are different from others [...] But, I like animals because they are part of who we are in that world. I'm prepared to put my energy into some of this, because I think it's important that we have at least some responsibility for the survival of species and things like that [...] Jack Cohen and Ian Stewart wrote a very famous chapter somewhere in one of their books, it's called "what would it be like to be a bat?" How would a bat think about being a bat? And the answer is you don't know, because you are not a bat. And you won't ever know [...] I think it's an interesting example with Termites, where they recently found out there's a whole different evolutionary path that we didn't know about, why they have soldiers going on searches, and the point would be to go and capture the other colonies and kill the king and inform. It's very complex. I mean, this is not something you can explain with very simple rules. So, yes, I like that [...] But I'm very uncomfortable to say because ants, termites or bees, or birds behave in a certain way that that tells me how humans behave. It's a very anthropocentric way of looking at the world and it doesn't quite work that way for me. It doesn't help."*

Research Participant 3: *"For example, now I know of the ants, ooh look at these, and they never clash with each other, then they work for one objective and they are so happy. They are so happy. And some of them die, and others are explorers that go and explore things, and then I don't know why, they call the others, and then they go too. And now I can't kill an ant for instance – I can't.*

*"And one thing that interested me, when I first started to investigate, was the biological system and things like this, the birds, and biology*

*and so on.*

*"For example, I have already read about the birds [...] and the formations that they do, and the things that they know, and things like that. And the other day I was really looking at it. Well it's amazing, and now this will be in my head forever [...] because it's an experience. You experience what somebody already experienced, because when people write about it, people report experiences. So they are expressing what they experience. But it's not the experience itself. And when you read it, you are not experienced, you are reading these things. But then when you experience what they experience, then it's yours also, it's part of you also.*

As mentioned above, the interest stimulated by ants, bats, birds, bees, and termites was wrapped up in a larger emotional experience. Emotional triggers of exploration into the domain of complexity science were different among all participants, but included such things as feelings of amazement, attraction, enjoyment, and generally having their interest stimulated or having "wow moments," as the following extracts show.

Research Participant 2: *"I graduated formally in 2002 I think [...] You start to see what appeals or doesn't appeal, in your way of thinking, what resonates [...] with my experience as a consultant, and as a human being basically. Then I started to make connections based on what I've learned there [...] There was one book I read years ago, Kevin Kelly's Out of Control, which I am sure you know, I'm not sure if you've read it, but you should, it's quite an interesting book. What he does, he describes clearly how when, he talks about machines, he said that when they interact the behavior emerging out of that is actually quite interesting. He calls it flocking behavior, or that sort of stuff, which is machines, it isn't human beings but he draws some parallels with that in his book, and I think it's quite an interesting book. And what he really describes is that [...] there is no form of control other than our own behavior [...] but we can pay attention to that on the micro level, and that's all we can do, and use that in order to make more sense. And he uses an interesting example that was kind of a "wow" moment for me; if we*

*do an excursion to Mars we send a multimillion expedition vehicle out there, a rover, that goes and crawls the planet and collects samples, it's very susceptible to one little failure somewhere, so why don't we use half of that money and send a hundred thousand little ant-like vehicles to Mars to crawl over it, and if 50% fails we still have 50,000 functioning machines, and what we do, what we create is weights in these little machines that can connect to each other, so that they know what each other is doing – which is of course a very powerful complexity principle. And, I thought, "golly, yes, it's very interesting, as a tax payer you worry about that they send these big things out there." Well, that's a shift. That's a shift in thinking, and that helped me big time, that sort of thing. So perhaps it was that book, I don't know, at least some of the reading.*

*"Similarly, some of the concepts that Mitchell Waldrop talks about, although very much from an economics point of view, very often, particularly at the beginning of the book, were a bit like that, so was it a wow moment? I'm not sure. But that was definitely a wow moment [...] Well, there were always wow moments, I mean, one other wow moment I had [...] was when I started to realize, that, and that's what Stacey taught me basically, is that the concept of a system is a very difficult concept to work with, because it implies a certain outsider looking in perspective, as if you can look at the world as something you can control without being affected by it in some generic sense. That did worry me in a way [...] and that's why I stopped feeling comfortable with that concept [...] You are always part of the conversation, whether you like it or not. And even worse, you've got a certain power position very often, so whatever you say and do, has a major effect [...] I think it's an interesting example with Termites, where they recently found out there's a whole different evolutionary path that we didn't know about, why they have soldiers going on searches, and the point would be to go and capture the other colonies and kill the king and inform, and it's very complex, I mean this is not something you can explain with very simple rules. So, yes, I like that."*

Similarly, research participant 3 described her and her colleague's amazement in what they had learned at a broader level:

"Chaos Theory interests me, because it is like whoa everything is chaos, it is amazing [...] when I arrived at this company, the first project that I did with innovation, we had to do some concepts about a technology that the client had. It was a thing on three dimensions [...] And this is, "Whoa, what is the 4th dimension?" And I started to look for the maths and so on [...] It was fantastic because it was so amazing these things about [...] everything depends on everything, and everything is changing, and so on. And then this related to complexity theory [...] It's because it's amazing how we know these things, by theory also. There's a gap, a very big gap between theory and how we do things. There's lots of people that know about this and they, it doesn't mean anything for their life, and this really changed my life. Really changed like respecting things [...] [One of my colleagues and I] have lots of conversations, really amazing. But he knows so much, and well, he knows lots of things and he links everything, and this is great because you can learn a lot from him."

Research participant 3 also described her like of and enjoyment in learning about patterns and behaviors through the natural sciences, stressing her emotional connection with this:

"And I like to observe a lot [...] Because, I like anthropology and sociology, and I also like object theory. And because it makes you think a lot [...] And so I, I read lots of things, but I personally like more philosophical things. And I think it's also, more than anything, I think is good to have other perspectives [...] Also to identify patterns of behaviors. Sometimes it's good for relationships. You find patterns, and it's like, "Ok, ok, this guy is a little bit like this, maybe it's because of this, this and this and this," and it makes you like people more, because you can understand them [...] Everything is intelligent. And we humans think that we are intelligent because we have information, and this is not true, intelligence is everywhere [...] Cells are intelligent, trees are intelligent and this is amazing, this is so, I don't know, but when I talk about these things, I feel

very happy. I don't know why it's something even emotional, I don't know, it's something that makes me happy. I don't know how or why things are like this."

Research participant 3 located the stimulation of her interest in the way she positioned herself in relation to what she was learning and seeking to understand, therefore making the experience a very personal one:

"Sometimes I read some point of view, "ah read this, this is very interesting," it is a very good book [...] Because I start to see how it's affecting me [...] because everything is connected, and this stuff interests me a lot, and it makes me change [...] I'm a designer, and a little bit ego-centric, because a product has always a little bit of you, of your personality. If I have to draw or to design a chair, it will be completely different than if it's you who designed it. Even if they have four legs and a thing to sit on and so on, it will be completely different. And this has to be about, your experiences, your influences, and what you are thinking.... So this always has to be, something behind the object, something behind the painting that you are seeing, behind the sculpture that you are seeing, behind anything that you are seeing. And this "behind" always interested me. What is behind things?"

Research participant 4 explained her need to develop new insights and have her interest stimulated:

"And I didn't really know anything and I think it was probably the fact that I wanted to... because I do feel that I mean there's like loads of energy in this town but I do sometimes feel that you know ideas can be too repetitive or people don't have enough kind of outside influences so I think it was very much the thing of getting new outside influences [...] I mean there's a lot of artists using computer programmes and if you think of the media there will be somebody in media art doing stuff. It's just finding the ones that are really doing interesting stuff [...] I think I just don't feel the artists are expanding enough, I think that's it [...] I was reading a biography, I was really, and they were talking in relation to economics and stuff like that, that really interested me."

Therefore, as these interviews show, individuals not only experienced an emotional connection with what they were learning, but sometimes actively sought that emotional connection out. Their subsequent intellectual interest generated in ants, termites, birds, and so forth was packaged in this emotional response. This was shown when, following the interviews, the research participants embarked on a personal, diary-writing exercise. These diaries, especially from six of the thirteen diarists, further revealed that the behavior of ants, termites, and birds stimulated thought, debate, contention, and inspiration for them.

Research participant 5 referred frequently to ants and termites and her interest in the topic:

*"Termite colonies and connected lives of ants, brains, cities, software and complex adaptive systems – coincidence or a pattern...? It does remind me of my rambly diary last week about the conflict between business outcomes and the personal needs of employees."* (Diary entry 14).

*"Emergence was my holiday book – and although I only managed a chapter on ants it was interesting to see that's exactly where I left off more or less with the diary as well [...] Anyway the piece I managed to read was about the greater scheme of things within the ant world that regulates and I was thinking that this is probably the root of religion/gods etc. Our need as a species to make sense of things – was Gods etc created as an explanation for things that people couldn't explain/rationalise [...]."* (Diary entry 15)

*"Ants seem to be quite interesting at the moment – the idea of an individual contributing to a wider context – simultaneously self organizing and being organized/regulated by reading the signs of other ants' self-organization. Kind of feels like a "glocal" approach – engage and take care of the local and the bigger picture looks after itself as the influences are felt on a micro level creating the macro-picture."* (Diary entry 22)

*"I was thinking again about ants – how they can't see the bigger picture and could this be one of the roles of artists/creatives, is this contradictory to "scratching your own itch" theory but I wondered if there was a relationship to laterality, abstract and spatial awareness that*

*enables a wider perspective other than the what's in front of your nose. Kandinsky has his theory of the triangle with artists at the apex pulling "society" forward [...]."* (Diary entry 23)

Research participant 2 commented on the analogies of ants and termites from a more critical perspective:

*"I can see the appeal of looking at termite mounds and be in awe with the self-organizing nature of it. I think it is quite another thing to then draw the parallel to human society [...]. For me, he makes the fundamental mistake that many people make that want to apply complexity science to human organizing. They apply it, per se. Take the rules [...] and import them in human society. I think one cannot just do that... Again, I come back to Stacey's recent work (this is no coincidence, because it really resonates with me). He builds up a theory of human relating (not ants or termites!) and then uses the principles of self-organization and emergence as an analogy to explain the pattern forming that we experience in social interaction [...]."* (Diary entry 6)

Research participant 3 discussed her feelings and thoughts about ants and termites:

*"[...] The mound is an architectural marvel [...] as a whole, members of the mound constitute a sophisticated society that makes it possible to meet the ever changing needs of the colony. [...] This is really amazing!!!! One thing that is bothering me, and that is making me think is: are they conscious of it? Is it done by habit by impulse? Even if it is marvellous and precise, we will never know [...] the why, how, and what for [...]."* (Diary entry 34)

Research participant 3 discussed the gap between instinct and action after reading an extract concerning the simulation of flocking birds:

*"Take a simple example, namely a flock of birds [...] Reynolds (1987) simulated the flocking behavior of birds with a computer program consisting of a network of moving agents called Boids. Each Boid follows the same three simple*

*rules – in my point of view they act by instincts, we humans, we have instincts but also a mind, that makes us think in all that we feel. In a flock of birds, each one acts on instinct, they don't think "aaaaaaaaaaaaaaaaa, I have to follow that guy" they just do it, there is no gap between action and instinct, and in humans there is a huge gap between thought and action, sometimes even action does not take place (which can be good or bad, judgement is not important now)."* (Diary entry 35)

Research participant 6 referred to the dominant themes in the literature pertaining to metaphors of bird and ants, and not people:

*"[…] I think it is interesting that in literature we have so many examples of the self-organizing of animals like flocks of birds or the ant examples but no one seems to use examples of self-organization of people like anarchism or the first unions."* (Diary entry 11)

## Discussion and conclusions

From the research findings presented, two main issues become clear. First, that analogies or metaphors relating to the natural sciences are of interest to some people, can stimulate their interest in complexity science further, and provide food for thought. Therefore, it is a reasonable assumption to make that when teaching or providing learning material on the topic of complexity science, it is of value to include metaphors and analogies on ants, termites, birds, and bees, and other phenomena from the natural sciences.

Second, the arguments around the validity of the congruence with such analogies and human relating are accepted by complexity science students, and this is acknowledged by them retrospectively as an important step in their learning. Once an individual has been introduced to this thought or makes the leap themselves, they are then ready to develop their ideas further and actively question the extent to which analogies about ants, termites, birds, or bees can be of use or relevance to them as humans. Following this, progression can be made to searching out theories more relevant

to human relating, such as, for example, Stacey's complex responsive processes of relating.

There is therefore some response needed to Stacey's assertions that simulations based on ants, termites, birds, and bees cannot provide a source domain for analogies with human behavior, because, he says, such simulations can only ever provide metaphors that may or may not provoke thinking about human interaction (Stacey, 2003b: 305). The findings in this paper acknowledge this point but also reiterate the value of that very point, emphasizing that it is precisely the fact that these simulations can provide metaphors that provoke thinking about human interaction that makes them of value to individuals learning about complexity science. There is justification in being presented with analogies and metaphors based on the natural sciences because they inspire and stimulate interest and the conversation needed in order to take a step further in developing an awareness and understanding about all that complexity science can offer.

In supporting the use of complexity science analogies that resonate strongly with human experience, and stressing the necessity of acknowledging the importance of feelings, the importance of reflection-in-action, and the importance of abstract thinking (Stacey, 2001), Stacey's critique of simulations, metaphors, and analogies based on ants, termites, birds, and bees misses the essence of what it is about complexity science that initiates such a process in the first place – a process that is often grounded in an emotional pull followed by intellectual stimulation.

In this paper, Stacey's position that "The complexity sciences can never be simply applied to human action: they can only serve as a source domain for analogies with it" (2003a: 53) is therefore acknowledged but rephrased as: "Complexity science can never be simply applied to human action, but can serve as an emotionally inviting, intellectually inspiring and stimulating source domain for metaphors and analogies with which to begin to develop further understanding of it."

In this way, complexity science metaphors and analogies based on ants, termites, birds, and bees are reaffirmed in their role as having value as images and vivid words. As Weick (1995) said, this can draw attention to new possibilities and provide the means by which to offer people, or organizations, access to more varied images in order to engage in sense making that is more adaptive than for those with more limited vocabularies.

## References

Bentley, P.J. (2001). Digital Biology: The Creation of Life Inside Computers and How It Will Affect Us, ISBN 9780747266549.

Bonabeau, E. and Meyer, C. (2001). "Swarm intelligence: A whole new way to think about business," Harvard Business Review, ISSN 0017-8012, May: 106-114.

Fuller, T. (1999). "Complexity metaphors and the process of small business foresighting," in M.R. Lissack and H.P. Gunz (eds), Managing Complexity in Organizations: A View in Many Directions, ISBN 9781567202854, pp. 336-351.

Fuller, T. and Moran, P. (2000). "Moving beyond metaphor," Emergence, ISSN 1521-3250, 2(1): 50-71.

Holland, J.H. (1992). Adaptation in Natural and Artificial Systems, ISBN 9780262581110.

Johnson, S. (2001). Emergence: The Connected Lives of Ants, Brains, Cities and Software, ISBN 9780684868769 (2002).

Kelly, K. (1994). Out of Control: The New Biology of Machines, Social Systems and the Economic World, ISBN 9780201483406 (1995).

Langton, C.G. (1996). "Artificial life," in M.A. Boden (ed.), The Philosophy of Artificial Life, ISBN 9780198751557, pp. 39-94.

Lewin, R. (1999). Complexity: Life at the Edge of Chaos, ISBN 9780226476551 (2000).

Lewin, R. and Regine, B. (2001). Weaving Complexity and Business: Engaging the Soul at Work, ISBN 9781587990434.

Lissack, M.R. (1997). "Mind your metaphors: Lessons from complexity science," Long Range Planning, ISSN 0024-6301, 30(2): 294-298.

Lissack, M.R. (1999). "Complexity: The science, its vocabulary, and its relation to organizations," Emergence, ISSN 1521-3250, 1(1): 110-126.

McMillan, E. (2004). Complexity, Organizations and Change, ISBN 9780415314473 (2005).

Morgan, G. (1986). Images of Organization: The Executive Edition, ISBN 9780803928305.

Price, I. (1999). "Images or Reality? Metaphors, Memes, and Management," in M.R. Lissack and H.P. Gunz (eds), Managing Complexity in Organizations: A View in Many Directions, ISBN 9781567202854, pp.165-179.

Ray, T.S. (1992). "An approach to the synthesis of life," in C.G. Langton, C. Taylor, J. Doyne Farmer and S. Rasmussen (eds), Artificial Life II, ISBN 9780201525717, pp. 371-408.

Resnick, M. (1997). Turtles, Termites, and Traffic Jams: Explorations in Massively Parallel Microworlds, ISBN 9780262680936.

Reynolds, C.W. (1987). "Flocks, herds and schools: A distributed behavior model," Computer Graphics, ISSN 0097-8930, 21(4): 25-34.

Sole, R. and Goodwin, B. (2000). Signs of Life: How Complexity Pervades Biology, ISBN 9780465019281 (2002).

Stacey, R.D. (1996). Complexity and Creativity in Organizations, ISBN 9781881052890.

Stacey, R.D. (2001). Complex Responsive Processes in Organizations: Learning and Knowledge Creation, ISBN 9780415249195.

Stacey, R.D. (2003a). Complexity and Group Processes: A Radically Social Understanding of Individuals, ISBN 9781583919200.

Stacey, R.D. (2003b). Strategic Management and Organizational Dynamics, ISBN 9780273658986.

Waldrop, M.M. (1992). Complexity: The Emerging Science at the Edge of Chaos, ISBN 9780671767891.

Weick, K.E. (1995). Sensemaking in Organizations, ISBN 9780803971776.

**Carol Webb** gained her first degree, BA Ancient History and Social Anthropology, at University College London (UCL) in 2001. More recently, and at Cranfield University, she completed her doctoral thesis. A key output of this study was a complexity science learning model focused on individual learning in the context of working life. While conducting her doctoral research Carol also worked on the EU co-sponsored RODEO project (www.e-rodeo.org), where she took a pivotal role in the development of the RODEO Starter Kit Calendar and Experience Game, led the project evaluation and validation process." Carol is now working on a UK Engineering and Physical Science Research Council (EPSRC) funded project to develop a complexity science taught course for research students.

**Fiona Lettice** is a senior lecturer in the Norwich Business School at the University of East Anglia. The main focus of her research and teaching is in new product development and innovation management. She has received funding from the European Commission and the Engineering and Physical Science Research Council (EPSRC) for her research in discontinuous innovation, knowledge management and innovation, complexity science, and innovation in regional clusters. Prior to her academic career, Fiona worked in industry as a project manager within Centrica's Business Development directorate, and for a small consultancy company, where she worked predominantly with BMW/Rover Group in design and engineering projects. In her work with multidisciplinary teams, Fiona uses graphic facilitation as a way to encourage dialogue and communication between different disciplines and organizations.

**Ip-Shing Fan** gained his doctorate in Computer Integrated Manufacturing at the Cranfield Institute of Technology and completed his Bachelor's degree in Industrial Engineering ar the University of Hong Kong. He is a Senior Lecturer and the Course Director of the MSc in Enterprise System Implementation at Cranfield University, UK. Taking a socio-technical approach, he works to develop understanding and methods to support the effective introduction and use of enterprise systems. He was the coordinator of the European Commission supported research project BEST (Better Enterprise Systems Implementation) – a €4 million project, with 12 partners in 10 countries – in which tools were developed to facilitate enterprise system readiness assessments relating to organizational and human factors, and to formulate management plans to implement change. People behavior and interaction in complex enterprise system projects have stimulated his interest in complexity science.

Forum

# From complicated to complex: On the relationship between connectivity and behavior

Kurt A. Richardson
ISCE Research, US

**A common assumption in the 'modern' era is that 'being connected' can only be a good thing for individuals and for businesses, and even nation states and continents. This short article aims to explore this assumption with the use of Boolean networks. Although the research presented here is in its early stages, it already demonstrates that there is a balance to be met between connectivity and performance, and that being well-connected does not necessarily lead to desirable network performance attributes.**

In the 'information age' there is a general belief that having access to as much information as possible is a good thing, leading to more effective decision making and thus allowing us to rationally design the world in our image. Of course, any sophisticated view of the information age has to acknowledge that having information for the sake of information is not much more useful than having no information. What is key is having access to the right information at the right time, where knowing both what is the 'right' information for the 'right' time are highly problematic assessments. We are slowly beginning to acknowledge that in a complex world, 'states of affairs' much be considered from multiple directions whilst maintaining a (constructively) critical disposition at the same time. This comes about because the external concrete reality we perceive is not quite as solid as our more recent scientific heritage would suggest. The relationship between our universe and our understanding of it is, dare I say it, very complex.

Along side this popular belief that information should be abundant and freely available, is that being connected is also the preferred state of existence. Like all ideas, 'being connected' has limits to its usefulness. Is there a preferred degree of connectedness? An

individual who was not connected at all could achieve nothing. Indeed, without some degree of connectedness, an individual could not even be recognized as such - we are, to a large extent, defined by our connections. At the other end of the spectrum, if an individual is too connected then it becomes also most impossible to achieve anything coherent. If too much is going on at once, and no stable patterns emerge (even if only temporarily) then again the notion of the individual and his/her identity is impossible to discern - the whole system becomes the only useful unit of analysis.

This short discussion article represents an early report into some research I have been performing that explores the relationship between connectivity and system behavior. The area I will be focusing upon herein is how a system's behavior develops as more and more inter-connections are added between individual system components. As in other articles I have written for *E:CO* (Richardson, 2004a, 2004b, 2005a) I will be using Boolean networks to explore this behavior. As I have suggested before, although Boolean networks are probably too simple to represent social reality in any complete sense, I believe that the lessons that can be learnt are still valid (albeit with some contextual restrictions) for more complex systems. I also tend to believe that some of the more general conclusions that can be drawn from the exploration of such systems are largely obvious. However, such models allow us to explore these behaviors scientifically rather than develop purely from the wisdom that comes with considerable experience. Even if science confirms what we think we already know, science allows us to investigate more thoroughly and rigorously our ideas in ways that more often than not lead to an enrichment in our understanding (especially if we can avoid getting too hung up on particular paradigms!).

## Basic parameters

I do not plan to go into great detail about Boolean networks and how they are constructed and simulated. The interested reader might read Lucas (2007), or Richardson (2005b). In this section I want to introduce a number of parameters that can be used to characterize the phase space of complex systems (Boolean networks in particular). I hope that after 8½ volumes of *E:CO* I do not need to spend time defining concepts such as 'phase space' and 'attractors' in detail. For the purposes of this article I would like to briefly describe the following measures:

1. Number of attractors, $N_{att}$;
2. The weight of the largest attractor as a percentage of the total size of phase space, $W_{max}$;
3. The maximum number of pre-images for a particular network configuration, $PI_{max}$;
4. The longest transient for a particular network, $T_{max}$;
5. The number of Garden-of-Eden states as a percentage of the total size of phase space, $G$.
6. The average robustness for a particular network, $R$;

## Phase Space Attractors

The number of phase space attractors is probably the most single important characteristic of a nonlinear dynamical system. In Boolean networks, all trajectories end up (after some transitory period) on periodic attractors. Given that Boolean networks are discrete networks one would never observe the type of chaotic behavior as seen in certain continuous systems. However, attractors with periods much larger than the size of the network are often referred to as quasi-chaotic or quasi-random. Indeed, it is a relatively trivial task to create Boolean networks that contain attractors with periods so large that for all intents and purposes (and by all standard tests of randomness) they are random. The primary interest in the number of attractors displayed by a particular network, is that this number corresponds directly with the number of qualitatively different behavioral modes that particular network can operate in. So, if a network only exhibits a single attractor then it only has one *function*. If it has many then it has many functions. This is overly simplistic of course. As we shall see, networks with huge numbers of attractors (as compared to the size of the network itself) are not very connected, and so they can easily be reduced to a number of independent (non-interacting) sub-networks that do not display very interesting behavior. The behavior of such networks can easily be explained analytically, i.e., with some quite simple mathematics. At the other extreme, are highly connected networks that exhibit few attractors that do behave in an interesting manner not easily considered from an analytical perspective, such is the nature of nonlinear dynamics. We shall explore how connectivity and the number and type of attractors relate to each other later in this article.

The attractors themselves generally only contain a small percentage of the number of states comprising the network's complete phase space ($2^N$). The remaining states describe trajectories from arbitrary points in phase space to particular attractors. The set of all attractor states and the states that comprise the various trajectories to a particular attractor form an attractor *basin*. The proportion of the total number of states comprising state space that comprise a particular basin is referred to as the basin's *relative weight*. An idealized at-

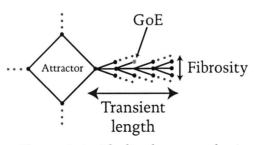

**Figure 1** *An idealized attractor basin*

tractor basin is shown in Figure 1. At the center of the attractor basin is the attractor itself containing a periodic loop of a relatively few states (although this is not always the case). From the attractor there are branches of states that branch off and form multiple trajectories to the central attractor. There are two parameters that are useful in describing the structure of these multiple trajectories, or branches. The first is the average number of *pre-images*.

## Pre-images

Although, for Boolean networks, the application of the rule table results in only one unique state (the networks are *forward deterministic*), reversing this algorithm may lead to more than one solution, i.e., any particular state may have more than one state that leads to it (so Boolean networks are not *backward deterministic*). A high average pre-image number results in fibrous-looking branches flowing to the central attractor. As such for the remainder of this article I will refer to average pre-image number as *fibrosity*, or F. Another important parameter is *maximum transient length*.

## Maximum transient length

The maximum transient length, $T_{max}$, is essentially a measure of the furthest distance one can get from the central attractor by applying the rule-based algorithm backwards. Let's say a network is started from a state that is ten states away from the central attractor. Once the network is simulated, it will take ten time steps before the central attractor (associated with the starting state) is reached. We might also refer to this transitory period as the network's *settling time*. If we assume that, in the real world, there is some degree of uncertainty in pushing a network to a particular state so that it adopts a particular mode of behavior, then (assuming we are even able to select a state on the correct basin) there will be a delay between the intervention and the desired (hopefully) response. There may in fact be a relatively long delay between the intervention and the network adopting the desired mode of operation, so long in fact, that it can be make the connection between cause and effect difficult to determine. (And, this of course ignores the possibility that

another intervention doesn't nudge the system towards another basin in the meantime). So long settling times are problematic for the intervener.

As phase space is finite, if settling times are long then fibrosity is relatively low. At one extreme we have short fibrous attractor branches that ensure that the central attractor is reached quickly from many possible starting points. At the other extreme we have long sparse attractor branches that can result in significant delays between action and desired response (although the system will respond immediately by following a trajectory toward the characteristic attractor).

## Gardens-of-Eden

Figure 1 also indicates a state labeled 'GoE' which is shorthand for 'garden-of-eden'. Mathematically, when rolling back time to construct these attractor basins a point is eventually reached for which there is no solution. These states cannot be reached from any other states – they are, in a sense, the beginning of time for the particular trajectory they 'create' – hence, the reference to the Garden of Eden (see Wuensche & Lesser, 1992; Wuensche, 1999). From a control perspective, internal mechanisms do not have any capacity to access GoEs – for all intents and purposes they do not exist, from an *internal* viewpoint. However, they can be reached from the outside by perturbing the network in a way that forces it to adopt a GoE state (from there the network will follow the trajectory that that state 'creates', although note that the particular trajectory will comprise states that are accessible from the inside). The practical upshot of the existence of GoEs is simply that if an external intervener (or, 'perturber') wanted to encourage the network towards a particular attractor s/he/it would have more states available to initiate the desired response. Of course, to take full advantage of this benefit the external intervener would have to have perfect knowledge of the network's phase space. In the absence of such absolute understanding, it still follows that an *external* intervener can potentially 'see' more of the network's phase space, than an *internal* intervener can, and arguably has a greater va-

E:CO Vol. 9 Nos. 1-2 2007 pp. 194-206

riety of maneuvers that s/he/it can execute to achieve designed ends.

### Dynamic robustness

I have already suggested that the number of phase space attractors is one of the more important attributes of a dynamic system. However, although two states may be next to each other on an attractor basin (i.e., in *phase* space), they may in fact be very far from each other in *state* space. For example, in a very small network containing only five nodes the state 00001 and 00010 are next to each other in state space, but in phase space they might actually lie on different attractor basins. As such, in order to have a better appreciation of a system's dynamics we need to understand how the states on a particular attractor basin are distributed across state space. We shall see such a state space portrait later on, but for now I want to consider a measure that takes into account both phase and state space structure. Dynamic robustness, $R$, is a measure of the chances of pushing a network into a different basin with a small nudge. In the case of Boolean networks, $R$ for single state is calculated by adding together the total number of 1-bit perturbations that do not result in a switch to a different basin, and dividing this number by the size of the network, $N$. For example, if we consider a network of size $N=5$ and the state 00010 then there are five 1-bit perturbations: **1**0010, 0**1**010, 001**1**0, 0000**0**, 0001**1** (the emboldened state is the reversed one). If three of these give states lie on the same basin then the dynamic robustness of state 00010 is 3/5. The network's overall dynamic robustness is simply the average of all the values of $R$ for a single state. If $R$ is high, say > 80%, then the network's qualitative behavior is relatively stable in the face of small external perturbations. If $R$ is low, say < 20%, then the majority of small external signals will result in a qualitative change in behavior. The dominant factor in this measurement is of course the number of attractors, but the distribution of the states lying in a particular basin also affects the overall measurement.

In one sense the total number of attractors is equivalent to the number of contexts, or *environmental archetypes*, a system 'sees' and

can respond to. As with many of the measures presented here, there is a balancing act to be performed. If a network 'sees' too many environmental archetypes, then it is essentially at the beck and call of the environment. If it 'sees' only one archetype, i.e., phase space is characterized by only one attractor basin, then the network has no variety in its responses to environmental changes whatsoever.

However, dynamic robustness also has an effect on a network's 'sight'. Dynamic robustness can be high if the states associated with each basin are distributed in such a way as to maximize $R$ for a particular number of basins (this is more likely when no one basin is significantly heavier than the others). However, networks that are characterized by many basins may also exhibit high dynamic robustness if one of those basins is considerably larger (heavier) than the others. In this latter situation, although the network has the potential to 'see' and respond to many environmental archetypes, it overly privileges one particular archetype and so effectively blinds itself to others.

The heart of this article is concerned with how the various parameters presented above vary with increasing network connectivity, but before moving on to consider these relationships a brief presentation of the computer experiment performed will be given.

### Growing Boolean networks

The computer experiment performed for this study starts with a network of $N=15$ nodes that contains no interconnections whatsoever (by most standards this starting point would not even deserve the label 'network'). In order to simulate a Boolean network, associated with each node is a rule table that determines what state a particular node will acquire on the next time step which is dependent upon the state of its input nodes for the current time step. For the starting point (completely disconnected nodes), each node simply maintains the same state from time step to time step (in essence there is no rule *table*, only the rule that the state of the node does not change over time). This results in $2^N$ point attractors that have no transient branches whatsoever (attrac-

*Richardson*                                                                                     197

tor weight = attractor basin weight = 1 state). Once the number of attractors and their branch structure have been determined, a connection is added between two randomly selected nodes (with the proviso that no connection already exists between those two random selected nodes). Once connections are made a process for evolving a node's rule table is required. For this study the following example illustrates the algorithm that was used.

The number of input combinations that a single node can respond is $2^k$, where $k$ is the number of inputs. For example, for a node with $k=2$ inputs there are four possible input configurations. The rule table for such a node may look like:

| Input B | Input A | State of node at next time step |
|---------|---------|--------------------------------|
| 0 | 0 | 0 |
| 0 | 1 | 1 |
| 1 | 0 | 1 |
| 1 | 1 | 0 |

The rule for a node with this response configuration can be expressed simply as 0110. Now let us consider that the node has now acquired another input with node C. There are now $2^3$ = 8 possible input configurations. For the algorithm used herein, when the state of node C is 0 (or off), the response to A and B is kept the same as it was before the connection from node C was added. The response to the additional four configurations that are formed when the state of node C is 1 (or on) are selected randomly. So,

| C | B | A | State of node at next time step |
|---|---|---|--------------------------------|
| 0 | 0 | 0 | 0 |
| 0 | 0 | 1 | 1 |
| 0 | 1 | 0 | 1 |
| 0 | 1 | 1 | 0 |
| 1 | 0 | 0 | 0 |
| 1 | 0 | 1 | 0 |
| 1 | 1 | 0 | 1 |
| 1 | 1 | 1 | 1 |

Simply expressed the rule changes from 0110 to 11000110 (where the emboldened digits represent the 'old' rule). As the number of connections, $C$, are increased the rule for a particular node may evolve as:

$C$ **Rule**
1 10
2 01**10**
3 1100**0110**
4 01100110**11000110**
5 1101000110101100**0110011011000110**
Etc.

When the network is fully connected ($C = 210 = N[N-1]$) the rule for each node is represented by a string containing a sequence of $2^{14}=16384$ '0's and '1's (note that connections to self are not included) with the basic structure illustrated above. The value of each parameter was determined as each additional connection was made. This process was repeated 1000 times and the results averaged across this sample set. The results of this computer experiment will presented and discussed next.

## Experimental results and discussion
### $N_A$ and GoEs

Figure 2 shows the relationship between the number of phase space attractors, $N_A$, and the percentage of GoEs with the number of connections, $C$. There are four distinct regions. The first region shows the number of attractors decreasing rapidly and the proportion of GoEs increasing rapidly. The rapid decrease in $N_A$ is due to the fact that as each new connection is made $N_A$ is halved. This is not always the case, but the important characteristic of this 'ordered' region is that the qualitative structure of phase space can easily be determined *analytically*. This is because in this region of low-$C$, no interacting feedback loops are formed amongst the interconnections.

The second region, which is labeled 'complex' sees a continued decrease (although at a much slower rate than in the ordered region) in the number of attractors, down to a minimum of around four attractors. The proportion of GoEs is also constantly high throughout this region, indicating that the vast

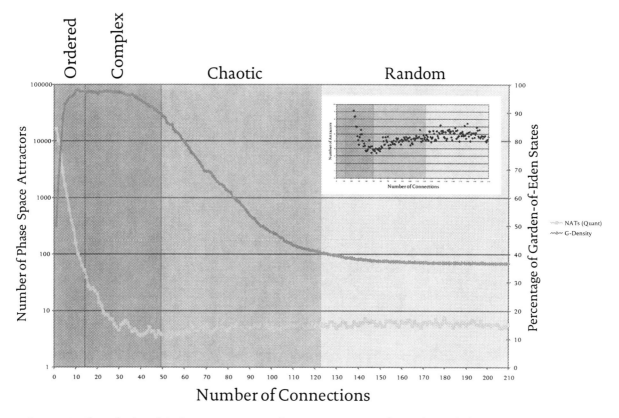

**Figure 2** *The relationship between network connectivity and number of phase space attractors / percentage of Garden-of-Eden states*

majority of states (over 90%) are only accessible via external intervention / perturbation. A further, and possibly more significant feature of this region, is that the number of emergent modules is greater than the number of topological, or structural, modules. A comprehensive set of data was not available at the time of writing, but Richardson (2007) explores the importance of emergent (dynamic) modules in significant detail. The emergence of dynamic modules is the principle mechanism by which certain (complex) networks restrict dynamics so that their dynamics is neither ordered or (quasi-) chaotic. When this article is 'upgraded' from a forum piece to a complete and more rigorous study this particular characteristic of the 'complex' region will be explored in greater depth. At this point in the study, it appears that a reasonable boundary between the 'complex' and 'chaotic' (to be discussed next) regions is where the number of structural (static) modules and the number of emergent (dynamic) modules are both equal to one. This occurs approximately around $C \approx 3N$.

The next region, termed 'chaotic', is characterized by a steady and relatively rapid drop in the proportion of GoEs, from around 97% to 40%, and a slow rise in the number of attractors from approximately four to six. It is difficult to say much about this region without calling upon other data (which we will do shortly), other than there is a significant increase in states that are not only accessible from outside the system. The same is true for the last region – 'random' – for which the number of attractors and the proportion of GoEs remain relatively steady at six and ~40%, respectively.

### $R$ and $W_{max}$

Figure 3 shows the relationship between network connectivity, $C$, and both dynamic robustness, $R$, and the weight of the largest attractor basin, $W_{max}$, i.e., the basin containing the most states. In the 'ordered' region there is a rapid increase in dynamical robustness that is attributable to the rapid decrease in the number of attractors (shown in Figure 2). Also of note is the very low weight of the 'heaviest' basin,

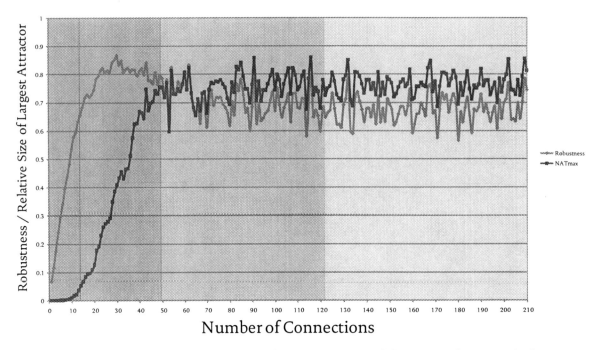

**Figure 3** *The relationship between network connectivity and dynamic robustness / relative size (weight) of the largest (heaviest) attractor*

which again is the result of the large number of attractors characteristic of networks in this region.

The 'complex' region is where it all happens within this particular dataset. The weight of the heaviest basin increases rapidly, and the dynamical robustness increases to 0.85 (at $C \approx 2N$) before decreasing rather slowly to ~0.70. The rapid increase in $W_{max}$ can be interpreted as an increase in *archetypal preference* – across this region the networks' behavior changes from having little preference for a particular mode of behavior (which means they 'see' many types of environmental context – indicatory of a relatively large number of attractors), to having a definite preference to the mode of behavior they exhibit (which means they are 'tuned' to one particular environmental context). Another way of expressing this shift is that the networks go from being overly flexible to being overly inflexible and that in the middle of the complex region there is a balance between qualitative pluralism and monism (or, dogmatism).

There is little to distinguish the 'chaotic' and 'random' regions in this particular dataset. Both $R$ and $W_{max}$ are relatively stable at 0.70 and 0.75, respectively, suggesting that

the phase spaces of networks existing in these regions are dominated by a single heavy attractor basin.

### Fibrosity and settling time

Figure 4 shows the relationship between network connectivity, $C$, and both $PI_{max}$ (or, fibrosity) and $T_{max}$ (transient, or settling time). If we consider the ordered region first then we observe that over this region fibrosity increases rapidly to a maximum of around 110, whilst at the same time, the maximum settling time remains very low. This indicates that whatever state a network in this region is initiated from, the trajectory will reach an attractor very quickly (bearing in mind that these attractors will be rather uninteresting as they are analytically trivial).

In the 'complex' region we see a rapid decrease in fibrosity along with a modest increase in maximum settling time[1]. The phase space of the average network in this region,

1 The fact that a large decrease in $PI_{max}$ is associated with only a modest increase in $T_{max}$ is simply that there are more states required to increase $T_{max}$ than $PI_{max}$. If $PI_{max}$ increases rapidly then state space quickly runs out of available states before a phase space trajectory can get too far from the central attractor.

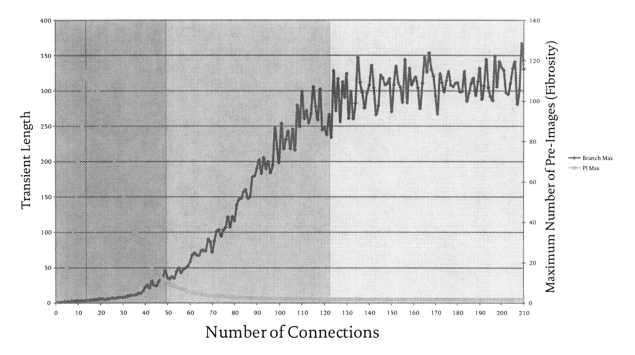

**Figure 4** *The relationship between network connectivity and transient length (settling time) / maximum number of pre-images (fibrosity)*

therefore, would contain attractor basins that exhibit a medium level of fibrosity and modest settling times. In a sense, this means that these networks balance the desire for having many routes to the same endpoint (*equifinality*) with that of getting to that same endpoint in a relatively short time. It should also be noted from the previous section that these networks also exhibit a range of non-trivial (i.e., interesting) behaviors that are not drowned-out by a preference for one particular mode (which is a direct result of dynamic modularity).

The 'chaotic' and 'random' regions, which contains networks whose phase space is dominated by a single heavy attractor, are distinguished by the quite different structure of the branches attached to the states on the central attractor. 'Chaotic' branches tend to be quite long and quite fibrous, whereas 'random' branches tend to be very long and sparse.

Now that we have considered each of the datasets separately, we can move on to constructing the 'bigger picture' by considering all the datasets together and developing a fuller appreciation of each network type. Before doing that, however, I want to highlight that the regional denotations presented herein relate to the characteristic networks' dynamics and not

necessarily their structural topology (although connectivity is an important structural parameter). Network theorists distinguish between ordered, small-world, scale-free and random networks. These *structural* denotations do not map directly to the *dynamic* denotations of ordered, complex, chaotic and random. For example, the (dynamically) 'random' that we shall see in the next section is far from random from a structural perspective. That being said, an interesting area for investigation, especially in the 'complex' region, would be how the *dynamic* structure (i.e., emergent modularity) maps to phase space structure.

### Considering all the data sets as one

Table 1 attempts to sum-up the observations made in the previous sections, by showing how each parameter changes qualitatively (e.g., ↑↑↑ ≡ rapid increase) over each region. Figure 5 brings presents the data visually (and arguably more effectively) by comparing the network structure, the largest phase space attractor basin, and the state space configuration (the online PDF version of this article is recommended so that full color can be observed) for a 'typical' network selected from each region. Figure 5 vividly illustrates the differences in attractor

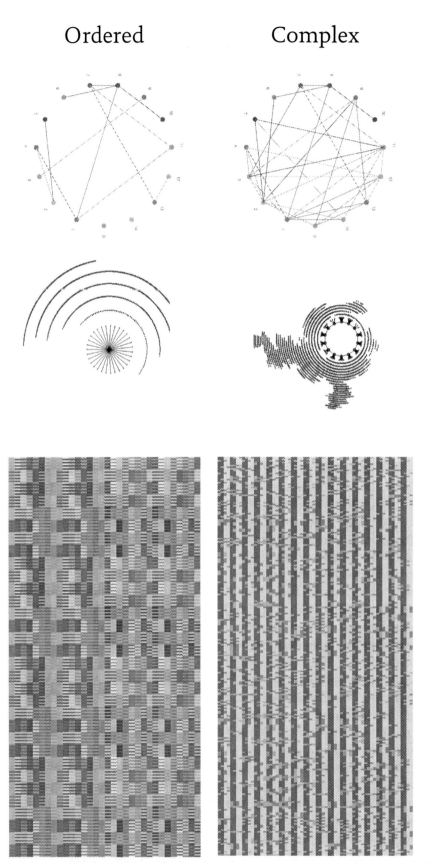

**Figure 5 (part 1)** *Structural topology, the largest phase space attractor basin, and the state space configuration for an ordered and a complex network*

Chaotic                    Random

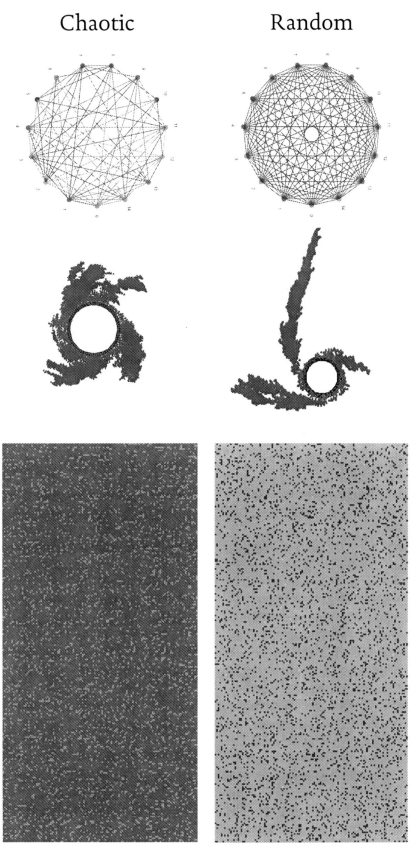

**Figure 5 (part 2)** *Structural topology, the largest phase space attractor basin, and the state space configuration for a chaotic and a random network*

| Network Type | $N_{att}$ | $PI_{max}$ | $T_{max}$ | GoE | $R$ | $W_{max}$ |
|---|---|---|---|---|---|---|
| Ordered | ↓↓↓ | ↑↑↑ | ↑ | ↑↑↑ | ↑↑↑ | ↑ |
| Complex | ↓↓ | ↓↓↓ | ↑↑ | ↔ | ↓ | ↑↑↑ |
| Chaotic | ↓ | ↓ | ↑↑↑ | ↓↓ | ↓ | ↔ |
| Random | ↔ | ↔ | ↔ | ↔ | ↔ | ↔ |

**Table 1** *Qualitative change in principle parameters across each dynamic region*

| Network Type | $N_{att}$ | $PI_{max}$ | $T_{max}$ | GoE | $R$ | $W_{max}$ |
|---|---|---|---|---|---|---|
| Ordered | H | M | L | M | M | L |
| Complex | M | M | L | H | H | M |
| Chaotic | L | L | M | M | H | H |
| Random | L | L | H | L | H | H |

**Table 2** *Qualitative value of principle parameters across each dynamic region (H=high, M=medium, L=low)*

| Network Type | $N_{att}$ | $W_{max}$ | $PI_{max}$ | $T_{max}$ | GoE | $R$ | $C$ |
|---|---|---|---|---|---|---|---|
| Ordered | 1 | 0.008 | 48 | 3 | 0.97 | 0.53 | 12 |
| Complex | 14 | 0.400 | 84 | 33 | 0.89 | 0.71 | 40 |
| Chaotic | 75 | 0.537 | 20 | 120 | 0.58 | 0.46 | 90 |
| Random | 75 | 0.870 | 7 | 335 | 0.37 | 0.78 | 210 |

**Table 3** *Actual values of principle parameters for an example network selected from each dynamic region*

basin structure and state space configuration and allows us to see directly the impact that parameters such as fibrosity and robustness have on these two 'spaces'.

### Missing data: $P_{max}$

$P_{max}$ refers to the period of the heaviest ($W_{max}$) attractor basin for a particular network. This additional data would be useful as the case of $P_{max} \gg N$ is often used to justify the term 'chaotic' for a Boolean network. A full analysis of how $P_{max}$ varies with $C$ was not available at the time of writing, but early indications show that $P_{max}$ increases with $C$. This trend is illustrated (amongst others) in Table 2 which reports the values of the $P_{max}$, and the other parameters discussed thus far, for the four networks depicted in Figure 5. This very small sample confirms that the period of the heaviest basins ($P_{max}$) for typical networks in the 'chaotic' and 'random' regions are indeed much larger ($\gg$) than the network size ($N$).

We can now attempt to make a 'standard' statement about each of the four dynamic regimes: ordered, complex, chaotic and random. It should be noted, however, that the statements that follow are of the 'on average' variety, in that there will exist networks in each region that look (in a dynamic sense) very much like networks in other regions. A more obvious limitation of such a categorization process is that the boundaries between each region are fuzzy and certainly not discrete. The statements are, therefore, no more than guidelines. They certainly do not allow us to make statements of the sort "All Boolean networks with $N=15$ and $C=60$ are dynamically chaotic." Although statements such as "Networks with $N=15$ and $C=60$ (with the same rule structure discussed herein) typically display dynamic traits that resemble chaotic behavior" are meaningfully efficacious. As with all of complexity thinking (and arguably all science and even all human thinking) we must resist the temptation is creating hard rules from fuzzy guidelines – guidelines need to balance the need to say something meaningful, without saying too much. To state this differently, one might also suggest that "to say something meaningful about complex systems, one must also be a little vague." The following characteristic statements illustrate this:

- A *dynamically ordered network* responds to **many** environmental changes **quickly** and without **preference**. The various behavioral modes available to the network are analytically trivial. Once in a particular mode, such networks are **quite** susceptible to external perturbations. Furthermore, a **modest number** of states can only be accessed from outside the system.

- A *dynamically complex network* responds **quite** quickly to a **modest** number of environmental changes with some **degree** of preference. The various behavioral modes available to these networks are analytically irreducible and innovative. Once performing a particular function, such networks are **very** robust to external perturbations. Furthermore, a **high** number of states can only be accessed from outside the system.

- A *dynamically chaotic network* responds **rather** slowly to a **modest** number of environmental contexts, but with a **high** preference for one particular archetype. The dominant mode is **very** complex to the point of being chaotic. Such networks are **very** robust to external signaling and a **significant** number of states can only be accessed from outside the system.

- A *dynamically random network* responds **very** slowly to a modest number of environmental contexts, but with a **high** preference for one particular archetype. The dominant mode is **very** complex to the point of being chaotic. Such networks are **very** robust to external signaling and yet only a **low** proportion of states can only be accessed from outside the system.

The emboldened terms are relative assessments that only gain meaning through comparison with the other types. We go even further with this process of data reduction. Consider the following slogans:

*Ordered* = fast, fickle and predictable;
*Complex* = swift, balanced and inventive;
*Chaotic* = sedate, dogmatic and incoherent;
*Random* = slow, stubborn and unfocused.

The more 'distance' however between the raw data and our summations, the more subjective dimensions play in our choice of words. For example, if a different slant was taken we might rewrite the slogan for chaotic as:

*Chaotic* = Thorough, strong-willed and sophisticated.

My point is simply that the process of categorizing complex datasets is problematic and requires a great deal of care.

## Final remarks

The motivation for this article was to explore the merits of a modern assumption that 'being connected' is unquestionably a good thing. The research presented here is still in its early phases, but it is clear that different levels of connectivity can be associated with different types of dynamics. One interpretation would suggest that being too connected is actually overly restrictive and that there is a balance to be maintained. Much of the complexity literature argues that "maintaining balance" is central to a sustainable approach for existing within a complex (eco-) system. Of course, we must take care in importing the lessons from abstract models such as Boolean networks into the realm of human organization. That being said, what is rather surprising to me is how narrow the desired 'balanced' (complex) region is relative to the (seemingly less desirable) chaotic and random regions. Furthermore, if we consider the width of the complex region, $C_{width}$, in relation to the whole of 'connectivity space' we can construct a measure of relative weight, $W_{complex}$, equal to the width of the complex region divided by the total number of a connections in a fully connected network. In this particular study $W_{complex} \approx 2N/(N[N-1])$. If we take the bold (and possibly wrong!) step of assuming this is true for increasingly larger networks then $W_{complex} \propto$

$N^{-1}$, and so as $N$ increases the relative width of the complex region becomes vanishingly small. Balance is achieved it seems, not by occupying 'the middle ground', but 'a narrow strip of ground off to one side'!

## References

Lucas, C. (2007). "Boolean networks: Dynamic organisms," http://www.calresco.org/boolean.htm.

Richardson, K. A. (2004a). "Systems theory and complexity: Part 1," *Emergence: Complexity & Organization*, ISSN 1521-3250, 6(3): 75-79.

Richardson, K. A. (2004b). "Systems theory and complexity: Part 2," *Emergence: Complexity & Organization*, ISSN 1521-3250, 6(4): 77-82.

Richardson, K. A. (2005a). "Systems theory and complexity: Part 3," *Emergence: Complexity & Organization*, ISSN 1521-3250, 7(2): 104-114.

Richardson, K. A. (2005b). "Simplifying Boolean networks," *Advances in Complex Systems*, ISSN 0219-5259, 8(4), 365-381.

Wuensche, A. (1999). "Classifying cellular automata automatically: Finding gliders, filtering, and relating space-time patterns, attractor basins, and the Z parameter," *Complexity*, ISSN 1076-2787, 4(3): 47-66.

Wuensche, A. and Lesser, M. J. (1992). *The Global Dynamics of Cellular Automata*, ISBN 9780201557404.

Forum

# New notes from Stellenbosch

Ken Baskin
ISCE Research, US

Call me irrational, but I can't help feeling that, at the 3rd International Workshop on Complexity and Philosophy, our attempts to apply complexity thinking to philosophy began to grow up. At the first two workshops, participants seemed to be in the human equivalent of phase transition, experimenting with a variety of only tenuously connected approaches and directions. In the most recent workshop, however, a deepened sense of what complexity thinking means for social systems seemed to emerge, creating a sense of coherence as gratifying as it was surprising.

This feeling that the conference had moved from phase transition into the early stages of a stable state was especially evident in a series of presentations on the issues of learning, ethics, and history. In each of these presentations, the issue of interconnection dominated, emphasizing a Post-Modernist recognition that complexity in human affairs demanded we transcend the Modernist focus on entities as analytically distinct and its search for the one right answer. Rather, each suggested we would do better to focus, not only on our interconnections, but also on learning to tolerate, if not embrace, the differences that have so often divided people.

Perhaps I misperceived what was going on, but, for me, this workshop felt as if many of the presenters were now speaking from the *experience* of complexity, rather than merely from *thoughts* about it.

Consider, for example, Aliki Nicolaides' presentation on the epistemology of learning. Her focus was an examination of what we mean by learning "in the context of intensifying complex reality." From a complexity point of view, learning becomes a dynamic process that demands the learner maintain relationship amid diversity. Such an attitude, she emphasized, is a far cry form the "show me the skill" approach in much of current, Modernist adult learning theory. Rather, complexity learning is, first and foremost, about discovering the "emerging model that defines the boundaries of action..." (Richardson & Cilliers, 2007). In this way, complexity learning generates self-reinforcing feedback loops in which one must discover emerging models in order to learn about the world coded in them.

As a result, rather than the objectivity demanded by Modernist learning, with its focus on the instrumental and technical, complexity learning requires a more relational connection in the learner. In this model of learning, one must focus on "embracing a multiple analytical and interpretive frame for creating meaning." Complexity learning is thus much more demanding than Modernist learning. For, rather than standing *outside* the subject of learning, Nicolaides continued, the learner must be in relationship to it. And that, in turn, requires a decree of openness, of mutuality and intimacy, that Modernist learning dismisses as "merely" subjective. It also requires the ability to hold different, even opposed positions. In many ways, Nicolaides appeared to be describing the same conditions that Stacey describes as necessary for creativity in *Complexity and creativity in organizations* (1996).

What made Nicolaides's presentation representative of the common position I perceived at the workshop was that it called, not merely for *thinking* differently, but for *living* differently. The two presentations on ethics and my own on history, all pointed to this need to transform ourselves and the way we live that a serious commitment to the principles of complexity thinking makes inescapable.

Even the more technical presentations enriched this sense that we were reaching deeper into what complexity meant for social systems. For example, anthropologist Dmitri Bondarenko offered a powerful framework for understanding the way social hierarchies function. After emphasizing that all societies are collections of hierarchies reflecting a variety of institutions – family, government, religion, education, etc. – he made a distinction between the two extremes on the continuum of hierarchy systems. On one hand are systems that are homoarchic – that is, one of the society's hierarchies is dominant, and its members' position in other hierarchies are largely dictated by their positions in the dominant hierarchy. Think for instance of Maoist China, where one's position in relation to the Communist Party hierarchy dominated his or her position in any other, as many of the most distinguished university professors learned during the Cultural Revolution. On the other are heterarchic systems, where no one hierarchy dominates. In American society, for instance, a person can be CEO, at the top of the hierarchy, of a major corporation, and, at the same time, a comparatively powerless person in the legal hierarchy.

This distinction, it seems to me, is much more illuminating than the distinction usually drawn between hierarchic and flat organizations. As we continue to learn, *all* complex systems are hierarchic. What distinguishes human societies is the simultaneous existence of many hierarchies. Bondarenko's presentation offered a powerful way to think about those human systems, reflecting their full complexity.

My sense that our discussions of human complexity were deepening was also reflected in the conversations provoked by the presentations. Bondarenko's, for instance, generated a discussion about whether organizations almost inevitably evolve from early stages where they are heterarchic to later stages where they become homoarchic. There was also a substantial amount of conversation about whether it was time for us to move beyond our use of the technical language of complexity science. This is a particularly important issue for me. For even though I have used the term "attractor" to describe such human phenomena as personality, culture, and *episteme*, I have become increasingly aware that such terms may create more problems than they resolve.

If you're interested in exploring any of these issues, the papers are available in the recently published collection *Explorations in complexity thinking*, edited by Kurt Richardson and Paul Cilliers. And if that whets your appetite, a fourth workshop may well be in the cards for 2009. Of course, the only way I'll be able to be sure my sense of the third workshop was accurate is to wait and see if the fourth continues moving in that direction. After all, the quickest way to figure out what a complex system will do is ... but we all know how that sentence ends.

## References

Richardson, K. A. and Cilliers, P. (eds.) (2007). *Explorations in Complexity Thinking: Pre-proceedings of the 3rd International Workshop on Complexity and Philosophy*, ISBN 9780979168819.

Stacey, R. D. (1996). *Complexity and Creativity in Organizations*, ISBN 9781881052890.

Forum

# Adjacent possibilities: Applied chutzpah

Ron Schultz
ISCE Research, US

I was looking for a job. A friend had suggested I contact the local economic development corporation and see what I could rouse. Since I've been working in the world of social entrepreneurs and social enterprise, I looked at the EDC web site with an eye to this particular form of social business making. Not too surprisingly, I found nothing approaching the idea of social interactions outside of an upcoming party. So, as a way to engage the CEO of the EDC so she might consider hiring me, I created a scenario about social enterprise, economic development and San Diego. To make it particularly San Diego-centric, I turned the scenario into a civic model. Since, in my mind, I was explaining this model to her with the sole intention of enticing her to consider making me her director of social enterprise, a position she neither had nor had ever considered, I needed nothing more than a brief elevator pitch and a few possible details to make my point.

As it turned out, this point was quite compelling. So compelling, that in the telling, as is wont to happen, I blurted out the possibility of creating a social enterprise zone in San Diego that would be a truly unique concept in the US and would make San Diego a model of progressive social action. The concept caught her off guard, and she immediately suggested I take the program to the City Council President Pro Tem and she gave me his number and told me to call him at her suggestion. I didn't get a job, but the next day, I went to visit the Council President Pro Tem on one of his open door days, and told him what I had in mind. He asked about a dozen questions, which being in the field, I was able to address, and he began nodding his head. "I like this," he said and repeated the phrase a second time. He then requested a more in depth meeting in a couple of weeks with more players at the table.

Now about three months down the line, after numerous meetings with the Councilman and many others, I find myself putting forward a new way of addressing the interaction of peer-to-peer lending, what we're calling community-based financing using neighbor-to-neighbor partner lending, micro-finance and the work of social entrepreneurs in the under-served areas of San Diego. Prominent people in the city have been taking my phone calls and agreeing to meetings and a new way of thinking about how we support social issues is developing.

Having mixed with you academics for a number of years now, I immediately started looking at process. I knew I was engaged in a series of interactions, initiated and furthered by a narrative out of which emerged a whole new realm of adjacent opportunities. But there was something that predated all of this that caught my attention. And that was the driving force to put the idea forward in the first place. For lack of a better term, I chose to call this force, *Applied Chutzpah*.

For those of you schooled in the finer delicacies of the Yiddish language, the way I am using the word chutzpah, or more correctly *khutspe,* might cause some affront. As pointed out in the book, *Born To Kvetch,* by Michael Wex (Harper Perennial, 2006) this word has come to mean a "laudable audacity or apparent effrontery that actually conceals a brave and often new approach to a subject or endeavor." Given what transpired with my series of phone calls in San Diego, I thought that an apt description. But Wex goes on to explain that khutspe is actually something "both stupid and mannerless, lacking in class and unpleasant," and he provides the example of propositioning a woman at her husband's funeral.

Whichever definition you choose, the point I wish to make holds true. And that is that this bit of applied chutzpah, I suggest, invariably leads to an emergent opportunity – chutzpah in either case implies an interaction of some sort - out of which a new way of thinking emerges – either an elevated conceptual possibility or utter amazement at the depth of human debasement. This new way of thinking promotes taking action – launching a unique civic model for social enterprise in one case or a well-deserved slap across the face in the other.

The case for applied chutzpah – while an argument could easily be made for its proximity to the latter definition of khutspe than the more popular laudable audacity – is worth considering. The important factor is that in audaciously engaging in an interaction with specific personal intention what emerges is a new way of thinking that initiates action, either good or bad. These audacious interactions differ from their less-in-your-face brethren, because as we all are well aware, what emerges from the majority of interactions does not create a new way of thinking. And without any evidence other than anecdote to support my contention, those precipitated by applied chutzpah, do.

If I were wiser I would leave this living example of that which I speak at that. Unfortunately, I am not. The program I am furthering to support social enterprise and social entrepreneurs demands continued applications of this 'Chutzpahtic' approach. Taking the audacious leap may produce moments that my colleague and friend Steve Farber refers to as OS!Ms (Oh Shit! Moments) when one finds oneself with nothing below and nothing above to grasp onto but one's awareness that something new and unexpected is about to happen that will radically change one's thinking no matter the eventual landing place. That's what it takes to change the world and create a new way of thinking about how to do so. And while there are no applications being taken for a course in applied chutzpah, it would be safe to say that this fact will not limit the variety of new ways of thinking, either laudable or mannerless, that will emerge because someone has exhibited their master status in applied chutzpah. Who knows, with a little applied chutzpah a new model might just emerge that could truly make a difference in how we operate in relationship to each other. How much chutzpah do you think it would take?

# Book Reviews

**A Review of** *A Complexity Perspective on Researching Organizations :Taking Experience Seriously*
**edited by Ralph Stacey and Douglas Griffin**
**reviewed by Shaun Coffey**
**published by Routledge**
**ISBN 0415351316 (2005)**

"Complexity as the experience of organization" focuses attention on how people cope with unknown consequences as they create organizational futures together. The basic argument advanced and supported in the book challenges the notion that organizations are systems. Rather, they are the ongoing patterning of interactions between people – the complex responsive process of relating. The perspective of complex responsive processes focuses on the experience of interaction which produces nothing but further interaction.

The book comprises two (2) introductory chapters that examine principles and methodologies and five (5) chapters contributed by consultants and managers who reflect on their experience of actual organizational events. Each chapter is introduced by the editors who conceptualize the experience and comment on key themes. The individual cases provide the authors stories of how they make sense of their experience – experience that range from long term leadership of an educational institution, to internal organizational development consultancies, to understanding consulting practice.

Collectively the accounts brought together address questions such as "what actually happens in organizations?" How do patterns of responses emerge?" What does this imply?" A strong element of the book is the contributors examination of how the perspective of complex responsiveness not just assist them in making sense of their experience, but also how this awareness leads to their own development (and often changes in the way they work). As one contributor records "If you can engage with the sense making and take the risk that you will inevitably be changed in the process as well, you have the foundation for a new practice.

The second chapter on methodology is a very valuable contribution, especially in the way it contrasts and distinguishes complex responsive processes approaching from action research. Key aspects are explored fully and particular care has been taken in defining and explaining concepts and terminology.

What is particularly useful in this explanation of methodology is the explanation of power relations, and the unconscious relationships sustained by ideology. The proposition is also developed that an organization is an evolving pattern of interactions emerging in local interaction of people and choice. No individual designs or controls the evolving patterns of organizations; rather the evolution emerges as the spontaneous choices of individuals and the amplification of small differences in the iteration of interaction from one present to another.

In the five contributed chapters, readers will find a range of situations to which they can relate, and result from work done in a doctoral or MA group at the University of Hertford-shire. The narrative methodology is particularly useful as it demonstrates different aspects of the complexity perspective: for example, the risk basis for reflection that brief accounts of usually ignored interaction with others can provide. Similarly, value is seen in going beyond the obvious and promoting conversation to surface issues. Choice of methodology for acting in organizations is important as it affects both what is done, and one's sense of self. Brief introductions from the editor's help focus the readers attention, and a very helpful.

If there is a weakness in the book it is the lack of a concluding chapter. That, however, can be a source of reflection for the reader and his/her experience of the book.

Whilst not an easy read, those who take the time to reflect on the narratives provided, and who then try to relate these to their own experience will find the book very useful. The book will have a ready audience in the academic community, and for practitioners versed in reflective processes for their development. For a novice to the field it may be less assessable.

As a practitioner I found the volume a useful and effective reminder that organizations change constantly and in unpredicted manners. Being open to the experience, and being aware of how one impacts on that change, is a constant challenge; as is the constant need to acknowledge the social nature of reflective practice and learning.

## A Review of *Small Worlds: the Dynamics of Networks Between Order and Randomness*
**written by Duncan J. Watts**
**reviewed by David McArthur**
**published by Princeton University Press**
**ISBN 0691117047 (2003)**

Tired after days of travel halfway across the globe, surrounded by the familiar masquerade of traffic on the "wrong" side of the street, strange currency, different faces, languages, and accents)? This is the complexity we endure to attend a conference on complexity. It is a relief when we spot a familiar someone in that strange location. Even spotting one of the "great names" at whose tables we are never asked to sit, makes us feel more connected. As academics, we share with each other and with the "great names" the ties of having read the same authors, having struggled with similar constructs, having survived the doctoral gauntlet. We take comfort in sharing a tie with others, in populating our immediate "neighborhood" with fellow "connected" attendees while surrounded by a city of "others" where the conference is being held to whom we feel no tie.

With an appetite for new explanations for order amid randomness – we live in densely connected, embedded networks at home. But in the sparsely connected network of a foreign conference location we intuitively welcome connecting ties that build a neighborhood, without critical analysis even if the ties are weak ties. We actively question one another ("You're at University of Warwick? I knew somebody there. Perhaps you know her?") to re-embed ourselves in a familiar small world ties to survive our stay at conferences where we are sparsely connected

Watts's book on the small world effect brings a mix of rigor (sometimes meaning mathematics) and vigor (enthusiasm, a broad range of applications, and playfulness) to this well-written but sometimes dense outgrowth (there are some 120 plots of the characteristics of his models) of his dissertation.

The book is divided into two parts. Part one introduces the reader to the small world effect and reviews graph theory, covering general measures of structure and developing some measures of graph topology (the qualitative structure) that are needed to support the claim that a network in a particular research domain is a "small world graph." He contrasts relational and spatial graphs in their ability to interpolate, as small world graphs do, between purely random and completely structured graphs. He examines three very different examples to see if they can be explained structurally as small worlds – the Kevin Bacon Graph (an example useful in sociology and organizations), the Western States Power Graph (from physics and electrical engineering), and the neural network of an commonly studied simple worm *C. Elegans* (from zoology and biology).

A social, engineering, or biological network (or a network in other disciplines) is a collection of nodes represented in a graph by vertices.[1] Edges represent the relationships that connect them, such as "acted in a film with" or "transmits neural signals to." Sparse graphs have many more vertices ($n$) than edges (M) and the average vertex is not highly connected ($k$). Additionally, in small world graphs the connected nature of vertices is that they form local clusters of adjacent vertices (neigh-

borhoods) which are thinly connected to other such neighborhoods. Indeed, the "characteristic path length" (the "median of the means of the shortest path lengths connecting each [vertex] to all other [vertices] (p. 29) is quite small relative to the size of the graph measured by either $n$ or M. But those structural characteristics don't model either random or ordered graphs well. The qualitative topology of small-world relational graphs is more completely described when *shortcuts* and *contractions* are explained.

Distance in a relational graph is measured by the number of edges traversed to connect with another vertex.[2] A shortcut is an edge that connects two vertices that otherwise would only be connected by a longer path length. The fraction of edges in the graph that are shortcuts ($\varphi$) is a topological measure of sparseness (p. 72). Vertices tend to cluster ($\gamma$) in neighborhoods that have few connections to other neighborhoods, thus satisfying the locally clustered, sparsely connected criterion of small world graphs.

Not all vertices or their neighbors are connected to others by simple ties or shortcuts – some are connected by contractions. A contraction is a vertex that, in concert with edges, connects two otherwise distant neighborhoods. The graph's composite measure of contractions ($\psi$) is the fraction of pairs of vertices in the graph which serve this bridging function (p. 73).

Using these measures Watts shows that both relational and spatial graphs interpolate between ordered and random graphs as functions of shortcuts and contractions. He demonstrates that these structural features are independent of any specific graph and are therefore not artifacts of the nodes or relationships being investigated. Relational graphs can be small-world graphs but spatial graphs cannot because their topology is driven by the spatial distribution of the vertices in the graph.

Watts develops a model that predicts characteristic (typical) path lengths and measures of clustering and length-scaling properties of graphs that interpolate between strictly ordered and random using the Graph or a

---

1 Watts makes many simplifying assumptions including that all graphs are connected – there are no isolates in the scope of this work. All edges are undirected (even though most think of neural and electrical power networks as directed). And all edges are unweighted – one edge or relationship is not more important than another.

2 Such as, "She acted in a film with someone who acted with someone who acted with Kevin Bacon." – A "Bacon number" of 2.

Moore Graph. Though Part One uses a static view of networks and their graphs, Watts has managed to develop a network-independent definition of small-world graphs and shown how they vary regularly as their topological characteristics change from those of random to those of ordered graphs.

In the final chapter in Part One, Watts evaluates three "real-world" networks by making some simplifying assumptions and developing and analyzing their graphs' topology – the "Kevin Bacon" version of a collaboration network, the electrical power grid in the Western USA, and the neural network of a simple worm, C. Elegans.

All three are small-world graphs, which supports the conjecture that small-world properties exist in real-world networks that are partly ordered and partly random (p. 161). The simple Kevin Bacon Graph is modeled quite well by Watts' model. The electrical power network, which is partly spatial, is modeled fairly well though the clustering prediction breaks down. The attempt to model C. Elegans' neural network is not well modeled by either Watts' models nor by either highly structured or random models – perhaps because the graph of the worm's neural system is too small (n or M) to generate reliable statistics (p. 161).

Watts's work and enthusiasm carry the reader into the world of applications of the network idea in Part Two. Here he explores the "So what?" question. Does the structure or topology of the small-world graph affect how some very different applications of network thinking act – their dynamic properties? He chooses applications from several disciplines that seem designed to stretch the abilities of even this current thinking in small-world graphs.

The spread of infectious diseases, the synchronization of cellular automata, the *emergence* of cooperation in graphed versions of the prisoner's dilemma game, and the global synchrony of coupled phase oscillators are examined. The travel of infectious disease, understood by earlier writers through spatial structure (distance), rates of migration between sub-populations, and how sub-populations are coupled, is shown by Watts to follow the small-world characteristic of characteristic

path length. Introducing the small-world topological measures into simplified graphs of the prisoner's dilemma provides insight into how researchers can empirically observe cooperation among human players of the game while the only rationally defensible position is one of betrayal (defection). Unlike true small-world graphs, poorly clustered graphs tend to have small populations of cooperators which "learn" from bad experience to betray the other player. As the fraction of shortcuts increases, the likelihood of a group of cooperators being betrayed by a defector increase and the core of cooperators collapses toward a strategy of defection. In a most important point, Watts points out that the reverse of this may be applicable to organizational theory where cooperation is desired and manipulating the edges connecting managers may create neighborhoods of cooperation.

Watts's book, which is an intellectual genealogy of his more popular Six Degrees, published in 2003, is a less accessible but more detailed description of the small world phenomena. It is well worth the read just to see how Watts builds a bridge between numerical and linguistic logic. If our social network extended to his, we would want to be at his table at the far away conference.

## A Review of *The Resilient Enterprise: Overcoming Vulnerability for Competitive Advantage*

written by Yossi Sheffi
reviewed by Max Boisot
published by The MIT Press
ISBN 0262195372 (2005)

What should companies do to recover from high-impact disruptions? What action should they take to lower their vulnerability and increase their resilience? These are the two key questions addressed by this book. Clearly, seven years into a new millennium confronting the twin challenges of climate change and of global security, they are timely.

The term 'resilience' is borrowed from the materials sciences to describe the ability of a material to recover its original shape following a deformation. In the book, it refers to the ability of a firm to return to its normal performance level following a high-impact/ low probability disruption. Security is about prevention. Resilience is about recovery. They must be thought of together. Both a firm's security and resilience may depend on the support that it receives from customer and suppliers when things go wrong. A support culture has to be built up, however, and this requires goodwill.

The book examines different kinds of disruptions – earthquakes, floods, and accidents, terrorist actions, etc. How should a company prioritise these? What do different types of disruptions have in common? How might a company prepare? In the case of terrorist attacks, the disruptive threat is *adaptive* – that is, the adversary works around your defences. And as we learn from game theory, a game against adversaries is not played in the same way as a game against nature. In exploring these issues, the book draws on the experience of many companies, both successful and unsuccessful at coping with disruptions. Since, as the author argues, a company is typically a citizen of its supply chain, the organization perspective adopted is that of the extended enterprise, the network of suppliers, manufacturers, distributors, retailers, that in concert with other participants in the supply chain, bring products to markets.

The book is subdivided into five parts. Part one discusses the nature of disruptions and one's vulnerability to them. The first chapter illustrates the nature of such a disruption by comparing Nokia and Ericsson's response to the consequences of a lightning strike that, on the 17th of March, 2000, hit the Albuquerque plant of one of their suppliers of semiconductors, Philips N.V., the Dutch electronic conglomerate. Although the effects of the strike seemed at first sight to be quite inconsequential, each company interpreted the disruptive event in a different way. On being informed of the strike, Nokia immediately swung into action to secure its future supplies, while the more laid-back and consensual Ericsson waited to see how things would develop. The result was that while Nokia secured for itself a first mover advantage in appropriating for itself all of Philip's spare capacity – it turned out that the plant's production capacity had been severely disrupted - Ericsson bore the brunt of the disruption because it could not secure secondary supplies of the affected parts. After incurring a US$ 2.34 billion loss in the company's mobile phone division, it ended up exiting from the phone handset production market.

Disruptions affect global supply chains. Today, tight supply chains – often implemented through 'lean' production systems – simultaneously improve efficiency and increase vulnerability to disruptions. Such chains create complex interdependencies that make it hard to know where the vulnerabilities to high impact-low probability events will lie. The dense connectivities these supply chains achieve ensure that the effects of a disruptive event will rapidly propagate beyond the site where it occurs.

Chapter 2 explores the nature of vulnerability. The Kobe earthquake of Jan 17, 1995 exposed the vulnerability of Japan's lean manufacturing paradigm. The connectivity of the international firms that were located in the region – Texas Instruments, Caterpillar, IBM, Procter & Gamble, etc – rapidly turned the earthquake into an event with global rather than local consequences. Yet companies vary in their vulnerability to high impact disruptions. A MacDonald franchise with a geographically extensive network of identical yet independent outlets, for example, is less vulnerable to a system-level disruption than, say, American Airlines, with its highly interconnected network of air routes. Sheffi points out that high impact disruptions are not as rare as they appear to be. *Singular* disruptive events are rare – ie, *this* particular earthquake of *this* magnitude in *this* specific place – but earthquakes, as a category, are not.

Anticipating disruptions is the subject of Chapter 3. Sheffi argues that disruptions result from a confluence of several factors that typically offer many precursory signs that a disruption is about to take place. Yet also typically, such signs can only be interpreted *ex post*, and this only where the confluence of factors is repeatable. *Re*-cognition presupposes some prior familiarity with the way that precursory signs are wrought into patterns. The reporting of 'near-misses' discussed by the author both relies on and focuses on events characterized by a high degree of recurrence. Only then can we follow Whitehead in seeing the familiar in the strange and the strange in the familiar.

In this chapter, Sheffi discusses power law distributions. He believes that these distributions can be used as the basis for estimating the probability that 'a big one' – a large disruptive event - will happen during a certain time interval. Yet the 'fat tails', unstable means and potentially infinite variance of such distributions makes any kind of effective prediction problematic, to say the least. Secondly there is a permanent temptation to assimilate such distributions to Gaussian thinking and to treat disruptive events as if they were the product of independent and 'additive' factors, rather than interconnected, and hence, multiplicative ones. Finally, and related to this, we may need to distinguish between having the relevant *data* before an event and having the *information* that is latent in the data. One can only really extract such information if one is armed with the right model – ie, distribution - of the situation at the outset.

How should one develop the required pattern recognition abilities? And how to get recognized patterns accepted by practical people in a timely fashion when these initially appear to be implausible? After all, reacting to a potential disruption can itself be as disruptive and costly as the disruption itself. Terrorists understand this. Historical data, for example, are of limited use when trying to forecast the nature of a new *intentional* threat – one that is the product of adversarial relationships rather than of natural forces - because of its adaptive nature. This may then call for another approach. If you cannot anticipate a disruption, then you need to build redundancy and flexibility into your systems. The problem is cultural and social – it is explored by Sheffi in chapters 10, 11, and 12.

The last chapter in the first part of the book, 4, discusses the effects of disruptions. Since we often lack the relevant experience, it is hard to estimate the effects of low probability-high impact disruption. Yet these go through several characteristic stages that allow one to frame some expectations so that one need not react to them passively as 'acts of God'. Furthermore, there are upsides to be captured by those who can anticipate and prepare. If Ericsson had to exit certain markets, for example, Nokia actually gained market share from the disruption.

Part two offers a brief primer on supply chain management. Chapter 5 discusses the vulnerability of tight supply chains and lean manufacturing and gives the basics – such as the amplification mechanism known as the bullwhip effect. Chapter 6 deals with demand-responsive supply chains and shows us how to build in flexibility through risk-pooling. This can be done by getting products to share common components and by reducing product variability. Concurrent engineering also allows firms to respond quickly to changing market conditions by shortening lead times between product conception and introduction. Finally, different kinds of collaboration with suppliers and customers (contracting) can also improve flexibility.

Part three explores different ways in which vulnerability might be reduced. Chapter 7 offers good sensible advice on ways to reduce intentional disruptions. This involves recognizing abnormalities or outliers – the strange in the familiar. Training will do this to some extent. Yet, as Sheffi recognizes, as systems become more complex, outliers become more difficult to spot. And human nature in the form of complacency then kicks in. We know that "the price of freedom is eternal vigilance" but are we really willing to pay that price? Indeed, are we even capable of doing so? Remember Long Term Capital Management. The problem is that while pattern recognition is the bedrock of all control functions, it only works on repetitive processes such as are found in a firm's productive activities. And repetition eventually bores us. Sheffi's advice here is useful, even though he confronts a catch-22 question: "How to put a value on avoiding a problem you don't have because you spent money to avoid it?" (p. 135)

Chapter 8 explores security-driven collaboration. Such collaboration requires information sharing; yet it is costly and goes against an organization's natural tendency. The failure to share information across organizations with respect to the Tsunami of December 26, 2004, for example, may sadly reflect the natural order of things . Information sharing is also highly uncertain in its outcomes: after all, what is information for you as a potential source, may be viewed as merely data for the recipient. The 'wisdom of crowds' that collaboration can achieve is nevertheless worth exploiting. It is an effective way of processing complex patterns even if this requires enlisting outside institutions and organizations – an expensive and time-consuming business.

Chapter 9 looks at how disruptions are detected. Texas Instruments knew about the Kobe quake before the Japanese Prime Minister did. So when can an organization be said to "know" something? The instinct of firms is to keep control of things by disconnecting interacting parts so as to minimize the complexity that they have to deal with. But in disruptive circumstances the need is to re-connect. How, then, to keep out the noise that threatens? High-impact, low probability events are refractory to routinization and yet in need routines if they are to be detected and responded to. Grasping the magnitude of an disruptive event may require in-depth understanding that this is business-not-as-usual. Often IT can provide the 'smoke detectors' and screening facilities.

Chapter 10 shows us how resilience can be built up through redundancy. Inventory is expensive as is spare capacity. Investing in both must therefore be selective and requires placing bets. Sheffi tells us that redundancy in IT systems has proved valuable to those financial firms that had it. But how does one place bets when dealing with power law distributions? Resilience can also be built up through flexibility and Part four introduces the concept of flexibility as a response. Chapter 11 demonstrates how flexibility can be achieved through interchangeability: the standardization and commonality of parts creates flexibility through making readily available alternatives. Chapter 12 shows how flexibility – and hence resilience - can be secured through postponement. This was the Benetton formula that delivered mass customizaton. Postponement can best be understood through an options lens: options maintain the right to take decisions at a later date, when the states of nature become better known. Chapter 13 extends the concept of flexibility to supplier relationships, pointing out that these need to be strong – as in the case of Kereitsus. The chapter also explores the merits of single versus multiple sourcing. Chapter 14 then looks at customer relationship management, showing how one can win customers over with a strong response to a disruptive that provides an opportunity to shine. The final chapter of Part four, Chapter 15, looks at the challenges involved in building a culture of flexibility.

The last part of the book, five, places resilience in a strategic context by associating it with competitive advantage. Resilience gives an enterprise buoyancy in the wake of *any* disruption in an increasingly uncertain world. But how do you build the business case for resilience? How do you justify the cost and effort involved? Experience a major disruption, argues Sheffi, and you will invest in mitigating future ones. But does this then not leave him preaching his message to the converted?

Sheffi's is a practical book for practical people, well written and full of sensible, down to earth advice. It claims to deal with any phenomena that could be disruptive for a firm - accidents and natural phenomena as well as terrorist activities. It does not however address the challenges posed by disruptive technologies or by the disruptive effects of a competitor's moves. Although these arise in the course of doing business – and therefore, arguably, firms ought to be addressing these anyway – it would have been nice to position the societal and natural disruptions discussed in the book in relation to these more mundane forms. Also, I think that the reader would have a better appreciation of the nature of low probability-high impact disruptions if these had been discussed in the context of the many other kinds of change that a firm needs to confront. Finally, what I missed in the book – apart from the odd hint here and there - is any sense that disruption has upsides. We may be dealing with significant discontinuities, but should we assume that they only presage bad things for a firm? Sheffi takes the ability to recover from disruptions as a source of competitive advantage. No one would quarrel with that proposition. But the extreme events described by power laws and discussed on pp. 48-50 are as likely to have upsides as they are to have downsides – in the case of disruptive innovation, Schumpeter frames the process as one of creative destruction. Could an exclusive focus on the threats posed by disruptive events and on the undoubted need for resilience screen out any latent opportunities that such events harbour? I certainly do not dismiss the value of Sheffi's focus, but I nevertheless ended up asking myself whether the concept of resilience would not benefit from being placed in a wider context. After all, one expects more from an entrepreneurial organization than just resilience, taken as an ability to recover an original posture. In response to radically changed conditions, one expects *creative learning* to take place as well. Hopefully, Sheffi will take on this expanded brief in future work.

## A Review of *Reengineering Health Care: the Complexities of Organizational Transformation*

written by Terry McNulty and Ewan Ferlie
reviewed by Christian L. van Tonder
published by Oxford University Press
ISBN 0199269076 (2004)

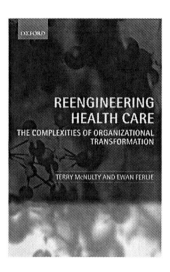

Reengineering health care is essentially a documented account of the authors' 'empirical case-study work' which attempted to bring about organizational transformation in a large National Health Service teaching hospital (the Leicester Royal Infirmary) in the UK between 1992 and 1998, using Business Process Engineering (or BPR as it is commonly known) as the change vehicle[3]. The authors further qualify the book's objective as one of producing an analysis of the experience of BPR implementation that is both empirically-based and theoretically informed.

The book is logically and clearly structured, commencing with an orientating chapter (chapter 1), which is followed with coverage of business process reengineering (BPR) as a model for planned organizational transformation (chapter 2), the changing context of health care in the United Kingdom (and research setting) in chapter 3, the research design and methodology pursued (chapter 4) and the various empirical results chapters (5 and 6) and discussion and contextualization chapters (chapters 7 to 10).

Except for the occasional carefully-worded statement of outcomes, it is clear that the authors are (impressively) direct and frank about the realities of a process that started out as a 'radical solution' and transformational ideal, but ultimately emerged as an incremental and evolutionary change endeavour. The latter, they concluded, was largely a consequence of the pronounced influence of the very organizational setting that it sought to change and as a result the change impact was 'uneven'.

The reader may not always subscribe to some of the positioning statements and supporting arguments the authors' offer but this is of course reader-specific and will naturally vary from reader to reader. As a case in point note for example that the authors' are particularly critical of the place and utility value of more quantitative / positivist methodologies in the field of change management and argue that quantitative approaches need to be succeeded by qualitative methodologies. This, it is submitted, depends entirely on 'where' (in a manner of speaking) the research question is located and 'how' it is detected, recognized and defined ...- an issue that cannot be disentangled from the researcher's ontology and epistemology, scientific education and many other idiosyncratic researcher attributes and variables (what you see is a function of how you see). This, however, does not detract from a well-substantiated rationale for the adoption of a qualitative approach, which is executed through a case study design and primarily process research. Viewed from a perspective that accords central importance to the research question, their methodological position is appropriate and clearly and substantially argued.

Of some concern, perhaps, is that the majority of cited perspectives on change and

---

3. The authors employ Hammer and Champy's (1993) definition of BPR as a '...*fundamental rethinking and radical redesign of business processes to achieve dramatic improvements in critical contemporary measures of performance such as cost, quality, service, and speed*' (see chapter 2, p. 22) and position it, again from Hammer and Champy's perspective as *a contemporary prescription to guide and accomplish organizational transformation* (see chapter 2, p. 17).

large scale change (in particular organizational transformation) are somewhat dated and contemporary developments (post 2000/2001) are exceptionally limited. From a purist perspective it can be argued that the definition of organizational transformation employed by the authors is an impoverished one...one that, for all practical intents and purposes, is imprecise and unhelpful. In the book organizational transformation is largely positioned as a desired *outcome* (as opposed to a 'change *strategy*'), which can be attained through business process reengineering (BPR). Fortunately the book's focus is on the latter and not the former.

The book and its primary theme, quite frankly, is everything but novel. It is hardly surprising that the authors state that the "...*process of change was highly contested and the outcome of change uneven*" and "...*that some of the implementation difficulties gained greater prominence as the process progressed...*" (p.1). As a result the intended 'big bang' change strategy eventually manifested merely as a gradual and emergent change process. This observation by the authors suggests, somewhat naively, that their expectations of the anticipated outcomes of the process extended substantially beyond that which was realistically attainable (if the success / failure rates of BPR as reported in the literature are used as point of departure). Of interest is that the authors do account for the poor returns of this form of change strategy but do so rather superficially. Against this, the literature on large scale change in general and BPR in particular, is replete with implementation challenges, problems and barriers, and the unavoidability of a change 'downside' and some unintended change consequences - regardless of the level of success achieved. Perhaps the greatest consistency in the application of BPR is the convergence of sentiment on its unlikely 'returns'.

The *typical criticisms* of large-scale change programmes apply as much to this "programmatic change strategy" (cf. chapter 6) and attempted radical change and its 'management', as it does to any other major change initiative. Clear evidence of an N-step philosophy

(cf. Collins, 1998[4]) and inadequate prioritization of the social component in socio-technical change approaches such as BPR, are noted. The authors for example conclude in chapter 8 (p.383) that... "*The difficulty of trying to transform existing organizing processes and arrangements is not simply a task of changing business processes. Transformation also involves changing existing structural forms with the associated values and interests*[5]". This statement does not convey the fundamental recognition that an organization, when viewed as a social collective (as the choice of research approach, design and methodology suggests), would indicate that transformation should *commence* with the socially constructed i.e. the *values and interests* of those who collectively define the organisation... rather than the *processes* or *existing structural forms with the associated* ..." This has been an enduring criticism of BPR and similar socio-technical change approaches and is born out by the many references to resistance among clinicians and nurses cited by the authors. In essence the social dimension should have served as starting point for the reengineering process, and in this setting should have been considered to a greater depth before commencing with the initiative.

However, from the perspective that the book clearly outlines a *typical* BPR endeavour with *typical* less-than-desirable outcomes, it is also contributing to the existing knowledge reservoir on BPR and large scale change. To this end it allows a more detailed and thorough consideration of the immediate and extended context(s) of the BPR application and reveals the micro implementation considerations and challenges to a greater extent than is usually the case with a journal article or management report.

While the central theme and the execution of the BPR process do not differentiate the book from practically any other on the shelf, it is *novel* in areas such as its strong scholarly orientation and the detailed account it offers on the qualitative research design and methodology followed in the study. What is decidedly different though, is that the book presents

4. Collins, D. (1998). *Organizational change: Sociological perspectives*. London: Routledge.
5. Underlining (emphasis) added.

the BPR initiative in the predominantly professional and highly sophisticated *setting of a hospital* - a subsystem of the broader *health care system*. Moreover, it does so in an elaborately detailed and systematic fashion. The authors' application of BPR to six clinical settings effectively translates into six micro-case studies rather than a single overarching case. These involved the redesign and reengineering of patient care processes, elective surgery, and outpatient services in several directorates or divisions of the hospital. The authors describe these in fair detail and provide ample narrative evidence in support of their knowledge claims. They systematically employ a common discussion frame that comprises the context and immediate history of the clinical setting, the reengineering process and / or objectives pursued, the chronological unfolding of the process, and the impact of the reengineering intervention, which serves to enhances comparison of these interventions across the different micro-cases. From the perspective of contextualizing the BPR construct for the health care industry, the book succeeds admirably. Moreover, the authors' careful delineation and thorough exposé of institutionalised managerial and clinical tensions and the powerful role of professional allegiance and dominance as a mediating paradigm for institutional functioning and large-scale change, are invaluable for researchers, managers and consultants that are involved in this industry.

The audience likely to benefit most from reading this book obviously embraces the medical and quasi-medical fraternity – in particular those concerned with the management and efficiency of health care institutions. Serious followers of the BPR movement and to a certain extent practitioners and academics that busy themselves with the idealistic (and messy) notion of 'change management' are likely to form part of the book's reach. The complexity reader is unlikely to be found within this group, except for those who intentionally focus on or a have a preference for work or research in the health care industry.

At a concrete and pragmatic level: the reading task, at times, becomes a bit tedious, which is not aided by the often over elaborated writing style and lengthy sentence construction. Whereas the former may impact motivation and impede reading progress, a particularly helpful structural feature of the book is the abundant use of fairly detailed section and chapter summaries which purposefully reflect on preceding sections and chapters and so maintain continuity in thought and argument.

In closing, the value of the book is bound to reside in its detailed and rich account of firstly the clarity and insightful portrayal of attempted large scale change in public health care institutions and, secondly, shedding some light on the multiplicity of factors that conspired to produce (yet another) typically less-than-successful BPR initiative. It is the former (and not the latter) that will ensure a place for the book on the shelves of medical administrators, managers and clinicians.

# A Review of *The Broadband Explosion: Leading Thinkers on the Promise of a Truly Interactive World*

edited by Stephen P. Bradley and Robert D. Austin
reviewed by Christian L. van Tonder
published by Harvard University Press
ISBN 1591396700 (2005)

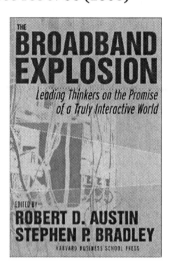

*T*he broadband explosion: Leading thinkers on the promise of a truly interactive world is the physical manifestation of the Harvard Business School's fourth colloquium on contemporary developments in information technology and telecommunications. It follows in the (by now established) tradition of earlier colloquia, which constitute important position markers in the evolution or rather unfolding revolution in these technology domains. The colloquia, and hence the edited works that followed in their wake, are important sources for influencing and directing technology development and utilization and in this regard this fourth colloquium, and *the broadband explosion*, is no different. Consistent with the three previous colloquia the book aims to capture contemporary perspectives and anticipated developmental thrusts in the areas of information technology and telecommunications.

The book's contribution is a function of the astounding mix of academic and industry leaders in the fields of information technology and telecommunications, which the edi-

tors managed to bring together in its compilation. With no less than 16 chapters, the book embraces a rich diversity of perspectives and commentary, that are broadly clustered under - what the editors term - the *promise of broadband, creating value* in a broadband world, *capturing the value* of wireless broadband and reflecting on *policy formulation* in the domain of broadband.

The book commences with a fascinating launch platform (Chapter one) from which the reader can begin to contemplate not only the stunning advances in information and telecommunications technology, but also the seemingly boundless prospects of the broadband explosion. It does so with a captivating account (on a large screen display at the conference site) of a music lesson between teacher and student in different physical locations. The lesson is enacted in the conference session in virtual real time with mere millisecond delays in communication and information transmission, and with such clarity and sensitivity to subtle behavioral nuances that it could be mistaken for reality. Moreover, the message and power of connectivity and interactivity was further driven home by the coincidental participation of a member of the audience who rapidly sourced a specific version of a piece of music referred to during the lesson, and promptly made it available to the teacher and student. As this example suggests, a core message of the *broadband explosion*, is that the pursuit of a truly virtual reality and virtual experience is not only plausible, but metaphorically speaking, merely a couple of milliseconds away. Indeed, on reading this work, the images of "I- robot" that it invoked seemed far too real for comfort!

Not entirely unanticipated, the work stuns the reader with extensive statistics on the dizzying rate of technology development. The magnitude of the trends conveyed by these statistics offers a thought provoking glimpse into the nature of the unfolding connectivity and interactivity revolution which is delivered to our doorstep – courtesy of the broadband explosion. It reveals the phenomenal pace of innovation and obsolescence, and in particular how the introduction of broadband and more

E:CO Vol. 9 Nos. 1-2 2007 pp. 211-227

specifically the concept of wireless broadband have, practically overnight, showered an already dense and complicated global information network with a dramatic and exponential increase in the data quantity and quality and the pace of data transmission. Something of this unbridled "tear away" nature of the broadband revolution (explosion) is suggested by the pace of technology development, which is indicated in part by the magnitude of the intellectual and financial resources invested for example in *Internet2* (and the Abilene network with its sustainable 10 gigabyte per second circuit), but is also conveyed by the astounding market *adoption* rate evidenced for example in the phenomenal and exponential growth in *DoCoMo's I-mode* technology (one million subscribers within six months of launching, 10 million subscribers after 18 months and so the story continues). In a sense then Austin and Bradley's statement that interactivity accelerates innovation in a new collaborative way (Chapter 1), appears to be somewhat of an understatement of the phenomenal revolution that is currently underway across the globe. If the astronomical connectivity rate and its impact in rural India (the *eChoupal* example - chapter 8) is related to Newman's statistics on broadband penetration (expressed as a percentage of households per country - Chapter 3), the reader is suddenly confronted with a new meaning of "developing" and "developed" countries. Examples such as these illustrate social change as a consequence of increasing connectivity, but at the same time global interconnectivity is stringing along human and social development and with it the promise of social change on an unprecedented scale and of nature not yet anticipated nor understood. The book unfortunately does not reach into this realm.

In general, the book will serve a useful purpose not only to the person who wishes to gain a quick sense and feel of the rapid and unfolding domain of telecommunications and information technology but will also prove useful to the reader who wishes to obtain a relevant snapshot of the state of development in these areas. This said, *different readers* for different reasons will find different parts of the book more valuable. It offers something for the technically-minded, the future-oriented, those operating in the policy and regulatory environment, and those in the business sector who would be primarily concerned with investment strategies and decisions. Understandably sections of the book will not appeal to the average "*complexity*" reader as complexity *per sé* is not part of the focus and is seldom if ever consciously raised. Notwithstanding this, the book has much to offer for the complexity scholar as the majority of the chapters in one way or another draws the reader into a consideration of both the mechanics and dynamics of some of the key drivers that promote the development of complex settings. Indeed, the treatment of information and telecommunications technologies in the various chapters conveys a powerful subtext that suggests rapidly escalating complexity. This is amply demonstrated by examples such as Upton and Fuller's eChoupal case (Chapter 8) with its accelerating and expanding density of interconnectivity, rapid growth in interactivity and increasing interdependence. It is from this perspective in particular that complexity theorists will find the book stimulating, interesting and above all thought provoking.

Against the sheer magnitude of the broadband explosion, its promised capabilities and in particular of course the hype and excitement that accompanies broadband, the reader is still left with the somewhat sobering realities of cyber crime and the paradoxical yet instinctive need to contain while every conceivable technology-based business application is taking strain and suggesting otherwise. Several of the book's chapters pose questions that will keep the IT manager in a pensive state far longer than s/he may wish to be. If s/he decides to embrace the rapid development of broadband enthusiastically, their companies may well be exposed to equally rapidly expanding risk, while a decision to contain and approach exploration and growth into this domain cautiously, may well create a lead-lag situation relative to competitors in the industry. This in itself may constitute an equally if not greater risk than that of embracing the technology. The book of course does consider the notion of risk, an exponential increase in cyber crime and the vulnerability of broadband to security threats (cf. Hunker, Chapter 14) and the increasing demands of security associated with the broadband explosion, as well as the form and nature that 'effective policy' could take, but it could have reflected to a greater extent on the shadow side of this technology phenomenon. The transportability of data, now greatly facilitated by broadband, accentuates the demands of information overload at various systemic levels and the dramatic challenges of protecting individual, institutional and national privacy and guarding against new, more sophisticated cyber threats that are bound to surface.

If points of criticism can be raised, it concerns the typical challenges that edited texts have to contend with and this book is no exception. With this many contributors and the wide range of discussion topics covered, the adequate integration of perspectives is bound to be difficult. However, more attention to some form of concluding synthesis (challenging as it may be) may have aided closure for the reader. At the same time, while individual chapters have touched on the implications of the broadband explosion from the specific vantage point of the chapter topic, the implications arising from an overarching and more integrative perspective could have been addressed more purposefully. The editors may well argue that it is for the reader to infer and conclude where this leads us but, most certainly for me, a more explicit and integrated reflection on the likely longer term implications (both challenges and real opportunities) of the different perspectives would certainly have been most useful.

The fundamental question of what the social and psychological impact and consequences of the rapid development of information and telecommunications technologies on the fiber of society might be, for all practical intents and purposes reside outside the scope of the book (it has not been an objective of both the colloquium and this book). However, in an increasingly integrated world it would be dangerous to ignore the medium and long term socio-psychological ramifications of accelerated technology development of this nature and magnitude. This may well prove to be an important and meaningful addition to future col-

loquia, for... implicit in "the promise of broadband" is also the "promise" of as yet unknown and new emergent social and psychological phenomena - with its benefits and burdens.

With writing styles often varying from chapter to chapter, and with some of the chapters at times very technical in their presentation, the reader is bound to experience some occasional frustration. For readers not directly involved in the telecommunications and information technology domains, this situation may be further compounded by the bewildering array of terminology employed, including such terms as "wireless ecosystem", "I-mode", "Wi-Fi", "3G". These terms are often overwhelming in their 'strangeness' and practically constitute a "new" language for these readers. In such circumstances a glossary may substantially aid the reading experience.

Finally, the book may not be regarded as a leisurely "read" by some and in its entirety may not keep every reader spellbound. However, there are several chapters that will capture the reader's attention and these will ensure a stimulating read and make the book a worthwhile addition to the reader's bookcase.

# A Review of *Science, Strategy and War: The Strategic Theory of John Boyd*

written by Frans P. B. Osinga
reviewed by Sean Lawson
published by Routledge
ISBN 0415371031 (2007)

The title of Osinga's book conveys well the overall focus of the study: the often overlooked but profoundly important relationships among science, military strategy, and war. It is a big topic, to be sure, so to ground his study Osinga has chosen to explore these relationships as exemplified in the strategic theory of the late USAF Colonel John Boyd, a former fighter pilot and intellectual core of the Military Reform Movement of the late 1970s and 1980s. He examines the role of science in shaping Boyd's thinking, and the impact that his thinking has had upon the U.S. military since Vietnam.

Over the last thirty years, Boyd's ideas have had a profound impact on the U.S. military, as well as the business community. He is most famous for his OODA (Observation-Orientation-Decision-Action) loop theory of knowledge formation. The OODA loop describes how humans interact with their environments to construct mental models of their environment that are shaped both by immediate observation and orientation (pre-understanding based on previous experience, culture, history, genetics, etc.). These mental models are used to decide upon and carry out courses of action. The results of action feed back into the system through observation. Yet, there is always a necessary tension between the mental model and reality, resulting from the fact that orientation shapes perception. As time passes, Boyd argued, a mismatch develops between mental models and reality. When individuals or organizations become internally focused, sticking to out-dated orientations, a breakdown occurs in understanding, leading to disorder, chaos, confusion, and panic. Thus, the process, according to Boyd, is always one of "destruction and creation," destroying old models and creating new ones in a never-ending cycle, with the goal of adapting to an ever-changing environment so as to promote individual or organizational survival by increasing the capacity for independent action.

Osinga's goal, then, is to "provide a better understanding of the strategic thought developed by John Boyd" (p. 1). In so doing, he aims to correct a number of misconceptions related to Boyd's thinking. He argues that "Boyd's OODA loop concept, as well as his entire work are more comprehensive, deeper and richer than the popular notion of 'rapid OODA looping' his work is generally equated with" (p. 7). Additionally, Osinga argues that Boyd's thinking is about more than "tactical and operational level war fighting," but "also about organizational agility, about the creation of organizations in general" (p. 7). As such, he asserts that we can learn as much from the way that Boyd thought, constructed arguments, and the sources he used, as from the content of his ideas.

To achieve his goal, Osinga has made the greatest use yet of Boyd's personal library and collection of personal papers archived at the Marine Corps University in Quantico, Virginia. For his research, he read the same books that Boyd himself read, using Boyd's handwritten notes, marginalia, and markings in those books to determine from where Boyd was drawing specific ideas, as well as which authors and books had the greatest impact upon Boyd's thinking. He uses his sources to take the reader on an intellectual journey through the "formative factors" that shaped Boyd's thinking, trying as much as possible to recreate the process of learning that led to Boyd's theory. With these formative factors in mind, he provides an exhaustive explanation of Boyd's thinking.

Osinga's second chapter is devoted to exploring three of the four "formative factors" which shaped Boyd's thinking. First, based on previous biographies by Robert Coram and Grant Hammond (Coram, 2002; Hammond, 2001), Osinga quickly summarizes Boyd's professional background, including his days as a fighter pilot, his educational background in both economics and industrial engineering, and his work in aeronautical research and fighter aircraft design. Next, he recounts Boyd's central role in the debate over military reform which took place in the United States in the aftermath of Vietnam. Finally, he examines the way that Boyd's study of military history shaped his thinking.

In an effort to trace the changes in science that influenced Boyd's thinking, chapters 3 and 4 "present a panorama of the scientific *Zeitgeist* of Boyd's lifetime" (p. 52). For its part, chapter three examines the impact on Boyd's thinking of early twentieth century developments in science, as well as the philosophy of science. Beginning with the philosophy of science, he examines the importance of Boyd's study of the writings of Karl Popper, Michael Polanyi, and Thomas Kuhn. He continues by tracing the emergence of a more nonlinear, holistic worldview within twentieth century science which, he argues, had its roots in scientific developments such as thermodynamics, the theory of evolution, relativity, quantum mechanics, the Heisenberg uncertainty principle, and Goedel's incompleteness theorem. He demonstrates the impact on Boyd's thinking of this shift, in addition to the impact of postwar developments in cybernetics and "systems thinking." Taken together, these developments served as the conceptual and metaphorical foundations of Boyd's 1976 essay, "Destruction and Creation," which formed the intellectual core of his subsequent work.

Chapter 4 demonstrates the importance for Boyd's thinking of the neo-Darwinist work of Richard Dawkins and others, Ilya Prigogine's work on dissipative structures,

and finally the emerging sciences of chaos and complexity. When combined, these ideas led Boyd to see militaries as open, complex, adaptive systems which exist far from equilibrium in the chaotic, unpredictable environment of war, in which change is constant and the effects of change are nonlinear. Finally, and perhaps most surprisingly, Osinga outlines the similarities between Boyd's thinking and the postmodern philosophy and social theory of scholars such as Jean-Francois Lyotard, Anthony Giddens, and Jacques Derrida.

The last three chapters put knowledge gained in the previous three chapters to good use by providing the most thorough and in-depth explanation of Boyd's thinking to date. In chapters 5 and 6 he takes the reader slide by slide through Boyd's fourteen-hour briefing, "A Discourse on Winning and Losing," explaining every idea, where it came from, and its importance to Boyd's overall theory. The last chapter argues for the continuing relevance and influence of Boyd's ideas by reviewing the recent works of a number of prominent U.S. military thinkers whose own theories either share an affinity with Boyd's ideas, or were directly influenced by Boyd's ideas.

Osinga's years of studying Boyd have paid off; there is no doubt that he accomplishes his objective. One cannot read this book without coming away with a deeper understanding of Boyd's thinking. He absolutely demonstrates the importance for Boyd's thinking of concepts and metaphors drawn from emerging science. In so doing, he helps to provide a needed, general corrective to the history of science literature which has been concerned mainly with the impact of the military upon science, but not the reverse. In particular, he invalidates the arguments made by a number of historians of science who have argued that the emerging sciences of chaos and complexity have had no impact upon U.S. military thinking (Gray, 1998: 2) and that the Military Reform Movement had no lasting impact (Edwards, 1996: 287-288).

The main weakness of Osinga's book is that it leaves the reader wanting more. First, while examining the "scientific *Zeitgeist*" during Boyd's lifetime helps to explain where his ideas came from, it does not explain why Boyd's ideas were successful, why they persisted while so many others failed.

Second, as previously mentioned, while Osinga provides a needed corrective to the literature on the relationship between science and the military, he may have gone too far in the other direction. In Osinga's account, science seems to come from out of nowhere to impact military thinking. However, there was (and still is) very much a circular relationship between the military and science. There is a need to better integrate the story of Boyd's thought and contributions with what historians of science have already written about postwar American science, particularly the histories of cybernetics, operations research, and systems analysis (see Fortun & Schweber, 1993; Galison, 1994; Ghamari-Tabrizi, 2000; Hughes & Hughes, 2000; Mindell, 2002), each of which were important to the military but receive too little attention in Osinga's account.

Finally, Osinga's treatment of Boyd's thinking is largely uncritical. If Boyd is correct (and Osinga makes a strong case that he is), then we should expect that there are mismatches between Boyd's theory and reality, imperfections and contradictions that will lead to its evolution over time. Otherwise, stagnation will lead to death. Thus, there is a need to explore those mismatches, imperfections, and contradictions, not to denigrate Boyd's theory, but to build upon and expand it. Osinga has proved himself most qualified to take on this task.

However, none of these criticisms can or should overshadow the success of Osinga's endeavor. They merely suggest that he has not, in fact, written the final word on Boyd, that there is much work left to be done where Boyd's ideas are concerned. That is one of the greatest tributes he could have paid to Boyd. Osinga's book should be read by military professionals and academics alike, but also by anyone interested in the social and cultural impacts of science in general, and chaos and complexity theories in particular. *Science, Strategy and War* will and should remain required reading for years to come.

## References

Coram, R. (2002). *Boyd: The Fighter Pilot Who Changed the Art of War*, ISBN 9780316881463.

Edwards, P. N. (1996). *The Closed World: Computers and the Politics of Discourse in Cold War America*, ISBN 9780262050517.

Fortun, M. and Schweber, S. S. (1993). "Scientists and the legacy of World War II: The case of operations research," *Social Studies of Science*, ISSN 0306-3127, 23(4): 595-642.

Galison, P. L. (1994). "The ontology of the enemy: Norbert Wiener and the cybernetic vision," *Critical Inquiry*, ISSN 0093-1896, Autumn: 228-266.

Ghamari-Tabrizi, S. (2000). "Simulating the unthinkable: Gaming future war in the 1950s and 1960s," *Social Studies of Science*, ISSN 0306-3127, 30(2): 163-223.

Gray, C. H. (1998). "The crisis of infowar," in G. Stocker and C. Schopf (eds.), *Infowar*, ISBN 9783211831915.

Hammond, G. (2001). *The Mind of War: John Boyd and American Security*, ISBN 9781560989417.

Hughes, A. C. and Hughes, T. P. (2000). *Systems, Experts, and Computers: The Systems Approach in Management and Engineering, World War II and After*, ISBN 9780262082853.

Mindell, D. A. (2002). *Between Human and Machine: Feedback, Control, and Computing Before Cybernetics*, ISBN 9780801868955.

# Calling notices and announcements

This section includes calling notices of events primarily hosted or cohosted by ISCE Events. Brief details of other relevant events are also given. If you are involved in the planning of an event and would like a notice to be included here then please contact us at events@emergence.org.

# Nonlinear Dynamics, Psychology, and Life Sciences

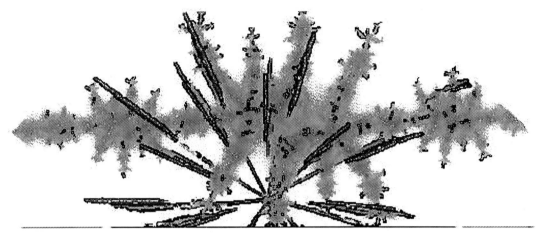

*Nonlinear Dynamics, Psychology, and Life Sciences* publishes original papers that augment the fundamental ways we understand, describe, model and predict nonlinear phenomena in psychology, the life and social sciences. Nonlinear concepts include attractors, bifurcations, chaos, fractals, solitons, catastrophes, self-organization, cellular automata, genetic algorithms and related evolutionary processes, and neural networks. The broad mixture of the disciplines represented here indicates that many bodies of knowledge share common principles.

*NDPLS* is a refereed journal and published quarterly. It is currently abstracted in *PsychINFO, Medline, JEL/Econlit* and other important data bases. For author information, abstracts and contents, and institutional subscriptions please visit: **www.societyforchaostheory.org/ndpls/** . For individual subscriptions please visit: **www.societyforchaostheory.org/membership.html**

**Topics Published in 2005 (Vol. 9):**
Missing third dynamics in Western philosophy
Dynamical models of happiness
Mapping knowledge in Bateson's epistemiology
Talent identification and development in sport
Perception of fractals in Jackson Pollack's art
Collectivities as simplex systems
Aggressive behavior of elementary school boys
Verbalizaion, replacement, group coordination
Convexity and general equilibrium in economics
Co-evolution of behavior, culture, and technology
Dynamics of tactile perception
Emergent leadership
Capital accumulation and education
**Special issue: NONLINEAR METHODS**
**Part 1: Broad Issues**

**Topics Scheduled for 2006 (Vol. 10):**
Chaotic dynamics in simple neuronal systems
EMG signals under two static work postures
Science education problem solving
Fractal analysis of Mesoamerican pyramids
Chaos, complexity and classic Hollywood cinema
Structure of Japanese dry rock gardens
**Special issue: NONLINEAR METHODS**
**Part 2: Domain-specific Issues**
ECG dynamics in flying phobia
Attractor lattices in mental models
Operant learning as a self-organized process
Physiological linkage during conversations
Bifurcations and action patterns in martial arts
Catastrophe model for adolescent substance use
Societies that self-destruct

 Published by the **Society for Chaos Theory in Psychology & Life Sciences**

# TECHNISCHE UNIVERSITÄT DRESDEN

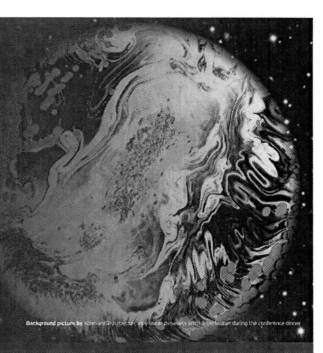

# ECCS'07

## EUROPEAN CONFERENCE ON COMPLEX SYSTEMS

Dresden, October 1-5, 2007

Background picture by voluntary Stutzbecher, a non-linear dynamics artist's performer during the conference dinner

Supported by:

ONCE-CS    Deutsche Forschungsgemeinschaft DFG

NEST    HORE IS DIFFERENT

**Program Committee Chair:**

**Jürgen Jost**
(MPI for Mathematics in the Sciences, Leipzig, Germany)

**Local Organization Committee:**

**Dirk Helbing**
(TU Dresden)

**Holger Kantz**
(MPI for Physics of Complex Systems)

**Andreas Deutsch**
(TU Dresden)

**Keynote Speakers on October 1-3, 2007:**

**Dario Floreano**
(École Polytechnique Fédérale de Lausanne, CH)

**Peter Fromherz**
(MPI of Biochemistry, Martinsried, D)

**Albert Goldbeter**
(Université Libre de Bruxelles, B)

**Neil F. Johnson**
(University of Oxford, UK)

**Stephan Mertens**
(Otto-von-Guericke-University, Magdeburg, D)

**Mark Newman**
(University of Michigan, Ann Arbor, USA)

**Denis Noble**
(University of Oxford, UK)

**Karl Sigmund**
(Faculty for Mathematics, University of Vienna, A)

**Steven Smale**
(UC Berkeley, USA)

Best Poster Awards in Complexity Science: 3,000 EUR

Pictures by
Guy Theraulaz, Hans J. Herrmann, and Martin Schönhof

**Satellite Conferences on October 4+5, 2007, for example:**

Self-Organization and Adaptive Control
Complex Dynamics and Interacting Agents
Systems Biology and Artificial Cells
Cognition and Consciousness
Emergence of Language and Communication
Artificial Intelligence and Autonomous Robots
Data Traffic and Information Networks
Non-Linear Dynamics and Time Series
Turbulence and Granular Flows
Traffic, Regional and Urban Systems
Group Dynamics and Organizations
Socio-Economic Systems and Financial Markets
Measuring and Modeling Complex Networks
Biological Regulatory Networks
Evolution and Game Theory
Engineering with Complexity and Emergence
Manufacturing and Supply Networks
Chemical Systems Design
Bioinspired Methods

We call for proposals for satellite conferences in these or other fields.

Registration and further information at:
http://complexsystems.lri.fr/eccs07 • http://www.trafficforum.org/dresden

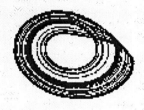

## OR CREATES BRIDGES

EURO XXII
PRAGUE

## CALL FOR PAPERS

## Prague July 8 - 11, 2007
### 22ND EUROPEAN CONFERENCE ON OPERATIONAL RESEARCH

### CONFERENCE TOPICS

We invite all researchers, academicians, practitioners, as well as students interested in all branches of operational research, mathematical modelling and economic analyses to participate at the conference and to present their papers in the following areas:

**Continuous Optimisation & Control**
**DEA and Performance Measurement**
**Data Mining & Knowledge Discovery**
**Decision Analysis & Decision Support Systems**
**Discrete Optimisation, Graphs&Networks, Scheduling**
**Energy & Environment**
**Financial Modelling & Risk Management**
**Fuzzy Sets & Expert Systems**
**Game Theory & Mathematical Economics**
**Logistics & Transportation & Traffic**
**Metaheuristics**
**Multiple Criteria Decision Making and Optimisation**
**OR Education, History, Ethics**
**OR in Health & Life Sciences**
**OR in Industries**
**Production Management & Supply Chain Management**
**Revenue Management**
**Simulation & Stochastic Modelling and Programming**
**Software for OR/Modelling Languages**
**System Dynamics and Modelling**

### SESSIONS

Invited and contributed papers will be organised in parallel sessions of 90 minutes, with three or four papers in each session. Abstracts can be submitted via the Conference web page – euro2007.vse.cz. Every participant can present no more than one paper at the Conference.

Invited and contributed sessions will generally be a part of Conference main streams. Their list together with two responsible organisers is presented on the Conference web page. The researchers who want to organise an invited session or contribute a paper within an invited session should contact the stream organiser or PC chair with their proposals.

### PRIZES AND AWARDS

During the EURO XXII conference the following prizes will be awarded:
**The EURO Gold Medal**
**The EURO Excellence in Practice Award**
**The EURO Management Science Strategic Innovation Prize**
**The EURO Doctoral Dissertation Award**

### IMPORTANT DATES

| | |
|---|---|
| On-line registration: | starts in October 2006 |
| Deadline for abstract submission: | February 28, 2007 |
| Deadline for early registration: | April 15, 2007 |
| Conference: | July 8-11, 2007 |

### CONFERENCE VENUE

The campus of the University of Economics, Prague is located within 15 minutes walking distance of the historic city centre of Prague. It offers up-to-date audio visual equipment.

### BOOK AND SOFTWARE EXHIBITIONS

Commercial exhibitors are welcome to display books, journals and computer software related to operational research. Tutorials and workshops organised by software exhibitors may also be arranged. Please contact the Organising Committee.

### SOCIAL PROGRAMME

A social programme including Welcome Party and Conference Banquet will be organised in distinctive and memorable places of the city. The conference organisers are also co-operating with an official travel agent offering tours to various places of interests located in Prague and its surroundings as well as pre- and post-conference tours to other interesting places in the Czech Republic.

E-mail: euro2007@vse.cz | http://euro2007.vse.cz

# THE 11TH WORLD MULTI-CONFERENCE ON SYSTEMICS, CYBERNETICS AND INFORMATICS
## JOINTLY WITH
## THE 13TH INTERNATIONAL CONFERENCE ON INFORMATION SYSTEMS ANALYSIS AND SYNTHESIS: ISAS 2007
### JULY 8-11, 2007 – ORLANDO, FLORIDA, USA.

**HONORARY PRESIDENTS OF PAST CONFERENCES**
*Bela H. Banathy, Stafford Beer, George Klir,
Karl Pribram, Paul A. Jensen, Gheorghe Benga*

**PROGRAM COMMITTEE CHAIRS**
*William Lesso and C.Dale Zinn*

**GENERAL CHAIR**
*Nagib Callaos*

**ORGANIZING COMMITTEE CO- CHAIRS**
*Jorge Baralt, Belkis Sánchez, Andrés Tremante*

**PROGRAM COMMITTEE**

Abd-El Malek, Yousef (Egypt); Aburatani, Sachiyo (Japan); Abusitta, Adel (Jordan); Acharya, Sushil (USA); Affenzeller, Michael (Austria); Alhamouz, Sadeq (Jordan); Alzamil, Zakarya (Saudi Arabia); Anshel, M. (USA); Aruga, Masahiro (Japan); Assaf, Mansour H. (Canada); Aukstakalnis, Nerijus (Lithuania); Baker, Emanuel (USA); Baniulis, Kazys (Lithuania); Banwet, D. K. (India); Barkana, Atalay (Turkey); Bãro, Thomas (Germany); Baryshev, Andrey (Netherlands); Bernley, Jesse (USA); Bezuglov, Anton (USA); Bhat, Talapady N. (USA); Bhattacharyya, S. (USA); Bingham, Nathan (USA); Bique, Stephen (USA); Bisdikian, Athanasios (USA); Bo, Wanjiu (China); Bolbouca, Sorana-Daniela (Romania); Bönke, Dietmar (Germany); Borchers, Carsten H. (Germany); Botto, Todd (USA); Bradl, Peter (Germany); Brothers, Timothy (USA); Carvalho, Marco (USA); Cerny, Vaclav (Czech Republic); Cha, Seung-Tae (South Korea); Chandra, V. (USA); Chávez, Rosa-Hilda (Mexico); Chen, Chin-Ti (Taiwan); Chen, Juzhong (China); Chen, Yli (Taiwan); Chen, Meihua (China); Chien, Steven (USA); Cho, Vincent (Hong Kong); Choi, Jun-Ho (South Korea); Choi, Young-Ho (South Korea); Choo, Jinboo (South Korea); Choudhury, D. Roy (India); Chowdhury, Masud H. (USA); Christidis, Konstantinos (UK); Ciftcioglu, Özer (Netherlands); Cipolla Ficarra, Francisco (Italy); Clark, Russell J. (USA); Cohen, Bernard (UK); Corvello, Vincenzo (Italy); Cote, Paul (USA); Crnkovic, Jakov (USA); Daneshmehr, Ali Reza (Iran); Das, Asesh (USA); Davison, Geoff (UK); Degardin, Annick (France); Dell'Osso, Louis F. (USA); Deng, Zhihui (China); DeVolder, Dennis (USA); Di Sciullo, Anna Maria (Canada); Diallo, Saikou Y. (USA); Doma, S. B. (Egypt); Du, Xuesong (China); Duan, Yunqing (USA); Eid, Mahmoud M. A. (Egypt); El-Badawy, El-Sayed (Egypt); El-Halafawy, Faraq Z. (Egypt); El-Sahn, Ziad A. (Egypt); El-Sherbini, Ahmed M. (Egypt); Eom, Ki-Hwan (South Korea); Erkollar, Alptekin (Austria); Ezekiel, Soundararajan (USA); Fang, Rong-Jyue (Taiwan); Fey, Ines (Germany); Franger, Sylvain (France); Fuhrer, Patrik (Switzerland); Fujikawa, Takemi (Australia); Fujita, Naoyuki (Japan); Gardezi, A. K. (Mexico); Gbadiesh, Ronald J. (USA); Goriachkin, Oleg (Russia); Geykadooh, A. (USA); Gsell, Heiko (Germany); Gunarathne, Gunti (UK); Guo, Liangqun (China); Gyíres, Tibor (USA); Ham, Chan (United States); Hansen, Elizabeth (USA); Hansen, John (USA); Hashimoto, Shigehiro (Japan); Higashiyama, Yoichi (Japan); Hochin, Teruhisa (Japan); Horimoto, Katsuhisa (Japan); Horimoto, Katsuhisa (Japan); Hrušák, Josef (Czech Republic); Ha, Bin (Japan); Huang, Sheng-He (USA); Huie, Carol (USA); Hunt, C. Anthony (USA); Hussein, Hossam A. (Egypt); Hwang, Yih-Feng (USA); Hyun, Kyo-Hwan (South Korea); Imamura, Nobuaki (Japan); Ishikawa, Hiroshi (Japan); Jacobs, Jonathan B. (USA); Jäntschi, Lorentz (Romania); Johnson, Mark (USA); Jung, Kyung-Kwon (S. Korea); Kamejima, Kohji (Japan); Kaneko, Takashi (Japan); Kazubiak, J. (Germany); Katsuyama, Tomoo (Japan); Khaled, Pervez (United States); Khurana, Amulya (India); Kim, Dong Hwa (South Korea); Kim, Tae-Kyun (South Korea); Kim, Geon-Hee (South Korea); Klingenberg, Frank (Germany); Kobayashi, Futoshi (Japan); Koike, Makoto (Japan); Kramer, Kathleen A. (USA); Kreisler, Alain (France); Kromrey, Jeffrey D. (USA); Kronreif, Gernot (Austria); Kruczynski, Klaus (Germany); Kuragano, Tetsuzo (Japan); Kwak, Bangmyung (South Korea); Kweon, Gyeong-Il (South Korea); Lalitha Bhaskari, D. (India); Lee, Wei-Bin (Taiwan); Lee, Chul-Kyun (South Korea); Lee, Hwajung (USA); Letellier, T. (France); Leung, Lin (USA); Li, Jiye (China); Li, L. (United States); Lipikorn, Rajalida (Thailand); Long, Changjiang (China); Lou, Shi-Jer (Taiwan); Loutfi, Mohamed (UK); Love, Gloria C. (USA); Löwe, M. (Germany); Luh, Guan-Chun (Taiwan); Lyell, Margaret (USA); Ma, Xiaojing (China); Magoshi, Jun (Japan); Mandagere, Nagapramod (USA); Manley, Denis (Ireland); Markowitz, K. (United States); Masuda, Giovanni Luca (Italy); Mathews, Brian (UK); Matsumoto, Katunori (Japan); Mayer, Daniel (Czech Republic); Mayer, Matthias P. (Germany); McDonald, Aaron (USA); Micceri, Theodore (USA); Michaelis, B. (Germany); Migliarese, Piero (Italy); Michael, Wasfy B. (USA); Miles, Joseph (USA); Mishra, Arabinda (USA); Miyahara, Tetsuhiro (Japan); Mohammed, Amina E. (Egypt); Mohammed, Ahd El-Naser A. (Egypt); Moreno, Carlos M. (Venezuela); Muknahallipatna, Suresh (USA); Muraleedharan, Rajani (USA); Nagai, Yasuo (Japan); Nagai akahmi, V. (India); Nagappan, Sarojini Devi (Malaysia); Nakamoto, Hiroyuki (Japan); Nam, Su-Chul (South Korea); Nazmy, Taymoor M. (Egypt); Nishigaki, Masakatsu (Japan); Nowak, Derek B. (USA); Oblitey, William (USA); Obrebski, Jan B. (Poland); Ocella, Tomas (Czech Republic); Ohkura, Tatsunari (Japan); Olson, Patrick C. (USA); Ong, Vincent Koon (UK); Oraby, Osama A. (Egypt); Osadciw, Lisa Ann (USA); Palesi, Maurizio (Italy); Pasqulet-Rocha, Jacques (Switzerland); Patel, Sandip C. (USA); Peng, Jian (Canada); Petkov, Emil (United Kingdom); Pitzer, Erik (Austria); Poon, Gilbert (Canada); Porteus, Jeremy (USA); Portnoy, David (USA); Postolache, Octavian (Portugal); Qi, Huan (China); Qureshi, Yasser (UK); Ramachandran, S. (India); Ramírez Caceres, Guillermo Horacio (Japan); Ranganathan, Raghuram (USA); Rani, Chigurupati S. (USA); Ratkovic Kovacevic, Nada (Serbia); Raut, Rabin (Canada); Rebielak, Janusz (Poland); Rehsi, Manmohan Singh (India); Ren, Meiqi (USA); Rohla, Stefan (USA); Rocke, Adam J. (USA); Rogers, Timothy J. (USA); Ropella, Glen E. P. (USA); Rossignol, R. (France); Ruan, Tongjun (USA); Ruthrauskas, Aleksandras V. (Lithuania); Saad, Abd-El-Fattah A. (Egypt); Sateesh Reddy, J. (India); Savaria, Yvon (Canada); Sax, Eric (Germany); Schaeffer, Donna M. (USA); Seok, Seung-Joon (South Korea); Shalaby, Hossam M. H. (Egypt); Sharaf, Abdallah M. (Egypt); Shayeghi, Hossien (Iran); Shin, Jeong-Hoon (South Korea); Shirasawa, Hidenori (Japan); Shirokov, I. B. (Ukraine); Sirmoon, Blair (USA); Singh, Karun (USA); Singh, Shveta (India); Sissom, James (USA); Sivasankaran, Gayathri (USA); Skstaric, Dobrila (Serbia); Sleti, Azzam Talal (Jordan); Song, Hong Jun (Australia); Srinivasan, S. (India); Staceyyte, Viktorija (Lithuania); Stöfleiss, Martin (Germany); Stubberud, Stephen C. (USA); Tsubaki, Michiko (Japan); Tumisa, Charles D. (USA); Ucal, Meltem (Turkey); Vaish, Anurika (India); Vasinek, Vladimir (Czech Republic); Verlinde, Patrick (Belgium); Wagner, Stefan (Austria); Wang, Zhong (USA); Warwick, Jon (UK); Wei, X. (USA); Weissenberger-Eibl, Marion A. (Germany); White, Joseph L. (USA); Wilkes, Mitch (USA); Winkler, Stephan (Austria); Wu, Qiong (Japan); Xu, Mark (United Kingdom); Yamaguchi, Akira (Japan); Yan, Yanjun (USA); Yan, Mu-Tian (Taiwan); Yan, Kuo-Qin (Taiwan); Yang, Zhuzhuan (China); Yang, Guohua (China); Yang, Sun-Cheol (South Korea); Yang, Hung-Jen (Taiwan); Yazawa, Toru (Japan); Yilmaz, Levent (USA); Yoon, Changwoo (USA); Yoshida, Eri (Japan); Yu, Zu-Guo (Australia); Zaleh, Jeff (USA); Zaretsky, Esther (Israel); Zeller, Andrew J. (Germany); Zhang, Xiaotheng (Jane) (USA); Zhao, Yi (China)

**ACADEMIC/SCIENTIFIC CO-SPONSORS**

- World Organization of Systemics and Cybernetics (WOSC) (France)
- International Federation of Systems Research (IFSR) (Austria/USA)
- Inter-American Organization for Higher Education (IOHE)
- Energy Institute of The Americas (USA)
- Marymount University, School of Business (USA)
- Vilnius Gediminas Technical University (Italy)
- Centre for Energy Environment Resources Development (Thailand)
- Journal Of Systemics, Informatics and Cybernetics (JSCI) (USA)
- Asociación Latina Interación Persona-Ordenador (ALAIPO) (Italy/Spain)
- International Association of Interactive Communication (AINCI -Asociación Internacional de Comunicación Interactiva)

Dear Kurt A Richardson

On behalf of the WMSCI 2007 Organizing Committee, I would like to invite you to participate in the 11th World Multi-Conference on Systemics, Cybernetics and Informatics (http://www.iiis-cyber.org/wmsci2007), Which will take place in Orlando, Florida, USA, from July 8-11, 2007.

We are emphasizing the area of Network Systems which is related to your specific area.

A multi-methodological review will be applied in the selection process of this multi-disciplinary conference. Submitted papers or extended abstracts will have three kinds of reviews: double-blind (by at least three reviewers), non-blind, and participative peer-to-peer review. These three reviews will support the selection process of those that will be accepted for their presentation at the conferences, as well as those to be selected for their publication in JSCI Journal. Details are given in the conference web site.

Authors of accepted paper/abstracts who registered will have access to the reviews made by the reviewers who recommended the acceptance of their papers/abstracts for their presentation at the conference, so they can improve their camera-ready paper and their presentations accordingly.

Pre- and post-conference virtual sessions will be held. These virtual sessions will be associated in a one-to-one relationship with the face-to-face sessions to be held at the conference. Details on this issue are provided at the conference web site.

The best 10%-20% of the papers will be published in Volume 7 of JSCI Journal (http://www.iiisci.org/Journal/SCI/Home.asp). 24 issues of volumes 1, 2, 3 and 4 of the Journal have been and will be sent to about 200 university and research libraries, and 6 issues of Volume 5 (2006) will be sent to a larger number of libraries. Promotional, free subscriptions, for 2 years, are being considered for the organizations of the Journal's authors.

Also, we would like to invite you to organize an invited session related to a topic of your research interest. If you are interested in organizing an invited session, please, fill out the respective form provided in the conference web page. We will send you a password, so you can include and modify papers in your invited session.

Invited sessions ' organizers with the best performance will be co-editors of the proceeding volume and the CD electronic proceedings where their sessions' papers were included. They will also be candidates for invited editors, or co-editors of a possible JSCI Journal issue related to their invited session's papers.

You can find information about the suggested steps to organize an invited session in the Call for Papers and in the conference web page.

If the deadlines are tight and you need more time, let me know about a suitable time for you and I will inform you if it is feasible for us.

Best regards,

Professor Nagib Callaos
WMSCI 2007 General Chair

Postal Address: Torre Profesional La California, Av. Francisco de Miranda, Caracas, Venezuela.

Torre Profesional La California, Suite PH-4, Av. Francisco de Miranda, La California Norte, Caracas, Miranda 1071, Venezuela
IIIS - WMSCI 2007, PMB – 115, 3956 Town Center Blvd., Orlando, Florida 32837, USA.
Phone: +58 (212) 272-9094   Fax: +1(407) 816-4909   E-mail: wmsci2007@iiis-info-cyber.org

Full submissions invited now. Submit early and have and opportunity to respond to the reviews and resubmit if necessary. Please use the APA style guide for paper formatting and citations.

The conference will be held in Accra, Ghana, for a three-day period during the week of 7-11 July 2008, details to be announced mid-2007. LMSSSA2008 will provide an opportunity to hear and present academic work that can build and inform good management practice in Sub-Sahara Africa. Emphasis will be upon indigenous African approaches, dissemination of best practice information, and discussions of the values and pitfalls of emulating Western practice. All topics must broadly relate to management and/or leadership in Sub-Sahara Africa.

Please submit your competitive paper/session full submission electronically to

lmsssa2008@yahoo.com

Proceedings will be published via a CD with an ISSN. If you have any questions, please feel free to contact us via this email address.

**LMSSSA2006**

**Makolo Market in Accra**

**Wildlife Parks-Ghana**

**Conference Chair:** Seth BUATSI, School of Business, Kwame Nkrumah University of Science and Technology, Kumasi, Ghana

Conference Facilitator: Romie LITTRELL, AUT Business School, Auckland University of Technology, New Zealand

# SASO 2007

## First International Conference on

## Self-Adaptive and Self-Organizing Systems

**Boston, Mass., USA, July 9-11, 2007**
http://projects.csail.mit.edu/saso2007/

Sponsored by IEEE Computer Society,
Task Force on Autonomous and Autonomic Systems

Technical co-sponsors: ACM SIGOPS, ACM SIGART,
and IEEE Systems, Man, and Cybernetics Society

General Co-Chairs
Ozalp Babaoglu
*University of Bologna, Italy*

Howard E. Shrobe
*MIT, USA*

Program Committee Chairs
Giovanna Di Marzo
Serugendo
*Birkbeck, University of London, UK*

J.P. Martin-Flatin
*NetExpert, Switzerland*

Mark Jelasity
*Hungarian Academy of Sciences & University of Szeged, Hungary*

Finance Chair
Paul Robertson
*MIT, USA*

Work-in-Progress and Applications Tracks Chair
Franco Zambonelli
*University of Modena and Reggio Emilia, Italy*

Industry Chair
Fabrice Saffre
*BT, UK*

Tutorial Chair
David Hales
*University of Bologna, Italy*

Panel Chair
Robert Laddaga
*BBN Technologies, USA*

Publicity Chair
Hermann De Meer
*University of Passau, Germany*

Sponsor Chair
J.P. Martin-Flatin
*NetExpert, Switzerland*

Local Arrangements Chair
Thomas J. Green
*MIT, USA*

The complexity of current computer systems has led the software engineering, distributed systems and integrated management communities to look for inspiration in diverse fields (e.g., robotics, artificial intelligence or biology) to find new ways of designing and managing networks, systems and services. In this endeavor, self-organization and self-adaptation have emerged as two promising facets of a paradigm shift.

Self-adaptive systems work in a top-down manner. They evaluate their own global behavior and change it when the evaluation indicates that they are not accomplishing what they were intended to do, or when better functionality or performance is possible. Such systems typically operate with an explicit internal representation of themselves and their global goals.

Self-organizing systems work bottom-up. They are composed of a large number of components that interact locally according to simple and local rules. The global behavior of the system emerges from these local interactions, and it is difficult to deduce properties of the global system by studying only the local properties of its parts. Such systems do not use internal representations of global properties or goals; they are often inspired by biological or sociological phenomena.

The aim of this conference series is to provide a forum for laying the foundations of a new principled approach to engineering systems, networks and services based on self-adaptation and self-organization. Achieving this requires the development of theories, frameworks, methodologies, tools, middleware, testbeds, best practices, etc. SASO will gather participants with different backgrounds to foster cross-pollination between different research fields and encourage technology transfers.

| Keynote 1 | Keynote 2 |
|---|---|
| Michael G. Hinchey, NASA, USA<br>*99% (Biological) Inspiration* | Gerald Jay Sussman, MIT, USA<br>*Designing for Applications Unanticipated by the Designer* |

| July 9, 2007 | July 10, 2007 | July 11, 2007 |
|---|---|---|
| **Research Track** | **Research Track** | **Research Track** |
| Session 1: Design Methodology, Foundations | Session 4: P2P Systems | Session 8: Security |
| Session 2: Provocative Ideas | Session 5: Data Collection and Aggregation | Panel 3: Self-Organizing and Self-Adaptive Networks |
| Session 3: Synchronization, Desynchronization | Panel 2: Engineering Emergence | **Work-in-Progress Track** |
| Panel 1: An Industrial Perspective on Self-Adaptive and self-Organizing Systems | Session 6: Combinatorial Optimization | Session 1: Software Engineering and Multiagent Systems |
|  | Session 7: Management and Control | Session 2: Self-Adaptation |
|  |  | Session 3: Self-Organization |
|  |  | **Applications Track** |

The proceedings of this conference are published by the IEEE Computer Society Press.

# Other titles from ISCE Publishing include:

## Managing Organizational Complexity: Philosophy, Theory, and Application
*Edited by Kurt A. Richardson*

*Managing the Complex* is an ambitious series title - and it would be an audacious one if we were not to begin the series with a frank admission: to date few to none of us have a skill set which includes managing the complex. We try various things, we write about others, and we wonder about still others. When a tool, perspective, or technique comes along which seems to evoke success, we emulate it, probe it, and recoil at the all too often admission that it was situation and context which afforded success its opportunity, and not some quality intrinsic to the tool perspective or technique.

Indeed, if the study of complexity has done anything for managers, and for those who espouse managerial theory, it is in providing a 'scientific foundation' for the notion that *context matters*. Those who preach abstract ideas have then to reconcile themselves to the notion that situation and embodiment matters. Those who believe in strong causality and determinism are left to wrestle with the role of chance, uncertainty, and chaos. Those who prefer to argue that men move history are confronted with the role of environment and affordances, while those who argue the reverse are left to contend with charisma, irrationality of crowds, and the strange qualities we know as emotions.

A series on complex systems has less ambitious goals to contend with than this. Such a series can deal with classifications, and categories, and speak of 'noise' as if it were not the central focus of the problem. *Managing the complex* is about managing noise or perhaps we should say it is about 'dealing with' 'accepting' 'making room for' and 'learning from' noise. The articles in this volume and in the series as a whole will each be considered as noise by some and as gems by others. Situation and affordance will dictate how each is perceived at any given time by any given reader.

## Organizations as Complex Systems: An Introduction to Knowledge Cybernetics
*Written by Maurice Yolles*

This book develops a cybernetic theory of the organization as a complex autonomous and self- organizing, self-producing and self-creating social community, and in so doing it will set the scene to discuss a variety of aspects of organizational and social processes and forms that arise from a systemic view. It begins by creating a philosophical foundation, it develops a viable systems approach that proceeds to cover a whole range of topics in a coherent and integrated way that are today seen to be important to social communities. Fundamentally developing as a knowledge management text, topics covered include community mission, purposes, interests, structure, politics, ethics, control, communications, management and conflict processes. It will also deliver an appreciation of the nature and use of information, knowledge and intelligence to assist the management of social communities.

## Emergence: Complexity & Organization Volume 6
*Edited by Kurt A. Richardson, Jeffrey A. Goldstein, Peter M. Allen, and David Snowden*

Organizations of all kinds struggle to understand, adapt, respond and manipulate changing conditions in their internal and external environments. Approaches based on the causal, linear logic of mechanistic sciences and engineering continue to play an important role, given people's ability to create order. But such approaches are valid only within carefully circumscribed boundaries. They become counterproductive when the same organizations display the highly reflexive, context-dependent, dynamic nature of systems in which agents learn and adapt and new patterns emerge. The rapidly expanding discussion about complex systems offers important contributions to the integration of diverse perspectives and ultimately new insights into organizational effectiveness. There is increasing interest in complexity in mainstream business education, as well as in specialist business disciplines such as knowledge management. Real world systems can't be completely designed, controlled, understood or predicted, even by the so-called sciences of complexity, but they can be more effective when understood as complex systems. While many scientific disciplines explore complexity through mathematical models and simulations, Emergence: Complexity & Organization explores the emerging understanding of human systems that is informed by this research.

E:CO Volume 6 includes articles from Isabelle Stengers, Julie Klein, Sandra Mitchell, Glenda Eoyang, Bill McKelvey, William Sulis and many more, which explore a range of complexity-related topics from philosophical concerns through to the practical application of complexity ideas, concepts and frameworks in human organizations. Also included are a series of four reproductions of classical papers in the fields of complexity and systems:

"Principles of Self-Organizing Systems" by Ross Ashby (originally published in 1962) "General Systems Theory: The Skeleton of Science" by Kenneth Boulding (originally published in 1956) "Science and Complexity" by Warren Weaver (originally published in 1948) "Emergence" by Stephen Pepper (originally published in 1926).

## Emergence: Complexity & Organization Volume 7
*Edited by Kurt A. Richardson, David Snowden, Peter M. Allen, and Jeffrey A. Goldstein*

Volume 7 includes articles from Max Boisot, Ken Baskin, Robert E. Ulanowicz, Heather Höpfl, Victoria Alexander, and many more, which explore a range of complexity-related topics from philosophical concerns through to the practical application of complexity ideas, concepts and frameworks in human organizations. Also included are a series of four reproductions of classical papers in the fields of complexity and systems:

"Futurology and the Future of Systems Analysis" by Ida R. Hoos (originally published in 1972) "A Form of Logic Suited for Biology" by Walter M. Elsasser (originally published in 1981) "Beyond Open Systems Models of Organization" by Louis R. Pondy (originally unpublished conference paper from 1976) "The Architecture of Complexity" by Herbert A. Simon (originally published in 1962).

## Emergence: Complexity & Organization Volume 8
*Edited by Kurt A. Richardson, Jeffrey A. Goldstein, Peter M. Allen, and David Snowden*

Volume 7 includes articles from Elizabeth McMillan, Carol Webb, Eve Mitleton-Kelly, Carlos E. Puente, Paul Cilliers, Kathleen Carley, Alfred Hubler and many more, which explore a range of complexity-related topics from philosophical concerns through to the practical application of complexity ideas, concepts and frameworks in human organizations. Also included are a series of four reproductions of classical papers in the fields of complexity and systems:

"The Philosophic Functions of Emergence" by Charles A. Baylis (originally published in 1929); "Novelty, Indetermisim, and Emergence" by W. T. Stace (originally published in 1939), and; "The Functions of the Executive, Chapter 2: The Individual and Organization" by Chester I. Barnard (originally published in 1938).

**For ordering details please visit: http://isce.edu/catalog/**

## Other titles from ISCE Publishing include:

### Reframing Complexity: Perspectives from the North and South
*Edited by Fritjof Capra, Alicia Juarrero, Pedro Sotolongo, and Jacco van Uden*

**Contents: Part I—Sources of Complexity: Science and Information** *Complexity and Life* Fritjof Capra; *Ecology, a Dialog between the Quick and the Dead* Robert E. Ulanowicz; *Complexity and Environmental Education* Carlos J. Delgado Díaz; *Key Issues Regarding the Origin, Nature, and Evolution of Complexity in Nature: Information as a Central Concept to Understand Biological Organization* Alvaro Moreno & Kepa Ruiz-Mirazo. **Part 2—Philosophical, Epistemological, and Methodological Implications** *Why We Cannot Know Complex Things Completely* Paul Cilliers; *From Paradigms to Figures of Thought* Denise Najmanovich; *Complex Dynamical Systems and the Problem of Identity* Alicia Juarrero; *Complexity, Society, and Everyday Life* Pedro Sotolongo. **Part 3—Organizational Implications** *Emergence Happens! Misguided Paradigms Regarding Organizational Change and the Role of Complexity and Patterns in the Change Landscape* James Falconer; *Modeling of Social Organizations: Necessity and Possibility* Raimundo J. Franco Parellada; *The New Complex Perspective in Economic Analysis and Business Management* Ruth Mateos de Cabo, Elena Olmedo Fernández, & Juan Manuel Valderas Jaramillo. **Part 4—Global and Ethical Implications** *Complexity, Ideology, and Governance* Roger Strand; *Globalization and the Complexity of Human Dignity* Ken Cole; *The Consolations of Uncertainty: Time, Change, and Complexity* Carl A. Rubino.

### Explorations in Complexity Thinking: Pre-Proceedings of the 3rd International Workshop on Complexity and Philosophy
*Edited by Kurt A. Richardson and Paul Cilliers*

This pre-proceedings contains the all the papers submitted for the two-day Complexity and Philosophy workshop held 22nd-23rd February 2007, in Stellenbosch, South Africa. The event was co-hosted by Stellenbosch Institute for Advanced Study (STIAS), ISCE Events, and the Cathedra for the Study of Complexity (Instituto de Filosofia de La Habana). As with previous meetings, the aim of this workshop was to explore the philosophical implications of the science and thinking of complex systems.

Attendees were encouraged to submit papers on the following topics: Status, limits and legitimacy of knowledge regarding complex systems; Relationship between linear and nonlinear philosophies; Complexity-based ethics; Frameworks for the analysis of complex systems; Complex limits to theories of everything; Complexity and the social sciences; Complexity and globalization; Complexity and human subjectivity.

**Contents:** Editorial - Kurt A. Richardson & Paul Cilliers; 1. Foucault, complexity, and myth: Toward a complexity-based approach to social evolution (a.k.a. history) Ken Baskin; 2. Complexity-based ethics: Martin Buber and dynamic self-organization - Deborah P. Bloch & Terrence Nordstrom; 3. Gaia, complexity, and American Indian Tribes: Common ground for compatible theories - Nicholas C. Peroff; 4. What is there in a word?: Heterarchy, homoarchy, and the difference in understanding 'complexity' in the social sciences and complexity studies - Dmitri M. Bondarenko; 5. Wittgenstein's Ladder in Prigogine's Universe - Tapio Muhonen; 6. To catch a falling star: Opening the middle path's hands of humility to science - Graham Schliebs; 7. Rhythmic entrainment, symmetry and power - John Collier; 8. The complexity of design as a wavefunction - Johann van der Merwe; 9. A-causality: A quantum ontology for complex systems - Walter Baets; 10. Modeling rationality and emergence in dynamic networks - Remo Pareschi; 11. Homeostasis, complexity, and the problem of biological design - Scott Turner; 12. Bios theory of physical, biological and human evolution - Hector Sabelli; 13. Two ways of reducing linguistic complexity - Josef Zelger; 14. The discrete challenge to theories of the continuum - Tony Smith; 15. The role of information 'barriers' in complex dynamical systems behavior - Kurt A. Richardson; 16. Non-quantitative modeling as a framework for the analysis of complex systems - Jan H. S. Roodt; 17. An epistemology of learning through life - Aliki Nicolaides & Lyle Yorks; 18. Towards a dialectic complexity framework: Philosophical reflections - Fredrik Nilsson; 19. Measuring complexity: Things that

---

## Publishing Opportunities at ISCE Publishing

In July 2005 the Institute for the Study of Coherence and Emergence (a *non-profit* research organization) developed the capacity to publish complexity-related books inhouse. We now, through ISCE Publishing, provide the necessary support for authors of complexity-related literature to get published in a professional and timely manner. Our publications are available through both Amazon.com and Barnes & Nobel. We are keen to maintain a close working relationship with our authors, allowing them to have much more influence over their book project than they would with larger more established publishers. One notable consequence of this is that the royalties achievable through ISCE Publishing are in the range 15-20% rather than 7-12% which is the norm (ISCE Publishing considers higher royalty rates if they are donated to non-profit organizations dealing with complexity-related issues).

If you are interested in publishing your book, or book series, through ISCE Publishing then please send your proposal to us at submissions@isce.edu. Or, if you have ideas relating to edited collections of previously published papers, or are keen to see a classic out-of-print text back in print, then contact us at the same address. Lastly, we also produce conference proceedings in both CD-ROM and bound print form (both with ISBN/EAN referencing).

## 'Net-worker' Opportunities at ISCE Publishing

As well as publishing complexity-based texts, we at ISCE Publishing are keen to incorporate the organizational insights published through our catalogue into our day-to-day operations. As such ISCE Publishing is a distributed (network-based) organization that maintains only a minimal full-time team. As our catalogue grows we plan to contract out certain activities (such as reviewing, typesetting, proofing, editing, etc.) to interested and able 'net-workers'. The benefit to ISCE Publishing from this networked, or adhocratic, set-up is that it will be a very flexible and adaptable enterprise, able to respond quickly to incoming requests and novel projects. The benefit to ISCE Publishing's 'net-workers' is that they can realize financial rewards greater than those on offer through more traditional publishing houses. For example, manuscript reviewing is rarely a paid activity with the publisher being reliant on the generosity of the reviewer. ISCE Publishing's profit-related reward scheme will ensure that the financial success of any project will be channeled back to all those that contributed to the realization of that project. For more details of becoming a 'net-worker' with ISCE Publishing please contact Kurt Richardson at kurt@isce.edu.

## ABOUT E:CO

*Emergence: Complexity & Organization* (E:CO) is an international and interdisciplinary conversation about human organizations as complex systems and the implications of complexity science for those organizations. With a unique format blending the integrity of academic inquiry and the impact of business practice, *E:CO* integrates multiple perspectives in management theory, research, practice and education. *E:CO* is a a quarterly journal published in print and online by The Complexity Society, the Institute for the Study of Coherence and Emergence, and Bookmasters in accordance with academic publishing standards and processes.

## INTELLECTUAL ECOLOGY

*E:CO*'s niche is the opportunity to bridge three gaps:

- The distance between academic theory and professional practice;
- The space between the mathematics and the metaphors of complexity thinking; and,
- The disparity between formal idealizations and actual human organizations.

Organizations of all kinds struggle to understand, adapt, respond and manipulate changing conditions in their internal and external environments. Approaches based on the causal, linear logic of mechanistic sciences and engineering continue to play an important role, given people's ability to create order. But such approaches are valid only within carefully circumscribed boundaries. They become counterproductive when the same organizations display the highly reflexive, context-dependent, dynamic nature of systems in which agents learn and adapt and new patterns emerge. The rapidly expanding discussion about complex systems offers important contributions to the integration of diverse perspectives and ultimately new insights into organizational effectiveness. There is increasing interest in complexity in mainstream business education, as well as in specialist business disciplines such as knowledge management. Real world systems can't be completely designed, controlled, understood or predicted, even by the so-called sciences of complexity, but they can be more effective when understood as complex systems. While many scientific disciplines explore complexity through mathematical models and simulations, *E:CO* explores the emerging understanding of human systems that is informed by this research. Engineered and emergent views of human systems can coexist, creating a useful tension that drives organizational evolution. However, neither academics nor practitioners can leverage complexity alone. Academic discussions about complexity are often biased towards quantitative research and mathematical models that are inappropriately prescriptive for systems comprised of actors endowed with free will, who are simultaneously part of and aware of the system. The metaphors of complexity have a usefulness of their own as well, but too often they are applied without adequate reference to the mechanisms, models and mathematics behind them.

## CONTENT IN CONTEXT

Readers of E:CO are managers, academics, consultants and others interested in developing and applying the insights of complex systems theories and models to analysis and management of private-, public- and social-sector organizations and applying insights derived from organizational experience to understanding complex systems theories.

*E:CO* encourages multidisciplinary contributions from all sectors of social and natural sciences and all sectors of organizational practice. The journal's unique format presents both reviewed and non-reviewed content from three overlapping sources. Peer-reviewed articles are at the heart of our content, but with an emphasis on communicating across boundaries. Academic articles pass double-blind reviews by two academics and one practitioner. When subject matter is theoretical or reporting research findings, authors will be encouraged to discuss practical implications of the ideas. Similarly, practitioner articles also will be double-blind reviewed by two practitioners and one academic. When appropriate, authors will be encouraged to connect to theory or research that has either already been done or needs to be done.

Additional non-reviewed content includes feature articles, essays, profiles, conversations and conference summaries, as well as news, commentary, book reviews, etc. Each article will be clearly marked according to which path it took to publication.

*E:CO* incorporates *Emergence* , originally published by the Institute for the Study of Coherence and Emergence.

### SUBMITTING MATERIAL TO *E:CO*

E:CO is interested in receiving work from a wide range of perspectives:

- theoretical and practitioner based
- both conventional and unconventional methodologies
- case study work
- approaches to teaching management or leadership
- work covering a variety of organizational types, size and ownership
- cross cultural studies and work from Australasia, Africa, Central and South America and the Far East as well as the USA and Europe.

We ask that authors set their paper clearly within the context of the notion of complexity and complex systems, however they chose to define such, and that the practical implications and transferable lessons from their work be clearly described.

Note that quantitative studies (including those which focus on survey results and related statistics) are not suitable for *E:CO*. Authors are limited to one mathematical formula per paper (additional formulae may appear in the technical appendix). If you wish to submit work of a quantitative nature, please represent it qualitatively. Figures and tables should be illustrative. Quantitative and statistically based submissions will be returned without review. Each article in *E:CO* will be accompanied by space on the E:CO web site for additional materials and discussion forums.

### FORMAT

*All submissions are electronic.*

Suggested length is 4000 to 5000 words. Review pieces and essays should be 2000 to 3000 words. Note: additional material considered relevant and/or related by the author(s) can be posted on the web site, which will be associated with each accepted article. The author(s) will be responsible for securing all necessary permissions for material to be posted on the web site.

All submissions must be in either MS Word (6.0 or later) or Corel WordPerfect (6.0 or later). All manuscripts should be formatted as typed, 11 or 12 pitch, double-spaced (including references) on 8 1/2 by 11 inch white paper with margins of at least one inch on all four sides; or if on A4 paper, with appropriately adjusted margins, as all origination for printing will be done in the USA. Electronic submissions should be sent simultaneously to: Kurt Richardson (Managing Editor), and Caroline Richardson (Administrative Assistant). No hard copies are required for submission.

## ORDER OF MATERIAL
### Front Matter
First Page: Title of paper, name and position of author(s), author(s') complete address(es), email contacts, fax and telephone number(s), and any acknowledgement(s) of assistance. Second Page: A brief biographical sketch of each author including name, degree(s) held, title or position, organization or institution, previous publications, and areas of research interest. Third Page: Title of paper without author(s') name(s) and a brief abstract of no more than 150 words.

### Body of Text
The text and page numbering will begin on the fourth page (as page #1), with major headings centered on the page and subheadings flush with the left margin. All headings and titles should be typed with upper and lower case. Do not use all capitals. Bibliographic citations should be integrated into the text as indicated below. In the extreme case that an explanatory note is needed, it must be formatted as an endnote. All endnotes must be approved by the editor before final submission.

### Technical Appendices
Technical appendices may be used to include mathematical or highly technical material which supports the main text but which is not critical to the reader's interpretation of the text. Note that technical appendices will only appear on the Emergence web site and not in print.

### Tables and Figures
Each table or figure should be placed on a separate page and numbered consecutively beginning with Table 1 and Figure 1. A table or figure should not be included unless it is referred to in the text of the article. Placement in the text should be indicated as follows:

[Figure 1 about here]

Footnotes in tables or figures should be designated by lower case letters. Each table and figure must have a title and a number. The table or figure number and title should be typed on one line, using upper and lower cases, as follows:

**Figure 1** *The interplay of competing frameworks*

Figures also need to be provided as separate files and in their native format, e.g., if a figure was designed using Power Point then please provide the .ppt files and not an exported JPEG. Our typesetters can deal with most file formats. EPS is one of the more popular for publishing purposes.

## References
References within the text (incl. notes and appendices) should include the author's last name and year of publication enclosed in parentheses, e.g. (Meddaugh, 1986). If practical, place the citation just before a punctuation mark. If the author's name is used within the text sentence, just place the year of publication in parentheses, e.g., "According to Meddaugh (1986)..." If a particular page or section is cited, it should be placed within the parentheses, e.g., (Meddaugh, 1986: 48). For multiple authors, use up to two names in the citation. With three or more authors, use the first author's name and *et al.* (even on he first appearance within the article, e.g., (Meddaugh, *et al.*, 1989).

An alphabetical listing of references should appear at the end of the manuscript, with each author's surname first and year of publication following all authors' names. Work by the same author with the same publication year should be distinguished by lower case letters after the date (e.g., 1983a). Works by the same author should be listed earliest to latest, and the author's name should appear with each reference (do not use underscores). Examples are as follows:

Crissy, W. J. E. and Kaplan, R. M. (1969). *Salesmanship: The Personal Force in Marketing*, ISBN 0471187550.

Richardson, K. A., Tait, A., Roos, J. and Lissack, M. R. (2005). "The coherent management of complex projects and the potential role of group decision support systems," in K. A. Richardson (ed.), *Managing Organizational Complexity: Philosophy, Theory, and Application*, ISBN 1593113188, pp. 433-458.

Ingram, T. N. and Bellenger, D. N. (1983). "Personal and organizational variables: Their relative effect on reward valences of industrial salespeople," *Journal of Marketing Research*, ISSN 0022-2437, 20(May): 198-205.

Note that all books and journals must have their ISBN and ISSN included, respectively, where known. From issue 9.1 (2007) the town, state and publisher are no longer needed for books for which there is a current ISBN. Only older books (pre-ISBN) require town, state, and publisher.

If you have trouble finding journal ISSNs then try entering the journal's name within inverted commas and "ISSN" into google. For example:

"Journal of Management" ISSN

Failure to format references correctly may create delays in the publication process.

## ACCEPTANCE PROCEDURE
The Editors and Managing Editor will review all submissions for suitability. Manuscripts deemed suitable are reviewed independently by members of the editorial review board, and their recommendations guide the Editors in their acceptance decision. The reviews are double blind - neither authors nor reviewers know the identity of each other.

All reviewing for *E:CO* is done electronically. Authors will be updated via email.

### Riddled Basin

The featured image is a slice in time of the destination space of a simple mechanical system depicted below:

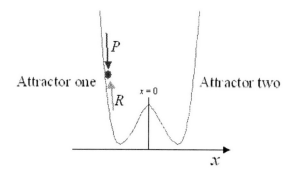

The system is a ball moving inside a double well under the influence of gravity and a sinusoidal perturbing force. The destination plot on the back cover is a snapshot in time indicating which side of the double well (left or right) the ball will be in depending on starting conditions (red for left, blue for right). Complexity thinkers will be more than familiar with the quantitative indeterminism more formally referred to as *chaos*. The significance of this particular example is that it illustrates not only quatitative indeterminism in a simple system, but also *qualitative* indeterminism, i.e., for this very simple mechanical system it is not even possible to predict, after some arbitrary period, which side of the well the ball will be on, let alone specific position and velocity information.

The image generated using a Runge-Kutta-4 approximation approach is rather granular. With sufficient computing power one would observe that as time progresses the blue and red regions would become more and more intimately mixed resulting in a structure known as a fractal.

*Kurt Richardson*

If you have an image - which may be a photograph, complex computer generated image, or some interesting data - that you'd like to have published in full color on a future issue of *E:CO* then please send it along to featured_image@emergence.org along with a paragraph or two describing what the image depicts and how it was created.

Printed in the United States
83377LV00002B/1-114/A

9 780979 168857